The Ideology of Creole Revolution

The American and Latin American independence movements emerged from distinctive settings and produced divergent results, but they were animated by similar ideas. Patriotic political theorists throughout the Americas offered analogous critiques of imperial rule, designed comparable constitutions, and expressed common ambitions for their new nations' future relations with one another and the rest of the world. This book adopts a hemispheric perspective on the revolutions that liberated the United States and Spanish America, offering a new interpretation of their most important political ideas. Joshua Simon argues that the many points of agreement among various revolutionary political theorists across the Americas can be attributed to the problems they encountered in common as Creoles – that is, as the descendants of European settlers born in the Americas. He illustrates this by comparing the political thought of three Creole revolutionaries: Alexander Hamilton of the United States, Simón Bolívar of Venezuela, and Lucas Alamán of Mexico.

Joshua Simon is Assistant Professor of Political Science at Columbia University, New York.

Problems of International Politics

Series Editors

Keith Darden, *American University*

Ian Shapiro, *Yale University*

The series seeks manuscripts central to the understanding of international politics that will be empirically rich and conceptually innovative. It is interested in works that illuminate the evolving character of nation- states within the international system. It sets out three broad areas for investigation: (1) identity, security, and conflict; (2) democracy; and (3) justice and distribution.

Titles in the Series

The Ideology of Creole Revolution

*Imperialism and Independence in American
and Latin American Political Thought*

JOSHUA SIMON
Columbia University

CAMBRIDGE
UNIVERSITY PRESS

University Printing House, Cambridge CB2 8BS, United Kingdom

One Liberty Plaza, 20th Floor, New York, NY 10006, USA

477 Williamstown Road, Port Melbourne, VIC 3207, Australia

4843/24, 2nd Floor, Ansari Road, Daryaganj, Delhi – 110002, India

79 Anson Road, #06-04/06, Singapore 079906

Cambridge University Press is part of the University of Cambridge.

It furthers the University's mission by disseminating knowledge in the pursuit of education, learning, and research at the highest international levels of excellence.

www.cambridge.org
Information on this title: www.cambridge.org/9781316610961
DOI: 10.1017/9781316665633

© Joshua Simon 2017

First published 2017

Printed in the United States of America by Sheridan Books, Inc.

A catalog record for this publication is available from the British Library.

Library of Congress Cataloging-in-Publication Data
Names: Simon, Joshua (Joshua David), author.
Title: The ideology of Creole revolution : imperialism and independence in American and Latin American political thought / Joshua Simon, Columbia University.
Description: Cambridge ; New York : Cambridge University Press, 2017. | Series: Problems of international politics | Includes bibliographical references and index.
Identifiers: LCCN 2016059493| ISBN 9781107158474 (hard back) | ISBN 9781316610961 (paper back)
Subjects: LCSH: United States – History – Revolution, 1775–1783. | United States – Politics and government – 1775–1783. | Latin America – History – Autonomy and independence movements. | Latin America – Politics and government – 1806–1830. | Creoles – United States – History. | Creoles – Latin America – History. | Hamilton, Alexander, 1757–1804 – Political and social views. | Bolívar, Simón, 1783–1830 – Political and social views. | Alamáan, Lucas, 1792–1853 – Political and social views.
Classification: LCC E210 .S56 2017 | DDC 973.3–dc23
LC record available at https://lccn.loc.gov/2016059493

ISBN 978-1-107-15847-4 Hardback
ISBN 978-1-316-61096-1 Paperback

Contents

Acknowledgments

The argument of this book, that the ideas of the American independence movements were more similar to one another than has usually been acknowledged, was not inspired by a document discovered in a dusty archive, or by an insight gleaned from a scholarly tome, but by a trip – a surf trip, to be specific, along the Americas' Pacific coastline. Traveling overland with a board under my arm, and riding waves from Pichilemu to Pacasmayo, San Juan del Sur to Puerto Escondido, and from Black's to Bolinas to Short Sands Beach, I caught sight of commonalities and connections underneath all of our Americas' differences and divisions. I decided to devote my studies to describing the shared origins, pervasive contradictions, and collective promise of the New World's distinctive political ideas. This book represents the first fruit of my efforts, so it seems fitting to begin by acknowledging my many hosts and fellow travelers, some of whose names I never knew, but whose *bienvenidas* have, more than anything, inspired my account of our hemisphere.

I have been the beneficiary of great intellectual generosity as well. In countless hours of conversation, going back to my time as a student at Reed College, Casiano Hacker-Cordón taught me to how to think about politics and political philosophy. Bruce Ackerman, Karuna Mantena, Paulina Ochoa Espejo, and Anthony Pagden advised the dissertation that became this book, which I wrote with the support of the Department of Political Science at Yale University. Seyla Benhabib, Tom Donahue, Adom Getachew, Philip Gorski, Stathis Kalyvas, Wim Klooster, Adria Lawrence, David Lebow, Andrew March, Jeff Miley, Aziz Rana, John Roemer, Andy Sabl, Stephen Skowronek, Susan Stokes, Brandon Terry, and Immanuel Wallerstein helped refine its arguments. A Fox fellowship at the Colegio de México allowed me to spend a year learning from José Antonio Aguilar, Roberto Breña, Moisés González Navarro, Andrés Lira, Erika Pani, Faviola Rivera Castro, Corina Yturbe, and Josefina Zoraida Vázquez. My time in Mexico was greatly enriched by the company of my good friend Juan Rebolledo and the hospitality of his gracious family.

Since leaving Yale, I have had the pleasure of teaching at the New School for Social Research, King's College London, and Columbia University, where I have learned an immense amount from my students, and profited from the advice of colleagues including Uta Balbier, Banu Bargu, Clare Birchall, Robin Blackburn, Jean Cohen, Sandipto Dasgupta, Max Edling, Jon Elster, Nancy Fraser, Roberto Gargarella, Ayten Gündoğdu, Turku Isiksel, David Johnston, Andreas Kalyvas, Tony MacFarlane, Dan Matlin, Eduardo Posada-Carbo, Jay Sexton, Hillel Soifer, Rogers Smith, Nadia Urbinati, Diego von Vacano, and Eric Van Young. Ian Shapiro offered consistently wise counsel throughout this project, and also helped me find a publisher. Camila Vergara provided excellent research assistance. I am thankful to Lew Bateman at Cambridge University Press and to two anonymous reviewers, whose comments on my manuscript greatly improved this book.

Some passages in Chapter 4 appeared previously in "Simón Bolívar's Republican Imperialism: Another Ideology of American Revolution," *History of Political Thought*, Vol. 33, No. 2 (2012), 280–304. Some passages in Chapter 6 appeared previously in "The Americas' More Perfect Unions: New Institutional Insights from Comparative Political Theory," *Perspectives on Politics*, Vol. 12, No. 4 (December 2014), 808–828. I thank the editors of both publications for permission to reprint this material here.

Still more profound thanks are due to my father, Jack Simon, who encouraged my intellectual curiosity at our dinner table; to my brothers, Aaron and Stevie, who remind me of where I have come from and ask the best questions about what I am doing now; and to my daughters, Sylvia and Madeleine, who fill me with more joy and pride every day than I ever knew I could feel in a lifetime. My deepest gratitude, though, is to my wife, Dawn Teele, the "inspirer, and in part the author, of all that is best in my writings ... whose exalted sense of truth and right was my strongest incitement, and whose approbation and love are my chief rewards."[1]

I hope this work will honor the heroes of our American past and inspire the heroes of our American future, but I dedicate it to Spin and Pow, personal heroes whom I have lost since I began.

Introduction: The Ideas of American Independence in Comparative Perspective

In the fifty years surrounding the turn of the nineteenth century, dissident inhabitants of colonial cities from Boston to Buenos Aires condemned, fought, and finally overthrew the European empires that had ruled the New World for more than three centuries, creating new, sovereign states in their stead. These American independence movements emerged from distinctive settings and produced divergent results, but they were animated by strikingly similar ideas. Patriotic political theorists throughout the Americas offered analogous critiques of imperial rule in the years leading up to their rebellions, designed comparable constitutions immediately after independence had been won, and expressed common ambitions for their new nations' future relations with one another and the rest of the world. This book adopts a comparative perspective on the revolutions that liberated the United States and Spanish America, offering a unified interpretation of their most important political ideas. It argues that the many points of agreement it describes amongst revolutionary political theorists in different parts of the Americas can be attributed to the problems they encountered in common as *Creoles*, that is, as the descendants of European settlers born in the Americas.

The institutions of European imperialism in the Americas placed Creoles in a difficult position. As the European inhabitants of American colonies, Creoles enjoyed many privileges, benefitting in particular from the economic exploitation and political exclusion of the large Indigenous, African, and mixed-race populations that lived in or near their colonies. However, as the American subjects of European empires, Creoles were socially marginalized, denied equal representation in metropolitan councils and parliaments, and subjected to commercial policies designed to advance imperial interests at the colonies' expense. Independence offered Creoles an escape from the vagaries of imperial domination, but posed a serious threat to the internal hierarchy of the colonies, so the political thinkers that organized and defended rebellions across the hemisphere were forced to confront a dilemma: How could they end European rule of the Americas without undermining Creole rule in the Americas? The ideology of Creole Revolution – the political ideas that I shall claim were common to all of the American independence movements – arose as patriotic Creole intellectuals sought to address this dilemma.

Scholars of North American and Latin American political thought have long sought, almost always in isolation from one another, to understand the contradictory qualities of the ideas they study. How can Americans invoke ideals of liberty and equality so passionately while passing over the oppression and exclusion that their societies impose on Indigenous, African, and other non-white populations? What ends are served by the odd mixtures of democratic and undemocratic institutions framed by the Americas' innovative and influential constitutions? Why are Americans so jealous of their own nations' autonomy, yet so eager to influence events elsewhere in the world? In the pages that follow, I argue that each of these contradictory ideological tendencies first emerged as revolutionary Creoles grappled with the problems posed by their independence movements. Seeking a way out from under imperial rule that would not require them to relinquish the privileges that imperialism had allowed, Creole political thinkers throughout the Americas embraced a contradictory ideology that incorporated both anti-imperialist and imperialist positions at the same time.

Anti-imperial imperialism took on distinct forms as the Creole Revolutions progressed, appearing first in defenses of revolution, then in constitutional designs, and finally in foreign policies. Creole patriots justified their rebellions by reference to arguments carefully tailored to impugn some, but not all of the inequalities that characterized their societies, claiming that their own right to rule themselves originated in their forefathers' conquest of the New World. Creole constitutional designers created political systems that conformed in some respects to revolutionary ideals of popular sovereignty, but also centralized authority and separated powers in order to limit the political influence that the Americas' heterogeneous populations could exert. Creole statesmen embarked on projects of external conquest and internal colonization, arguing that they could only assure the Americas' independence by expanding their new states' frontiers and consolidating their control over often resistant populations. In the following text, by comparing the political ideas of three carefully chosen Creole revolutionaries, I demonstrate that the institutional context within which the American independence movements unfolded exerted a decisive influence on the ideologies that the movements' intellectual leaders expounded, producing convergence around anti-imperial imperialism in these three forms, even amongst Creole thinkers who were influenced by very different intellectual traditions.

By showing that the American independence movements were similar in their institutional origins and political ideas, this book challenges established accounts not only of North American and Latin American political thought, but also of the Americas' comparative political and economic development, and the history of inter-American relations. It reconstructs a critical period in the Americas' history: a period of institutional change and evolving hemispheric affairs in which it was not yet inevitable that the United States would become the world's largest economy and foremost military superpower, or that Latin America would experience persistent political instability and economic underdevelopment; a period in which all Americans were struggling to resolve similar problems. Recognizing and understanding the many points of ideological convergence across the Creole Revolutions prompts us to reconsider the causes of the United States and Latin America's subsequent political and economic divergence, raising a broad set of questions about the long-term legacies of the Americas' transition to independence.

1.1 COMPARING REVOLUTIONS

Despite their geographic and historical proximity, comparative studies of the American independence movements have not been common. Scholars have usually approached the revolutions that liberated the United States and Latin America using different interpretive frameworks, with the result being that when they are compared at all, the American independence movements have been compared to different sets of non-American rebellions and revolts, rather than to each other. The concept of the "Creole Revolution" that I develop here offers a new, unified interpretive framework capable of explaining features of the ideology of the American independence movements that more established alternatives have ignored or misunderstood.

A tendency to separate and distinguish the North American and Latin American independence movements emerged early. In a series of letters written after his retirement, the Massachusetts patriot, political theorist, and US President John Adams reflected on the extraordinary period of global history that he had observed during his career in politics. Even as he was "plunged head and ears in the American revolution from 1761 to 1798 (for it had been all revolution during the whole period)," Adams wrote, he had been "eye-witness to two revolutions in Holland" and "ear-witness to some of the first whispers of a revolution in France." Taken together, he wrote, the "last twenty-five years of the last century, and the first fifteen years of this, may be called the age of revolutions."[1]

Adams pointedly declined to list the colonial rebellions that had already shaken off Spanish rule in the Southern Cone, which would soon demolish the entire mainland edifice of the Spanish American empire, as defining events of the age of revolutions. The problem, for Adams, was that the "people of South America are the most ignorant, the most bigoted, the most superstitious of all the Roman Catholics in Christendom." The idea that "a free government, and a confederation of free governments, should be introduced and established among such a people, over that vast continent, or any part of it" appeared to Adams "as absurd as similar plans would be to establish democracies among the birds, beasts, and fishes."[2] Adams's eminently English aversion to Catholicism made it impossible for him to conceive of Spanish Americans' struggle for independence as of a piece with the broader age of revolutions that he credited himself and his fellow British North Americans with initiating.

Though the prejudices underpinning it would evolve, Adams's "age of revolutions" proved to be a durable analytical apparatus. His European contemporaries, including figures like Edmund Burke and Alexis de Tocqueville, wrote about England's Glorious Revolution, the independence movement of the United States, and the French Revolution as passages, more or less tortured, to the modern world.[3] Later, scholars retained the same basic set of comparisons even as they refined the categories they used it to illustrate, describing the Glorious Revolution, the North American independence movement, and the French Revolution as paradigmatic "bourgeois" or "democratic" revolutions,[4] and tracing the intellectual lineage of "republican" political ideas from ancient Greece, through Renaissance Italy and seventeenth-century England, to the rebellious colonies of British North America.[5]

Even authors who have insisted on the United States' exceptionalism have done so almost exclusively with reference to Europe, arguing that the "absence of feudalism" in North American history made the constellation of political forces that arose in the independence movement and shaped the early republic's institutions utterly unlike any European analogue.[6] From the first, then, the independence movement of the United States has been treated as either an exemplary or an exceptional event in a north Atlantic age of revolutions: a wave of agitation unified, primarily, by Enlightened philosophies and anti-monarchical aims.

Latin Americans have rarely been regarded as important participants in this period of trans-Atlantic upheaval.[7] Instead, their roughly contemporaneous break with European rule has been treated as the consequence of an early or "incipient" nationalism: a sense of separate American identity and a resulting desire for independence, which formed gradually over the course of the colonial period and crystallized in the decades surrounding the turn of the nineteenth century.[8] According to this view, European persecution inspired Spanish Americans to think of themselves as Peruvians or Chileans, for example, rather than as Spaniards, and then to seek independence for these administrative subunits of the Spanish Empire in order to bring political sovereignty into alignment with their new national identities.

The identification of nationalism, as opposed to anti-monarchism, as the central motivation of Latin America's independence movements has long governed scholarship on their intellectual history. The clearest evidence of its influence is a historical and social-scientific literature that largely adopts the region's present-day national boundaries as natural units of analysis.[9] In the rare instances when this approach has inspired comparison with cases outside contemporary Latin America, it has pointed scholars toward the twentieth-century anti-colonial movements of Asia and Africa. Like these later uprisings of colonized peoples, the Latin American independence movements overthrew a foreign ruler, creating a "model" of "national liberation" that subsequent freedom fighters would follow.[10] After achieving independence, Latin American political thinkers confronted a set of political and economic difficulties akin to those experienced by other "post-colonial" societies. Ultimately, and perhaps inevitably, the Latin American countries assumed a place on the global periphery, as primary goods producers frequently subject to foreign interventions.[11]

The dominance of these distinct interpretative frameworks in the literature on the independence movements of the United States and Latin America has limited inter-American comparisons, but this is not their only flaw. Both the "age of revolutions" and the "incipient nationalism" theses fail to account for certain distinctive features of the political thought of the American independence movements, and both lead to problematic depictions of the societies that independence produced in the Americas.

In order to establish an analogy between the Glorious Revolution, the French Revolution, and the British North American independence movement, proponents of the age of revolutions thesis tend to deemphasize the fact that the North American effort was, inescapably, a rebellion directed by the inhabitants of a collection of colonies against an empire, stressing anti-monarchical currents of its ideology instead.[12] This makes it difficult, though, to account for patriotic Americans' loyalty to their monarchs, which persisted even in the late stages of their disenchantment with empire, or their embrace of quasi-monarchical institutions after independence had been won. The age of revolutions thesis also tends to pass over the "peculiar institutions" present in British North America but absent in Europe at the end of the eighteenth century, reducing the important roles that concerns with African slavery and Indigenous expropriation played in the ideology of the independence movement, and in the political struggles of the early republic.[13]

Meanwhile, the incipient nationalism thesis implies incorrectly that, prior to their independence movements, Latin Americans had already adopted national identities corresponding to the states that the endemic infighting of the nineteenth century would eventually produce.[14] As a result, it cannot explain the differences between the region's present-day political boundaries and the geographic outlines of independent states that the leaders of Latin America's independence movements originally envisioned. In particular, it tends to obscure the ubiquitous, though mostly unsuccessful efforts that Latin Americans, like their North American counterparts, made to unify former colonies under common governments after winning independence. The incipient nationalism thesis also exaggerates the extent to which the leaders of the Latin American independence movements rejected their own European identities in favor of nationalist alternatives that incorporated African and Indigenous Americans on equal terms, assuming that the valorization of *mestizaje* and *democracia racial* that emerged later in Latin American political thought preceded or accompanied the region's independence.[15]

If the age of revolutions thesis downplays the imperial context of the American independence movements, then, the incipient nationalism thesis mischaracterizes it. The empires that Europeans established in the Americas differed importantly from the ones they built later in Asia and Africa. The mainland American territories of Britain, Spain, and Portugal were "settler colonies," inhabited by large, permanent populations of European settlers, who had complicated, and often conflictual relationships with both metropolitan authorities, on the one hand, and

Indigenous and enslaved or free African and mixed-race communities on the other.[16] With the single, important exception of Haiti, it was the descendants of these settlers – *criollos*, as they were known in Spanish, or Creoles, as I shall call them here – who liberated the Americas from European rule and established the Americas' newly sovereign states. The American independence movements were Creole Revolutions, and this fact had important consequences for the political ideas that arose in their course.

Creole leadership not only distinguished the American independence movements from the European, Asian, and African revolutions with which they are usually compared, but also made the ideas of the American independence movements more similar to one another than has usually been acknowledged. The American independence movements did not overthrow European rule because it was either monarchical or foreign. Their Creole leaders did not, at least originally, aim to usher in a new era of human history or to rectify the historical injustice of European conquest. Indeed, they initially demanded nothing more than to be recognized as the subjects of legitimate monarchs, and to have the rights they bore as the descendants of the Europeans who conquered the New World respected in their respective metropoles. When metropolitan intransigence in the face of these demands finally convinced Creoles to seek independence, they were anxious to escape European rule without relinquishing the privileges that their European ancestry had given them. Thus, far from eliminating the monarchical and imperial institutions from the independent societies they created, after independence Creoles reshaped their institutional inheritances in ways that helped them consolidate control over the Americas' heterogeneous populations. Once in power, Creoles pursued territorial expansion and colonization as avidly as their European predecessors, insisting all the while that their aim was not to dominate, but to liberate the populations that they conquered and forcibly integrated into their independent states. By treating the American independence movements as Creole Revolutions, I shall argue, we can better understand why these paradoxical, simultaneously anti-imperial and imperial ideologies appeared in important writings produced throughout the hemisphere.

1.2 COMPARING CREOLES

My use of the term "Creole," in this book, to describe the descendants of European settlers born in the Americas may cause some confusion. In the United States, Creole usually refers to the residents of former French colonies in North America, particularly Louisiana, and to their culture and language, especially insofar as it retains strong French influences. The term is also used more broadly in English to describe persons of mixed European and African descent born in the Caribbean basin, and their languages and cultures, especially insofar as they syncretize European and African influences.[17]

As indicated in the preceding text, the sense of the word that I intend is that of the original, Spanish term *criollo*, which was used as early as 1581 to distinguish persons of specifically European descent born in the Spanish Americas from *peninsulares*, or Europeans born on the Iberian peninsula, and from the Indigenous and African inhabitants of Spanish America.[18] Creole is still used in this way in both Spanish- and English-language histories of Spanish America,[19] but it is rarely applied to British America. Indeed, the only instance of which I am aware in which the term "Creole" has been used to structure a comparative account of the Americas is in Benedict Anderson's masterpiece *Imagined Communities*, which exerted an early and profound influence on the arguments developed in this book.[20]

I have chosen to follow Anderson, and incur the risk of misunderstanding, not only to acknowledge my debts to his work, but also in order to avoid describing the subjects of this study as "settlers." Though the latter term has framed very insightful studies of settler colonial societies, particularly in the former British Empire,[21] I find it inapt as a description of political thinkers whose families had, in many cases, passed many generations in the Americas, and whose place within the empires under which they lived was, as Anderson notes, determined as much by the "shared fatality of trans-Atlantic birth" as by the act of migration and settlement that their predecessors had undertaken.[22] I think "Creole" better conveys the contradictory qualities of the institutional context inhabited by the leaders of the American independence movements, which I shall describe in more detail in the next chapter, and which I shall argue had important effects on their political ideas.

One regrettable implication of this terminological choice is that, for purposes of this study, the Haitian Revolution, which produced the Americas' second independent state, but which was led by slaves of African descent and free people of color, was not a Creole Revolution in the sense intended, and will not form a major area of focus. I shall not expand here upon how the socio-racial and institutional factors that distinguished the Haitian Revolution from the independence movements of mainland British and Spanish America influenced its ideology.[23] For different reasons, this book will also have relatively little to say about Brazil, which followed a very distinctive path to independence under the leadership of a legitimate heir to the Portuguese throne, or about Canada and the Caribbean, which became independent much later than the United States and mainland Spanish America.

I.3 COMPARATIVE POLITICAL THEORY

To support the interpretation of the political thought of the American independence movements advanced in this book, I adopt an approach inspired by the growing field of comparative political theory. In recent years, political theorists have devoted greater attention to traditions of political thought that have traditionally been excluded from their canon. Studies of East and South Asian, Islamic, African, and Latin American political thinkers have uncovered surprising areas of consensus across cultures we often assume are worlds apart, and stark disagreement on ideas we often assume should command universal assent.[24] These important findings suggest that even as it improves our historical understanding of unfamiliar political ideas, comparative political theory will also revitalize critical political theorizing, exposing long-settled opinions to new challenges and undermining the intellectual hegemony that has accompanied Western Europe and North America's economic and military dominance of the rest of the world.[25]

These are central motivations for the present study. Despite its immense internal attractions and clear potential as a source of critical insights, Latin American political thought has not been the subject of extensive study in Anglophone political theory.[26] Here, by examining a range of influential Latin American political thinkers alongside their better-known British American counterparts, I hope to arouse interest in a rich, but unfamiliar tradition, while also gaining new historical perspective and critical purchase on some canonical texts and ideas.

At the same time, though, I aim to advance beyond existing approaches in this exciting field. For the most part, comparative political theorists have confined themselves to the interpretive-historical task of establishing *what* a given piece of non-Western political thinking argues and the evaluative-philosophical task of asking *whether* what it argues is compelling. They have not taken advantage of the comparative method's unique capacity to accomplish the social-scientific task of explaining *why* the political thinkers they study thought what they did, rather than something else. In other words, they have not used the comparisons they make to identify the factors that cause ideological convergence or divergence amongst political thinkers or across traditions of political thought. In this book, I compare the ideas of three carefully chosen Creole revolutionaries in order to argue that the contradictions characteristic of the American independence movements' ideology were caused by contradictions inherent in their Creole protagonists' institutional situation.

Of course, this formulation raises some difficult questions: In what sense can political ideas be said to have been caused? What is entailed in explaining why a given thought appeared where and when it did? I propose a simple and, I hope, relatively uncontroversial answer to these questions: Political ideas are caused by the background problems that their thinkers set out to solve. Explaining why political thinkers thought what they did involves reconstructing the background problems that they aimed to address when they wrote or spoke.[27] I shall suggest that these background problems are, in turn, products of an interaction between two contexts that all political thinkers always occupy: an institutional context and an intellectual context.

By institutional context, I mean the formal and informal rules that structure social interactions in the community where the political thinker whose thoughts we wish to explain lives, thinks, and writes or speaks. Following Jack Knight and James Mahoney, I assume that, in general, institutions exist not because they represent cooperative solutions to collective action problems, but because they are the contingent outcomes of conflicts over the distribution of political power, economic resources, and social prominence. Actors or groups of actors devise and enforce the rules that make up an institutional context in order to secure distributional advantages at the expense of other actors or groups of actors.[28]

In this sense, Mahoney notes, institutions create collective actors: "A shared position as privileged (or not) within institutional complexes provides a basis for subjective identification and coordinated collective action."[29] Groups that derive advantages from existing institutions will have interests in maintaining those institutions. Groups that are disadvantaged by existing institutions will have contrary interests in reforming or abolishing those institutions and replacing them with others. The presence, within any given community, of groups with contrary interests causes conflicts. In the course of these conflicts, spokespersons emerge from the contending groups to offer arguments as to why existing institutional arrangements should be maintained, reformed, or abolished and replaced by others that would distribute advantages and disadvantages differently. These spokespeople are political thinkers; their arguments are political thoughts.[30]

By intellectual context, I mean the opinions and beliefs that influence individuals' and groups' appraisals of the institutional contexts that they occupy, and the conceptual frameworks and languages that political thinkers draw upon as they make arguments on behalf of their groups' preferred institutional arrangements. Political ideas, in other words, do not simply reflect the interests of groups privileged or underprivileged by institutions, they also mediate the translation of institutions into interests, shaping groups' perceptions of their own advantages and disadvantages, the justice or injustice of a given distribution of power or wealth or prestige, and the possibility or impossibility of alternative institutional arrangements.[31] As they intervene in conflicts, political thinkers do not make new arguments out of whole cloth, but rather adapt and repurpose preexisting arguments, conceptual frameworks, and languages.

Intellectual historians like Quentin Skinner and J. G. A. Pocock have described "languages," or "discourses," or "broader traditions and frameworks of thought," which supply the set of terms and concepts that individual political thinkers employ, and consequently shape or limit what it is possible for them to think.[32] Mark Bevir offers a related, but distinct definition of intellectual "traditions" as "webs of beliefs" passed from teacher to pupil and subsequently modified by pupils before being passed on again. He argues that an individual political thinker, or an aspect of his or her thought, can be partially explained by "locating" it in the tradition that provided the "starting point" from which he or she departed.[33] Finally, Michael Freeden outlines an approach to analyzing the "distinctive configurations of political concepts" that constitute political "ideologies," such as "liberalism," "conservatism," and "socialism."[34] Though each of these approaches makes different assumptions about exactly how, and how much, existing "discourses," "traditions," or "ideologies" influence the thinking, writing, and speaking of individual political thinkers, all of them offer useful ways of characterizing the intellectual contexts within which different political thinkers thought and wrote or spoke, and which, in interaction with those political thinkers' institutional contexts, produced the background problems that caused them to think and write or speak as they did.

Different thinkers may be more or less explicit about the background problem or problems that caused them to think about politics in the way that they did. Indeed, they may even be more or less conscious of those problems, depending on how deeply they interrogate their own interests, presuppositions, prejudices, and inherited vocabulary and concepts. Thus, often, the background problems to which a text responds cannot be simply read out of the text itself; they must, rather, be inferred, and it is here that the method of comparison becomes useful.

John Stuart Mill described what remains the basic logic of the comparative method in 1843, describing two ways of choosing cases for comparison that make causal inference possible. Mill's "method of agreement" involves comparing cases that are as different as possible in all respects, but which all display the phenomenon or outcome one aims to explain. His "method of difference," by contrast, involves comparing cases that are as similar as possible in all respects, but in which the phenomenon or outcome one aims to explain appears in some cases and not in others. Both methods serve to highlight the patterns of variation across cases, and when successful, identify the factor or factors responsible for causing the phenomenon or outcome one aims to explain.[35] Both methods can be used to infer the background problems that caused political thinkers to think what they did: By comparing thinkers situated in similar institutional contexts but different intellectual contexts, or by comparing political thinkers influenced by similar intellectual contexts but situated in different institutional contexts, we can isolate the ways in which each factor helped shape the background problems that caused their political ideas.

In the following chapters, I compare the ideas of three prominent Creole political theorists: Alexander Hamilton of the United States (1755–1804), Simón Bolívar of Venezuela (1783–1830), and Lucas Alamán of Mexico (1792–1853). I have chosen Hamilton, Bolívar, and Alamán according to Mill's method of agreement.[36] Hamilton, Bolívar, and Alamán came from societies shaped by different versions of the settler colonial model European empires imposed upon the Americas, and they inherited different stations within those societies' Creole elites. Even more importantly, for present purposes, they were each influenced by different philosophical traditions. But, as I shall endeavor to show, Hamilton, Bolívar, and Alamán all converged on an important set of ideas, defending American independence as a response to the unequal conditions imposed on Creoles by European imperial rule, proposing constitutions designed to protect Creole privileges within independent societies by unifying former colonies and granting executives extensive authority, and seeking to consolidate their states' sovereignty through territorial expansion and internal colonization. These differences and similarities provide a basis for inferring that Hamilton, Bolívar, and Alamán's ideological convergence was caused by the convergent background problems they each faced, as Creoles who sought and won independence for their respective colonies.

The colonial predecessors of the United States, Venezuela, and Mexico illustrate the wide range of forms settler colonialism took in the Americas. British rule and a Protestant majority sharply distinguished the thirteen colonies from their Spanish American counterparts, but the latter were by no means homogenous. Venezuela was a classic plantation colony, with an economy dominated by the export of agricultural primary goods and a relatively small, relatively rural population, of which a majority was comprised by the enslaved and free descendants of Africans forcibly transported across the Atlantic. The colony enjoyed a metropolitan policy of benign neglect for much of its history, permitting its Creole elites extensive autonomy in the oversight of local affairs, and allowing the development of dense illicit networks of trade with European powers other than Spain.

Meanwhile, Mexico – known as New Spain before independence – was the crown jewel of Spain's American possessions, home to roughly half of the empire's overseas population, densely urbanized, and much more economically diversified than colonial Venezuela. While some slaves were brought to New Spain, Indigenous communities and *mestizos* made up most of the non-European population. Spanish sovereignty was also much more present in New Spain, where for centuries newly arrived Spanish immigrants married into established Creole families, creating a local ruling class with a distinctly trans-Atlantic, but exclusively Hispanic, character.[37]

Deeply shaped by the differences between their societies, Alexander Hamilton, Simón Bolívar, and Lucas Alamán were also biographically dissimilar. Hamilton was the illegitimate offspring of a wandering Scottish nobleman and a French Huguenot exile who met in the Caribbean. He married into the colonial upper class of British North America and rose quickly up the ranks of first the military and later the political hierarchies of his adoptive country by virtue of his extraordinary energy, administrative genius, and formidable rhetorical talent. Bolívar, meanwhile, was born into Caracas's Creole elite, inherited a huge fortune and a large estate, and assumed a leadership position in the movement for Spanish American independence virtually from the start, displaying throughout adept military strategy, powerful personal charisma, and a singularly expansive vision of his revolution's potential world-historical import. Alamán, finally, was the scion of a long-established New Spanish family whose financial fortunes had declined somewhat by the time of his birth.

Of the three, only he had an extensive formal education, which made him an indispensable statesman and technocrat during Mexico's early independence, and then his country's premier historian in his mature years.[38]

Perhaps most importantly, Hamilton, Bolívar, and Alamán differed in their dominant philosophical influences. Hamilton's political thought owes deep debts to the authors of the Scottish Enlightenment, especially David Hume, from whom he derived a historical method for learning about politics, a focus on the interaction of individual interests within different institutional settings, and a clear sense of the importance of commerce in international affairs. Bolívar, meanwhile, was steeped in the classical republican tradition developed by figures from Machiavelli to Montesquieu, whose influence is visible in Bolívar's concerns with the cultivation of civic virtue, his concept of collective liberty, and his attraction to mixed models of government and territorial expansion. Finally, Alamán lived long enough to absorb the conservative reaction to the French Revolution, especially the writings of Edmund Burke. He offered a reformist solution, short of independence, to the "American Question" at the *Cortes* of Cádiz, opposed and criticized the largely indigenous rebellion that preceded Mexico's independence movement, and was keenly aware of the advantages that preserving some colonial political institutions might hold for an independent Mexico.

As we will see, these divergent influences deeply colored each author's intellectual contributions to his respective country's independence and early statehood. I do not claim that the American independence movements were similar in all respects, or that Hamilton, Bolívar, and Alamán were ideologically identical. Rather, I show that despite their differences – and especially their philosophical differences – Hamilton, Bolívar, and Alamán's ideas display a common set of core contradictions: the anti-imperial imperialism that I claim was characteristic of the ideology of Creole Revolution. I argue that these three important figures converged in this sense because they all addressed background problems structured by the common institutional context that each occupied as a Creole revolutionary.

1.4 ORGANIZATION OF THE BOOK

Chapter 2 states the main historical and interpretive contentions of the book. I describe the overlapping imperial institutions that structured the interests shared by Creoles in different parts of the Americas, and the changes to these institutions that eventually drove Creoles to seek independence throughout the hemisphere. I argue that Creoles occupied a "contradictory" institutional position, which imparted to them a set of internally adversarial interests, and caused the Creoles who organized and led struggles for independence to develop an ideology that was both anti-imperial and imperial at the same time. I show how anti-imperial imperialism appeared in Creoles' revolutionary, constitutional, and international political thought, drawing illustrations of its distinctive tenets from intellectual leaders of the independence movements in the United States, Mexico, Venezuela, Colombia, Argentina, and Chile.

Chapters 3, 4, and 5 are dedicated to case studies of Alexander Hamilton, Simón Bolívar, and Lucas Alamán, respectively. Each chapter provides enough background history and biography to give readers a sense of the unique paths the United States, Andean South America, and Mexico, respectively, followed to independence, and to contextualize each figure's political thought. In each case, I also document a characteristically Creole mode of political thinking, showing how the contradictions of anti-imperial imperialism appear within the works of single authors. In Hamilton's writings, analyses of individual interests and commercial interactions serve as the basis for a critique of British imperialism and a defense of a renewed, American imperial project. For Bolívar, the same, classically republican self-reinforcing cycles of liberty and virtue, tyranny and corruption, justify both Spanish American independence and the conquest and forced assimilation of a continent. Finally, Alamán's conservative preference for gradual political change provides grounds for the establishment of a New Spanish empire that maintained many of the qualities of the old one.

Together, the three case studies are intended to substantiate, in a systematic fashion, the general claims made about the ideas of American independence in Chapter 2, but along the way, the general concept of the Creole Revolution permits new insights into the political thought of these three important individuals, and interventions in the large literature dedicated to each. Each case study offers an account of how American political thinkers have adapted different European traditions of political thought to address problems arising in their hemisphere. This productive feedback between theory and evidence, between a general interpretation of Creole political thinking and close readings of the distinctive versions produced by particular Creole political thinkers, strongly recommends the comparative method I adopt.

Chapter 6 addresses a puzzle that emerges from the arguments made in earlier chapters: If the Americas were so similar at the time they achieved independence, why are they so different today? When and why did ideological convergence give way to economic and political divergence? I describe the rise of organized opposition parties within the ranks of Creole revolutionaries, and compare the ideological divisions that underlay partisan conflict in the newly independent Americas. I suggest that the United States' relatively peaceful first transfer of authority from an incumbent to an opposition administration contributed to its relatively stable politics and relatively fast economic growth, especially by leaving the union intact. By contrast, postcolonial conflicts led to the breakdown of the United Provinces of the Río de la Plata (comprising present-day Argentina, Uruguay, Paraguay, and Bolivia), Gran Colombia (comprising present-day Venezuela, Colombia, Ecuador, and Panama), and the Empire of Mexico (comprising present-day Mexico, Guatemala, Honduras, El Salvador, Nicaragua, Costa Rica, and the western United States), leaving smaller states less capable of defending their interests abroad and stimulating economic development at home. In this way, I show how the comparative study of political thought, in general, and the ideology of Creole Revolution, in particular, can help reframe long-standing questions in comparative politics and economic history about the origins of the Americas' disparities of wealth and power.

The Conclusion traces the divergent intellectual influence of the ideology of Creole Revolution in Latin America and the United States through the nineteenth century. I show that anti-imperial imperialism informed the original articulation of the Monroe Doctrine in 1823, and describe how the United States' increasing capacity to project authority throughout the hemisphere and the rise of scientific racism contributed to more aggressive invocations of the doctrine by US presidents in the context of the Mexican–American and Spanish–American Wars. I also discuss Latin American political thinkers' response to these developments, suggesting that José Martí's influential critique of scientific racism and call for Latin American unity in the face of North American aggression can be read as an alternative iteration of anti-imperial imperialism, marking a shift in the evolution of an intellectual tradition that has persisted throughout the twentieth century and up to the present day.

2

The Ideology of Creole Revolution

Today, Simón Bolívar is widely regarded as the greatest hero of Spanish America's struggle for independence, but his road to eternal fame and glory was rocky. The summer of 1815 found Bolívar struggling to overcome a serious reversal. Only two years after its founding, the Second Republic of Venezuela had followed the First into ruin, succumbing to simultaneous assaults by the regular forces of the Spanish Empire and an undisciplined, but effective loyalist insurgency spearheaded by *pardo* – or mixed-race – cattlemen from the colony's eastern plains. Bolívar retreated with what remained of his army from Caracas to the Caribbean port city of Cartagena before sailing into exile on the island of Jamaica. There, he published an account and defense of his efforts in pursuit of independence to date, emphasizing an important problem that he and his fellow patriots had encountered:

We are neither Indians nor Europeans, but a species midway between the legitimate owners of the land and the Spanish usurpers. Being Americans by birth and Europeans by right, we must both dispute the claims of natives and resist external invasion. Thus, we find ourselves in the most extraordinary and complicated situation.[1]

Bolívar did not face this extraordinary and complicated situation alone. Here, he describes a dilemma that arose in each of the revolutions that freed the Americas, North and South, British and Spanish, from imperial rule. The Creoles – descendants of European settlers, born in the Americas – who led the American independence movements were, as Bolívar relates, caught between two worlds and torn by conflicting interests. They were deeply attached to the rights and privileges they enjoyed as Europeans, but resentful of the political, economic, and social subordination that their American birth sometimes entailed. As a result, they were enthralled by the idea of exercising greater autonomy in the Americas, but also wary of the turmoil that severing ties with Europe might unleash. They knew that their colonial societies rested in delicate balance, always in danger of tipping over into tyranny or anarchy – toward, that is to say, more complete domination from across the Atlantic, or toward chaotic conflict with the African Americans, Native Americans, and mixed-race Americans that they lived amongst.

Ultimately, the task of defining and defending Creoles' distinctive interests fell to the political theorists of their revolutions, intellectuals and statesmen like Bolívar, who justified the Americas' independence movements before the court of global opinion, designed the Americas' first constitutions, and conducted the Americas' early foreign policies with an eye to sheltering Creoles' cherished rights from both foreign and domestic threats. As they grappled with the two-sided dilemma they faced in common, Creole revolutionaries across two continents developed a common ideology, marked by its contradictory embrace of both anti-imperialist and imperialist commitments. I analyze Bolívar's particular version of this ideology extensively in Chapter 5. In the following text, I describe the general form that Creole political thinking took throughout the hemisphere, showing how anti-imperial imperialism emerged from the extraordinary and complicated situation that the institutions of European imperialism imposed upon Creoles in every part of the Americas.

2.1 IDEOLOGY AND INSTITUTIONAL CONTRADICTION

It is worth beginning by clarifying exactly what is meant here by "ideology," a term that is used quite diversely even in scholarly writing, not to mention political debate.[2] Contemporary political scientists use "ideology" to describe the usually unexpressed political beliefs or preferences that underlie individuals' political behavior, usually conceiving of ideologies as arranged along a spectrum defined by one or more axes, observable in patterns of roll-call voting (amongst elites) or survey responses (amongst masses).[3] Meanwhile, contemporary political theorists and historians of political thought use the term, often with pejorative intent, to describe written or spoken political ideas that fail to achieve, or even to strive for, the standards of internal consistency and rational persuasiveness characteristic of political philosophy. Ideologies, in this definition, are ideas developed for merely instrumental purposes, in defense of particular partisan interests, and not in pursuit of timeless truths.[4] The second usage comes closer to the one I intend, though as in the first, here I shall treat ideologies as social phenomena susceptible to systematic explanation. To this end, I make a virtue out of ideology's defining vice, explaining the contradictions present in the ideas I examine by reference to the partisan interests they were developed to defend. This approach recalls an older, but still influential use of the term ideology, most closely associated with Karl Marx.[5]

In 1845, Marx argued that the idealist German philosophy of his day fundamentally misunderstood the relationship between material reality and human thinking, treating the world as if it were a product or artifact of our understanding when their true relationship was the reverse. "Life," as he put it, "is not determined by consciousness, but consciousness by life." Hegel and his followers fetishized ideas, ascribing to them an autonomous existence and historical evolution that severed the connection between thought and the context in which it occurred, covering over the conditions in which particular ideas arose and thus failing to grasp the specific functions that they served. Properly understood, Marx wrote, "Morality, religion, metaphysics, all the rest of ideology and their corresponding forms of consciousness ... have no history, no development" of their own. Rather, "men, developing their material production and their material intercourse, alter, along with this their real existence, their thinking and the products of their thinking."[6] A history of ideologies, then, should begin with a history of ideologues, and of the societies in which they lived.

Marx provided an outline for such a history, describing progressive stages of social development, distinguished one from another by the "forms of ownership" that structured economic production and exchange. As these forms of ownership evolved along with advances in productive technologies, societies divided and redivided into classes: groups of individuals owning similar amounts of the raw materials, machines, and labor power that comprised their societies' "means of production." In all but the most primitive societies, Marx argued, disparities of ownership between classes permitted some classes to benefit at others' expense, generating an "antagonistic" system of opposed interests and an inherently unstable social dynamic, prone to disruptive conflict. Ideologies emerge out of this conflict.

In Marx's account, dominant classes, interested in the maintenance of advantageous forms of ownership, seek stability by building a "legal and political superstructure ... to which correspond definite forms of social consciousness" upon the "real foundation" provided by the economic structure of society.[7] In other words, political thinkers associated with dominant classes develop ideologies in order to contain the conflicts that class divisions cause, legitimizing or disguising the exploitation of dominated classes by misrepresenting contingent features of society as if they were natural and inevitable, or by suggesting that existing institutions satisfy universally valid ideals. Meanwhile, in moments of "social revolution," political thinkers associated with insurgent classes employ the same strategies in order to attract support for the reform or abolition of the institutions that facilitate their exploitation:

Each new class which [would] put itself in the place of [the] one ruling before it is compelled, merely in order to carry through its aim, to represent its interest as the common interest of all the members of society, that is,... it has to give its ideas the form of universality, and represent them as the only rational, universally valid ones. The class making a revolution [presents itself] from the very start,... not as a class but as the representative of the whole of society; it appears as the whole mass of society confronting the one ruling class.[8]

Thus, the political and philosophical debates that occupied the intellectuals of Marx's day, "the struggle between democracy, aristocracy, and monarchy, the struggle for the franchise, etc., etc.," could be better understood as "the illusory forms in which the real struggles of the different classes are fought out among one another."[9] For the most part, Marx himself was interested in the strategic implications of this conclusion, but his concept of ideology offers scholarly direction as well. It suggests that in order to account for the emergence of a particular ideology at a particular time within a particular setting, one should reconstruct the economic structure of the society, noting its characteristic forms of ownership and class divisions, asking what institutions the ideology in question was meant to legitimize and which class's interests those institutions would serve.

By describing the political ideas of the American independence movements as an "ideology," then, I mean to suggest, following Marx, that they should be understood as products of a conflict between classes with opposed interests. The political theorists that helped define and defend these struggles developed their arguments in order to defend institutional arrangements that would "advance the interests of [their own] particular party or class,"[10] as they thought, wrote, and spoke. However, in applying this concept of ideology to the American independence movements,

I make two important qualifications to Marx's original exposition of the term.

First, and most fundamentally, in order to develop an account of the class struggle that gave rise to the American independence movements, I replace the traditional Marxian schema of classes distinguished by their disparate ownership of economic assets, evolving in a prescribed series of historical stages, with a more flexible theory, which allows other forms of inequality, varying over space as well as in time, to structure class conflicts and the ideologies to which they give rise. Specifically, as noted in Chapter 1, I reject Marx's distinction between "illusory" conflicts over political institutions and the "real struggles" of economic classes, allowing political institutions themselves to create class distinctions and invest the members of different classes with opposed interests, causing conflicts amongst classes and influencing the political ideas of their participants.[11] The institutions that most proximately structured the American independence movements were the institutions of European imperialism in the Americas.

It is useful, heuristically, to consider the institutions of European imperialism in the Americas in terms of three "constitutions" – written and unwritten arrangements of authority that allotted unequal political power and privileges to groups of people: (1) within European, or metropolitan, societies; (2) within American, or colonial, societies; and (3) between European metropoles and their American colonies, or, said another way, within the empires as wholes.[12] Each of these three constitutions created classes with conflicting interests: Members of distinct social estates and orders contended within metropolitan societies; representatives of separate racial castes struggled within colonial societies; and the European- and American-born grappled within the empires as wholes. The three constitutions also overlapped, subjecting individuals and groups to institutions that sometimes reinforced and sometimes cut across lines of privilege characteristic of metropolitan, colonial, and imperial societies. The Creoles whose political thought forms the subject of this study occupied an institutional position structured by cross-cutting benefits and burdens, which invested them with interests different from those of fellow Europeans born in Europe, on the one hand, and from fellow Americans of African or Indigenous descent, on the other.

This leads to a second necessary qualification. In his programmatic statements, Marx depicted class relations in polarized, binary terms, with each stage of social development in his progressive history defined by conflict between two opposed classes. The *Communist Manifesto* famously described the "history of all hitherto existing society" as "the history of class struggles" waged by "freeman and slave, patrician and plebeian, lord and serf, guild-master and journeyman, in a word, oppressor and oppressed." The advent of capitalism only intensified this Manichean tendency, creating "two great classes directly facing each other, Bourgeoisie and Proletariat."[13] Applying this framework, modified according to the terms in the preceding text, to the American societies that form the subject of this study would yield a polarized binary – colonizer and colonized, perhaps – incapable of accommodating Creoles, who, as Benedict Anderson aptly observed, "constituted simultaneously a colonial community and an upper class."[14] To more precisely describe the unique institutional position of the American Creoles, we have to attend to the ways in which the empires' three constitutions overlapped.

Over the more than three-hundred-year-long course of European imperial rule in the Americas, the specific institutions governing the internal socio-racial hierarchy of the colonies took on a range of forms, and important variations also existed both within and between the territories claimed by different imperial powers.[15] In the early years of settlement, colonial constitutions in British and Spanish America tended to reproduce the institutional arrangements of their metropoles, recreating "societies of orders" across the Atlantic, in which corporate memberships and inherited properties defined political, economic, and social privileges. Eventually, though, in every part of the Americas claimed, colonized, and ruled by Europeans, "a concept of nobility based fundamentally on the notion of purity of blood arose in contrast to one which reserved the title and status of nobles to an inevitably small number of families whose members had in the economic system and in society very clearly defined functions."[16] The specific institutions that accomplished this separation between European settlers and American-born Creoles of European descent, on the one hand, and African, Indigenous, and mixed-race Americans, on the other, facilitated the latter groups' simultaneous economic exploitation, political exclusion, and social marginalization.

For example, as African slaves replaced white indentured servants as laborers on plantations across southeastern North America in the late seventeenth and early eighteenth centuries, colonial assemblies adopted laws that prohibited even free men of African descent from voting in local elections, holding offices, or testifying in court. Other laws and city ordinances punished miscegenation and intermarriage, and discouraged the baptism of African and mixed-race children.[17] At the same time, land-grant policies, franchise laws, and naturalization procedures, lowered barriers to economic advancement, political participation, and social equality for poor whites, including those who had only very recently arrived from Europe. In this sense, as Rogers Smith has argued, "[British] Americans went beyond any explicit provisions in English law and gave legal expression to an increasingly racialized sense of their identity so powerful that the very humanity of these outsiders was denied."[18] Both formal and informal institutions shaped British America's emerging racial hierarchy, with written laws and vigilante justice reinforcing a conflictual division of colonial identities and interests.

Similarly, the Spanish imperial practice of governing indigenous communities through separate *Repúblicas de Indios*, a form of indirect rule, and the *encomienda*, a tribute system, not only excluded Native Americans from the colonies' political and civil society organizations, but also facilitated the extraction of their labor and their forced conversion to Catholicism, giving juridical effect to the elevation of *peninsulares* and *criollos* over *indios*, *negros*, and *castas*, or mixed-race Americans.[19] Creoles fiercely defended these institutions against admittedly less than philanthropic metropolitan efforts to diminish the social and legal distinctions between the colonies' racial castes and ameliorate exploitation and abuse, rioting against the abolition of the *encomienda*, and protesting late colonial-era policies that offered mixed-race Americans the opportunity to purchase certificates attesting to their racial purity.[20] Examples such as these could be multiplied, further illustrating the myriad ways in which the colonial constitutions of all the European empires in the Americas endowed Creoles with rights and privileges that were denied to indigenous, African, and mixed-race Americans, creating differently interested classes of colonial inhabitants.

But the American Creoles' institutional position was defined not only by the constitutions of their colonies but also by the constitutions of their empires, which placed all Americans, Creoles included, in a subordinate position with respect to Europeans. The British and Spanish American empires were both, formally speaking, "composite monarchies": assemblages of separate territories united by a common sovereign in the person of the king.[21] This implied a fundamental legal equality between the empires' subjects in the Old World and the New – between, for example, *Valencianos* and *Novohispanos*, or Bristolians and Bostonians. However, what this equality should mean in practice was a question subjected to near-continuous contestation in both the English and Spanish Americas virtually from the moment the empires were first established.

Much debate centered on a fraught distinction between the colonies' "internal" and "external" affairs, or between domestic matters on which colonists demanded a degree of autonomy, and matters relating to foreign policy and commerce, which colonists conceded were rightfully regulated by metropolitan governments.[22] In instance after instance, colonists and metropolitan governments disagreed about exactly where the line between internal and external affairs should be drawn, and about what sacrifices it was reasonable to expect the colonies to make on behalf of the empires to which they belonged. All too often, colonists saw metropolitan preferences imposed by royal proclamation or parliamentary legislation, and lamented their lack of representation or the disadvantages distance imposed on their lobbyists. Worse yet, imperial policies were enforced by ecclesiastical, military, and administrative organs of imperial government within the colonies, whose empty posts were frequently filled by new arrivals from overseas rather than established settlers, leading colonists to conclude that their trans-Atlantic isolation produced more malign than benign neglect.[23]

It is clear, then, that Marx's classic conception of conflict between binary sets of polarized classes cannot account for the social position of the American Creoles. At once dominant as Europeans within American colonies, and dominated as Americans within European empires, Creoles were neither colonizers nor colonized, but both. In this sense, their institutional position resembled what the sociologist Erik Olin Wright, in his attempt to account for the distinctive interests and ideologies of the "middle classes" of managers and professionals common in advanced capitalist societies, called a "contradictory class location." Individuals in this category, who work for a wage but also possess substantial endowments of financial or human capital, are neither bourgeois nor proletarian, in Marx's terms, but both. Their position is "contradictory," Wright argues, "precisely in the sense that [it] partakes of both sides of ... inherently contradictory interests."[24] In thought and deed, then, the middle class exhibits contradictions that cannot be captured by Marx's polarized binaries.

The overlapping constitutions of European imperialism placed Creoles in a position with analogous contradictions, offering simultaneous advantages and disadvantages, opportunities to exploit and to be exploited. As a result, Creoles developed interests in the maintenance, reform, or abolition of imperial institutions that sometimes pushed them into alliance with Europeans and sometimes pushed them into alliance with Indigenous or African Americans, but often pushed them into simultaneous conflict with both. Creoles' contradictory institutional position, and the contrary allegiances and interests it inspired, would be reflected in ideological contradictions as institutional changes in their societies moved them gradually toward revolution and independence.

2.2 THE INSTITUTIONAL ORIGINS OF THE CREOLE REVOLUTIONS

Despite its contradictions, European rule of the Americas persisted and advanced for almost three centuries, aided and abetted by the expansion of Creole communities across two continents. Over the course of the eighteenth century, however, reforms to each of the European empires' three constitutions were perceived by Creoles as threats to their cherished institutional advantages, and portents of further despised institutional disadvantages, hastening their disenchantment with imperial rule and causing the conflicts that ultimately exploded into the American independence movements. The most fundamental revisions were occasioned by warfare between Europe's imperial powers, the costs of which caused metropolitan governments in both Spain and Britain to expand authority they wielded within their empires, and to curtail the autonomy of colonial assemblies, city councils, and other Creole-dominated political institutions.

The War of the Spanish Succession, fought between 1701 and 1714, ended Spain's long-standing Habsburg dynasty and installed a Bourbon successor, while also dramatically reducing the claims of the Spanish Crown within Europe, leaving the new monarch, Felipe V, with an empire consisting mainly of present-day Spain and Spanish America. Felipe V and his heirs, Fernando VI and Carlos III, sought to reverse Spain's relative decline amongst Europe's great powers by instituting a broad set of economic and administrative reforms, both within Spain itself and its overseas possessions.[25] In order to increase returns from the Americas to the royal treasury, some outdated restrictions on intercolonial trade were relaxed, but at the same time much more stringent oversight of colonial agriculture, industry, commerce, and tax collection was established by the creation of new territorial divisions and the installation of a new layer of bureaucracy – an intendancy system modeled on the one Felipe V's grandfather, Louis XIV, had imposed on France.

As the historian Jaime Rodriguez writes, the Bourbons generally "rejected the Habsburg concept of *federated* kingdoms, insisting instead upon a united and centralized Spain ruling over its overseas possessions."[26] The Bourbon reforms were not implemented with even intensity over the entirety of Spanish America, and particular policies had disparate effects on different regions, depending on the nature of their economies and the effectiveness of enforcement.[27] Speaking broadly, though, the shift to Bourbon rule and its attendant reforms had negative implications for Spanish America's Creoles, who found themselves completely excluded from posts they had previously occupied in the colonial *audiencias* – supreme judicial and administrative courts with broad territorial competence – and thus deprived of the autonomy they thought they deserved as equal subjects of Spain's composite monarchy.[28]

A few decades later, following their triumphant, but expensive, engagement with France and Spain in the Seven Years' War – actually fought over a longer period, from 1754 to 1763 – the British were also seized by a reformist impulse. While the war inspired a new sense of loyalty amongst the Creoles in the colonies, who viewed its outcome as a result of their own military efforts and an important step toward their predestined expansion over the North American continent, metropolitan Britons emphasized, instead, the colonists' "vexatious" habit of citing their "rights and privileges" in order to avoid fulfilling fiscal and material requisitions made for the war effort, and colonial merchants' refusal to cease trade with neutral and enemy powers. At the same time, the war heightened the British government's awareness of the importance of the colonies and colonial trade to Britain's rise amongst the world's ranks of great powers, and redoubled their commitment to stamping out any signs of colonial disposition to "independency" before it could spread.

Thus, as Jack P. Greene notes, "The experience of the Seven Years' War ... sent the postwar expectations of men on opposite sides of the Atlantic veering off in opposite directions."[29] Just as Creoles expected to be rewarded for their service with an augmented representation in London and greater autonomy in colonial affairs, an overseas ministry under George Grenville was doing its best to "restrict [the colonies'] scope for economic and political activity," while reducing the costs of maintaining the empire and imposing a greater share of the remainder on the colonists themselves.[30] To this end, new taxes and customs controls were adopted, and old ones were more energetically enforced by new cadres of excise men, enlarged squadrons of Royal Navy ships, and the permanent stationing of some 7,500 professional soldiers in the colonies. As in Spanish America, these innovations aroused passionate resentment, and at times, determined resistance, amongst British American Creoles.[31]

Eighteenth-century modifications to imperial constitutions coincided with a series of pseudoscientific publications that cast Americans in a distinctly negative light. The French naturalist Georges-Louis Le Clerc, Comte de Buffon, claimed in a work published at mid-century that there were fewer animal species in the New World than the Old, and that American animals were smaller, weaker, and less sexually active than their European counterparts. He attributed these differences to the presence of "moist and poisonous vapors" and lower average temperatures in the Americas, providing a climatic explanation of American underdevelopment, which was well received by Europeans confident of their global superiority and recently impressed by Montesquieu's observations on the connection between climate and political institutions. Buffon's ideas were pursued further by Cornelius de Pauw, a Dutch naturalist, who advanced the field mainly by extending Buffon's observations to the humans of the New World. De Pauw claimed that Americans were smaller, weaker, less hirsute, and less libidinous than Europeans.

While remaining focused on humidity and temperature as root causes of American inferiority, de Pauw described the New World as degenerate rather than underdeveloped, noting that even European species achieved a smaller size and adopted a more passive demeanor when transplanted across the Atlantic. This set the stage for the Abbé Raynal and his fellow *encylopédiste* Denis Diderot to draw out the political implications of Buffon and de Pauw's climatic theories, bringing them back, in a way, to where they began with Montesquieu, by arguing that climate-driven degeneration could explain some of the famous crimes committed by European settlers in the New World, as well as the tendency of its peoples to be governed by despotic governments.[32]

Of course, Europeans had long described Indigenous Americans as backward and uncivilized, employing these observations to justify the conquest, with its forced religious conversions, violent territorial acquisitions, slavery, and other forms of exclusion and domination.[33] Creoles also relied upon this image of the savage to justify their expropriation of Indian lands and labor. However, the pseudoscience of climate and geography that de Pauw, in particular, had used to reframe this familiar theme presented clear and problematic implications for Creoles: If the American climate, rather than race or culture, was responsible for Native Americans' civilizational deficits – if, indeed, European species degenerated upon exposure to the New World's temperature and vapors – then Creoles, too, could be described as inferior, and justifiably subjected to the treatment Europeans accorded their inferiors.

Predictably, the Creole response to the threat implied by the new naturalism was furious, their cause championed by luminaries including the New Spaniard Francisco Javier Clavigero, the Chilean Giovanni Ignazio Molina, the Quiteño Juan de Velasco, the Pennsylvanian Benjamin Franklin, and the Virginian Thomas Jefferson.[34] As they churned out reams of criticism of Buffon, de Pauw, and Raynal, these intellectuals contributed to the development of class consciousness amongst the Creoles within each empire,[35] heightening awareness of the imminent threats not only to the equality with European-born Britons and Spaniards enshrined in their imperial constitutions, but also to the superiority vis-à-vis nonwhite Americans enshrined in their colonial constitutions.

Creoles were particularly concerned with the ways in which reforms to imperial constitutions might change colonial constitutions as well – the prospect, in other words, that increased metropolitan oversight might impinge upon their own interactions with African, Indigenous, or mixed-race inhabitants of the colonies. They had grown accustomed to broad autonomy in this area, a consequence of the difficulty involved in enforcing policy across an ocean without the cooperation of local elites. The humanitarian "New Laws," imposed by Emperor Charles V in 1542, forbade the granting of new *encomiendas,* or rights to the labor and tribute of indigenous communities, revoked the perpetuity of existing grants of *encomienda,* and imposed stricter new regulations on conditions under which Indigenous Americans could work. They were met by furious protest in the Americas. Rebellious *conquistadores* beheaded the Viceroy of Peru when he informed them of the empire's new policies. His counterpart in New Spain escaped a similar fate only by declining to enforce the New Laws until their main provisions were repealed.[36]

By the second half of the eighteenth century, much had changed. In 1763, George III issued a royal proclamation that dramatically revised the procedure by which British American colonists could acquire new land from Indigenous communities. Seeking to restrain the often fraudulent or forced purchases that land speculators had come to rely on as means of increasing profits, the Proclamation established a line running through the colonies of New York, Pennsylvania, Virginia, North Carolina, South Carolina, and Georgia. All future settlement west of the line was forbidden, and existing settlers were directed to decamp immediately. East of the line, settlers were prohibited from bargaining or transacting personally or on their own behalf with members of Indian tribes; all future land purchases would be made in the name of the Crown, by Crown-appointed colonial governors.[37]

To be sure, even with the fortified administrative apparatus installed in the colonies in the course of the Seven Years' War, the Proclamation of 1763 was not perfectly enforced, and the Crown's efforts to intercede on its Indigenous subjects' behalf had some perverse unintended consequences. Nonetheless, the law caused sufficient inconvenience for British American speculators, and represented a real enough threat to American Creoles' cherished privileges, that it was cited amongst the "long train of abuses" perpetrated by the king against his American subjects that the signers of the Declaration of Independence felt authorized their break with imperial rule.[38]

Ultimately, however, and interestingly, for both British and Spanish American Creoles, the most proximate impetus to rebellion were not reforms that modified either imperial or colonial constitutions, but shifting balances of power in the metropoles. In British America, as is well known, the growing authority of Parliament, vis-à-vis the Crown, became central to the arguments that Creoles made against taxes and duties imposed upon their colonies by Parliament in the late 1760s and 1770s. In the years leading up to their revolution, colonists, who would soon call themselves patriots, appealed to King George III to assert his prerogative and veto acts affecting the colonies but originating in a legislature where colonists had no representation. Though this "patriot royalism" has often been dismissed as a rhetorical or legal contortion, recent scholarship has shown that in rejecting Parliament's assertion of authority, British North Americans were fighting "to preserve a constitutional structure that they had assumed to be permanent – or at least not alterable without their consent – and which now seemed under deadly assault."[39] Creoles viewed the king's prerogative as a critical bulwark of the formal legal equality they cherished, and which Parliamentary sovereignty threatened to overturn.

The parallels present in the lead-up to Spanish America's struggles for independence are likely less well known to English-language readers. In the first decade of the nineteenth century, Napoleon's conquests rearranged alliances amongst Europe's great powers, placing Spain in league with France against Britain and Portugal. In 1807, King Carlos IV gave French troops permission to cross Spanish territory on their way to Portugal, an important gap in Napoleon's "continental system." Soon after, a palace coup by the Spanish heir apparent, Fernando VII, provided Napoleon with a pretense for imprisoning both claimants and placing his brother, Joseph Bonaparte, on the Spanish throne. Spaniards rose in resistance to this imposition, with local notables in urban areas meeting in provisional committees, or *Juntas*, to collect funds and empower officers.

In order to better organize the resistance nationwide, a *Junta Central Suprema* was formed in 1808 and calls were issued for deputies to be elected from all of Spain's provinces, including the American colonies. However, there was a problem: while the *Junta Central* asked each Spanish province to send two deputies, only one deputy each was allotted to the nine American kingdoms and captaincies-general. The result was thirty-six peninsular deputies versus nine from the Americas, which had a population equal to or even greater than Spain. Thus, while Spanish Americans responded to Napoleon's invasion with declarations of loyalty to Fernando VII, many refused to recognize the authority of the *Junta Central*.[40] In the Spanish Empire, as in the British Empire, then, colonial rebellion was preceded and inspired by a shift of authority within the metropole from a monarchical to a representative institution. The unequal basis on which metropolitan Spaniards proposed to represent their overseas countrymen in the *Junta Central*, like the complete exclusion of British Americans from Parliament, caused Spanish American Creoles to conclude that their metropole considered them second-class citizens, and prodded them into revolt.

Though retrospect tends to surround the events that most profoundly shape history in an aura of inevitability, it is important to recognize the counterintuitive and contingent qualities of the Creole revolutions. There were Americans with much more profound grievances to air, and much stronger interests to pursue than the Creole patriots that overthrew the empires of the New World, as the slaves of Saint Domingue would demonstrate. Only a complex conjuncture of institutional reforms, simultaneously affecting the imperial, colonial, and metropolitan constitutions of British and Spanish America, could have convinced Creoles throughout the hemisphere to desert the familiar inconveniences of imperial rule for the much more menacing uncertainties of independence. That the Americas were freed by the descendants of European colonists was not inevitable, but the fact that the American independence movements *were* Creole Revolutions explains much about the ideas and institutions they produced.

2.3 ANTI-IMPERIAL IMPERIALISM

If we adopt the foregoing analysis of the American Creoles' contradictory institutional position, and the modified Marxian understanding of the relationship between institutional position and ideology developed in the preceding text, what expectations should we have regarding the ideologies that would emerge in the course of the Creole Revolutions? Perhaps obviously, we might expect that they will be *contradictory*, advancing mutually exclusive projects, and defending them by reference to opposed principles or ideals. We should also expect to observe convergences amongst Creole political thinkers on ideas and institutional arrangements that advanced their class's particular interests, reconciling the internal antagonism of colonizer and colonized. Here, I argue that as they grappled with the philosophical and political dilemmas imposed by their contradictory institutional position, Creole political theorists converged upon an ideology that was both anti-imperialist and imperialist at the same time.

Here again, some terminological reflection is in order. Michael Doyle's definition of empire – "relationships of political control imposed by some political societies over the effective sovereignty of other political societies" – is a common touch point, admirable for its ability to capture a wide range of cases without describing "all forms of international inequality" as ipso facto imperial.[41] But Doyle's parsimonious concept does not convey some of the connotations that "empire" has carried in the history of political thought, and, by describing empire as a relationship between two or more "political societies," Doyle's discerning definition rules out patently imperial forms of territorial expansion that abolish borders and erase distinctions by eliminating or assimilating conquered communities.

As Anthony Pagden shows in his comparative history of imperial ideologies, the immense influence of Rome as an exemplar of *imperium* lent the term *empire* itself a sense not only of domination or control, but also of assimilation. An empire is a "kind of political, and cultural, unity created out of different states widely separated in space." The medium of imperial assimilation is "civilization." For its Roman ideologues, the "ethical purpose" of imperial expansion was the "exportation" of *civitas*: the forceful induction of outsiders into a set of customary practices and, crucially, a system of laws that enabled those subject to them to pursue uniquely human ways of living. Empire "had the power to transform all those who entered it. So long, that is, as you were outside it, a barbarian or a provincial, you were in some sense less than human. Once inside, you would in time become 'civilized.'"[42]

Importantly, imperial expansion transformed not only Rome's provinces, but also its metropole, enabling the Roman emperors to rise on the ruins of the Republic. For subsequent theorists of empire, Rome demonstrated that a republic could be or become an empire, but also illustrated what Hannah Arendt would describe as imperialism's "boomerang effect" – the tendency of territorial expansion abroad to promote political centralization at home.[43] Consequently, as Pagden notes, empire also came to mean consolidated and especially monarchical authority.

Doyle's definition of empire as an inter-national control and Pagden's Rome-centered intellectual history of imperialism must be supplemented, finally, with an account of the internal dynamics of imperial societies, aptly described by Jane Burbank and Frederick Cooper as the "politics of difference." For all their assimilative effects, empires are "polities that maintain distinction and hierarchy as they incorporate new people ... the concept of empire presumes that different people will be governed differently."[44] Not all empires are colonial, settling specially privileged metropolitan émigrés in conquered territories amongst indigenous or other populations. But social stratification and legal pluralism, either within conquered territories or between conquered territories and the metropole, is characteristic of imperial rule.[45]

In all these senses of the term, the ideology of Creole Revolution was anti-imperial. The polities that Creole political theorists sought first to reform and then to destroy were empires, products of territorial conquests that united widely separated communities under a single, overarching authority. It was precisely the imperial features of those polities – the inequalities that they imposed upon peripheral populations – that formed the central object of Creoles' condemnation and eventual case for independence. Even after American Creoles won their independence, their political thinking remained anti-imperial, focused on crafting domestic political institutions and approaches to foreign policy that would insulate their societies against reconquest, and aid other Americans in their own efforts to overthrow European rule.

However, the ideology of Creole Revolution was also imperial. Creole political theorists aimed, from the outset, to preserve the privileges that, as the descendants of Europeans, they enjoyed at the expense of Indigenous and African Americans, often making the threat posed to these privileges by continued submission to Europe an important part of their calls to arms. They designed constitutions with an eye to containing the conflicts that they knew their still-stratified colonial societies might produce. To this end, they adopted modes of organizing authority over immense territories and dividing powers within central governments modeled on the constitutions of their imperial predecessors. And they defended efforts to expand their new states' territories beyond existing borders and to consolidate control over previously unincorporated populations as means of spreading what they regarded as a uniquely enlightened way of living under political institutions animated by ideals they had discovered in the course of fighting for their freedom.

Thus, the ideology of Creole Revolution can be described as anti-imperial imperialism, and this contradiction can be understood as the product of the distinctive two-sided struggle that Creoles encountered as they fought to extricate themselves from European rule. Anti-imperial imperialism took on different forms as the Creole Revolutions progressed, appearing clearly in three ubiquitous problems of Creole political thought: (1) justifying rebellion against European rule in the Americas; (2) designing constitutions to govern independent American states; and (3) defining an approach to foreign relations both within the hemisphere and around the world.

2.4 CREOLE RIGHTS

Throughout the Americas, the years leading up to declarations of independence were characterized by profound reflection on basic questions in political theory: the origins and purposes of government, the reciprocal obligations of sovereign and subjects, and most importantly, the conditions under which individuals could legitimately dissolve the political entities to which they belonged. Much scholarship has centered on whether the rights that colonial patriots denounced their respective metropoles for violating and eventually fought to preserve were particular, grounded in Creoles' historical and legal understandings of their rights as Englishmen and Spaniards, or universal, emerging from early modern natural rights theories and Enlightenment rationalism, and claimed by Creoles simply as persons. Most scholars agree that, in the course of the American independence movements, particularist rights were found inadequate, offering too narrow a foundation for the broad autonomy Creoles wished to claim.[46] Meanwhile, as some studies have noted, universalist accounts were too broad, carrying implications for the internal reform of colonial societies that few Creoles would wish to endorse.[47]

Though this dilemma has been described before, few works have highlighted the middle ground upon which many canny Creoles ultimately converged on in their attempts to justify American independence. Both British and Spanish Americans argued that rebellion against European rule was a legitimate means of preserving a set of privileges more expansive than the particular rights of Englishmen or Spaniards, but less inclusive than the universal rights of man – a set of rights that the ideologists of Creole

Revolution claimed specifically *as Creoles*, that is, as the descendants of the conquerors of the New World.

In 1774, the Virginian planter and polymath Thomas Jefferson drafted instructions for his colony's delegates to the first Continental Congress, directing them to propose that a petition be sent to King George III. The petition should request, Jefferson wrote, that "as chief magistrate of the British empire," George III intercede on the colonists' behalf, exercising his royal prerogative to negate the "many unwarrantable encroachments and usurpations, attempted to be made by the legislature of one part of the empire" – that is, Parliament – "upon those rights which God and the laws have given equally and independently to all." Jefferson's instructions, later published as *A Summary View of the Rights of British Americans*, took pains to remind the king that the colonists' "ancestors, before their emigration to America, were the free inhabitants of the British dominions in Europe," emphasizing that by choosing to cross the Atlantic, they did not divest themselves or their descendants of their rights as Britons, or consent to any "claim of superiority or dependence asserted over them by the mother country from which they had migrated." To the contrary, Jefferson argued, "America was conquered, and her settlements made ... at the expence of individuals, and not of the British public. [The settlers'] own blood was spilt in acquiring lands for their settlements, their own fortunes expended in making that settlement effectual."[48] Thus, in the process of settling the New World, settlers had acquired new rights for themselves and for their descendants: rights to the lands they conquered, rights to use or trade the products of their own and their dependents' labor as it suited their interests, and the right to consent to the laws that governed their societies, through representatives seated in colonial assemblies and legislatures.[49]

Parliament's attempts to legislate for the colonies – to change the terms upon which British Americans acquired lands or contracted labor, paid taxes, or stood trial – abrogated these hard-won rights and introduced a profound threat to Creole's cherished liberties. For what reason, Jefferson asked, should "160,000 electors in the island of Great Britain give law to four millions in the states of America, every individual of whom is equal to every individual of them, in virtue, in understanding, and in bodily strength?" Here, Jefferson's insistence on Creoles' moral, mental, and physical equality to metropolitan Britons hearkens back to the debates on Buffon's theory of degeneration and foreshadows the grounds upon which he himself would later defend Indigenous expropriation and African slavery.

Indeed, Jefferson seems concerned that he and his fellow Creoles might share these unfortunate peoples' fate if Parliament's overreach was not stopped. "History has informed us," he wrote, "that bodies of men, as well as individuals, are susceptible of the spirit of tyranny." If the colonies failed to resist Parliament's assertion of authority, "instead of being a free people, as we have hitherto supposed, and mean to continue ourselves, we should suddenly be found the slaves not of one but of 160,000 tyrants." The *Summary View* closes by insisting that "it is neither our wish, nor our interest, to separate from" the British empire, asking only that the King "[n]o longer persevere in sacrificing the rights of one part of the empire to the inordinate desires of another; but deal out to all equal and impartial right."[50] Of course, Jefferson did not yet know that only two years later, he would cite a similar list of complaints before declaring independence on behalf of British America's Creoles.

In 1809, a lawyer from the kingdom of New Granada (present-day Colombia) named Camilo Torres penned one of the most famous Spanish American responses to institutional shifts occasioned by the Napoleonic Wars in Spain. Like Jefferson's *Summary View*, Torres's *Memorial de Agravios* was the draft of a petition to be sent by the Creole-dominated *Cabildo*, or city council, of Santa Fe de Bogotá to the recently established *Junta Central* in Sevilla. Torres opens the *Memorial* by describing the "joy" that he and other Americans had felt upon learning of the formation of the *Junta Central*, and being informed of its intention to invite representatives from overseas. This plan appeared to offer what Torres described as "true fraternal union between European and American Spaniards, upon the basis of justice and equality." He noted perceptively that, "If the government of England" had followed a similar plan, "maybe it would not today lament the loss of its colonies ... [whose residents] did not understand how, being vassals of the same sovereign," they could be subject to laws "not sanctioned with their approbation."[51] Here, the example of a previous Creole Revolution affords Torres an insight into the range of possible conclusions the conflict in which he was involved might have, an insight that was unavailable to his British North American counterparts.

Nonetheless, Torres felt compelled to add that "in the midst of their just pleasure," *Novogranadinos* had "not been able to see without profound pain that, while the provinces of Spain, even the most inconsiderable, have sent two representatives to the *Junta Central*, the vast, rich, and populous dominions of America are only allowed one each." Torres could see no grounds upon which this inequality could be sustained. He hastened to remind the members of the *Junta Central* that "The Americas are not composed of foreigners to the Spanish nation. We are sons, and descendants of those who spilled their blood to acquire these new dominions for the Spanish Crown." Spanish America's Creoles were "as Spanish as the descendants of Don Pelayo" – the eighth-century Spanish nobleman who initiated the reconquest of the Iberian Peninsula from the Moors – "and as deserving, for this reason, of the distinctions, privileges, and prerogatives of the rest of the nation,... with this difference, if there is one, that our parents, as I have said, by means of indescribable labors, discovered, conquered, and populated this New World for Spain."[52] Here, like Jefferson, Torres insisted that his ancestors trans-Atlantic voyage had, far from depriving them of old rights, actually invested them with new ones. And like Jefferson, Torres would shortly assert that Spain's violation of those rights justified the creation of an independent state, The United Provinces of New Granada, which he led as president until he was captured and executed by Spanish troops in 1816.

For both Jefferson and for Torres, as we've seen, America's absent or unequal representation in metropolitan legislatures was an affront to the rights they each claimed, in strikingly similar language, as Creoles: rights their Spanish and British ancestors brought with them across the Atlantic and won in the process of subjugating the New World. In both empires, Creoles originally sought not independence but the recognition and equality they felt was their due. Only after years of metropolitan intransigence would they take the risky step of wresting their societies out from under the protective shadow of European rule. In these influential writings, it is clear that the American independence movements did not originate in calls for national liberation or the end of monarchical government, as the alternative interpretations discussed in Chapter 1 would suggest, but rather in demands for the reform of imperial institutions that granted European Britons and Spaniards privileges that they denied their American-born counterparts.

Creoles' claims of injustice, then, though at times decorated by appeals to natural law or universal rights, were made on behalf of a colonial elite, and rested on rights derived from the conquest. As the historian Simon Collier observed, even as Creoles invoked "the language of the rights of man, of representative government, of popular sovereignty ... they did not – and could not – cease to be what they had been in the colonial period: aristocrats, landowners, the leaders of society."[53] Thus, anti-imperial imperialism appears first in Creole revolutionaries' attempts to justify revolt against Europe. Though the Creole Revolutions were directed against empires, they did not attack the idea of empire itself, but only a form of imperialism that distinguished between Europeans born in Europe and those born in the Americas. Creole political theorists justified their own independence by citing rights that their forefathers had won by depriving other Americans of theirs.

2.5 CREOLE CONSTITUTIONALISM

As military victories brought independence within reach, the prospect of actually governing independent societies became central to Creole political thought. British and Spanish American patriots feared that, even if they managed to wrest freedom away from their respective metropoles, their new states would be exposed to the threat of reconquest by both the old imperial powers across the Atlantic and the new ones emerging within the Americas. At the same time, having mobilized large and diverse groups of people to confront their opponents, Creoles were forced to consider how they would reestablish social order and stable governance after victory. Thus, the two-sided dilemma inherent in the American independence movements persisted even after independence had been won.

To confront it, the ideologists of Creole Revolution turned to constitutional design. What Americans needed, Simón Bolívar wrote, were institutions capable of "withstanding the blows of two monstrous enemies ... who both attack at once: *tyranny and anarchy.*"[54] His colleagues throughout the hemisphere frequently invoked the same two specters,[55] as they converged around two institutional arrangements that seemed uniquely suited to resisting reconquest and reestablishing internal order within postcolonial American societies.

The first was the "union," a multi-level system of nested territorial authorities, which united former colonies under common governments.[56] Only within such unions, Creole constitutional theorists would argue, could Americans hope to maintain the independence they had fought so hard to win, and only within such unions could Creoles hope to preserve the privileged position within the Americas that they had sought independence to protect. The second was presidentialism, a system of separated powers that granted significant authority to an executive that did not depend upon the legislature for either election to or tenure in office.[57] Like union, Creole constitutional theorists argued, presidentialism would make the American states more formidable in foreign affairs and less susceptible to the volatile contentions of their heterogeneous populations.

Here, the relative timing of the American Revolutions becomes important. Because British North America's independence movement occurred first, the ideas and institutions developed in its course were deeply influential for the later Spanish American independence movements, and nowhere was this truer than in the realm of constitutional design. The US Constitution of 1787 enjoyed great prestige amongst Spanish American patriots, not only as the first document of its kind, and not only as the end product of an analogous struggle for independence, but also because Spanish Americans believed that the institutional arrangements the Constitution created were the cause of the United States' rapidly growing prosperity and global prestige.[58]

Nonetheless, its impact was not straightforward, particularly with respect to the idea of union. The US Constitution was most often invoked by Spanish American *federalistas*, proponents of decentralized systems in which component provinces or states were recognized as sovereign and a general government exercised only limited legislative authority, while being left entirely dependent upon the states for the execution of its policies. Ironically, then, the Spanish American champions of the US Constitution used its imprimatur to argue for a position similar to the one taken by Antifederalists in the United States, who opposed its ratification.

By contrast, factions that questioned the wisdom of imitating the US model, known variously as *unitarios, centralistas,* or, maddeningly, *antifederalistas*, insisted that conditions in Spanish America were fundamentally different from those in North America, that even if "federalism" had produced good results there, it could not do the same in a new context. Thus, they recommended a system in which the general government exercised sovereign authority in foreign and interstate relations, while the states were limited to administering their own internal affairs – in other words, a system not unlike the one defended by the Federalist Party of the United States and embodied in the US Constitution.[59]

Thus, British and Spanish American Creoles' convergence upon union as an institutional ideal cannot be explained as imitation, because the supposed imitators seem to have largely misunderstood the original.[60] Rather, union was attractive to Creole political theorists across the hemisphere because of the advantages it offered in the conduct of foreign and domestic affairs, advantages that were ideally suited to the dilemmas presented in the later stages and early aftermath of Creole Revolution.

As the New Yorker Alexander Hamilton argued, in a striking statement of postcolonial defiance, union would enable Americans to resist "the arrogant pretensions of the European,... to vindicate the honor of the human race, and teach that assuming brother moderation ... Disunion will add another victim to his triumphs."[61] His Virginian collaborator, James Madison, in elaborating a domestic counterpart to this defense of union, exposed the other edge of Creoles' concern. Divided by differences of "faculties," religions, and vast inequalities of wealth, the Americas' heterogeneous societies would be torn apart by factional conflict unless institutional measures were taken. Amongst the "numerous advantages promised by a well constructed Union," he emphasized the system's capacity to "refine and enlarge the public views, by passing them through the medium of a chosen body of citizens, whose wisdom may best discern the true interest of their country, and whose patriotism and love of justice will be least likely to sacrifice it to temporary or partial considerations."[62] Union, in other words, would place governments securely in the hands of the Creole Revolutions' enlightened and virtuous leaders, limiting the influence of the multi-racial masses they led.

Without ever reading the *Federalist Papers*, Spanish American Creoles voiced similar arguments after independence. Simón Bolívar spoke of the union he hoped to forge out of Spain's former colonies as a "shield for our new destiny ... a base upon which these governments might hope, if it is possible, to last eternally."[63] As for Hamilton, for Bolívar the advantages of union were first and foremost related to foreign affairs: Under the auspices of a common government, the Spanish American republics could combine their military forces to complete the wars for independence, negotiate as a unit for recognition in Europe and beneficial terms of trade, and eliminate the prospect of inter-American conflicts, "establishing a perfect equilibrium within a new order." And like Madison, Bolívar noted that union would lessen the danger posed by the "differences of origin and color" that divided American societies, and, in particular, allow Americans to "put aside their fears of the tremendous monster that has devoured the island of Santo Domingo" – that is, slave insurrection – and of "the masses of primitive inhabitants" on the peripheries of their new societies.[64] For Creoles throughout the hemisphere, then, union served a double purpose, fortifying American independence against external threats, while preserving the internal hierarchies the American states inherited from their imperial forebears.

The relatively late dates of the Spanish American independence movements facilitated constitutional influences not only from the north, but from across the Atlantic. The French Revolution and its global reverberations – the Haitian Revolution, the rise of Napoleon, and the liberal Spanish Constitution of 1812 – all figured prominently in early Spanish

American constitutional thought. But as with the United States, their effects were not straightforward. While many Creole patriots eagerly read French revolutionaries' writings and incorporated their slogans into their own work, they were, generally speaking, appalled by the execution of Louis XVI and the anarchy of the Terror. Creoles were uncertain of Napoleon's plans for the Americas, and deeply unsettled by the prospect of a slave revolt like the one that had arisen shortly after the French Revolution in Haiti.[65] Thus, they were skeptical of what was perceived to be the characteristic constitutional innovation of the French Revolution: simple popular government through a single supreme legislature – or what contemporary political scientists would call a parliamentary system. The Mexican statesman Lucas Alamán wrote in 1834 that

> The constitution which the Constituent Assembly gave France, which was copied in a servile manner by the Cortes of Cádiz, not only did not distinguish properly between the powers, not only did not establish a well-balanced equilibrium amongst them, but in excessively debilitating the Executive, transferred all authority to the Legislature, creating in the place of the absolute power of the monarchy a power as absolute and entirely arbitrary, not even having to contain it the brakes that can in some manner impede the arbitrariness of monarchs. France and Spain, by means of similar constitutions, did nothing more than pass from the tyranny of one to the infinitely more unbearable tyranny of many.[66]

Spanish Americans connected the untrammeled authority of the legislature in the French Constitution with the social upheaval that followed the French Revolution, arguing that that their own societies should adopt constitutions modeled on the English system of separated and balanced branches of government, where the crown's executive authority served to check the more directly popular will of Parliament.

In this, of course, they converged neatly with their British North American counterparts. In 1787, John Adams addressed French criticisms of the systems of separated powers that had already made their way into the particular constitutions of several states, citing literally hundreds of historical examples wherein "mixing the authority of the one, the few, and the many, confusedly in one assembly" had produced "wide-spread miseries and final slavery of almost all mankind." Adams emphasized, like many other Creoles, that the primary threat to social stability in the newly independent Americas was not an overzealous executive but an unchecked legislature. Because it more directly represents the opinions of the populace, "the legislative power is naturally and necessarily sovereign and supreme over the executive." Thus, Adams argued, in order to avoid the anarchy that would inevitably result from popular rule, the executive should be made "an essential branch of the [Legislative power], even with a negative," that is, a power to veto the legislature's decisions. Otherwise, "it will not be able to defend itself, but will be soon invaded, undermined, attacked, or in some way or other totally ruined and annihilated."[67]

Creole constitutional designers were often so concerned to constrain the latent potential for anarchy they associated with their most representative institutions, that, as I shall detail in subsequent chapters, they divided their legislatures into two or even three chambers, and carved out a role in the legislative process for third and even fourth branches of government alongside the legislature and the executive. Like union, then, presidentialism served in Creole constitutional theory as a means of limiting popular influence on government.

Of course, presidentialism served not only domestic purposes, contributing to the reestablishment of social order after independence by balancing the excessively democratic tendencies of legislatures, but also promised to bring efficiency and consistency to the conduct of foreign affairs. "Energy in the executive," Alexander Hamilton argued, "is a leading character in the definition of good government ... essential to the protection of the community against foreign attacks." Only a unitary executive, serving a substantial term in office, elected independently of the legislature could, in his analysis, muster the energy necessary to defend the United States from the ambitious European powers whose empires still encircled the new nation's territory.[68] Though he had, in the Philadelphia Convention, suggested that the "English model" of executive authority – that is, hereditary monarchy – "was the only good one" and recommended that the president be elected for life, Hamilton later retreated from this position.[69]

However, Hamilton's Spanish American counterparts did not scruple to endorse quasi-monarchical solutions to the problem of their societies' exposure to invasion, particularly from enemies closer to home. In 1840, as the US Congress considered whether to annex the Mexican province of Tejas, the Yucatecan diplomat and politician José María Gutiérrez Estrada addressed a public letter to the president of his republic, arguing that unless Mexicans invested their executive with monarchical authority, "perhaps not even twenty years will pass before we see the North Americans' stars and stripes flying above our National Palace."[70] With similar concerns in mind, Creoles throughout Spanish America incorporated strong, independent executives into their constitutions, though even these measures did not prevent Gutiérrez Estrada's prophecy from being realized, less than ten years after he wrote.

Creole political theorists defended their constitutional designs in sweeping terms, often adopting a rhetorical posture of speaking to the ages and resolving problems that plagued all societies. If we allow ourselves to be taken in by this presumption, it is easy to lose sight of the very specific two-sided dilemma reflected in Creole constitutional thought. Both union and presidentialism were novel creations, representing Creoles' most important, and lasting, contributions to global constitutionalism. But both were adopted because they promised to solve particular problems: resisting reconquest and reestablishing internal order within heterogeneous American societies. Both addressed these problems by mixing earlier constitutional models. Union offered a midpoint between the total dependence imposed upon colonies under an empire, and the total independence of sovereign states within an international system.[71] Presidentialism offered more Americans greater opportunities to govern themselves than they might have enjoyed as the subjects of a monarch, but placed greater limits on their actual influence than they would have encountered in a classical or parliamentary democracy. In this sense, both constitutional designs embody the anti-imperial imperialism characteristic of Creole political thinking in general.

2.6 CREOLE CONQUEST

As we saw in the preceding text, inter-imperial conflicts were important precipitants of the American independence movements, giving rise to the institutional reforms that eventually spurred the Creole Revolutions. The warfare associated with the Revolutions only deepened contention amongst Europe's great powers. Spain and France aided British North Americans in their war for independence, hoping that by weakening the United Kingdom they would assure or expand their own American holdings. Conversely, British ministers explored allegiances with Spanish American dissidents, hoping to forestall French and North American incursions on the continent and to secure new markets for their manufactures. Even as successively larger parts of the New World became independent, Britain, Spain, France, Portugal, and Russia continued their battles over western North America, South America's interior, and the Caribbean.[72]

In the famous "Farewell Address" he published when he declined a third term as president of the United States, George Washington piously warned Americans against "interweaving [their] destiny with that of any part of Europe," insisting that nations so recently freed from imperial rule should not "entangle [their] peace and prosperity in the toils of European ambition, rivalship, interest, humor or caprice."[73] But the Creole founders of new American states did not hesitate to enter the fray. Rather, they announced their own imperial programs, defending territorial expansion and internal colonization as means of assuring their independence and spreading their ideals throughout the hemisphere and around the world.

From the beginning, the Creole Revolutions were expansionist affairs. Small groups of men gathered in conventions, congresses, and committees to declare independence on behalf of large populations with whom they consulted only in the most perfunctory fashion. On June 9, 1816, from the city of Tucumán, the self-declared "Representatives of the United Provinces of South America" took it upon themselves to enunciate the "unanimous and indubitable will" of people inhabiting a region stretching from the mouth of the Rio de la Plata across the continent into the highest Andean plateaus.[74] Their representative pretensions were based on a late-colonial-era administrative reform, which had placed nearly all of present-day Argentina, Uruguay, Paraguay, and Bolivia under the control of a new viceroyalty seated in Buenos Aires. Declaring themselves heirs to this authority, *porteño* patriots organized campaign after campaign against royalist holdouts throughout the former imperial subunit, forging an independent state one conquest – or "liberation" – at a time.[75]

The United Provinces were not the first or last to follow this procedure, or to fail in the process. One of the Continental Army's first outings was an unsuccessful attempt to liberate the oppressed peoples of Quebec, and to bring a fourteenth British colony forcibly into the fold that would become the United States.[76] The Creole elites that declared the independence of the "Empire of Mexico" in 1821 claimed the entirety of the former viceroyalty of New Spain, encompassing all of present-day Mexico, Guatemala, Honduras, El Salvador, Nicaragua, Costa Rica, and the western United States.[77] In its original form, the polity historians now refer to as "Gran Colombia" contained the former viceroyalty of New Granada, comprising present-day Venezuela, Colombia, Ecuador, and Panama.[78]

Nor were Creole revolutionaries content to remain within territorial boundaries established under European imperialism. In the first year of his presidency, while his representative in Paris negotiated terms for the Louisiana Purchase, Thomas Jefferson had even grander ambitions in mind, noting in a letter to James Monroe, then the governor of Virginia, that "it is impossible not to look forward to distant times, when our rapid multiplication will expand itself beyond those limits, & cover the whole northern, if not the southern continent, with a people speaking the same language, governed in similar forms, & by similar laws."[79] The United States was not the only American nation gripped by such expansive zeal. As the secretary to the *Junta* of Buenos Aires notables who assumed provisional authority over the viceroyalty of the Río de la Plata in 1810, Mariano Moreno circulated a private *Plan de Operaciones* for the government of what he called the "United Provinces of the Río de la Plata," specifying the measures that should be taken, "now that South America has proclaimed its independence, so that it can enjoy a just and complete liberty." Moreno's *Plan* contained detailed strategies, not only for the liberation and unification of the former viceroyalty, but also the "dismemberment of Brazil," and the annexation of a substantial portion of the Portuguese colony to the United Provinces.[80]

The arguments Creole political theorists made on behalf of these efforts to enlarge their new states mixed familiar themes. On the one hand, territorial expansion would serve defensive ends, helping to consolidate independence by depriving European and American competitors of a foothold that could be used to launch a reconquest. Before he took his army across the border of Gran Colombia and into the viceroyalty of Peru in 1823, Simón Bolívar insisted that he "should be permitted to advance on territories occupied by the Spanish in Peru, because the enemy will come here if I do not contain him there, and because enemy territory should not be considered foreign territory, but conquerable territory."[81] He would make similar arguments two years later on behalf of his plan to unite Peru and Upper Peru (present-day Bolivia) – which his armies had by then occupied – with Gran Colombia under a single central government.[82] In the same year James Monroe, by now president of the United States, informed Europeans that that his administration would "consider any attempt on their part to extend their system to any portion of this hemisphere as dangerous to our peace and safety." This statement formed the basis for later administrations' frequent interventions in Latin America and, indeed, informed a lasting, and distinctively American, approach to foreign policy that the historian William Appleman Williams described as "imperial anticolonialism,"[83] perfectly capturing the contradictions involved.

Creole revolutionaries' interest in territorial expansion was not merely defensive. As I noted in the preceding text, Creoles responded aggressively to Enlightenment naturalists' theories of climate-driven degeneration, insisting that the Americas' flora and fauna were actually healthier and more abundant than their European counterparts, and that men born in the New World were possessed of stronger constitutions, quicker intellects, and surer morals than those born in the Old, having avoided exposure to the latter's corrupting influence.[84] Successful revolution and the achievement of independence added new, more political dimensions to Americans' confidence in their own exceptionalism.

Before independence had even been declared, Thomas Paine's famous pamphlet *Common Sense* inspired British North Americans to believe that the opportunities available to them had not arisen "since the days of Noah." They "had the power to begin the world over again" – to tear down the crumbling edifices of European imperialism and refashion global institutions in the image of their own.[85] Half a world away and half a century later, the Chilean patriot Bernardo O'Higgins expressed similar sentiments:

> It is evident that the Republics of the New World bear the vanguard of the freedom of the whole world, and that destiny is leading them on to break the chains of the human race; for in the example of America may be found the most encouraging hopes of the philosopher and the patriot. The centuries of oppression have passed; the human spirit yearns for its freedom; and now there shines the dawn of a complete re-ordering of civil society through the irresistible progress of opinion and enlightenment.[86]

For the ideologists of Creole Revolution, the republican virtues displayed in their independence movements and the enlightened ideals embodied in their political institutions served as the premises for arguments that justified not only continued efforts to expel European empires from the New World, but also the progressive expropriation of the Americas' "uncivilized" Indigenous communities, and eventually, the conquest of territories claimed by other Creole revolutionaries. In this way, Creoles' convergence upon foreign policies marked by territorial expansion and internal colonization, the final form of anti-imperial imperialism, brought the Creole Revolutions into conflict with one another, and, as I argue in Chapter 6, ultimately brought the Creole Revolutions to an end, opening a new era of hemispheric divergence that would drive American and Latin American political thinking in two very different directions.

2.7 CONCLUSION

In the anti-imperial imperialism characteristic of the Creole Revolutions, we confront a contradictory ideology similar in many ways to the "liberal imperialism" that political theorists and intellectual historians have recently described in nineteenth-century European political thought.[87] In both cases, we have political thinkers committed to a set of seemingly anti-imperial principles – independence and popular sovereignty in the case of the Creoles, equality and individual liberty in the case of the European liberals – employing them in defense of imperial policies of expansion, exclusion, and expropriation. Anti-imperial imperialism displays the same internal tension that Uday Mehta has described in liberal imperialism. The problem for interpreters of each case is to "account for how a set of ideas that professed, at a fundamental level, to include as its political referent a universal constituency nevertheless spawned practices that were either predicated on or directed at the political marginalization of various people."[88]

However, while many contributors to the large, and very valuable literature on liberal imperialism have sought to show that "the imperialistic urge is internal to liberalism, that inherent in the very structure of liberal rationalism and abstraction is a propensity for colonial domination,"[89] here I offer a different way of understanding how anti-imperial and imperial commitments could simultaneously occupy the center of the ideology of Creole Revolution. Rather than interrogating liberal ideas to see how they could end up providing a defense for illiberal practices, I show that, because of the contradictory position they occupied amongst the overlapping institutions of European imperialism in the Americas, the political theorists that defended the Creole Revolutions converged on a set of contradictory ideas, which were both anti-imperial and imperial. Here, contradictions are not a result of the ideas themselves, but of the interests that they were developed to defend, and of the institutions that structured those interests.

In the following chapters, I provide a more systematic demonstration of this theory, through the comparison of three ideologists of Creole Revolution. None of the three was a "liberal" in the sense intended in the preceding text, but all three evinced philosophical commitments, and engaged in concerted political activities, which were anti-imperial. Alexander Hamilton analyzed the perverse incentives of a legislature that represented only a specific, geographically constrained, portion of the population subject to its laws, attacking in this way the inequality between center and periphery that defines imperial rule. Simón Bolívar denounced the corruption that Spanish tyranny had induced in Spanish America, insisting that only independence would enable Spanish Americans to develop the virtues requisite for self-rule. And Lucas Alamán argued that the colony of New Spain had, through the gradual progress stimulated by Spain itself, reached a point of maturity at which the continuation of Spanish rule could not but become stifling and counterproductive.

At the same time, Hamilton, Bolívar, and Alamán all defended independence without impugning the imperial hierarchies within their own societies, sought to constrain popular sovereignty in unionist and presidentialist constitutions, and defended territorial expansion and internal colonization after independence had been won. These latter positions, clearly at odds with the former, were not logical entailments of Hamilton's empiricism, of Bolívar's republicanism, or of Alamán's conservatism. Rather, these three political thinkers stitched together their paradoxical philosophies in response to the dilemmas presented by the extraordinary and complicated situation that, as Creole revolutionaries, they encountered in common.

3

Alexander Hamilton in Hemispheric Perspective

This book is not the first to describe the political ideas of the American founding as an ideology, or to argue that the institutions structured by the US Constitution served the interests of the early republic's dominant class. But it departs from earlier work in this vein by describing the founders of the United States as Creole revolutionaries, and suggesting that they occupied an institutional position with closer contemporary analogies elsewhere in the Americas than in Europe. In this chapter, I argue that the political thought of the particular founder upon whom I focus, Alexander Hamilton, can be better understood when considered from a hemispheric perspective, informed by comparisons drawn with other parts of the Americas and attentive to inter-American relations, than from the Atlantic perspective that has, to date, framed the debate on the relationship between class interests and ideologies in the independence movement of the United States.[1]

As I noted in the Introduction, comparisons drawn between British North America and Europe have informed scholarly analyses of the American founding since the founding itself, with figures like John Adams and Alexis de Tocqueville tracing trans-Atlantic connections between the signal events that defined the "Age of Revolutions." The advent of the discipline of political science in the United States at the end of the nineteenth century only encouraged this approach. The nation's first political scientists cut their teeth debating the comparative merits of the US Constitution, with some asserting that the protection of individual liberties its institutions offered placed it well in advance of the prevailing political systems of Germany, Great Britain, and France, while others insisted that the complex system of checks and balances it framed had impeded development toward a democratic ideal that was, by then, better realized on the other side of the Atlantic.[2]

To explain points of similarity and difference in European and North American political development, scholars influenced by materialist theories of society and politics compared the economic classes that confronted each other in the American Revolution and its aftermath to the ones that contested roughly contemporaneous revolutions in Europe. In his 1913 classic, *An Economic Interpretation of the Constitution of the United States*, Charles Beard cited James Madison, not Karl Marx, as the inspiration for the "theory of economic determinism in politics" that he employed, but Marx might have sympathized with his conclusions. Beard depicted the ratification of the US Constitution as the triumph of a "consolidated group" of manufacturers, merchants, shippers, commercial agriculturalists, and financial speculators over a coalition of "manorial lords" and indebted "small farmers,"[3] drawing a direct analogy between the factions of the early American republic and the urban and rural classes at war in Europe's "bourgeois" revolutions.[4] Like its analogues across the Atlantic, in Beard's account, the expansion of federal authority effected by the Constitution cleared the way for the rise of capitalism in the United States, and consolidated the influence of capital-owners in American government.

Though it remains an influential point of reference,[5] by midcentury Beard's account of the American founding faced two important critiques. First, historians Robert Brown and Forrest McDonald reanalyzed the framing and ratification debates using new data and methods, finding little evidence to support Beard's characterization of the class interests in contention over the Constitution.[6] Second, the political scientist Louis Hartz attacked Beard's basic approach, insisting that no concept of class struggle imported from Europe could be applied to the United States. Having been settled by "men who fled from the feudal and clerical oppressions of the Old World," British North America lacked both the landed aristocracy and the landless peasantry that bookended Europe's class structure and drove its class conflicts. In Hartz's telling, every stratum of the early republic's foreshortened social hierarchy pursued their aims in terms dictated by a pervasive "Lockian" liberalism, which limited the scope of possible political dissent. Attempts to discover a "social revolution" analogous to the ones that shook England or France within the American founding were misguided, Hartz argued; any plausible interpretation of American political thought had to begin by acknowledging the United States' fundamental uniqueness within the wider Atlantic world.[7]

Like its progressive predecessors, Hartz's liberal consensus enjoyed widespread influence even as it encountered significant criticism.[8] Beginning in the late 1960s, a group of intellectual historians led by Bernard Bailyn, Gordon Wood, and J. G. A. Pocock argued that the American founders were, in fact, neither exceptional nor liberal. Rather, their writings evidenced deep engagement with an "Atlantic republican tradition" of political thought, whose roots extended back to Renaissance Italy.[9]

Wood paired this revisionist intellectual history of the early republic with a new account of its class structure that also reincorporated European categories.[10] To be sure, no one could accuse Wood of employing "economic interpretation" as a method. His account of the founding depicts a "social struggle" in which the combatants are "middling people" and a "gentry-aristocracy" defined less by their financial interests or occupations than by their political outlooks.[11] The Constitution itself, for Wood, was not the culmination of a bourgeois revolution but "an aristocratic remedy"[12] – a last, desperate bid by a backward-looking elite to hold back the bustling, commercial democracy being created beneath their feet by the "thousands upon thousands of middling artisans and craftsmen" that eventually came into their own within Thomas Jefferson's Democratic-Republican party.[13]

Over the past century, then, leading interpretations of the American founding have shifted dramatically. But whether they've emphasized conflict or consensus, and however they've characterized the era's dominant classes, castes, or groups, Beard, Hartz, and Wood's many followers have all focused intently on economic and ideological divisions, or lack thereof, amongst the early republic's European-descended colonist-citizens. As a result, they have neglected relations between these colonist-citizens and the Europeans whose rule they repudiated, and between colonist-citizens and the politically excluded, economically exploited African and Indigenous people who also inhabited North America. In recent years, historians have highlighted both lacunae, calling attention to the centrality of international and racial ideologies in the American founding.

"Internationalist" interpretations of the American founding have restored foreign policy and international relations to the heart of the founders' political thought, exposing the interpretive problems that have resulted from Beard, Hartz, Wood, and others' exclusive focus on domestic concerns and party politics.[14] These scholars have described the international legal context of British Americans' struggle for autonomy, highlighting the diplomatic purposes of the Declaration of Independence and the imperial ambitions of the new nation's leading patriots.[15] They have recast the Constitution of the United States as a "peace pact" – a novel solution to a long-standing problem in international relations, which allowed the states to coexist in close proximity without resorting to war – and as the institutional basis for a program of territorial expansion and global power projection more successful than any previously attempted in history.[16]

These internationalist interpretations of the founding undermine the image of an exceptionally isolated and peaceful country that Americans have long cherished, replacing it with an account attentive to the extraordinary war-making capacity forged at Philadelphia and the frequency with which the United States deployed military means in pursuit of its interests throughout its early history. As the historian Max Edling notes, this new research has moved us closer to understanding the "most interesting feature of the American polity," namely, "the combination of, on the one hand, a fundamentally liberal regime in the domestic sphere with, on the other hand, a government possessing the ability and willingness to regularly mobilize and project powers of coercion on an enormous and unprecedented scale beyond the nation's pale."[17]

From a different, but related angle, the political scientist Rogers Smith has argued that if Hartz and others were right in emphasizing the absence of feudalism as an important source of differences between European and American political institutions, they were wrong in insisting that American institutions were pervasively liberal as a result. "Feudalism" in Europe, Smith pointedly observes, "did not include chattel slavery, race-based immigration and naturalization restrictions, ineligibility of women and the foreign-born for the highest political offices, segregation, or many ... other forms of civic hierarchy" unique to the United States.[18] Similarly, in an important recent book, Aziz Rana argues that scholars who have described exceptionally radical republican currents in the ideas of the American Revolution "fundamentally mistake what in reality was exceptional about the Revolution." Though British-American colonists did develop "a remarkably robust account of freedom," and aimed to extend its blessings to a wider swathe of society than would have been possible in Europe, both the settlers' vision of freedom itself and their egalitarian aspirations were premised upon "the expansion of [African] slavery and the expropriation of indigenous groups," forms of domination and exclusion that supplied the material requisites – land and labor – for white settlers' freedom.[19]

By showing that imperial expansion and racial discrimination were as central to American political thought in the period of the founding as liberalism and republicanism, the recent literature has fundamentally reoriented scholarship on the relationship between class structure, ideologies, and institutions in the early republic. But even as they have, with very good reason, rejected the grounds on which Hartz and others based their narratives of American exceptionalism, these works have not rejected exceptionalism itself, or escaped the Atlantic perspective that has always framed the debate on class conflict in the American founding. They show, convincingly, that if America was exceptionally egalitarian, it was also peculiarly racist, and that if relations amongst the American states were exceptionally peaceful, the United States also was unusually apt to conquer and annex neighboring territories. Indeed, for some, though not all of these scholars, America was exceptionally egalitarian and peaceful *because* it was peculiarly racist and unusually expansive.[20] But in these accounts, the United States' exceptional egalitarianism, its peculiar racism, and its unusually effective expansion appear exceptional, peculiar, and unusual specifically in contrast to Europe.

The account offered here incorporates the important insights offered by studies that center race and foreign relations in the American founding, but seeks to advance their critiques by showing that the paradoxical combination of liberal, republican, imperial, and racist ideologies that arose in the independence movement of the United States was not exceptional, unusual, or peculiar, but comparable and even analogous to the ideologies voiced by Creole revolutionaries throughout the Americas. In the pages that follow, I illustrate the fruitfulness of this hemispheric approach in an examination of the political thought of Alexander Hamilton.

3.1 HAMILTON IN HIS HEMISPHERE

Cogent cases could be made, of course, for focusing on one or another of his colleagues, but four features make Alexander Hamilton a particularly apt subject for this study. First, Hamilton's manifestly influential ideas have proven unusually difficult for scholars working within any of the frameworks described in the preceding text to explain.[21] Charles Beard described Hamilton as the "colossal genius of the new system" established by the Constitution, but had to admit that no personal financial interest could explain his devotion to the Federalist cause.[22] Louis Hartz's Hamilton is a "gloomy" advocate of aristocratic government in a land without an aristocracy.[23] Likewise, for Gordon Wood, Hamilton was a thinker out of sync with his era, pursuing a vision that was "already anachronistic and ill-adapted to the restless democratic and capitalistic society that was rapidly emerging in America."[24] Others, though, have hailed Hamilton as "the prophet of the capitalist revolution" that was yet to come in America,[25] and credited him with envisioning an age of global "American ascendancy ... much closer to his countrymen's understanding of their role in the world in the twentieth than in the eighteenth century."[26]

By treating Hamilton as idiosyncratic in each of these very different – or even mutually exclusive – ways, all of these scholars fail to account for his enormous intellectual influence on the American founding. Here, I will show that precisely the paradoxes of Hamilton's thought – the ideas that lead interpreters to treat him as both ahead of and behind his times – tie him tightly to his period and place, reflecting the dilemmas he confronted as a Creole revolutionary. Examining Hamilton in hemispheric perspective helps us to return him to his rightful place within the pantheon of the United States' founders.

Second, Hamilton was, almost uniquely amongst his contemporaries, intimately involved in every stage of the American founding. His critiques of the British Empire, penned while he was still an undergraduate, are as cogent and compelling as those written by more senior figures, like James Wilson, John Adams, or Thomas Jefferson. When these elder statesmen had retired from the scene, or left the country to serve as ambassadors to foreign courts, Hamilton joined James Madison and a younger generation of revolutionaries to lead a lobbying effort that culminated in the constitutional convention of 1787. Afterward, he wrote the lion's share of the *Federalist Papers*, penning opinion pieces now considered the most authoritative guide to the meaning of the Constitution itself. Finally, as secretary of the treasury under President George Washington and as the effective leader of the Federalist Party throughout the presidency of John Adams, Hamilton had an outsize influence on the early republic's fiscal and foreign policies.

It is true that Hamilton had intellectual and political adversaries in each of these roles, and that, as a result, his writings can only incompletely represent the ideas of the American founding. But, as I noted earlier, overemphasizing intra-Creole divisions can cause us to lose sight of the larger contours of conflict in the independence movement of the United States. Here, I show that Hamilton's defense of American independence, his contributions to constitutional design, and his aspirations for the United States in inter-American and international affairs all display the same contradictory embrace of anti-imperialist and imperialist arguments that characterized the ideologies of Creole revolutionaries throughout the Americas.

Third, Hamilton's Caribbean origins and path to prominence in the American founding gave him firsthand experience with imperial affairs and colonial hierarchies unlike any other founder's, making his intellectual engagement with the international and racial issues that arose in the United States' bid for independence especially revealing.[27] No documents survive that conclusively testify either to the time or the place of Hamilton's birth, but his most recent biographer places it on the tiny island of Nevis, in the British West Indies, in 1755.[28] After moving the family to the nearby Danish island of St. Croix in 1764, Hamilton's father, the fourth son of a minor Scottish noble, abandoned his wife and two young sons to pursue a business opportunity. Hamilton's mother, a descendant of French Huguenot émigrés, opened a general store and managed in this way to support the family for a time, but then succumbed to a fever in 1768. Legal complications surrounding the termination of his mother's first marriage prevented Hamilton's parents from marrying, so he and his brother were technically illegitimate and inherited nothing from their mother's small estate. Hamilton found work as a clerk in the merchant company that had supplied his mother's store, quickly distinguishing himself as a master of languages, an able accountant, and a keen administrator, to the point that he was left in charge of the business for extended periods while its owners were away. From this vantage, Hamilton would have had an excellent introduction to the interlocking imperial institutions that shaped economic exchange in the hemisphere, and an opportunity to observe the social hierarchies that supported it; at the time, St. Croix was the main sugar-producing island in the Danish West Indies, and slaves made up more than 90 percent of its population.[29]

Hamilton might have had a successful career in business, but even his earliest correspondence betrayed broader ambitions. In one infamous letter, written at about age fourteen, Hamilton confessed to wishing "there was a War" that would give him an opportunity to "exalt [his] station."[30] Though war was to become central to Hamilton's rise, another sort of disaster got him off St. Croix. In the late summer of 1772, a major hurricane decimated much of the island. Hamilton wrote an account of the storm and showed it to his minister, who had it published in an English-language newspaper.[31] Impressed by the young man's prose, a group of local businessmen created a subscription fund to pay for Hamilton's education. Hamilton traveled to Elizabethtown,

New Jersey, in the fall, and began preparing for the College of New Jersey's entrance requirements. Ultimately, though, he chose to matriculate at King's College (now Columbia University) in New York, where the faculty agreed to let him pursue an accelerated course of study.[32] In New York, Hamilton found himself at another nexus of economic exchange and in the company of a substantial coterie of British imperial officials. Slavery was less pervasive in New York City than on St. Croix, but slaves still constituted one-fifth of the city's population, and the broader Proprietary Colony of New York contained an important frontier, where European settlers were advancing on areas controlled by well-organized Indigenous communities, especially the Iroquois.[33] To the extent that the habitually itinerant Hamilton had a home, it was New York, and his experiences there with international commerce, slavery, and indigenous expropriation definitely shaped his contributions to the ideology of the independence movement.

It was also likely in New York that Hamilton encountered the works that would shape his philosophical outlook: English authors like Hobbes, Locke, Harrington, Trenchard and Gordon, and Blackstone, as well as continental authors including Vattel and Montesquieu, but most of all the Scottish philosophers, historians, and political economists, and amongst these, above all, David Hume. Much more thoroughly than his colleagues, Hamilton rejected what he described as the "abstract calculations" and "utopian speculations" present in some of the Enlightenment's rationalist strands, preferring Hume's skeptical, empiricist "science" of politics. From Hume, he adopted a method of analyzing politics, which involved assembling multiple historical instances in order to infer, from their commonalities, generalizable rules of individual and group behavior, and then using these rules to predict what consequences might follow from alternative institutional arrangements. Hamilton also accepted Hume's resignation to the inevitable corruption and selfishness of politics, abandoning the efforts of his more classically republican colleagues to preserve or cultivate Americans' civic virtues and aiming instead to create institutions that would channel self-interested persons and spirited parties toward serving what he perceived to be the public good. Finally, like his master, Hamilton was attentive to the ways that established social conventions shaped actions and interactions. He was at once wary of how excessively rapid changes could destabilize societies and attuned to the difficulty of shifting even the most deleterious of long-standing habits.[34]

Hamilton's Humeanism forms the fourth and final reason I've selected him for this study. As I show in the following text, Hamilton applied his

distinctive philosophical framework to a set of problems that he shared
with other figures throughout the hemisphere. Hume's methods, observations, and conclusions underlie Hamilton's critique of British imperial
rule, his defenses of the political union and presidentialist system of separated powers framed by the Constitution, and his approaches to domestic economic development and international relations, distinguishing his
arguments in each realm from the ones that Simón Bolívar and Lucas
Alamán, whom I consider in later chapters, offered in support of similar positions. This juxtaposition of ideological difference and similarity,
I will suggest, allows us the clearest possible view of the influence that
Hamilton's institutional position as an American Creole exercised on his
political ideas.

3.2 CRITIQUE OF AN IMPERIAL CONSTITUTION

Though he emigrated to British North America to pursue an education,
and by all accounts devoted himself with singular intensity to his studies
after settling in New York, Alexander Hamilton never acquired a college
degree. Instead, he became deeply embroiled in the contentious politics
sweeping his adoptive colonies. While he was still a student, Hamilton
published a series of pamphlets that criticized the evolving institutions of
the British Empire and built a case for American independence. Hamilton's
pamphlets incorporated and elaborated arguments developed by other
Creole pamphleteers, who, in the decade since the end of the Seven Years'
War, had been engaged in a continuous effort to define and defend the
rights of British colonists against perceived encroachments by the British
Parliament. Though familiar, this background is worth briefly recounting.

From the middle of the eighteenth century, the British officials most
directly involved in the oversight of North American affairs expressed
growing anxiety about the future of their empire's overseas possessions.
The colonial population increased dramatically in the first half of the
century, and the colonies became more and more important to the British
economy, both as sources of raw materials and as markets for manufactured goods. The idea of an independence movement furrowed some
British brows, but this distant prospect was overshadowed by a much
more proximate concern that either France or Spain might try to conquer
choice parts of Britain's North American claims. For a century, English
writers had effusively praised their country's unique approach to imperial
rule, ascribing both economic advantages and ethical superiority to its
light administrative touch and emphasis on commercial cooperation, as

contrasted with the baroque supervisory apparatus and violent obsession with conquest exemplified, in their minds, by the Spanish.[35] The specter of interimperial competition shook this self-satisfaction, inspiring metropolitan ministers and colonial administrators to raise alarms about the precarious state of affairs that the British approach had brought about. They argued that only a much firmer hand could assure the colonies' future adhesion to their metropole, initiating a series of institutional reforms designed to fortify colonial defenses, enforce commercial regulations, and curtail the relative autonomy that the Creoles who sat in colonial legislatures had come to enjoy.[36]

These reformist efforts accelerated in the aftermath of the Seven Years' War, a wide-ranging conflict fought in the North American theater by French and Spanish troops and allied Indigenous communities against British regulars fortified by colonial militiamen. The war ended in 1763 with a decisive British victory and the transfer of France's North American claims to British control. British patriotism surged in the colonies, and colonists looked forward with great anticipation to settling the new territories they had helped secure.

But the British saw things differently. Officers complained that the colonial legislatures had refused to meet troop requisitions, and ultimately fielded undertrained and poorly supplied soldiers, contributing little to the war effort. Metropolitan taxpayers complained about the cost of the conflict, demanding measures that would shift more of the financial burden of defending the colonies onto the colonists themselves. The results were now-infamous pieces of parliamentary legislation designed to reallocate the costs of protecting the colonies onto the colonists themselves. The Sugar and Stamp Acts, amongst others, imposed new tariffs on colonial trade and government transactions. New taxes were accompanied by new restrictions on colonial legislatures' authority to issue paper money and new measures meant to curtail smuggling and customs evasion. In order to limit future conflicts with Indigenous communities, the Crown issued a royal proclamation that forbade colonists from negotiating new property acquisitions directly, and entirely prohibited new settlements in the North American interior, granting the territories newly acquired from France to the "Indian Nations ... for their hunting Grounds."[37]

The reforms introduced after the Seven Years' War battered British North American Creoles from above and from below, subjecting them to more stringent imperial oversight and depriving them of privileges they enjoyed in relation to Indigenous Americans. Each measure exposed basic disagreements between Europeans and Americans regarding the constitution of the British Empire.[38] Most colonists at midcentury readily conceded Parliament's right to impose what they referred to as "external" taxes upon colonial trade, while reserving at least in theory the power to levy "internal" taxes on income or consumption to the colonial assemblies. Debates on post-war parliamentary legislation gave rise to a new, more stringent distinction, which tied the legitimacy of acts to the intentions of their authors: Parliament could enact tariffs for the purpose of "regulating trade" between the colonies and the rest of the world, but the ancient, unwritten English constitution stipulated that only legislatures in which colonists were represented could impose taxes meant to "raise revenues." The Sugar and Stamp Acts, many pamphleteers insisted, crossed this fine line, denying Creoles rights they felt they were entitled to as Englishmen, and illustrating the disdain with which metropolitan Britons had come to regard their North American counterparts.

The Royal Proclamation of 1763 embodied a different sort of offense, pressing Creoles on the sensitive point of their relations with the non-white and non-Protestant inhabitants of their colonies' frontiers. The lines separating the crown's North American subjects by religion, race, and national origin were not always clear. As Aziz Rana writes, "Early Anglo settlers did not necessarily enjoy a unique plethora of ancestral rights and privileges." The land they lived on was formally regarded as conquered territory, and the colonists themselves "were often treated legally and politically as no different than any other conquered population, confronted by martial law and coercive forms of labor discipline."[39] Over time, though, as the colonies steadily expanded, and as chattel slavery replaced indentured servitude, Creoles came to think of themselves as a caste apart. They developed novel descriptions of their colonies' legal status, referring to the land as "discovered" or "settled," rather than as conquered, in order to claim all the customary rights of Englishmen, while insulating the colonies' peculiar institutions – like indigenous expropriation and chattel slavery – from interference by metropolitan courts and ministers.[40] The Proclamation, by extending the king's protection to Indigenous communities at the colonists' expense, undermined the status and privileges, not to mention the economic advantages, that Creoles claimed as the descendants of settlers and the bearers of Christianity and civilization on a continent of conquered heathens and savages. It seemed to some to portend a ministerial plot to reduce Creoles to the submissive position due a conquered population.[41]

These twin affronts brought the tensions inherent in British North American Creoles' contradictory institutional position into clear focus, inspiring the petitions, protests, and acts of resistance classically described as the "prologue to the Revolution."[42] Colonial tax collectors were burned in effigy and British imperial administrators had their houses demolished by angry mobs. Settlers continued pouring over the proclamation line, and speculators continued to deal in Indigenous lands with impunity. Colonial legislatures discussed, and in some cases passed, resolutions defying Parliament, and, at the behest of the Massachusetts Assembly, delegates from nine colonies met in New York to organize a unified response. It was in this context that luminaries including James Otis, Daniel Dulany, John Dickinson, John Adams, James Wilson, and Thomas Jefferson composed and published pamphlets that began making a legal and philosophical case for American independence.[43]

Tensions built for ten years before finally boiling over. In May 1773, Parliament passed the Tea Act, a subtle piece of legislation meant to lower the price of East India Company tea in the colonies while preserving a standing duty of three pence per pound, thereby enticing colonists into abandoning a boycott without conceding the boycotters' arguments regarding Parliament's authority to impose revenue-raising taxes. But when shipments of newly cheapened tea arrived in four North American harbors, colonists, on principle, refused to unload their cargo in two, and refused to pay the newly lowered tax in a third. In the fourth harbor, Boston, the tea's arrival pushed colonists and colonial administrators into a standoff, which was broken on the evening of December 16 by fifty men "dressed in the Indian manner," who boarded the ships and dumped 90,000 pounds of East India Company tea into the water.

In response, Parliament passed four laws between March and June 1774, referred to in the colonies as the "Coercive" or "Intolerable Acts," which closed the Port of Boston, asserted more absolute royal authority in the Massachusetts colony, and modified legal and military regulations throughout the colonies in general. Between June and September of the same year, twelve colonies (all save Georgia) sent delegates to the first Continental Congress, which met in Philadelphia in September and October. The delegates passed three important acts: a Declaration of Rights, stating that colonial law should be limited by natural law, the British constitution, and the colonial charters; a nonimportation "association" boycotting British goods; and an agreement to meet again in May 1775 should British intransigence continue.[44]

These events became the subject of debates throughout the colonies. In New York, a prominent Anglican priest named Samuel Seabury published a pamphlet under the pseudonym "A Westchester Farmer," condemning Congress's acts, denying the legitimacy of its claim to represent the colonies, and warning that rebellion could only lead to more punitive laws, economic disruptions, and ultimately a war that the colonies could not win. In response, the nineteen-year-old Alexander Hamilton published "A Full Vindication of the Measures of the Congress," a thirty-five-page pamphlet reprising the main lines of the colonists' criticism of parliamentary taxation and defending the nonimportation association as both just and sound policy. Seabury responded with "A View of the Controversy Between Great-Britain and her Colonies," a well-argued piece that probed the underlying principles and implications of Hamilton's position. As scholars, we are fortunate that Seabury chose to respond, and in this way, because his second pamphlet inspired Hamilton, in his own eighty-page reply, "The Farmer Refuted," to state the Creole case clearly and completely.

Hamilton elaborates two distinct lines of argument. One was familiar from the pamphlets published by his fellow Creoles throughout the preceding decade. As Eric Nelson has shown in his striking recent book, on the eve of their independence movement, colonists turned to a rather surprising source of precedents for their case against Parliament's authority to tax the colonies: the royalist defense of the Stuart monarchy in the period of the English Civil War. According to this view, the origins of the rapidly escalating imperial crisis lay in the steady accretion of powers Parliament had accomplished at the expense of the monarchy, which had lost any effective role in legislation and thus no longer served as an effective constitutional check or balance. Echoing other "patriot royalists," Hamilton drew upon both metropolitan legal sources and colonial charters to frame his call for the king to reassert his rightful place by exercising his prerogative to veto Parliament's recent, illegitimate tax acts.[45]

As Nelson notes, David Hume's *History of England* served as an important guide for Hamilton and his fellows, as they made this complex legal case.[46] But Hamilton also developed a second, more original argument in parallel with this one, analyzing how the British Empire's institutions channeled individuals' interests on each side of the Atlantic, and demonstrating exactly why Creoles should expect to be harmed by policies originating in a legislature where they were unrepresented. This argument also drew on Hume, citing at length from this famous passage in his essay "Of the Independency of Parliament":

In contriving any system of government, and fixing the several checks and controuls of the constitution, every man ought to be supposed a *knave*, and to have no other end, in all his actions, than private interest. By this interest we must govern him, and, by means of it, make him, notwithstanding his insatiable avarice and ambition, co-operate to public good. Without this, ... we shall in vain boast of the advantages of any constitution, and shall find, in the end, that we have no security for our liberties or possessions, except the good-will of our rulers; that is, we shall have no security at all.

Here, Hume clearly rejects the classical republican tradition of political thinking, which made the cultivation of civic virtue, or public spiritedness, central to the creation and preservation of good government. Inverting that tradition, Hume insisted that "men are generally more honest in their private" affairs, where they can be observed and honored by their fellows. In politics, particularly within the context of a large, modern state, "this check is, in a great measure, removed; since a man is sure to be approved of by his own party, for what promotes the common interest; and he soon learns to despise the clamours of adversaries."[47]

In his pamphlet, Hamilton followed extensive excerpts from the preceding passages with the exclamation, "What additional force do these observations acquire, when applied to the dominion of one community over another!"[48] That is to say, when applied to the relationship between a metropole and its colonies. Within Britain, the House of Commons provided some assurance that the government would serve the public good. A representative chosen by election, Hamilton noted, "is bound by every possible tie to consult the advantage of his constituent." Not only are representatives grateful for and honored by their election, but the ambition to be reelected also "demands a return of attention and regard to the advancement of his [electors'] happiness." Thus, "Self-interest, that most powerful incentive of human actions, points and attracts" representatives to work in their constituents' interests.[49]

However, when the same representative institution assumed the right to pass legislation directly affecting the American colonies, extending its "jurisdiction ... over countries that have no actual share in its legislature," these advantages were not merely mitigated, but reversed. Because a "vast majority of mankind is intirely biassed by motives of self-interest," the voting public in England would be "glad to remove any burthens off themselves, and place them upon the necks of their neighbours." Lacking representation, the American colonists had no means of assuring that their own interests were weighed in legislation. In the end, "the British Parliament, with a view to the ease and advantage of itself, and its constituents, would oppress and grind the Americans as much as possible."[50] From Hume's first principles, then, Hamilton derives a critique of the inequalities imposed upon Creoles by the constitution of the British Empire, emphasizing, alongside historical and legal arguments concerning prerogative powers and the rights of Englishmen, how the institutional arrangement of parliamentary sovereignty would tend to produce policies systematically biased against colonial interests.

Seabury was quick to recognize the implications of Hamilton's arguments and point out how radical the rejection of parliamentary sovereignty in the colonies was: "The British colonies make a part of the British Empire. As parts of the body they must be subject to the general laws of the body." If "every English colony enjoyed a legislative power independent of the parliament," he continued, "this absurdity will follow – that there is no power in the British empire, which has authority to make laws for the whole empire." If Parliament was sovereign on the British Isles, as the Glorious Revolution and nearly a century of subsequent precedents had established, then it must also be sovereign in the colonies, or else they were no colonies at all, but a separate country entirely. To deny Parliament's authority to legislate for the colonies was tantamount, then, to denying the existence of the empire itself.

Neither Hamilton, nor any of his fellow patriots were willing to endorse this conclusion yet, but Seabury highlighted a difficult philosophical dilemma. According to the established political theories of the time, sovereignty could not be divided or subordinated. As Hamilton himself conceded, some single agent or institution had to be sovereign in the British Empire; the contrary could not be maintained "without falling into that solecism of politics, of *imperium in imperio*."[51] The solution to the problem lay in returning to and radicalizing the "patriot royalism" developed over the preceding decade. Not Parliament, Hamilton wrote, but the "person and prerogative of the King" provided a "connecting, pervading principle," uniting the empire's far-flung possessions. Once again, both metropolitan legal precedents and the colonial charters provided evidence for this account of the empire's constitution.[52]

Asserting that the king alone was ultimately sovereign in the colonies had the additional advantage of avoiding the biases inherent in parliamentary sovereignty. The king, untied to any particular constituency, was interest-bound to preserve the "*mutual* connection and dependence" of the colonies and the mother country, and would thus assure that "all co-operate to one common end: the general good."[53] That Hamilton's critique of the British Empire was not based on opposition to monarchical government should by now be clear. To the contrary, Hamilton insists that parliamentary authority in the colonies, precisely because it incorporated a popular element, was "a more intolerable and excessive species of despotism than an absolute monarchy."[54] Hamilton did not object to being ruled by a monarch. Rather, he spoke for a colonial community that wished to avoid becoming "vassals of their fellow-subjects in Great Britain."[55]

Here, Hamilton's Humean account of how political institutions can channel private interests in positive or perverse ways returns to serve as the argument for a British Empire reimagined as a commonwealth system, in which multiple, mutually autonomous territories were united under the authority of a single sovereign monarch. As we'll see, though Hamilton's philosophical approach is unique, his conclusion was not; Creole revolutionaries throughout the hemisphere proposed similar solutions to imperial crises before ultimately deciding upon independence, and afterward adapted the idea they could induce their respective metropoles to adopt to frame the unions of former colonies their wars would forge.

Seabury was not quite out of ammunition, though. He also pointed out the implicit radicalism in the claim that affording unequal representation to different groups of subjects was inconsistent with the English constitution, the colonial charters, or the natural rights of men. The principle "that an Englishman is bound by no laws but those to which he hath consented in person, or by his representative" was denied to "great part of the people in England" because they lacked the property requisite for the franchise.[56] No one would claim that Parliament had no authority to tax or govern the vast majority of the metropolitan population. In Seabury's view, it was perfectly natural for colonists, in particular, to lack representation in Parliament: "the dependence of the colonies on the mother-country has ever been acknowledged."[57] He challenged Hamilton with some troubling facts: the charters, where they existed, did not speak uniformly of colonists' rights, and some colonies, like New York, did not even have charters, having been created by a cession of territories from the Dutch. Thus, even if one conceded that some colonies had been granted rights to local representation, there could be no general right of colonists derived from the charters.

Hamilton's reply to these arguments, by turns anti-imperial and imperial, illustrates the contradictions central to the ideology of Creole Revolution. He began by confronting Seabury's account of colonial dependency:

The term colony signifies nothing more than a body of people drawn from the mother country to inhabit some distant place.... As to the degrees and modifications of that subordination which is due to the parent state, these must depend upon other things besides the mere act of emigration.

For Hamilton, the "mere act of emigration" undertaken by the British set-tlers of North America did not divest them of their rights as Englishmen. To the contrary, in the course of settling the New World, they had won new rights for themselves and their descendants.

As to the disenfranchised masses of the metropole, Hamilton notes that England's freehold qualification for the franchise was meant to exclude persons who "are in so mean a situation, that they are esteemed to have no will of their own" and are therefore held to be incapable of participating in self-government. However, within the metropole, institu-tions assured that even this poor souls would see their interests served by their government. Because propertyless Englishmen "compose a part of that society to whose government they are subject," they have "rela-tions and connexions among those who are privileged to vote." But this acceptable sort of vertical dependency, of the poor upon the rich, dif-fered from the unacceptable horizontal dependency created by parlia-mentary sovereignty in the colonies. The latter placed American colonists, "of all ranks and conditions, opulent as well as indigent" in a state of dependency upon the British electorate.[58] While Hamilton and his fellow Creoles were willing to countenance inequalities, and indeed would seek to preserve the socio-racial hierarchy of their own colonies after indepen-dence, they would not submit to a system that made them second-class subjects within the British Empire.

Like his counterparts throughout the hemisphere, Hamilton was particularly attentive to the ways that reducing the British colonies' autonomy, vis-à-vis the metropole, might undermine colonists' privi-leges in relation to the non-British and non-European inhabitants of the Americas. Though he is often credited by his biographers with unshak-able abolitionist commitments, in fact, Hamilton did not devote much time or energy to thinking or writing about slavery. His scant remarks on the subject reveal ambiguous ideas and a clear willingness to let other considerations – whether personal or political – determine his attitude toward particular slaves and slave owners, and toward slavery in general.[59] Thus, his revolutionary-era pamphlets did not address, as some other Creoles' pamphlets did, the threat posed to the institution of slavery by British abolitionism, or by Chief Justice Mansfield's deci-sion in the case of *Somerset v. Stewart*, which declared slavery illegal in England and permitted its continuation in the colonies only by imply-ing, contrary to Hamilton and his fellows' arguments, that the colo-nies lay outside the jurisdiction of English common law.[60] Hamilton was more concerned with the settlement of indigenous lands, and this issue did arise in his newspaper editorials in response to the Quebec Act of 1774.

Passed soon after the Intolerable Acts, and often included amongst their number, the Quebec Act modified the system of government established for Britain's new territories in Canada by royal proclamation at the end of the Seven Years' War. Declaring the precedents set in its other North American colonies "inapplicable to the State and Circumstances" of a colony so recently ruled by France, the bill imposed British criminal law but left French civil law – including a seigneurial land tenure system – in effect in Quebec, created a government of officials appointed directly by the Crown, with no locally elected assembly, and established toleration for the Catholic religion, allowing individual Catholics to vote and hold office, and the Catholic Church to collect compulsory tithes. At the same time, the boundaries of Quebec were greatly expanded to encompass some territories formerly lying within the western claims of the colonies of Virginia, Massachusetts, and New York. Like the Royal Proclamation of 1763, the bill served several purposes simultaneously: increasing the discretionary power of the metropolitan government within its colonies, accommodating the French and Indigenous inhabitants of the territory, and discouraging British colonists from settling beyond their colonies' existing frontiers.[61]

The act aroused protests from British colonists that associated the Catholic religion with tyranny, and who had expected that the exclusion of Catholics from public life that characterized their own societies would extend into newly acquired Canada.[62] These protests were particularly fierce in colonies – including Alexander Hamilton's New York – that were full of Creoles eager to stake claims to western lands, who were now concerned that the claims they staked would not be governed according to established principles of English property law.[63] Hamilton gave voice to these concerns in two newspaper editorials, each full of the usual denunciations of the "Romish clergy" empowered by the act and the "arbitrary government" they would surely establish. But Hamilton focused his critique on the new territorial borders established by the act. "However justifiable this act may be in relation to the province of Quebec, with its ancient limits," he wrote, "it cannot be defended by the least plausible pretext, when it is considered as annexing such a boundless extent of new territory to the old." The coupling of the expansion of Quebec with the preservation of French civil law and the toleration of Catholicism "develops the dark designs of the ministry more fully than any thing they have done." No less a purpose than denying British Americans their rightful claim to the "natural advantages of this fertile infant country" lay behind the act's promulgation. As such, Americans should consider it "as being replete with danger to ourselves, and as threatening to our posterity."[64]

As with the Intolerable Acts, Hamilton's critique of the Quebec Act was meant to encourage Creoles to resist Parliament's impositions, not to encourage their outright revolt. But in both works, he implied that if Creoles' legitimate demands were not met, more drastic measures might be necessary. His defense of those measures, as we've seen, mixed invocations of liberty with attachments to hierarchy, but ultimately rested upon a Humean analysis of the inequalities that British rule imposed specifically upon America's Creoles. In this sense, as we will see in subsequent chapters, despite the different philosophical traditions that informed its first principles, Hamilton's argument on behalf of American independence closely resembled others offered throughout the hemisphere.

3.3 CONFEDERATED EMPIRE

As word of armed conflict and American casualties at Lexington and Concord spread across the colonies, Creoles began organizing local militias to defend their communities. In New York, Alexander Hamilton joined a unit and threw himself wholeheartedly into the work of preparing for war, drilling with his fellow students before classes in the mornings and devoting hours to the study of tactics and artillery science at night. The second Continental Congress, assembled in Philadelphia, authorized the raising of a Continental Army in June 1775, appointing George Washington commander-in-chief.

British American Creoles still remained open to a solution to the imperial crisis short of independence. In July, Congress sent a final petition across the Atlantic, offering to negotiate differences regarding trade regulations and taxation with the metropole. King George III, doubting the sincerity of the offer, and denying the legitimacy of the assembly that sent it, declined to answer the petition, issuing instead a "Proclamation for Suppressing Rebellion and Sedition" and thus, in effect, declaring war upon his colonies.

Hamilton received a commission as captain of a provincial artillery company in February 1776 and soon found himself in the midst of the fighting as the war, and the Continental Army, shifted from Boston to New York. Throughout the protracted siege of the city that followed, he published anonymous dispatches on the war in a St. Croix newspaper, lauding the heroism of the patriotic troops and the justice of their cause.

Neither was sufficient to resist the British advance, but it was during the Continental Army's withdrawal from the city that the young artillery captain caught the attention of General Washington, who was so impressed with Hamilton's performance as an administrator and a soldier that he invited him to join his staff as an aide-de-camp.

Joining Washington's general staff put Hamilton in the very center of the military arm of the revolutionary cause. From this vantage, he gained a thorough familiarity with the difficulties involved in coordinating the war efforts of thirteen polities that, considering themselves sovereign, only begrudgingly conceded men and money to the Continental Army. He was one of the first and most vocal critics of the Articles of Confederation, arguing from early on that by making Congress dependent upon the states to carry out its laws and to provide its revenues, the Articles had entrusted responsibilities to a government that was not endowed with the powers it needed to discharge them.[65]

Hamilton's earliest critiques of the Articles focused on the Congress's membership, despairing that the country's "men of weight and understanding" preferred "the emoluments and conveniences of being employed at home," within the state governments, to service in the "grand council of America." "How," he asked, signaling the centrality of international affairs in his thinking, "can we hope for success in our European negociations, if the nations of Europe have no confidence in the wisdom and vigor of the great Continental Government?"[66] In a long 1780 letter to James Duane, a congressional delegate from New York, Hamilton forged a deeper, institutional critique, arguing that the "confederation itself is defective and requires to be altered; it is neither fit for war, nor peace." The central problem was not the character of congressmen but "a want of power in Congress," which had prevented the general government from acting in the "instances without number, where acts necessary for the general good, and which rise out of the powers given to Congress, must interfere with the internal police of the states."[67]

Aware of the fact that the British government's meddling in its colonies' "internal police" had so recently provoked the latter into rebellion, Hamilton sought to draw a clear distinction between the spurned British Empire and his own incipient plans for an independent America:

There is a wide difference between our situation and that of an empire under one simple form of government, distributed into counties, provinces, or districts, which have no legislatures but merely magistratical bodies to execute the laws of a common sovereign. Here the danger is that the sovereign will have too much power to oppress the parts of which it is composed. In our case, *that of an empire composed of confederated states* each with a government completely organized within itself, having all the means to draw its subjects to a close dependence on itself – the danger is directly the reverse. It is that the common sovereign will not have power sufficient to unite the different members together, and direct the common forces to the interest and happiness of the whole.[68]

Here, we can already see rudiments of Hamilton's mature constitutional thought. His novel formulation – "an empire of confederated states" – anticipates the novel political form that he and other Creoles throughout the Americas would conclude represented the best way to organize their newly independent states: a union of former colonies that incorporated elements of both empire and an international system.[69]

During the final year of the war, Hamilton fell out with Washington and left his staff. Free from his former responsibilities, he finally committed his critiques of the Articles of Confederation to print. In a series of six essays, titled *The Continentalist*, Hamilton aired for the first time many of the arguments that would later reappear in his coauthored defense of the US Constitution. Here, as in his pre-revolutionary pamphlets, the influence of David Hume's skepticism is clear. "It would be the extreme of vanity," he began the first number, "not to be sensible that we began this revolution with very vague and confined notions of the practical business of government."[70] In the heady early days of the struggle, "chimerical projects and utopian speculations" had won approval, though they were premised on outdated political ideas. "We might as soon reconcile ourselves to the Spartan community of goods and wives, to their iron coin, their long beards, or their black broth" as to their political institutions. "There is a total dissimilarity in the circumstances as well as the manners of society among us, and it is as ridiculous to seek for models in the small ages of Greece and Rome, as it would be to go in quest of them among the Hottentots and Laplanders."[71] If Americans hoped to achieve and sustain their independence in a world of great powers and global empires, they would require institutions adapted to that purpose rather than relics from the past.

Primary amongst the problematic inferences drawn from ancient examples was a belief in the "necessity of disinterestedness in republics." Experience and subsequent history had shown that selfishness and ambition, not disinterestedness, were the dispositions that should be assumed in designing political institutions. In any shared endeavor, such as the one the American states were currently undertaking, "Many cases may occur where members ... have, or seem to have, an advantage in things contrary to the good of the whole, or a disadvantage in others conducive to that end." In these instances, "the selfishness of every part will dispose each to believe, that the public burthens are unequally apportioned, and that itself is the victim." This tendency will be abetted by the "ambition of men in office in each state," who "think their own consequence connected with the power of the government of which they are a part," and who, as a result, "will endeavour to encrease the one as the mean of encreasing the other."[72]

These impulses could not be eliminated, but they could be channeled by "enlarge[ing] the power of Congress." By giving the common government the power to regulate interstate trade in view of the common good, by granting it a permanent, and reliable source of revenues, independent of the states, by entrusting it with the authority to dispose of "unallocated land" in the west, and by allowing it to appoint its own customs and military officers, Americans would overcome provincial shortsightedness and pave the way to a free and prosperous future.[73]

Hamilton neatly tied this general argument against loose confederations, derived from Humean premises and European precedents, back to the particular dilemma faced by British North America's Creole revolutionaries: "Nothing but a well-proportioned exertion of the resources of the whole, under the direction of a Common Council, with power sufficient to give efficacy to their resolutions, can preserve us from being a CONQUERED PEOPLE now, or can make us a HAPPY PEOPLE hereafter."[74] As the war raged on, the union's capacity to resist reconquest naturally occupied the center of Hamilton's thinking, but here it is clear that he has already grasped the peacetime advantages of the union that he would spend the next five years pursuing.

3.4 ELECTIVE MONARCHY

After covering himself in glory by leading a successful assault on a British redoubt in the decisive patriot victory at Yorktown, Alexander Hamilton returned to New York to complete his legal education and begin a private law practice. Having made an advantageous marriage to Elizabeth Schuyler, daughter of Philip Schuyler, the scion of a long-established and wealthy Creole family. The Schuylers owned a large Hudson River estate worked by slave labor, and Philip Schuyler was an influential figure in New York politics. Through his connections, Hamilton soon became a regular fixture at the city's elite salons and dinner parties. He also won a few prominent cases and began a family, but he did not abandon his broader political interests, particularly his critique of the Articles of Confederation.

In 1786, Hamilton sought and won a seat in the State Assembly in order to oppose the policies of Governor George Clinton, who had imposed steep tariffs on goods entering New York, whether from overseas or from neighboring states, that some observers feared might spark an interstate war.[75] Hamilton believed that so long as the states retained the power to profit at each others' expense, they would do so, and with disastrous political and economic consequences. Thus, he eagerly seized the opportunity to pursue an institutional solution to the problem when delegates from five states met at a convention in Annapolis to make new agreements concerning the navigation of rivers that touched more than one state. There, working closely with a young Virginian delegate named James Madison, Hamilton wrote and convinced the convention to adopt a resolution, which declared that

The power of regulating trade is of such comprehensive extent, and will enter so far into the general System of the federal government, that to give it efficacy, and to obviate questions and doubts concerning its precise nature and limits, may require a correspondent adjustment of other parts of the Federal System.[76]

In other words, without substantial reforms to the structure of the Confederation itself – which lay beyond the remit the delegates at Annapolis were given to consider – it would be impossible to actually make the changes necessary to improve interstate commerce and remove a potential source of serious interstate conflict. Thus, the resolution called upon the state legislatures to send delegates with much broader mandates to a new convention, to be held in Philadelphia in the summer of 1787.

Considering his prominence in the lobbying efforts that led to the Constitutional Convention, Hamilton played a surprisingly small role at the convention itself. Though elected as a delegate, his law practice in New York forced frequent absences, and when he was present, Hamilton's influence was muted by the opposition of his fellow delegates from New York – Clintonites strongly opposed to strengthening the federal government. Hamilton did deliver one long speech at the convention on June 18. He spoke for six unbroken hours, outlining and defending a complete "Plan of Government" to serve as an alternative to the Virginia and New Jersey proposals already under consideration.[77]

Hamilton's plan was distinguished, first, by the extent of authority it would shift from the state governments to the common government of the union. He spent much of his time on the convention floor exhaustively illustrating the many difficulties encountered by the historical "fœderations" – from the Amphictyonic Council of ancient Greece to the Old Swiss Confederacy – that his fellow delegates had cited as models for the United States. He argued that without a common government invested with "compleat sovereignty," the American states would, like their predecessors, fail to take advantage of the political and economic opportunities available to them, and eventually fall to fighting amongst themselves.

Issues particular to the former colonies' situation argued in favor of union as well. Absent a greatly empowered union, Americans would have no reliable recourse when their statehouses were beset by revolts of slaves or taxpayers, or when their settlers were attacked by hostile Indians. As isolated polities, insignificant as either economic or military powers, the individual states would ultimately be denied "respect" and "reciprocity" in international affairs, becoming dependent upon the protection of some foreign power if they were not actually reconquered.[78] According to James Madison's notes on the speech, Hamilton demurred from suggesting that the state governments be "extinguished" entirely only because he did not wish to "shock the public opinion by proposing such a measure." Thus, he recommended that the state governments be reduced to "district tribunals" and limited in their legislative and administrative authorities to purely "local" matters, leaving the common government to oversee interstate and international affairs and to offer a backstop against domestic unrest of all kinds.[79]

Hamilton's plan also included extensive considerations of the form that the common government of the union should take. As a basic principle, he argued that the convention ought to "go as far in order to attain stability and permanency, as republican principles will admit." In practice, this meant adopting a lightly modified form of the classic "mixed" regime exemplified by the "British constitution," which Hamilton did not demur from pronouncing the "best in the world."[80] He outlined a bicameral legislature, in which one house held their positions for life and the other served three-year terms. These two institutions would represent "the few and the many, who have distinct interests." Their conflict should thus be balanced, as in Britain, by a life-term executive with the power to veto legislation.[81]

Hamilton was prepared for the opposition his plan would arouse. "It will be objected probably, that such an Executive will be an elective monarchy, and will give birth to the tumults which characterise that form of Gov[ernment]." "Monarch," he replied to this anticipated objection, "is an indefinite term. It marks not either the degree or duration of power. If this Executive Magistrate would be a monarch for life – the other proposed [by the delegates from Virginia] would be a monarch for seven years. The circumstance of being elective was applicable to both."[82] Hamilton's willful terminological flexibility is strongly reminiscent of his pamphlet debate with Samuel Seabury. Like "empire," "monarch" could take on many meanings. The delegates should not shy away from adopting institutions that bore some resemblance to monarchy – or to empire, for that matter. Rather, they should seek as far as possible to incorporate the advantages of monarchism and imperialism into the republican system of government they were designing.

Hamilton's defense of "elective monarchy" at the Constitutional Convention has frequently furnished grounds for criticism of his character and political commitments. When his fellow New York delegate and political opponent Robert Yates broke the convention's rules by releasing his notes in order to expose Hamilton as a monarchist, the lifetime executive proposal caused a scandal. Hamilton conceded that his convention speech represented the "highest toned propositions" that he had ever made, but he maintained his insistence that the plan was "conformable with the strict theory of a Government purely republican."[83] Notably, even Hamilton's most determined scholarly sympathizer has characterized the plan he outlined as "atrociously misguided."[84] Other commentators simply dismiss it as hopelessly out of step with the political thought of the moment.

In these apologies and dissmissals it is rarely noted that at the convention itself, four state delegations voted in favor of Hamilton's call for a life-term presidency, including Virginia's, which as Hamilton himself deduced, meant that James Madison himself "must have concurred." "Thus," Hamilton wrote later, "if I sinned against Republicanism, Mr. Madison was not less guilty."[85] At the time, Hamilton's plan also attracted praise from patriot notables including George Washington and John Adams.[86] It would be difficult to argue that an idea that won the assent of these luminaries was totally out of step with the ideas of the American founding.

The hemispheric perspective adopted in this book permits us an even broader insight: The plan of government Hamilton recommended in the Constitutional Convention looks remarkably like a number of constitutions adopted in the Spanish Americas following independence. As I will show in the following chapters, not only the specific institutions Hamilton preferred – a lifetime executive and senate, a strongly consolidated central state – but also the reasons he cited for his preference – stability, permanency, protection against foreign invasion, and insulation against the uncertainties of democratic governance – reappear in the political thought of Colombia and Mexico's revolutionary leaders. The problem of overcoming the common difficulties inherent in the Americas' postcolonial condition, while conforming to republican principles was to be a common concern for Creoles throughout the hemisphere, and within this frame Hamilton's proposals appear, if anything, moderate by comparison.

3.5 FORMING A MORE PERFECT UNION

Of course, Alexander Hamilton's most systematic statements on constitutional design were signed "Publius" and written in order to convince New Yorkers to support ratification of the Constitution drafted by the Philadelphia Convention. Hamilton was not entirely pleased with the system of government the Constitution framed, but he was gravely worried by what might occur if it were not established: "[I]t is probable the discussion of the question will beget such animosities and heats in the community that this circumstance conspiring with the *real necessity* of an essential change in our present situation will produce civil war." Thus, he lent his pen, and his considerable energy, to the ratification effort, while cherishing hopes that time would move the system closer to his original preferences. "A good administration will conciliate the confidence and affection of the people and perhaps enable the government to acquire more consistency than the proposed constitution seems to promise for so great a Country." Ultimately, he thought, the federal government would "triumph altogether over the state governments and reduce them to an intire subordination, dividing the larger states into smaller districts."[87]

In the more immediate term, the Constitution was worth defending for the two major advantages it had over the Articles of Confederation: First, it created executive and judicial organs of the federal government, enabling it to give direct effect to its laws, without state intermediation. I discuss Hamilton's defense of the Constitution's presidentialist system of separated powers in the next section. Second, it endowed the federal government with virtually unlimited authority in several particularly important realms, including foreign policy, interstate commerce, and westward expansion, while also allowing the federal government to impose taxes for the purpose of funding its activities in these spheres. This transfer of authority created the union of former colonies that Hamilton used most of the initial numbers of *The Federalist* to defend.

Citing precisely these two features of the Constitution, the historian Max Edling's valuable recent account of the framing and ratification debates argues that the ideal Hamilton and his fellow "nationalists" had in mind was a "fiscal-military state" analogous to the ones that had formed in Europe during the early modern period.[88] On this reading, Hamilton sought reforms to the Articles of Confederation in order to "Europeanize" the United States – expanding the federal government's extractive and war-making powers and thereby making the nascent republic viable in a competitive international system of "national-states."[89] There is much to recommend this account, and I would not wish to deny, in particular, that international concerns were central to Hamilton and his fellow Creoles' contributions to constitutional design.

However, I do think that something important is missed in reading the Constitution as an attempt to make the United States into a European national-state. One of the main arguments employed in the *Federalist*'s defense of the Constitution, especially the numbers written by Hamilton, was that the more perfect union it promised to form would prevent the emergence of European-style national-states in America. The critical objective pursued by Hamilton's constitutionalism was to avoid the interstate conflicts, fettered economic development, demagogic politics, and popular uprisings that he argued were inevitable products of the European state system, with its always precarious balance of sovereign powers.

Thus, we might say that if Hamilton did seek to "Europeanize" the United States, he did not have the European national-state in mind, but rather Europe as the domain of a never-quite-realized universal empire.[90] The Constitution, he hoped, would frame a government for an American union, combining features of previous European confederations and empires in order to rule a territory already much larger than that of any European nation, under institutions better suited to reconciling the diverse interests of its heterogeneous subjects. This ideal was neither European nor uniquely North American, as I shall show in subsequent chapters, nor was it uniquely North American. Rather, it emerged in local variations as a solution to the analogous background problems that arose in the aftermath of Creole Revolutions throughout the hemisphere.

From the first number of the *Federalist*, Hamilton makes his conception of the stakes at play in the ratification debate clear: "The subject speaks its own importance; comprehending in its consequences, nothing less than the existence of the UNION, the safety and welfare of the parts of which it is composed, *the fate of an empire*, in many respects the most interesting in the world."[91] A stronger federal government was the indispensable means of forestalling the states' alarming progress toward becoming either "wholly disunited, or only united in partial confederacies," and thereafter falling into "frequent and violent contests" amongst themselves. To deny that war would follow from the separation of the states into sovereign entities, Hamilton claims, "would be to forget that men are ambitious, vindictive and rapacious."[92] Here, Hume's science of the interaction of private interests returns, not to justify revolution against an empire, but to support the construction of a new one. Absent an overarching authority, ineradicable human selfishness would drive the states into conflict over any one of a number of possible disagreements: Territorial disputes over undivided lands and the vast unsettled frontier, commercial conflicts over transport and protectionism, debt policy, foreign policy, immigration policy, almost any issue could form a pretense for conflict.

Even the mere possibility of war would have devastating consequences for the American states, leading them to create large standing armies, financed by excessive taxation and presenting a constant threat of internal repression. A "state of continual danger," Hamilton argued, "will compel nations the most attached to liberty to resort for repose and security to institutions which have a tendency to destroy their civil and political rights ... we should in a little time see established in every part of this country, the same engines of despotism, which have been the scourge of the old world."[93] The only way to avoid this outcome was to deprive the states of some portion of their sovereign authority. Only "visionary [read: utopian], or designing men" could propose "the paradox of perpetual peace between the States, though dismembered and alienated from each other."[94]

Against fashionable theories promising that commerce and republican government would bring world peace,[95] Hamilton insisted that "in practice," republics are no "less addicted to war than monarchies." Trade could as easily become a cause of conflict as of peace: "Have there not been as many wars founded upon commercial motives, since that has become the prevailing system of nations, as were before occasioned by the cupidity of territory or dominion?"[96] Thus, only a new empire, standing above and apart from the local interests and conflicting claims of the provincial legislatures, could smooth over the "differences that neighbourhood occasions,"[97] and thereby assure peace amongst the states.

Commerce and relations between "commercial republics" formed a particular concern of Hamilton's political thought, lending them an air of precocious "modernity."[98] In his view, a system of sovereign states with no common commercial oversight not only promised to produce armed conflict, but also "fettered, interrupted and narrowed" trade, stifled economic growth, and thus diminished prosperity.[99] Again, it is useful to consider the position Hamilton sought to undermine. The pamphleteer "Agrippa" clearly stated what is still a familiar view, according to which

The freedom that every man, whether his capital is large or small, enjoys, of entering into any branch that pleases him, rouses a spirit of industry and exertion that is friendly to commerce. It prevents that stagnation of business which generally precedes publick commotions. Nothing ought to be done to restrain this spirit. The unlimited power over trade, however, is exceedingly apt to injure it.[100]

Hamilton did not deny that some government interventions into trade were injurious. He thought that "Commerce," like other forms of human interaction, "has its fixed principles, according to which it must be regulated," and he acknowledged that when these principles were "unknown, or violated" by policy makers, commerce would be damaged. His argument was, rather, that when competitive sovereign states bore the authority to regulate trade, they tended to violate the principles of commerce in pursuit of short-term advantages over rivals. Thus, the removal of this authority upward into the hands of an overarching regime – the "empire of confederated states" Hamilton had contemplated since the Revolution – would produce better policy.

As an insightful Hamilton scholar recognized, the indispensable premise of all of these claims is a "belief in a genuine public good or national interest apart from and above the bargaining processes of conflicting private interests." Though Hamilton was deeply concerned with the way that institutions structured the interaction of private interests, he did not "neutralize the dimension of *public* interest to a mere market place for the realization of private interests."[101] His political theory preserved a place for a genuine public interest, different from a mere aggregation of private interests, and his constitutional theory was centrally an effort to assure that this public interest be realized in government policy.[102]

For Hamilton, it was precisely the "ENLARGEMENT of the ORBIT" of government, the expansion of territory through the "association of two or more States into one State"[103] that would achieve this aim, not only by preventing sovereigns from competitively pursuing policies destructive of collective goods, but also through its effect on the quality of elected representatives. "The extension of the spheres of election will present a greater option, or latitude of choice to the people," thereby promising "greater knowledge and more extensive information in the national councils," making officials "less apt to be tainted by the spirit of faction, and more out of the reach of those occasional ill humors or temporary prejudices and propensities, which in smaller societies frequently contaminate the public councils."[104] In short, then, assembling a relatively smaller number of representatives to legislate for an enlarged citizenry would serve the public good by putting the right kind of men – men of enlarged views, extensive learning, and property – in offices where they would be able to resist the self-interested appeals of their constituents.

It is hard to read these passages without recalling the concerns Hamilton himself raised in his pre-revolutionary pamphlet debate with Samuel Seabury: What, the radical young student might ask his more mature self, is to become of those excluded from office for their lack of "broad dispositions"? Wouldn't they suffer from a re-orientation of government away from service of their particular interests? In *Papers* thirty-five and thirty-six, Hamilton takes up an objection voiced against the Constitution, that "the House of Representatives is not sufficiently numerous for the reception of all the different classes of citizens." Dismissing the premise of the objection – that all classes should be represented – as "altogether visionary [again, read: ridiculous]," Hamilton returns to the refrain I remarked on in the preceding text. "Mechanics and manufacturers will always be inclined," he wrote, "to give their votes to merchants, in preference to persons of their own professions or trades," since they "know that the merchant is their natural patron and friend; and they are aware, that however great the confidence they may justly feel in their own good sense, their interests can be more effectually promoted by the merchant than by themselves."[105] In 1774–1775, he argued that the "connexions" between enfranchised and disenfranchised Englishmen, the vertical ties of responsibility and mutual interest between the propertied and their unpropertied dependents, made the former effective advocates for the latter's interests. Similar ties would bind in the independent United States, with Creole merchants, professionals, and large property owners deciding upon the policies that best served the good of a public composed of stratified races and classes.

3.6 THE POWERS OF PRESIDENTIALISM

Even within a political union that would help assure, by virtue of its size and centralization of authority, that Creoles with "broad dispositions" would man the levers of government, Hamilton was concerned that excessive popular influence in government might destabilize the postcolonial United States. Thus, alongside the union, he defended the proposed Constitution's presidentialist system of separated powers as a complementary means of consolidating the authority of the Creole elite.

Two main features of this system allowed the Senate, the president, and the Supreme Court to check the most democratic branch of the federal government, the House of Representatives. First, the members of each were independent of the House for both their election to office and their terms in office. In the *Federalist Papers*, Hamilton praised the Constitution's provisions for the indirect elections of both senators and the president, as well as the president and the Senate's joint roles in the appointment and confirmation of Supreme Court justices. He also supported vesting the power to try impeached officers of the federal government in the Senate.

Second, these coordinate branches of government had to have a role in the lawmaking process, a means of actually stopping problematic policies from going into effect. Again, Hamilton described and defended the president's veto power under the Constitution and provided an innovative account of the Supreme Court's power to review and invalidate unconstitutional legislation. In the end, then, though the "highest-toned" institutional proposals Hamilton put forward at the Philadelphia Convention were not embodied in the Constitution, the United States would adopt a modified version of the "mixed" regime he described as uniquely capable of diffusing the tensions that its heterogeneous population would produce.[106]

The roles played by the president and the Supreme Court in the federal government's legislative process aroused particular dissent from the opponents of the proposed Constitution, who argued that it did not delimit strictly enough the boundaries of the executive and judicial authorities.[107] In response, Hamilton adapted David Hume's infamous defense of "corruption" in the English Constitution for American purposes,[108] arguing that a "partial intermixture" of the authorities of the separate branches was "in some cases not only proper, but necessary to the mutual defence of the several members of the government, against each other."[109] Because he thought the main danger to be avoided in the United States was the "tendency of the legislative authority to absorb every other,"[110] Hamilton was greatly concerned to enhance the relative powers of the executive and the judicial branches, and to ensure that these offices would be filled by men with "characters pre-eminent for ability and virtue." Thus, assuring the independence and authority of the executive and judicial authorities, while granting them some capacity to intervene in the acts of the legislature, was for Hamilton another means of insulating politics from popular involvement.

In electing a president, Hamilton felt that "it was desireable that the sense of the people should operate in the choice," not directly, but rather through a group of men "chosen by the people ... capable of analizing the qualities adapted to the station." In his evaluation, a "small number of persons, selected by their fellow citizens from the general mass, will be most likely to possess the information and discernment requisite to so complicated an investigation."[111] The executive authority should not be divided, because "unity is conducive to energy" and "[e]nergy in the executive is a leading character in the definition of good government."[112] Moreover, the president should serve a long enough term to remove his decision making from excessive regard for public opinion:

> The republican principle demands, that the deliberate sense of the community should govern the conduct of their affairs; but it does not require an unqualified complaisance to every sudden breese of passion, or to every transient impulse which the people may receive from the arts of men, who flatter their prejudices to betray their interests. It is a just observation, that the people commonly *intend* the PUBLIC GOOD. This often applies to their very errors.[113]

Hamilton's defense of presidentialism, then, like his defense of union, proceeds from a strong belief in the existence of a true public interest, combined with a deep skepticism regarding the capacity of the people, in their masses, to either know or seek that interest. The indirectly elected, long-termed, powerful president was designed specifically to provide a check upon the capricious will of the populace and their most immediate representatives in the legislative branch.

Similar considerations lay behind the structure of the judicial branch proposed by the new Constitution. Here, a particular point of contention concerned the life term allotted to judges, which Hamilton viewed as "one of the most valuable of the modern improvements in the practices of government. In a monarchy it is an excellent barrier to the despotism of the prince: In a republic it is a no less excellent barrier to the encroachments and oppressions of the representative body."[114] So that the courts might provide such a barrier, Hamilton carved out an important new role for the judiciary in the regulation of interbranch relations, primarily exercised through the power of judicial review. With the power to declare legislative acts void, the unelected, life-term members of the federal judiciary could

> guard the constitution and the rights of individuals from the effects of those ill humours which the arts of designing men, or the influence of particular conjunctures, sometimes disseminate among the people themselves, and which, though they speedily give place to better information and more deliberate reflection, have a tendency in the mean time to occasion dangerous innovations in the government.[115]

As regards domestic politics, then, all of Hamilton's primary contributions to constitutional design answer to a single question: how to construct a system of government in which sovereignty can credibly be said to emanate from the people, but in which policy making is effectively insulated from popular passions. As we will see in subsequent chapters, both this construction of the problem, and Hamilton's preferred solutions – union and presidentialism – were common in Creole constitutional theory.

3.7 AIMING AT AN ASCENDANCY IN AMERICAN AFFAIRS

The union and presidentialist system of separated powers created by the US Constitution were not designed for merely domestic purposes. At the close of the eleventh *Federalist*, Hamilton proposes to lead his readers "into the regions of futurity," revealing his vision of the longer-term prospects for the consolidated union of states forged by the new Constitution. Here, he reveals his conception of the world-historical importance of the American Revolution and the global influence that he felt was its due. The passage is worth examining at length. First, for Hamilton, as for other Creole political thinkers, the history of all hitherto existing society is the history of European imperialism:

The world may politically, as well as geographically, be divided into four parts, each having a distinct set of interests. Unhappily for the other three, Europe by her arms and by her negociations, by force and by fraud, has, in different degrees, extended her dominion over them all. Africa, Asia, and America have successively felt her domination.[116]

As Europeans spread their influence over a greater and greater portion of the globe, their ideologists defended the continent's success as a natural product of its inhabitants' special character:

The superiority she has long maintained has tempted her to plume herself as the Mistress of the World, and to consider the rest of mankind as created for her benefit. Men admired as profound philosophers have, in direct terms, attributed to her inhabitants a physical superiority; and have gravely asserted that all animals, and with them the human species, degenerate in America – that even dogs cease to bark after having breathed a while in our atmosphere.[117]

Europeans' insufferable arrogance and pseudoscientific rationale for the continued marginalization of American Creoles – precisely those "members of the human species" who had "breathed a while" in the American atmosphere – gave the revolution a particular urgency. Hamilton uses this stirring call for anti-imperial struggle to underline, once again, the proposed Constitution's capacity to consolidate American independence and, now, to expand its revolutionary mission:

Facts have too long supported these arrogant pretensions of the European. It belongs to us to vindicate the honor of the human race, and to teach that assuming brother moderation. Union will enable us to do it. Disunion will add another victim to his triumphs. Let Americans disdain to be the instruments of European greatness![118]

Here, it is clear that Hamilton's call for unity in the face of foreign oppression is not an early assertion of subaltern identity, an incipient Creole nationalism with aims limited to the independence of a conquered community. Rather, the Creole Revolution in British North American will "vindicate the honor of the human race," laying down a decisive marker against European imperialism, ushering in a new stage of global politics.

It quickly becomes apparent, though, that Hamilton's international program was, as Gerald Stourzh has observed, "only superficially clothed in the terminology of self-determination."[119] Even as he denounced the history of European domination throughout the world, Hamilton proposed the construction of what can only be described a new, hemispheric empire with the newly independent United States as its metropole:

I shall briefly observe, that our situation invites, and our interests prompt us, to aim at an ascendant in the system of American affairs.... Let the thirteen States, bound together in a strict and indissoluble union, concur in erecting one great American system, superior to the controul of all trans-atlantic force or influence, and able to dictate the terms of the connection between the old and the new world.[120]

It is, of course, of immense interest here to point out that it was precisely over the rest of the Americas that the United States began to cast its gaze, even within the first decade of independence. Hamilton's comments evidence a distinctly proprietorial attitude toward the as-yet unliberated Spanish Americas, more than a quarter century prior to the more famous assertion of an American sphere of influence coinciding with the New World in President James Monroe's 1823 State of the Union address.[121]

Hamilton's plan to establish "an ascendant in the system of American affairs" for the young United States had two distinct elements: (1) an internal civilizing mission that would employ the powers of the newly established federal government to encourage the development of industry and thereby decrease the reliance of the United States on European, and particularly English, manufactured goods and (2) an external policy of patronage and conquest that would forestall steady European, and particularly French, incursions into the Spanish Americas, allowing the United States to establish itself as the preeminent power in the New World. He pursued the first relentlessly, and the second more subtly during his term as secretary of the treasury in the administration of the first president elected under the new Constitution, George Washington.

Washington's election itself was probably a foregone conclusion, but that did not stop Hamilton from making every effort to assure his by-then longtime patron and mentor's accession to the office. In private letters, Washington expressed real hesitation at the prospect of leaving retirement to reenter politics once again. Hamilton responded by emphasizing the importance of the first presidency, noting that the population would regard it as a test of the system framed by the Constitution, and arguing that only Washington could "sufficiently unite public opinion" to discharge this weighty role.[122] Hamilton was also attentive to the mechanics of electing a president, and particularly, to the unfortunate fact that the Constitution's procedure for electing its executive officers made it possible for the country to mistakenly elevate their intended choice for vice president to the presidency, as would be demonstrated in the election of 1800.[123] Thus, he worked behind the scenes, encouraging electors to withhold votes from the presumptive vice president, John Adams, in order to give Washington a clear majority. The effort worked, but also earned Hamilton the eternal enmity of the prickly Adams, a consequence that would come back to bite him in short order. Washington did not originally intend to appoint Hamilton to the Treasury, and Hamilton did not expect a cabinet appointment at all, but when Washington's first choice, Robert Morris, turned him down, he recommended that Washington choose Hamilton instead. The president – apparently surprised that his former aide-de-camp was not only an adept of military strategy and political theory, but of public finance as well – followed this advice, and brought Hamilton once again into the very center of the period's political life.[124]

Hamilton's desire to see the United States become an important player in global commerce is well known, and the reports he delivered to Congress in his capacity as secretary of the treasury between January 1790 and December 1791 are justly famous documents in the history of American economic thought.[125] Here, I propose to consider them from the perspective we have been developing throughout this chapter, as part of a set of ideas reflecting the distinctive institutional position occupied by the American Creoles.

That Hamilton believed that his economic policies would serve the aims of the revolution is clear. In his "Report on Manufactures," he writes that "Not only the wealth; but the independence and security of a Country, appear to be materially connected with the prosperity of manufactures.... The extreme embarrassments of the United States during the late War, from an incapacity of supplying themselves, are still matter of keen recollection."[126] But Hamilton saw more than economic self-sufficiency in an industrial America. The creation of a manufacturing sector would increase domestic demand for agricultural produce, providing a more stable market than Europe for what would long remain the United States' primary commodities. Manufacturing also offered better prospects for growth than agriculture, because of its relatively greater susceptibility to the division of labor.[127] Manufacturing could incorporate newer technology, and create employment for populations left out of an agricultural economy:

Persons who would otherwise be idle (and in many cases a burthen on the community), either from the byass of temper, habit, infirmity of body, or some other cause, indisposing, or disqualifying them for the toils of the Country. It is worthy of particular remark, that, in general, women and Children are rendered more useful and the latter more early useful by manufacturing establishments, than they would otherwise be.[128]

Thus, Hamilton argues, manufacturing is "necessary to the perfection of the body politic," the useful incorporation of its various classes and castes into the shared project of providing for the commonweal.

Not only the ends, but also the means of Hamilton's economic policy lend it the distinctive character of a civilizing mission. He was concerned to refute not only those who would prefer that the United States remain an agricultural society, but those who, conceding the advantages of industrial development, would leave its initiation to the "quick-sighted guidance of private interest," thinking that any attempt by government "to give direction to the industry of its citizens" was bound to produce perversions of the "natural course of things."[129] Hamilton, as we've already seen in the preceding text, strongly disagreed with this perspective. His "Report on Manufactures" is, in large part, an elaboration of his earlier arguments for charging the federal government with the oversight of the economy. Here, however, government intervention not only serves to coordinate the pursuit of long-term interests, but also to counterbalance the weight of traditional practices that impede progress:

Experience teaches, that men are often so much governed by what they are accustomed to see and practice, that the simplest and most obvious improvements, in the most ordinary occupations, are adopted with hesitation, reluctance and by slow gradations.... In many cases they would not happen, while a bare support could be ensured by an adherence to ancient courses; though a resort to a more profitable employment might be practicable. To produce the desireable changes, as early as may be expedient, may therefore require the incitement and patronage of government.[130]

Like the "liberal imperialists" who "justified European imperial rule as a benefit to backward subjects" whose enslavement to superstition prevented them from achieving civilization by their own initiative,[131] Hamilton recommends a systematic program of government encouragement for industrial development as an indispensable means of overcoming the stifling forces of habit active in the United States. In this light, the "Report on Manufactures," long famous for its prescient political economy, can be seen as the outline for a program of internal colonization, the domestic portion of Hamilton's more expansive commercial imperialism.

3.8 IMPERIAL INTERVENTIONS

Just as he was unwilling to limit stimulation of manufacturing within the United States to the "natural" forces of the market, Hamilton thought that an active foreign policy was the only way to assure a broad base of consumers for the United States' manufactured goods. Even before they extricated themselves from Spain's restrictive commercial domination, he saw the inhabitants of Spanish America as a particularly attractive prize. In a world where legal trade was determined by alliances with Europe's great powers – especially England and France – positioning the United States to become a major commercial power within its own hemisphere entailed complex international considerations, which would lead Hamilton into a series of exchanges with the Venezuelan dissident Francisco de Miranda, known as the "precursor" of Latin American independence, and mentor to Simón Bolívar, whom we will consider in the next chapter.

The background of Hamilton's exchange with Miranda was the global perturbation provoked by the French Revolution. Like many of his fellows, Hamilton felt a "warm zeal" for the Revolution in its early stages,[132] but when news arrived in the spring of 1793 that King Louis XVI had been executed, that riots had become daily occurrences in Paris, and that the Revolution's early leaders, including Hamilton's good friend, the Marquis de Lafayette, had been forced to flee the country, he experienced a change of heart. By 1794 he had become convinced that "the cause in which [the French] are engaged is not the cause of Liberty, but the cause of Vice, Atheism, and Anarchy."[133]

But even more than the radical ideas of the French Revolution, Hamilton feared the revitalization of France's expansionist ambitions. In February 1793, France had declared war on England, bringing the matter of the US allegiances sharply into question. French representatives, and their American sympathizers, pressed the view that the treaty of alliance that had been concluded between France and the United States in 1778 made American support for France obligatory. Hamilton leapt into print to deny this view, publishing a series of seven essays titled "Pacificus" in support of a neutral stance on the conflict. The case he makes here is multitiered, but perhaps the most interesting argument was the first, concerning the nature of the conflict itself.

The treaty of 1778, he noted, was a defensive treaty, requiring the United States to aid France in the defense of her American colonies should these be threatened by a rival power. In the present conflict, however, France had taken the offensive, thereby relieving the United States of its responsibility to intervene.[134] France "gave a general and just cause of alarm to Nations," when the "Convention, in the name of the French Nation, declared that they will grant *fraternity* and *assistance* to every People who *wish* to recover their liberty ... [and] *defend those citizens who may have been or who may be vexed for the cause of liberty.*" While, Hamilton averred, "it is justifiable and meritorious in another nation to afford assistance to the one which has been oppressed & is *in the act* of liberating itself," as France had done for the United States during its own revolution, it is quite another thing "for any Nation *beforehand* to hold out a general invitation to insurrection and revolution, by promising to assist *every people* who may *wish* to recover their liberty." The latter amounts to "an interference by one nation in the internal Government of another," an aggressive act tantamount to a declaration of war.[135]

The notion that France sought to clothe imperial ambitions in a rhetoric of liberty was to become the centerpiece of Hamilton's denunciation of the Revolution as the former allies drew closer and closer to open conflict.[136] In 1797, he warned that the "conduct of France from the commencement of her successes, has by gradual developpements betrayed a spirit of universal domination," resting upon a claimed "right to be the legislatrix of Nations." The "specious pretence of enlightening mankind and reforming their civil institutions" that France's champions asserted was, in fact, nothing more than a "varnish to the real design of subjugating" the world. In this aim, Revolutionary France was no different from any other ambitious European state bent on conquest. Indeed, the "vast projects of Louis the XIV dwindle into insignificance compared with the more gigantic schemes of his Republican successors."[137] France's defenders in the United States argued that French and American revolutions shared the same principles, and that this should make the countries natural allies. But Hamilton saw France as just another European power desirous of supremacy in the Americas. The "true and genuine spirit of 1776," he insisted, should inspire Americans to "maintain inviolate the rights and unsullied the honor of the Nation." The United States "did not break the fetters of one foreign tyranny to put on those of another,"[138] republican or otherwise.

It might be possible to read Hamilton's attitude toward France, his aversion to the "spirit of proselytism" he saw as fundamental to the French Revolution, and his warnings of the directory's "desire of new modeling the political institutions of the rest of the world according to her standard,"[139] as attempts to "counter internationalist ideology with nationalist ideology,"[140] to assert the justice of the United States' autonomy as a sovereign nation-state. But to categorize Hamilton's position as nationalist would be to substantially miss the point, for Hamilton intended to oppose French designs in the New World with more than rhetorically charged calls to defend the homeland. As a Creole revolutionary he sought, paradoxically, to undermine European imperialism by building an empire of his own, to spread the principles of the American Revolution throughout the hemisphere as a means of forestalling the imminent arrival of French ones. And his main co-conspirator in this project was "The Precursor," Francisco de Miranda.

Miranda was born in Caracas to a wealthy family, educated in Spain, and served as an officer in the Spanish Army during operations to recover the Floridas from England during the American Revolutionary War.[141] After the war, he traveled in the United States, becoming enthralled by the figure of George Washington and resolving to play a similar role himself in South America. He befriended Hamilton, amongst others, during his time in New York in early 1784. At the time of their first meeting, Hamilton provided Miranda with a list of American officers who might be interested in joining a campaign to liberate South America.[142] Later, Miranda traveled to France and, with the aid of sympathizers amongst the Girondin leadership, secured a post as an officer in the French Army, hoping it would provide a platform from which to carry out his plans in Spanish America. He wrote to Hamilton in 1792, conveying in his uneven English that

The affairs & Success of france take a happy turn in our favour. I mean in favour of our dear Country America, from the North to the South.... things are grown ripe & into maturity for the Execution of those grand & beneficial projects we had in Contemplation, when in our Conversation at new Yorck the love of our Country exalted our minds with those Ideas, for the sake of unfortunate Columbia.[143]

Miranda clearly perceived that he had found in Hamilton a kindred spirit, a Creole revolutionary with a hemispheric conception of the American cause. He also shared Hamilton's late change of heart on the French Revolution. With the fall of the Gironde, Miranda was accused of conspiring against the Revolution, stripped of his commission, and imprisoned. Now thoroughly disillusioned with the French, he switched his allegiances, applying to England and the United States for aid in his emancipatory venture.

In 1798, he wrote to Hamilton again, warning that "the establishment of liberty throughout the New World seems to have been assured by Providence! The only danger I can foresee is the introduction of French principles."[144] In order to forestall this outcome, he recommended a three-way alliance between England, the United States, and himself in his self-declared capacity as the "principal agent of the Spanish American colonies." Hamilton replied, using the US minister to England, Rufus King, as his emissary:

With regard to the enterprise in question I wish it much to be undertaken but I should be glad that the principal agency was in the UStates – they to furnish the whole land force necessary. The command in this case would very naturally fall upon me – and I hope I should disappoint no favourable anticipation. The independency of the separated territory under a *moderate* government, with the joint guarantee of the cooperating powers, stipulating equal privileges in commerce would be the sum of the results to be accomplished.[145]

The seamless quality of Hamilton's transition, from denouncing the French Directory's ambition to "new model" the world's institutions according to their specifications to establishing a "moderate government" in Spanish America, from exposing imperial aims disguised with revolutionary rhetoric to securing trade privileges by offering independence, is astonishing. Here, once again, a deep contradiction emerges in the heart of American revolutionary thinking: a simultaneously anti-imperial and imperial ideology unique to this period and place and finding perfect expression in the ideas of Alexander Hamilton, Creole revolutionary.

3.9 CONCLUSION

The "Quasi-War" with France provided a necessary context for Hamilton's plans for hemispheric expansion. The perhaps overestimated threat of invasion and very real threats to American commercial interests in the Caribbean motivated Congress to expand the naval and military establishments of the young republic and increased the popularity of politicians, like John Adams, who supported a strong stand against France. The crisis allowed Hamilton to rise to the highest military post he would hold in his career – inspector-general of the US Army – a position from which he could, with some credibility, forecast interventions in the Spanish Americas.

However, with the end of hostilities, these plans fell apart. In the elections of 1800, to which we will return in Chapter 6, Thomas Jefferson's Republicans would sweep to victory on a platform centered on opposition to Hamilton's accomplishments. Hamilton himself continued to play a prominent role in politics, which was sometimes constructive, as with his reforms of the manner in which the president and vice president were elected (which became part of the Twelfth Amendment), his protest of Republican attempts to repeal the Judiciary Act of 1801 (unsuccessful), and his jurisprudential innovations in the law of libel (truth remains a defense against libel to this day).

It also must be said that Hamilton increasingly became the party politician that his opponents had long accused him of being, publishing a destructive attack on the character of John Adams, frequent screeds against the Jefferson administration, and, of course, engaging in the electoral machinations that would culminate in his fatal duel with Aaron Burr on July 11, 1804.[146] The night before that fateful day, Hamilton revised his will, explaining his reasons for following through with a duel that he considered contrary to his "religious and moral principles," and penning a final expression of his political ideas, now in response to secessionist threats leveled by his own Federalist Party:

I will here express but one sentiment, which is, that Dismemberment of our Empire will be a clear sacrifice of great and positive advantages, without any counterballancing good; administering no relief to our real Disease; which is Democracy, the poison of which by a subdivision will only be the more concentrated in each part, and consequently the more virulent.[147]

He was perhaps never more clearly an ideologist of Creole Revolution.

4

Simón Bolívar and the Contradictions
of Creole Revolution

The American independence movements produced many heroes: stirring writers and rhetoricians whose words raised peoples in rebellion; adepts of military strategy and international diplomacy who overcame opponents at home and abroad; and great legislators and statesmen who placed new nations on firm foundations. In retrospect, it is easy to romanticize these individuals, to treat their ideas and accomplishments as strokes of transcendent genius rather than as efforts, more or less successful, to address problems arising in their particular place and time. No figure has proven more susceptible to such retrospective romanticization than Simón Bolívar, by far the best-known and most widely revered leader of the Spanish American independence movements, whose graven image, often on horseback, can be found in cities throughout the world.

Bolívar's first equestrian statue was erected in Caracas in 1874 by Venezuelan President Antonio Guzmán Blanco, as part of an effort to add nationalist appeal to his program of economic modernization and authoritarian politics. Since then, Bolívar has been invoked by Venezuelan politicians from every conceivable point on the ideological spectrum, from the petro-capitalist Juan Vicente Gómez to the international socialist Hugo Chávez Frías.[1] A frequent subject in Latin American literature, Bolívar was elegized by José Martí, versified by Pablo Neruda, and novelized by Gabriel García Márquez.[2] Opinions from outside Latin America have been more varied: Bolívar was widely celebrated as the "George Washington of the South" in the United States,[3] and exchanged expressions of mutual admiration with Jeremy Bentham,[4] amongst other European luminaries. But Benjamin Constant thought that Bolívar's ambitions were more reminiscent of Napoleon than Washington,[5] and Karl Marx found even this less flattering comparison too generous.[6]

Similarly stark divisions characterize the vast scholarly literature on Bolívar's political thought. Appearing alternately as a committed democrat and a cynical dictator,[7] a pragmatic leader and a utopian dreamer,[8] a post-racial scourge of empire and a defender of the colonies' racial order,[9] it is difficult to discern the central theoretical tendencies of a thinker who, after almost two hundred years of analysis, has come to represent all things to all people. It is also difficult to argue that some of these accounts are simply wrong, since Bolívar's voluminous intellectual production provides ample evidence for each. Still, nearly every portrayal of Bolívar's political thought errs by omission, emphasizing the particular texts and periods of activity that support a given reading, while ignoring others that might suggest an alternative or even antithetical interpretation.[10] Thus, the approach taken in this chapter is different, seeking to explain the very contradictions in Bolívar's ideas by showing how they reflect the contradictory institutional position of a Creole revolutionary. In particular, I argue that Bolívar's political thought exhibits the simultaneous commitment to both anti-imperialism and imperialism that was characteristic of his colleagues throughout the hemisphere.

Biographically, Simón Bolívar was perhaps the finest flesh-and-blood instance of the Creole ideal type. Born in 1783 in Caracas, Venezuela, his was the seventh generation of American Bolívars, continuing a line led by his namesake, Simón de Bolívar, a minor Basque noble who emigrated to America in 1589 and received a grant of *encomienda*, or forced indigenous labor, from the king of Castile. Two hundred years later, upon the early death of his parents, the young Simón Bolívar inherited a substantial estate, with diverse holdings in commercial agriculture, cattle ranching, and mining, mostly operated by slave labor. From an early age, Bolívar received an excellent private education, with tutors including the noted radical intellectual Simón Rodríguez and the well-known poet and essayist Andrés Bello. He continued his education and was first exposed to politics in Europe, making two trips during his youth and young adulthood, and a third just after Venezuela took its first halting steps toward autonomy. There, he came to know a number of contemporary intellectuals and political figures personally, including Alexander von Humboldt and the aforementioned Bentham. He was in Paris on the day Napoleon I crowned himself in Notre Dame, though accounts differ as to whether he actually witnessed the event.[11]

During the fifteen years of warfare that preceded Andean South America's independence, Bolívar became the most prominent military and political leader in the region, as well as its most influential intellectual. His armies eventually freed the present-day countries of Venezuela, Colombia, Panama, Ecuador, Peru, and Bolivia from Spanish rule, earning him the title "The Liberator" (*El Libertador*) from his civilian supporters, and the nickname "Iron Ass" (*Culo de Hierro*) from the soldiers that followed him, on horseback, back and forth across the continent. With every victory, and every setback, Bolívar published newspaper articles and discourses, penned an incredible number of private and official letters, and made his opinions known to a close circle of aides and admirers, leaving excellent evidence of his opinions on the Spanish imperial system, the justice of the cause of independence, and the proper forms of government for newly established American polities. Bolívar's writing was thoughtful and beautifully composed, displaying a classical erudition and knowledge of contemporary European thinking as impressive as that of any of the founders of the United States.

However, perhaps because Bolívar achieved an individual prominence beyond that of any single North American revolutionary, his writings were rarely directed at refuting specific arguments from identifiable opponents, as were Alexander Hamilton's or, as we will see, Lucas Alamán's. Instead, his style tends toward bold pronouncements on the promise the future held for an independent America, distraught treatises on difficulties faced in the present, and detailed discourses on constitutional designs intended to effect the transition from the difficult present to a promising future.

Bolívar's philosophical influences also differed from Hamilton's and Alamán's, drawing deeply on the tradition of "classical republicanism" or "civic humanism" that intellectual historians have traced from renaissance Italy, through England's Glorious Revolution to Enlightenment France and the North American independence movement.[12] From this literature, Bolívar adopted a distinctive language for discussing politics, often contrasting his ideals of virtue, liberty, and freedom with their opposites: corruption, servitude, and slavery. Like other American republicans, he was prone to applying the latter terms collectively, speaking of entire colonial societies oppressed and debased by Spanish rule as enslaved, while neglecting what might seem a more obvious, individual application of the term to the Americas' many indentured servants, debt peons, and chattel slaves.

Along with its distinctive language, Bolívar adopted the classical republican tradition's concern with the maintenance of collective liberty against internal and external threats. Like his philosophical influences, Bolívar focused on the particular threat posed by the effects of long-term servitude or dependence on subject populations: the habits of servility or corruption thought to be typical of populations accustomed to authoritarian rule. He was convinced that Spanish Americans, because they had been denied an active role in imperial politics, lacked the civic virtues that would induce them to risk their own lives and fortunes to maintain their countries' freedom from foreign conquest and domestic anarchy. As we will see, escaping the vicious cycle of corruption for the virtuous circle of liberty was the central aim of Bolívar's constitutional thought, driving his interest in ancient and modern models of mixed government and his attraction to moral exemplars, including both individually heroic founders and lawgivers, and institutional guardians of public spiritedness and the rule of law.

Though well versed in the classics, Bolívar read less Aristotle and Machiavelli than Montesquieu and Rousseau, whom he often referenced in his writings.[13] From these authors, he absorbed mixed messages about the appropriate size of republics, about the probable effects of territorial expansion upon political stability and individual liberties, and about the propriety of forcibly assimilating new citizens to putatively republican regimes.[14] But the source of Bolívar's own inconsistencies on these issues was political rather than philosophical. Bolívar brought the framework of classical republicanism to bear on the distinctive dilemmas arising in a Creole Revolution, using the tradition's concepts of freedom and citizenship, virtue and corruption, monarchy and mixed government to justify a rebellion against European rule that left Creoles' ascendance within America undisturbed, to design innovative constitutions meant to contain the potentially explosive caste conflicts an inherited imperial social hierarchy could produce after independence, and to assert and pursue power and influence for his new state within hemispheric and global affairs. Thus, while his language was distinctive, Bolívar's core commitments closely coincided with those of Alexander Hamilton and Lucas Alamán.

In the following text, in Bolívar's early writings, I describe a familiar ambiguity between universalist claims made in defense of American independence and more particular claims made on behalf of a European-descended elite whose rightful place atop the colony's social hierarchy appeared to be under threat. In his well-known constitutional discourses of the late 1810s and early 1820s, I show that the Liberator, like other Creole constitutional designers before and after him, proposed a presidentialist system of separated powers and sought to create a union of former colonies that would fortify American independence against external enemies and limit popular influence on government internally in order to consolidate Creole rule after independence was won. And in Bolívar's calls to expand the theater of the war for independence and his famous projections of supranational, even global, political entities, I discern an imperial aspiration, premised like other Creoles' comparable ambitions on impressions of the world-historical importance of the revolutionary cause and the depraved condition of its opponents. In short, I present Bolívar as an exemplary ideologist of Creole Revolution and demonstrate that the theoretical tensions present in his defense of Spanish American revolution, his constitutions, and his foreign policy were directly related to the contradictory institutional position he occupied as an American Creole.

4.1 SPANISH AMERICA'S FIRST DECLARATION OF INDEPENDENCE

Beginning in 1776, a program of economic modernization and political centralization implemented throughout the Spanish American Empire transformed Caracas from a bustling, but distinctly peripheral port city into a central node of imperial authority. Caracas became first the seat of an intendancy and a captaincy-general, fiscal-economic and political-military administrations, respectively, and then of an *audiencia*, or imperial appellate court, and a *consulado*, a merchant and planter guild charged with organizing relations between metropolitan traders and colonial producers. These changes solidified the city's dominance of its immediate surroundings, with the new institutions exercising jurisdiction over a region roughly corresponding to the present-day country of Venezuela. But they also brought the city itself, and its prosperous and growing cacao, coffee, and indigo exports, under increased imperial scrutiny. As such, the reforms received mixed reviews from *Caraqueño* elites, who generally saw financial returns from their landholdings rise under a streamlined regulatory regime, but also resented the cadres of newly arrived administrators, bearing freshly minted qualifications from metropolitan universities, who presumed to regulate a colony accustomed to a degree of benign neglect.[15]

There was much less ambiguity in Creole responses to another policy introduced in 1795, designed to recognize the increasing wealth and social prominence of some Venezuelan *pardos* – free persons of mixed racial backgrounds – while fattening royal revenues at the same time. Added to a long list of royal dispensations offered for sale was a certificate attesting to the racial purity of its bearer, which would permit *pardos* with 500 *reales* in disposable cash to purchase entitlement to privileges and immunities previously enjoyed by Creoles and peninsular Spaniards exclusively. The City Council of Caracas, a Creole-dominated institution, petitioned the king to withdraw the offer, citing the threat it posed to the "present subordination" of the *pardo* plurality in the colony, and cautioning him against accepting further advice from colonial officials ill-disposed to the interests of "*españoles americanos*."[16] With new imperial administrators curtailing their autonomy from above, then, and new imperial policies undermining their status from below, at the end of the eighteenth century some Venezuelan Creoles came to think that continued subordination to imperial Spain had begun to imperil the "internal power structure" of the colony.[17]

This was to remain a minority view for more than a decade, though, even as Spain's entanglements in European conflicts caused the Crown to impose ever-more extractive trade and tariff policies on its American colonies. As late as 1806, when Francisco de Miranda, whom we met in the last chapter, landed a small number of ships and a rag-tag company of soldiers on the northern coast of South America with plans to begin a revolution, the Creole and peninsular elite of Caracas were unified in their fidelity to Spain. Indeed, the Creole-dominated City Council denounced Miranda as a traitor and contributed funds to support his swift expulsion.[18]

Matters shifted decisively only in 1808 when Napoleon's invasion of Spain plunged the entire empire into crisis. *Caraqueños* were amongst the first Americans to learn of their monarch's forced abdication and the resistance their peninsular counterparts were making against French rule. In conformity with the program followed in Spain, the city's elite, peninsular as well as Creole, petitioned the captain-general for permission to form a *Junta*, a temporary committee to bear sovereign authority in the king's absence. Despite its moderation – the petitioners even proposed to include the captain-general, the intendant, the archbishop, and the regent of the *Audiencia* in their *Junta* – this request was rejected. When it was resubmitted, its signers were arrested and the captain-general sent envoys into *pardo* communities with warnings that Creole autonomy would bring worse conditions for the colony's non-whites, thus raising the specter that the city's Creole elites dreaded most: a race war like the one they had heard about in Haiti.

Cowed by the captain-general's aggressive tactics, the *juntista* movement retreated, reemerging once again in 1810, when news arrived that the Spanish resistance had suffered a series of devastating defeats. On April 19, the city's Creole leaders peacefully deposed and deported the captain-general, declaring that sovereign authority within the colony would rest, until the king returned to the throne, in a *Junta Conservadora de los Derechos de Fernando VII* – a Committee for the Preservation of the Rights of Fernando VII. As indicated by this name, the formation of this committee did not represent a rejection of Spanish rule, or, even less, a denunciation of monarchical government. Rather, like other parts of the Americas, Caracas began down the road to revolution with a modest assertion of autonomy driven mainly by an unwillingness to be simply swept along by events unfolding across the Atlantic.

However, by this time more radical sentiments had begun to emerge, particularly amongst the younger generation of *Caraqueño* Creoles, who started to speak amongst themselves of independence and republican government. Two brothers from a wealthy and well-established family, Simón and Juan Vicente Bolívar, soon established themselves as prominent spokesmen of this faction. In response, more moderate elders had both Bolívars conveniently absented from the scene, sending them as representatives from the *Junta* to the governments of England and the United States, respectively. In London, Simón Bolívar and his fellow delegates promptly sought the counsel of Francisco de Miranda, recently returned from his ill-fated expedition. Miranda not only provided introductions to leading figures in the British foreign-policy establishment, but also supported and deepened his countryman's convictions regarding Venezuelan independence. Though his negotiations in London proved fruitless, Bolívar returned to Venezuela with a clearer sense of purpose. Along with Miranda, who joined him shortly afterward, he became a forceful advocate for a complete and final break with Spain.

In order to assure the support of the provinces subject to its authority, the Caracas *Junta* called for representatives to meet in a National Congress, which opened in March 1811. Meanwhile, under Bolívar and Miranda's influence, the *Sociedad Patriótica de Agricultores y Economía*, an organization originally created by the *Junta* to stimulate economic modernization in the colony, became the central forum for the radical separatist faction of Venezuela's Creoles, who steadily won over a greater and greater proportion of congressmen to their cause. It was in front of the *Sociedad Patriótica*, in the early morning hours of July 4, 1811, that Simón Bolívar made his first extensive public argument on behalf of an immediate declaration of independence:

In the National Congress they discuss what should already be decided. And what do they say? That we should begin by forming a federation; as if we were not already federated against foreign tyranny! That we should await word from Spain;

as if it matters to us whether Spain sells its slaves to Bonaparte or keeps them for herself, when we are resolved to be free! That we should prepare great projects with patience; as if three centuries of patience weren't enough! These doubts are the sad effects of ancient bondage. The Patriotic Society respects, as it should, the Congress of the nation, but the Congress should also attend to the Patriotic Society, center of enlightenment and of all revolutionary interests. Together, we will lay the foundation stone of South American liberty: to hesitate is to perish.[19]

In these early remarks, we can see the outlines of the arguments that would comprise Bolívar's case for Spanish American independence. Here, already, he identifies imperial rule with slavery and attributes the hesi- tation of his more moderate fellows to the corruption of their civic vir- tues caused by long-term subjugation. Here, already, Bolívar identifies the patriotic cause with progress and enlightenment, and presents the liberation of Caracas as a mere first step in an ultimately continental undertaking. The day after Bolívar's address to the *Sociedad Patriótica*, the National Congress voted to publish a short statement that – though more moderate than Bolívar might have hoped – made Venezuela the first Spanish American colony to declare its independence.[20]

Over the next decade, in personal letters, newspaper editorials, and official proclamations, Bolívar would elaborate his case, beginning with first principles: "States are enslaved either by virtue of their constitution or through the abuse of it," he asserted. Similarly, "a people is enslaved when the government, by its essence or through its vices, tramples and usurps the rights of the citizens or subjects." Spanish Americans were enslaved by their exclusion from any role in the administration of the colonies they inhabited. "For centuries," Bolívar insisted, "the position of those who dwell in this hemisphere has been purely passive; their political existence has been null." Never "Viceroys, or Governors, except in extraordinary cir- cumstances, rarely Archbishops or Bishops, never diplomats, and always military subordinates," Americans "do not occupy any position in society except as laborers and simple consumers." Thus, they "face the greatest difficulties in rising to enjoy the goods of freedom."[21] Here, Bolívar's clas- sical republican intellectual influences are clear. As noted in the preced- ing text, he conceives of freedom and slavery collectively – as qualities not of individuals but of "states" and "peoples" – and positively – as the opportunity to participate in self-government by occupying the highest ranks in the institutions of colonial rule. By denying Americans access to these offices, Spain essentially denied them the opportunity to fully realize themselves as humans. This, for Bolívar, was the central wrong in imperial rule that American independence would make right.

The fact that Bolívar himself owned other humans, whose life of labor supported his personal consumption and travel, as well as his intellectual and political pursuits, lends his use of terms like "slavery" and "servitude" a certain ironic quality. He was not, of course, the only patriotic American slave owner to characterize his position thus, but Bolívar made the tensions present in this grievance clearer than most of his contemporaries. He argued that under Spanish rule, Creoles "were not only deprived of their freedom, but also of an *active tyranny*" – an opportunity to perform a subordinate role in the colonial administration. Even under the Ottomans, Persians, and Mongolians, he notes, "subordinates participated according to the authority they were allotted. They were charged with civil, political, and military administration, with [the collection of] rents, and [regulation of] religion." By contrast, Spanish Americans were denied even the oversight of "domestic matters and internal administration," with the result being that they "were left in a kind of permanent infancy with respect to public affairs," deprived of both "familiarity with the process and workings of" government and "the personal esteem in the eyes of the people that derives from a certain habitual respect."[22]

Here, the limitations of Bolívar's anti-imperialism come into view. He attacked Spanish rule in America not because it was alien or absolutist, but because it denied Creoles any autonomy in the management of colonial affairs. He emphasized not only the personal developmental defects this position imposed, but also the ways in which it undermined would-be leaders' ability to attract the deference of colonial populations. Making free use of Montesquieu's well-known accounts of "oriental despotism"[23] as a foil against which he highlighted Spanish Americans' plight, Bolívar suggests, in effect, that Venezuelan Creoles would have to declare independence in order to attain the "active tyranny" that was their due.

Like other ideologues of Creole Revolution, Bolívar was prone to rhetorical flourishes and fond of framing his complaints about Spanish rule in universal terms, describing imperial policies as violations of rights borne by Spanish Americans simply as humans, or the empire itself as a departure from the ideal political order decreed by nature or by eternal philosophical truths. These passages have become favorites of Bolívar's progressive followers, and, in practical terms, have made the Liberator's works a potent archive of arguments on behalf of freedom and equality.

But, like his counterparts elsewhere, whenever Bolívar sought to define the basis for his patriotism precisely, and especially legally, the close connection between his own institutional position atop a colonial hierarchy and his political thought was made clear. In the early sixteenth century, he alleged, "The Emperor Charles V formed a pact with the discoverers, conquistadors, and settlers of America," providing that "since they carried out these acts at their own cost and risk, and without drawing support from the royal treasury, they would be conceded the right to rule the land [*les concedía que fuesen señores de la tierra*] ... as a sort of feudal property for themselves and their descendants." In addition, Charles V promised to "favor almost exclusively the Spaniards born in this country [*los naturales del país originarios de España*]," that is, Bolívar and his fellow Creoles, "for civil and ecclesiastical posts and rents." The contemporary practice of appointing peninsular Spaniards to new and vacant posts was, then, "a manifest violation of subsisting laws and pacts, depriving these Creoles [*naturales*] of the constitutional authority they were given by their code."²⁴ In the end, then, Bolívar's case for American independence rested on a Spanish breach, not of universal and inalienable human rights, and not of an ideal institutional order, but of a specific agreement concluded between the Holy Roman emperor, his well-armed emissaries, and their descendants, which entitled the latter to a "sort of feudal" lordship in the Americas and over their colonies' Indigenous and African inhabitants.

Combining classical republican concepts with an account of the legal rights Creoles bore as the descendants of the New World's conquerors, Bolívar built a case for American independence. Though his philosophical and legal references were often ancient, he was clearly conscious of the novelty of his political undertaking. In a telling passage, Bolívar compared "the present state of America" to the final days of the Roman Empire, "when each dismembered part formed a nation according to its unique situation and interests, or by following the particular ambitions of their chiefs, leading families, or corporations." One fact critically distinguished the Americas from the former Roman periphery, though: "[W]hile those provinces reestablished their ancient nations," resurrecting polities that pre-dated Roman rule, Americans "have retained only the barest vestiges of what [they] were in other times." Bolívar did not seek to connect the struggle for independence to a pre-Hispanic past, or to defend his rebellion as an effort to rectify the injustice of the conquest. He did not oppose empire in the name of any nationalism, incipient or otherwise. Americans, in his account, simply had no ancient nations to reestablish.

This problem presented itself with particular force for the Creole leaders of the independence movements. Bolívar and his fellows were "neither Indians nor Europeans," but a caste apart, situated by the institutions of

Spanish rule "in between the legitimate owners of the country and the Spanish usurpers." As "Americans by birth and Europeans by right," the Creoles' fight to rule themselves while preserving their colonial privileges forced them to confront "both Native Americans [*los del país*] and external invaders."[25] Here, Bolívar offers an extraordinarily clear understanding of the contradictions inherent in Creoles' institutional position. His writings just as clearly betray the entwined imperial and anti-imperial strands that characterized Creoles' revolutionary ideology.

4.2 MACHIAVELLIAN MOMENTS AND THE MORAL POWER

Taken, perhaps, by the profundity of his own insight, Bolívar repeated the passage comparing the incipiently independent Americas with post-Roman Europe almost word-for-word in his 1819 "Discourse at Angostura," regarded by most scholars as the single most complete statement of Bolívar's mature political thought. Once again, Bolívar emphasizes the peculiarities of Creole Revolution: the absence of a usable, pre-colonial past; the two-sided nature of the struggle to preserve imperial privileges while escaping imperial rule. In its later appearance, however, the passage's function shifts. After eight years of intense fighting, Bolívar is no longer concerned to defend a rebellion whose success is almost assured on the ground, but rather to characterize the difficulties he worried would arise after his armies had defeated Spain. The question now was not how to wrest freedom away from the Americas' oppressors but how to maintain American independence against its internal and external enemies. In this sense, Bolívar found himself face-to-face with the dilemma J. G. A. Pocock has described as the "Machiavellian moment":

The moment in conceptualized time in which the republic was seen as confronting its own temporal finitude, as attempting to remain morally and politically stable in a stream of irrational events conceived as essentially destructive of all systems of secular stability.[26]

Like many of his predecessors in the republican tradition, Bolívar sought a solution to this dilemma in constitutional design, drawing inspiration from the ancient and modern models of "mixed government" that Pocock traces from Aristotle to the North American independence movement. Like his counterparts in the northern half of the hemisphere, Bolívar modified these models in order to apply them to the novel problems posed by the Americas' postcolonial position in global affairs and internal socio-racial hierarchy. Thus, despite his distinctive philosophical starting point, as we'll see, Bolívar's ideas ultimately converged in important respects with those of Creole constitutional designers throughout the hemisphere.

In Venezuela, persistent legacies of imperial rule, the political inexperience of the Creole elite, and the volatility of a racially heterogeneous populace all combined to make the problem of maintaining freedom particularly pressing. Independence did not come easily, and it twice proved fragile indeed. The National Congress that declared independence in July 1811 produced a constitution in December, but its provisions had little time to go into operation before counter-revolution enveloped the First Republic from all sides. The Spanish, though mired in European conflicts, proved capable of launching effective attacks from bases in Puerto Rico and Santo Domingo, and they found willing collaborators amongst the mainly *pardo* population concentrated along the Caribbean coastline northwest of Caracas, whose loyalty the Creole revolutionaries did little to court.[27] After establishing a base of support in the city of Coro, the Spanish Commander Domingo Monteverde armed *pardo* rebellions against the republic throughout the interior, which proved difficult to suppress. Slaves fought on both sides of the battle, but skewed royalist as well, especially because Monteverde was quicker to promise manumission in exchange for military service than were his patriotic opponents, many of whom were slave owners with economic, as well as strategic, interests at stake in the matter.[28]

Already under siege, the republic's capacity to respond to external attacks and internal rebellions was devastated by two earthquakes, which struck Caracas in late March and early April 1812, killing an estimated twenty thousand people. Royalist clergy seized the propaganda opportunity presented by this tragedy, portraying the earthquake as divine retribution for *Caraqueños'* lack of fidelity to their monarch. The Congress appointed Francisco de Miranda *Generalissimo*, granting him dictatorial powers in the prosecution of the war, but by July, he concluded that the cause was hopeless and surrendered to the royalist forces. Bolívar, who had overseen the unsuccessful defense of an important arms cache and prison on the Caribbean coastline, considered this an act of cowardice and personally led a plot to have his mentor arrested and turned over to the Spanish authorities. This betrayal secured Bolívar's safe passage out of the colony to fight another day, but it has supplied grounds for sharp criticism of his character ever since. Miranda spent the last four years of his life imprisoned in Cádiz, Spain, eventually succumbing to exposure and malnourishment.

Bolívar made his way to Cartagena, a patriotic redoubt in the neighboring province of New Granada, where revolution had initially been spurred by a broader coalition of Creoles and *pardos*, and where independence proved somewhat more stable.[29] There, he offered his services as a soldier, distinguished himself in a number of battles, and finally prevailed upon the provisional government to provide him with a small force with which to undertake the liberation of Venezuela. Convinced that Miranda's excessive mercy lay at the root of the First Republic's failure, Bolívar adopted on this campaign a policy of "war to the death," under which American prisoners of war were spared, but Spaniards who did not join his army were immediately executed. His forces were also particularly brutal, however, with *pardo* regiments fighting for the royalist cause, despite their American birth. Monteverde adopted similar tactics, executing thousands of patriot prisoners, but ultimately failed to stop Bolívar's advance. The patriot army entered Caracas on August 6, 1813, where it was greeted by the welcome news that exiled patriots had routed royalists throughout the eastern plains. Bolívar was granted the title "Liberator of Venezuela," and, after hastily convening a National Assembly, gained supreme command of the patriot forces and temporary dictatorial authority over a resurrected Republic of Venezuela.

The Second Republic enjoyed an even shorter life than the First. This time, counter-revolution came from the eastern *llanos*, or plains, and was led by José Tomás Boves, a naval pilot from northern Spain who had fled smuggling charges to become a cattle dealer in Venezuela, joining a diverse company of poor Creoles and Canary Islanders, Indians, *pardos*, and fugitive slaves, who lived by rounding up and selling unbranded cattle, which they grazed on lands traditionally regarded as commons. The *llaneros* were ill-disposed toward independence from the start, associating the movement with its urban leadership. They moved decisively into the opposition when the congress of the First Republic introduced legislation meant to establish uniform private property in land and cattle, and to limit labor mobility by forcing workers to register with landowners and carry identification at all times. Boves organized this disaffected population into an effective lance cavalry, offering his forces the opportunity to loot wealthy republicans and the prospect of reestablishing the customary entitlements that made their livelihood possible.[30]

Boves quickly became the most feared man in the country, and in battle after battle, republican forces broke before his attacks. In July, Bolívar led a frantic evacuation of *Caraqueño* Creoles north and west to the coast, and gradually ceded ever more territory to royalist control. Boves fell fighting in December, but by the beginning of 1815, his forces had finished dismantling the Second Republic, leaving only disparate bands fighting for independence when the restored Fernando VII dispatched a giant expedition to firmly reestablish Spanish rule in northern South America. Bolívar decamped first to Jamaica and then to Haiti, where he was taken in by President-for-Life Alexandre Pétion, a veteran of the Saint-Domingue Revolution, who provided Bolívar with provisions, arms, soldiers, and ships for a third and finally successful campaign.[31]

These serial revolutionary triumphs and disappointments, the rapid construction and destruction of two republics, each incapable in its own way of containing the social and racial divisions of Venezuela, and neither effective in directing individual energies into collective external defense, furnish the essential context for Bolívar's reflections on the maintenance of liberty. In 1819, addressing an assembly gathered in the city of Angostura to draft "organic laws" for yet another new republic, he asked, "How, having broken the chains of our ancient oppression, can we perform the miracle of preventing their iron remnants from being reforged as freedom-killing weapons [*armas liberticidas*]?"[32] As this formulation vividly conveys, Bolívar considered the legacies of Spanish imperial rule – its "iron remnants" – a primary impediment to the consolidation of American independence:

Under the triple yoke of ignorance, tyranny, and vice, we have been unable to acquire or even to know virtue. Disciples of pernicious masters, we have studied the most destructive examples and learned the most awful lessons.... An ignorant people is the blind instrument of its own destruction; ... adopting illusions for reality, mistaking license for liberty, treason for patriotism, and vengeance for justice ... A corrupted people, if it wins its liberty, can quickly lose it.[33]

Here, as in his defense of revolution, Bolívar's intellectual debts to the classical republican tradition are clear, but as I noted in the preceding text, he now deploys the same concepts to a new end. Because of the deprivations they suffered under Spanish rule, especially the absence of any opportunity to participate in government, upon gaining their independence, Americans lacked the "virtues" necessary to sustain their freedom. Under the influence of "illusions" – mistaken understandings about individual and collective freedom – they were unwilling to put aside their many petty squabbles and work for the public good. Deeply "corrupted" by their imperial experiences, Bolívar argued, Spanish Americans' "Moral Constitution did not yet have the consistency necessary to receive the benefits of a completely representative government." He thus recommends that the legislators before him think of their task as essentially educative, concerning themselves with "laying a foundation" upon which future freedoms could rest.[34]

One of Bolívar's most famous institutional innovations was designed for precisely this purpose. At Angostura, he suggested that Venezuela's constitution should create, alongside the by-then traditional legislative, executive, and judicial branches of government, a new "fourth branch" he called the "*Poder Moral*" or "moral power." This branch was charged with the specific task of "regenerating the character and the customs that tyranny and the war" had suppressed in Spanish America. Citing ancient models – the Athenian Areopagus, the Spartan Ephors, and the Roman Censors – Bolívar described an authority with "dominion over childhood and men's hearts, the public spirit, good customs, and republican morality." Specifically, the distinguished members of the moral power would have the authority to reward heroic actions in service of the republic, or to accuse citizens of "ingratitude, egoism, frigidity toward the fatherland, idleness, and negligence." They would also oversee the education system, and provide public support for the arts and sciences. In all, Bolívar hoped, the moral power would cultivate a citizenry capable of sustaining republican liberty in Venezuela, and "restore to the world the idea of a people who is not content to be being free and strong, but also wants to be virtuous."[35]

Bolívar's proposal immediately acquired great esteem amongst his contemporaries in Spanish America and has remained ever since a point of special interest amongst his interpreters.[36] It captures the essential character of Bolívar's constitutionalism, being overtly authoritarian in its design – resembling a sort of "laicized Inquisition," in one scholar's memorable phrase[37] – but intended at the same time to eventually bring about its own obsolescence, after Spanish Americans had acquired the requisite virtues to rule themselves. This temporary educative despotism was Bolívar's best plan for escaping the vicious circle of tyranny and corruption his classical republican philosophical influences suggested a newly liberated people must inevitably confront.[38]

Though Bolívar framed the problem of maintaining liberty in classical republican terms and offered a solution with ancient precedents, distinctively Creole concerns appeared in his thinking as well. He tended to elide a distinction between two related difficulties: the shortage of civic virtues in Spanish America that was, on his account, a consequence of centuries of imperial rule, and the challenges involved in governing a racially stratified society renegotiating its terms of existence after the shock of independence. Americans who failed to dedicate themselves to the struggle for liberty were corrupted by their experience under absolutist government, their servility evidenced by their prioritizing personal interests rather than the common good. Bolívar applied the same terms, though, to indigenous and African Americans who refused to defer to Creole leadership in the struggle for independence, faulting their leaders for pursuing "factional" interests rather than the common good, and suggesting that racial conflict presented, if anything, an even greater threat to stable freedom than Americans' habituation to tyrannical government.[39]

At Angostura, Bolívar insisted that the formal exclusions of *pardos*, *mestizos*, and other *castas*, the separate "*repúblicas de indios*" with their communal lands and tribute systems, and, most of all, the chattel slavery that had characterized Spanish rule in the Americas, should be abolished, arguing that "the fundamental principle of our system requires immediately and inescapably that equality be established and practiced in Venezuela." But he was deeply concerned that equality be established and practiced properly, stressing that "although all men are born with equal rights to the goods of society,... not all are born equally able to occupy the highest posts."[40] He feared, most of all, that Venezuela's *pardo* plurality would fail to grasp this subtlety, that the "legal equality" he was willing to offer would "not satisfy the spirit of the people who want absolute equality now in both public and private, and will later seek *pardocracia*, and the extermination of the privileged classes."[41] Suppressing such radical demands, and, in general, "managing this heterogeneous society, whose complicated balance can be dislocated, divided, and dissolved by the slightest disruption," Bolívar argued, "will require an infinitely firm hand."[42]

Thus, racial diversity and the potential for race-based factional politics served as another premise in an argument against immediate adoption of "fully representative" government. Venezuela's political system needed to be designed in such a way that it would discriminate informally, concentrating the power of an enlightened Creole elite and limiting the influence of an unlettered, mostly propertyless *pardo* plurality, without recurring to the overt discrimination of the empire and thereby inciting racial conflict. Like other Creole constitutional theorists, Bolívar thought that two institutions would help achieve this balance: political union and a presidentialist system of separated powers.

4.3 FEDERALISM AND THE NORTH AMERICAN MODEL

The most consistent tenet of Bolívar's constitutionalism was opposition to decentralized, federal systems of government. As early as 1812, in the course of explaining the demise of the First Republic to an audience in Cartagena, Bolívar argued that "what most weakened the government of Venezuela was the federalist form it adopted." Though he conceded that "the federal system may be the most perfect, and the most capable of achieving human happiness in society," it was also "the one most inimical to the interests of our emerging states,... [whose] citizens haven't the aptitude to exercise for themselves a wide range of rights, because they lack the virtues of the true republican."[43]

Ironically, the main example Venezuelan advocates of federalism cited as evidence of the system's advantages was another emerging state: the United States of America, where, they argued, a federal system had permitted a colonial backwater to transform itself into a rising commercial power over the course of less than half a century.[44] In his efforts to address this argument by example, Bolívar made an analysis of the contrasting character of British and Spanish rule in the Americas the cornerstone of his argument on behalf of a more centralized union of Andean South America's former colonies:

The more I admire the excellence of the Federal Constitution of [the First Republic] of Venezuela, the more I am persuaded of the impossibility of applying it to our State. Indeed, to my mind, it is a miracle that its model in North America has subsisted so prosperously, and not broken down at the first sign of trouble. Although the people [of the United States] are a singular model of political virtue and moral enlightenment; although liberty has been their cradle, they were born into liberty, and fed on pure liberty; and although in many respects they are unique in the history of the human race, it is, I repeat, a miracle that a system so weak and so complicated as federalism has managed to govern them the difficult and delicate circumstances as they have experienced.[45]

Here, Bolívar takes a large measure of rhetorical license, reproducing the blackest possible legend of Spanish imperialism as the premise of his argument on behalf of a centralized political union. He also fails to acknowledge that the United States' first experiment with federalism did actually "break down at the first sign of trouble," giving way to a new constitution that assigned substantially greater authority to the central government than its predecessor. Apparently unaware of these parallels,[46] which might have supported his position, Bolívar cited Montesquieu's dictum that laws "must be adapted to the physical geography, climate, soil quality, situation, extension, and style of life of a people, to its religion, inclinations, riches, numbers, commerce, customs, and habits," arguing that "these are the Codes we must consult, not those of Washington!"[47] It is hard not to read these lines as another reference to Venezuela's racial heterogeneity, and to see centralism as an element of the "infinitely firm hand" Bolívar thought managing his countrymen would require.

When Bolívar's unionist ideal was eventually put into practice, it was applied to an area much larger than Venezuela, where concomitant increases in racial and regional diversity brought new complications and challenges. Bolívar began his third campaign in the far eastern plains of Venezuela, near the mouth of the Orinoco River, in late December 1816. This decision made both strategic and economic sense, allowing him to establish a base of operations away from the main concentrations of Spanish forces along the Caribbean coastline, and to exploit a ready source of steady income: the semi-wild cattle of the *llanos*. Through contacts he had made while in Jamaica, Bolívar began trading livestock and hides for arms, ammunition, and uniforms with English smugglers.

Though it provided a source of income and the security of distance from any concentration of Spanish forces, Bolívar's base of operations in the llanos carried a singular difficulty as well: dealing with the fiercely independent cattlemen that inhabited the plains. After the fall of the First and Second Republics of Venezuela, a number of patriots fighters in exile had established themselves in as regional strongmen, organizing bands of *llanero* cavalry men that carried out guerrilla attacks on Spanish forces, motivated as much by profits as by politics. Though sympathetic to the cause of independence, many of these caudillos were reluctant to surrender their authority, and refused to submit their forces to Bolívar's overall command.

Again, social and racial issues had a role to play. One of the most recalcitrant caudillos was Manuel Piar, who led a mainly *pardo* force that had won major victories against royalist forces, acquiring a wide area of influence in the eastern plains. Morillo, the Spanish general holding Caracas, expressed concerns in official dispatches that Piar might be establishing relations with Alexandre Pétion, and preparing the way for a Haitian-supported rebellion of *pardos* and slaves in Venezuela, revealing the deep anxieties Haiti inspired in royalists as well as Creole patriots. For his part, Bolívar treated Piar cautiously until he had assembled superior forces of his own, and then demanded that Piar pledge allegiance to the republican project under his direction. When Piar returned an ambiguous reply, Bolívar had him arrested, imprisoned, and executed, on charges of inciting a "race war."[48] Though Bolívar also took less punitive steps to quiet racial resentments, offering manumission to slaves who volunteered to serve in his armies, and promoting *pardo* officers whose loyalties were clear, racial factionalism within the revolution and the prospect of *pardocracia* continued to haunt him,[49] strengthening his already strong opposition to federalism as time went on.

By the middle of 1818, through tenuous arrangements built on flattery, bribery, and brute force, Bolívar controlled the patriot caudillos of the Venezuelan south from the Atlantic to the border with New Granada. To impose military discipline, he filled the officer ranks of his armies with experienced English and Irish soldiers, unemployed since the end of hostilities in Europe, and willing to face the unfamiliar climate and brutal warfare of Spanish America for adventure and the prospect of a paycheck.[50] These troops proved indispensable to the success of Bolívar's next maneuver: an attack on the Andean highlands of New Granada, where Spanish forces were less entrenched than on the Caribbean coast, and the population was more susceptible to republican arguments. He entrusted the oversight of early operations to Francisco de Paula Santander, a law student turned patriot who had been forced to flee his native New Granada for the Venezuelan plains after Spanish forces overran republican forces. In May 1819, Santander reported that conditions were ripe for revolution, and over the course of a few months, Bolívar marched his troops through high passes and low valleys, winning a decisive victory in August that sent the Spanish back into retreat.

Ties between the independence movements of Venezuela and New Granada, forged in the heat of Bolívar's successive cross-border campaigns, were formalized after patriotic forces occupied Santa Fe de Bogotá, the seat of a Spanish viceroyalty with supreme authority over all of northern South America. In December 1819, the Venezuelan National Congress assembled in Angostura passed a Fundamental Law [*Ley Orgánica*] giving the name "Colombia" to a unified state comprised by all of the former viceroyalty's territories: the captaincy-general of Caracas (present-day Venezuela), the kingdom of New Granada (present-day Colombia and Panama), and the presidency of Quito (present-day Ecuador). By convention, historians refer to this entity as "Gran Colombia" to distinguish it from the present-day country of the same name.

The National Congress also established election procedures for a constituent assembly, permitting all heads of households in the liberated territories with modest property holdings or a scientific, liberal, or mechanical profession, as well as all soldiers in the patriot armies, native or foreign, literate or not, to vote for deputies. As David Bushnell notes, these were "in some respects the most democratic elections ever held in Gran Colombia," distinguished not only by their broad franchise but also, given the circumstances, a surprising absence of irregularities.[51]

Deputies began arriving in the city of Cúcuta, on the border between Venezuela and New Granada, in January 1821.

Once a quorum had assembled and deliberations got underway, federalism and centralism were primary subjects of discussion. Deputies elected from the interior provinces of New Granada, many of whom were active in their province's first movement for independence, were wary of Bolívar, his army, and of the consequences a Venezuelan-led liberation might have for New Granada. They argued that Gran Colombia's component colonies should retain sovereignty within an independent federation whose central government was limited to the conduct of external relations and the war. Well-educated lawyers, doctors, and clerics, these Colombian federalists fluently cited fashionable philosophers, suggesting that overly large states tended to become monarchies, while citizens of small states could be free.

Having departed by this point to lead a campaign against remaining royalist strongholds in Venezuela, Bolívar was forced to reply from the sidelines: "One hears little here of the Assembly or of Cúcuta, but it is said that many in Cundinamarca want a federation," he wrote to Santander. "We may have to banish these *letrados*," or professionals, "from the Republic of Colombia, as Plato banished the poets from his Republic." Their mistakes, he argued, derived from a limited understanding of the country and its inhabitants:

These Gentlemen think that Colombia is full of the simple men they've seen gathered around fireplaces in Bogotá, Tunja, and Pamplona. They've never laid eyes on the Caribs of the Orinoco, the plainsmen of the Apure, the fishermen of Maracaibo, the boatmen of the Magdalena, the bandits of Patia, the ungovernable Pastusos, the Guajibos of Casanare and all the other savage hordes of Africans and Americans that roam like deer throughout the wilderness of Colombia.[52]

Bolívar did not believe federalism could establish and maintain freedom amongst such people. Colombia's complex, racially diverse population, accustomed to despotic Spanish rule and lacking the virtues of true republicans, required a firm, unified government. Union would allow the educated, Creole elite to exert direct control during the critical period of transition from colony to republic.

The federalist deputies, "more out of ignorance than malice,... speak of Lycurgus, Numa, and Franklin," but they were wrong to think that they could establish "republics like Greece, Rome, or the United States" in Colombia. In their naivety, they would succeed only in "accumulating rubble from fantastical creations," the ruins of "Greek buildings, built on Gothic foundations, standing at the edge of an abyss."[53] Here, Bolívar provides us with clear insight into the concrete social context that furnished the central problems for his political thought. His federalist opponents sought to build *"repúblicas aéreas"* – republics in the sky, drawing their principles from philosophical abstractions or worse, imitating irrelevant foreign models. By contrast, Bolívar's Creole unionism – simultaneously pragmatic and prone to learned flourishes – sought to reconcile opposing aims, establishing independence and republican liberty, while limiting popular sovereignty and social instability.

Ultimately, whether on the strength of their arguments or the implicit threat presented by Bolívar's armies, unionists won the day at Cúcuta. The constitution adopted by the Congress in October 1821 abolished Gran Colombia's colonial component states, replacing them with smaller departments, designed de novo with an eye to easing administration and diminishing the force of regional political identities that undermined unity. The departments were, in turn, subdivided into provinces, cantons, and parishes, which formed the basis of a multilevel system of indirect election for national officeholders. The internal administration of the republic was entrusted to a governor in each province and overseen by an intendant in each department, both of whom served at the will of the president.[54]

It is important to emphasize the novelty of this arrangement. To be sure, Gran Colombia arose within the boundaries of a former viceroyalty and could claim a legal precedent for its borders,[55] but the unification of its component colonies under a centralized government was not, as in Mexico, a continuation of colonial-era practices. Under its own captaincy-general, Caracas had been legally independent of the viceregal administration based in Bogotá, and even Quito and Panama, though formally subordinate, were accustomed to relative autonomy. Unlike Mexico's unionists, whom I will discuss in the next chapter, Bolívar was uninterested – to a fault – in basing his new state's legitimacy on colonial legacies. Gran Colombia was established, undiluted by federal devolution, as a republican solution to the dilemmas inherent in Creole Revolution.

4.4 PRESIDENTIALISM AND THE BRITISH MODEL

Bolívar had reason to be pleased with the results of the Congress at Cúcuta, but the deputies did not carry out all of his designs. When it came to distributing authority amongst the branches of the national government, they followed the example of the United States, dividing authority between three branches: a legislature comprised of two houses, one apportioned according to population and serving four-year terms, and the other apportioned by department, serving eight-year terms; an executive comprised of a president and vice president, serving four-year terms with one opportunity for reelection; and a judiciary headed by a supreme court of at least five ministers serving life terms.

Interbranch relations were slightly different than in the United States, though, ultimately tilting the balance of powers in favor of the legislature. No provisions were made for a presidential veto or judicial review of legislation in times of normal politics, but "in cases of armed interior commotions that threaten the security of the republic or sudden external invasions," the president was authorized to "dictate such measures as are indispensable that are not comprehended by the normal sphere of his attributes."[56] Bolívar's rather ample interpretation of this article during his own administration would eventually become a point of contention, but at the time of its promulgation, he deplored the fact that it made the executive "either a gentle stream or a devastating torrent,"[57] rather than the consistent, stabilizing force he thought the republic required.

In his address to the deputies at Angostura, Bolívar had considered alternative models of separated powers at some length. Athens, he argued, "provides the first, and most brilliant example of absolute democracy, but at the same time, the most melancholy demonstration of the extreme weakness of this sort of government." Even the constitution of Sparta, despite the "chimera" of its double monarchy, "produced better results than the ingenious masterpiece of Solon." Rome, meanwhile, "achieved the greatest power and fortune of any people in the world," even though its constitution "did not strictly distinguish between the powers," allowing "the consuls, the senate, and the people to be legislators, magistrates, and judges." However, its "only inclination was conquest," which "did not assure the happiness of the nation."

More recently, the French Revolution, "like a radiant meteor, has showered the world with such a profusion of political enlightenment, that every thinking man has learned the rights and duties of man, and the virtues and vices of government." Perhaps most remarkable of all, "this star, in its luminous passage, has sparked fires even in the hearts of the apathetic Spanish," inspiring the temporary adoption in 1812 of a constitution with strict limitations on executive authority.[58] But Bolívar was skeptical of French revolutionary constitutionalism and viewed the Spanish imitation as an apt illustration of its deficits: "the Spanish Constitution is a monster of indefinable form, similar in effect to the regime of Grand Turk but entirely opposite in appearance. What the Great Sultan does in Constantinople an assembly with infinite members does in Madrid. Its will is as absolute as that of the greatest despot in the world."[59] This opposition to legislative supremacy à la française was characteristic of Creole constitutional theorists, whose fear of a tyranny of the majority was only heightened by the racial divisions in their American societies.

Thus, after offering a familiar injunction to "never forget that the excellence of a government consists not in its theory, its form, or its mechanism, but in it appropriateness for the nature and character of the nation for which it is instituted," Bolívar recommended that the assembly adopt the British Constitution as a model, deeming it the "most apt ... for those who aspire to enjoy the rights of man and as much political freedom as is compatible with our fragile state of affairs." He seems to have been aware that this might seem an incongruously counter-revolutionary choice, hastening to declare that "in speaking of the British Government, I refer only to its republican elements." However, the first institution he proposed to imitate was the House of Lords:

It would not require a fundamental alteration for us to adopt a legislative power like the British Parliament. We have already divided our national representatives into two houses.... If the Senate, instead of being elected, were hereditary, it would be come the base, the fastener, and the soul of our Republic. During political tempests, this body would deflect lightening bolts from the government and repulse waves of popular dissent.[60]

Colombia's long period of subordination to Spain had left the country full of "men who do not know their own true interests"; who pursued selfish, sectional, or racial interests rather than dedicating themselves to the collective good; and whose frequent rebellions presented a constant threat to the stability of elected governments. The destructiveness of these mass movements could be minimized by a "neutral body" of hereditary senators whose authority was independent of both the current government and the people, in a position suited to mediating the conflicts that might arise between "these two founts of authority."[61] Future senators could be trained from birth in special schools designed to inculcate political virtues along with the "arts, sciences, and letters that adorn the spirit of a public man." Again, Bolívar insisted that a hereditary senate would "in no way be a violation of political equality," and that he "did not wish to establish a nobility." Rather, given Colombia's difficult circumstances, "not everything should be left to the chance and fortune of elections."[62]

The echoes of Alexander Hamilton's "high-toned" proposals in the Constitutional Convention here are clear. Like Hamilton, Bolívar struggled to reconcile the oligarchic measures he thought Colombia's situation required with the republican ideals he still hoped to achieve. This remarkable convergence was not a result of direct intellectual influence – none is apparent in the record – but rather a shared apprehension of a similar political situation. As in Hamilton's, the marked tensions in Bolívar's political thought, the contradicting imperial and anti-imperial impulses that underlie his hereditary senate and other institutional innovations reflect an attempt to safeguard the authority of a colonial upper class in the unstable circumstances of the Americas' early independence.

Turning next to the presidency, Bolívar argued that "however exorbitant the authority of the Executive Power appears in England, it would not be so in the Republic of Venezuela." Indeed, contrary to common misperceptions, dispensing with the trappings of royal authority called for an increase in the power of the executive: "In a republic, [the Executive] must be all the stronger, because everything conspires against him." Unable to rely upon the "superstitious veneration people instinctively accord their Royalty, ... the splendor of the throne, the crown, and the purple; ... the immense riches accumulated in generations of dynastic rule; [or] the reciprocal fraternal protection that all kings give and receive from one another," a republican executive required even more plenary powers than a king.

In Venezuela, the president would need "sufficient authority to overcome the inconveniences attendant on our present situation, the state of war from which we suffer, and the sorts of enemies, foreign and domestic, against which we have long struggled." Here, Bolívar explicitly ties the expansion of executive authority he sought to the double conflict inherent in Creole Revolution. Colombia's president would have to complete and consolidate a struggle for independence, while also suppressing the caste conflicts that independence had unleashed.

As numerous scholars of the classical republican tradition have shown, the model of mixed government developed first by Aristotle, and elaborated by the statesman-philosophers of republican Rome and Renaissance Italy, the British commonwealthmen, and British North American patriots was ideally suited to this purpose. These constitutions offered separate forms of representation to distinct classes of citizens and subjects, balancing their powers in an effort assure that no faction could dominate the others.[63] Bolívar faithfully echoed this conception, noting that a system of separated powers, generally, had to "maintain the balance, not only amongst the branches that comprise our government, but also the different fractions that comprise our society."[64] Venezuelans could do no better than to adapt Montesquieu's exemplar of modern mixed government, the British constitution, to their own special circumstances.

We get a much fuller picture of the way Bolívar hoped to structure such a system in the constitution he wrote seven years later for the newly established nation of Bolivia. There, he proposed a government divided into four branches: an "electoral power" comprised by representatives directly chosen by each of the ten active citizens of the republic, and responsible for choosing legislators; a tricameral legislature, including a chamber of censors, resembling the *poder moral* Bolívar had described at Angostura; a supreme court; and, most notoriously of all, a *presidente vitalicio*, or life-term president.

In the Bolivian Constitution, the balance of powers swung decisively in favor of the executive branch, which conducted war and determined foreign policy, convened or extended congressional sessions, initiated and vetoed legislation, appointed ambassadors, cabinet members, finance ministers, regional administrators, and the Church hierarchy, and could even "suspend ... pontifical bulls, briefs, and rescripts" if necessary. Upon his death or incapacitation, the president was to be automatically succeeded by a handpicked vice president, whom he chose with the advice and consent of the legislature.[65] In his presentation of the constitution to the Congress of Bolivia, Bolívar summarized the institution of the *presidente vitalicio* thus:

Under our Constitution, the President of the Republic will be like the sun: an unmovable core, radiating life throughout the universe. This supreme authority should be perpetual, because societies without hierarchies need even more than others a fixed point around which magistrates and people, men and things, can rotate. *Give me a fixed point*, said an ancient, *and I will move the world.* For Bolivia, this point is the life-term President.[66]

What was the immense undertaking for which Bolívar thought such a stout fulcrum was required? He viewed Spanish America's situation as analogous to that of Rousseau's "young people" – a populace too inexperienced in self-rule to recognize a good regime when they saw one. For a new, self-governing sovereign to become stable, Rousseau argued, "the effect would have to become the cause; the social spirit, which should be created by institutions, would have to preside over their very foundation, and men would have to be before law what they should become by means of law." He suggested that this problem could only be overcome by the intervention of "the Legislator," a founding father possessed of superior knowledge and virtue, whose charismatic qualities attract the adherence of a still-unformed citizenry.[67] Bolívar's *presidente vitalicio* is a permanent institutionalization of Rousseau's Legislator, a means by which the young peoples of Spanish America could sustain their independence, and the Creole elite could retain its privileges and power.

The *presidente vitalicio* never received the same level of acclaim as the *poder moral*. Many of Bolívar's contemporaries, upon learning of the life-term president, denounced him as a would-be Bonaparte, and later observers have continued to make the same association.[68] To be sure, there were commonalities between the constitution for Bolivia and the constitutions of Napoleonic France, but Bolívar named an inspiration closer to home: Haiti, the "most democratic Republic in the world," where Alexandre Pétion had taken permanent power in 1816. Upon declaring its independence, Bolívar explained, "the island of Haiti found itself in permanent insurrection." After experimenting with "all the known forms of government and a few unknown ones, they were forced to apply to the illustrious Pétion for salvation." The consistency of a president-for-life calmed Haiti's persistent instability, allowing politics to proceed "with the calm of a legitimate kingdom." This proved decisively that "a *presidente vitalicio* ... is the most sublime innovation for the republican system."[69] Bolívar could hardly have chosen a more resonant illustration of the possible evils attendant upon independence in the Americas than Haiti, which embodied the caste warfare many Spanish Americans worried might destroy their own societies.

For the principle of succession, Bolívar chose another interesting model, appealing now to the legislators' aspirations rather than their fears: "The United States has, in recent years, observed a practice of naming the First Minister [the secretary of state] to succeed the President." Indeed, when Bolívar wrote, the then president of the United States, John Quincy Adams, had been secretary of state under his predecessor James Monroe, who was secretary of state to his predecessor James Madison, who was secretary of state to his predecessor Thomas Jefferson, who was secretary of state to his predecessor, once removed, George Washington. For Bolívar, no other method of selection "could be as convenient in a Republic." Having the president succeeded by someone already serving in an important office not only assured that the new occupant would be "experienced in the management of the State," but also "avoided elections, which produce the great scourge of republics: anarchy."[70] Connecting this institutional innovation to an implicit practice in the United States, Bolívar came full circle from his earlier arguments against federalism. Though Spanish Americans seeking to imitate the latter were sadly misinformed, they would do well to observe how a streamlined system of presidential selection could smooth a country's transition to independence.

4.5 IMPERIALISM AGAINST EMPIRE

In September 1821, the Congress of Colombia, having completed its constitution but still seated as a constituent assembly in Cúcuta, named Bolívar the first president of the republic. In what would become a ritual exercise, he initially declined the post, explaining that he wished to concentrate on overseeing the war effort in the country's still-royalist south. Once Congress offered assurances that he would not be detained by his domestic duties, he was installed in office and then promptly departed for the front.

His aim now was to liberate Quito, capital of Gran Colombia's third component colony, where the Spanish forces occupied a defensible position and had managed to hold off republican forces from the surrounding regions. While a trusted lieutenant, Antonio José de Sucre, began a campaign from the south, Bolívar led his Army of Liberation down the spine of the Andes from the north. This path took him across the province of Popayán and through the city of Pasto, a persistent thorn in revolutionary sides since Quito's short-lived autonomous *Junta* movement in 1809–1810. As in the Venezuelan *llanos* and the Caribbean coast, the royalist resistance in Popayán had a strong popular element, drawing widespread support from the region's numerous Indigenous communities and from slaves employed in mining operations. Many members of both groups, quickly grasping that the colonial government's desperate position presented an unprecedented opportunity to renegotiate the terms of their relationship to the Spanish regime, served in loyalist militias, which again and again repulsed republican attacks, harassed supply lines, and threatened to spread popular royalist rebellion throughout Colombia as a whole.[71]

Bolívar's forces encountered fierce opposition as they made their way southward, taking heavy losses, both to death and desertion, over the entire first half of 1822. When, finally, in June, Bolívar occupied Pasto and obtained the *Pastusos*' reluctant capitulation to Colombian rule, he addressed them as follows:

Colombians of the South: the blood of your brothers has delivered you from the horrors of war. It has opened for you the way to the enjoyment of sacred rights, liberty, and equality. Colombian laws establish a balance between social prerogatives and natural rights. The Constitution of Colombia is a model of representative government, both republican and strong. You will not find a better one in all the political institutions of the world, until [the Colombian Constitution] itself achieves its own perfection. Rejoice in the fact that you belong to a great family, which can rest now in the shade of a forest of laurels, and can desire nothing more than to look on as the march of time brings to fruition the eternal principles of right that underlie our laws.[72]

In his recent book, Diego von Vacano suggests that Bolívar broke, decisively, with the expansionist version of classical republicanism most famously expounded by Machiavelli in insisting that a republic could not be imperial. "Bolívar's chief intellectual concern," von Vacano argues, "is freedom." For a republic to engage in imperial conquest "would mean to take away the freedom of others, which is self-contradictory." Understanding this contradiction, Bolívar developed, in von Vacano's account, a consistently anti-imperialist republicanism, which, while celebrating "martial" virtues, did not embrace territorial expansion and forcible assimilation of new populations as means of assuring the internal stability and external safety of the states he liberated from Spanish rule.[73]

While von Vacano rightly notes the deep tension – indeed, contradiction – between promoting freedom and imperial conquest, Bolívar's treatment of Pasto's popular royalists, and the arguments he made to justify his actions, clearly evidence his willingness to pursue republican ends by imperial means. Bolívar describes the brutal conquest and forced pacification of a predominantly indigenous community as "opening the way" to their freedom and equality. He describes the expansion of Gran Colombia's sovereign territory as the spreading of enlightened political ideals and institutions. In a very clear sense, then, he thought of imperialism as a weapon against empire.

As with his arguments on behalf of independence and his various innovations in constitutional design, the classical republican tradition provided the basic philosophical framework of Bolívar's attempts to unify ever more expansive portions of the former Spanish Americas under a single independent state. The same concepts of collective freedom, virtue, and corruption reappear here to justify the forced liberation of an ever larger and more diverse population.

An early formulation appears in the "Cartagena Manifesto" of 1812, where, in explaining the demise of the First Republic of Venezuela, Bolívar tells his audience that "[t]he most consequential error Venezuela committed ... was undoubtedly the fatal adoption of a policy of toleration" toward a royalist rebellion in the city of Coro, which I've already described in the preceding text. "Rather than subjugating that defense-less city," when they had a chance, Venezuela's leaders assumed a defensive stance, hoping the rebels would eventually come round to the cause of independence. Instead, this "allowed [the rebellion] to fortify itself" and receive Spanish assistance, "so that it was later able to subjugate the entire confederation." The *Junta's* error derived, Bolívar asserts, from certain "poorly understood principles of humanitarianism, which prevented them from *liberating by force a people too stupefied to recognize the value of its own rights*."[74] Machiavelli could not have put it better himself.

Even at this early stage, Bolívar realized that the basic doctrine underlying his attitude toward Coro would eventually carry his revolution across the continent. He submitted a telling "syllogism" to the consideration of the New Granadan legislators assembled before him: "Coro is to Caracas as Caracas is to the whole of America." So long as Venezuela remained under Spanish military occupation, it posed threat to other independent portions of South America similar to the one Coro posed to independent Venezuela. Thus, he recommended "as an indispensable measure for the security of New Granada, the immediate re-conquest of Caracas."[75] This sort of offensive, border-crossing, expansionist republicanism was to become Bolívar's trademark and would eventually lead, as we saw previously, to the permanent unification of Venezuela, New Granada, and Quito under the aegis of a new state "named Colombia in fair and grateful tribute to the creator of our hemisphere."[76] Bolívar's hearty embrace of the Americas' original *conquistador* was shared by his fellow Creole revolutionaries throughout the hemisphere, a tendency reflected to this day in the numerous political and geographic landmarks named for Columbus across both continents.[77]

Like other Creole revolutionaries before him, Bolívar invested American independence with world-historical importance and saw the unification of former colonies after independence as an essential step toward assuring Spanish America's ascendance into the global vanguard. From his military encampment in Angostura, in 1819, "upon contemplating the reunion of the immense region" that would make up Gran Colombia, he found his "imagination fixed on future centuries," observing from there a country

Extended between two far-flung coastlines, which nature has separated and which we will connect with deep, wide canals. I can see her as the connection, the center, the emporium of the human family, sending out to the four corners of the earth not only the silver and gold treasures of its mountains, the healthful bounty of its agriculture,... but also precious secrets unknown to those supposedly wise men ignorant of how much more valuable enlightenment is than the wealth of natural resources. I can see her now, seated on the throne of liberty, grasping the scepter of justice, demonstrating to the Old World the majesty of the New.[78]

Thus, for Bolívar, as for Alexander Hamilton, the independence and unification of Europe's former American colonies would hasten and consolidate a transition, from an epoch of brutal, extractive imperialism to a more enlightened era of prosperous global commerce.

Before Colombia could conquer the world, it had to consolidate authority in the territories it already claimed. Bolívar's conquest of Pasto's popular royalists and Sucre's victory over the Spanish at Quito cleared the country of internal threats to its independence, but not all of the new nation's residents were eager to recognize the sovereignty of the government in Bogotá. The city of Guayaquil, in the south of present-day Ecuador, had declared and won its own independence in October 1820, and had been ruled since that time by an autonomous *Junta*. Many of its members saw no reason why a colonial arrangement that had subjected them to the *audiencia* in Quito, and by extension to the viceroyalty in Bogotá, should be allowed to dictate the terms of their independent existence. Still another substantial faction within Guayaquil's patriotic leadership aimed for eventual annexation to an independent Peru, which was at the moment in the process of being liberated by José de San Martín, an Argentine general who hoped to establish new kingdoms with European monarchs in the Americas. Some of Guayaquil's Creoles thought this system would provide surer security for their property and privileges than Colombia's often-fractious republicanism.

Bolívar saw things differently. Guayaquil was an indispensable entrepôt for Quito and the rest of southern Colombia. Even more importantly, allowing Peru to annex the city would open the question of allegiance to other discontented regions, generating instability within the Gran Colombian union. He addressed a terse letter to the president of Guayaquil's *Junta*, expressing his disappointment at the latter's hesitation to recognize Colombia's claim, and informing him that under no circumstances would Guayaquil be permitted to retain autonomy or attach itself to an independent Peru. "Even on the broadest understanding," he wrote, "a people comprehended under an association has only a right to free and equal representation in the National Assembly. Any other pretension is against social justice."[79] He then proceeded to back up this interpretation by personally marching his army into Guayaquil, and decreeing the city's formal recognition of Colombian sovereignty, allowing Guayaquileños to vote afterward for ratification. Like his forced liberation of the popular royalists of Pasto, then, Bolívar's suppression of Guayaquil's separatists demonstrates a clear willingness to employ imperial means for putatively anti-imperial ends.

This bold military maneuver in Guayaquil placed Bolívar in an advantageous position when San Martín arrived from Lima for a meeting of the minds. By this time, San Martín had been weakened by serial setbacks in Peru, where Spanish forces drawing substantial support from local indigenous communities had forced him into a draining and dangerous stalemate. He came to Guayaquil resigned to the latter's incorporation into Colombia, and hoping to secure reinforcements from Bolívar's armies for his own continuing operations in Peru. He also planned to sound his counterpart out on the idea of establishing European princes on American thrones. He found Bolívar emphatically opposed to a monarchical solution to Spanish America's endemic instability, and unwilling to make any significant commitment of troops to San Martín's command. What alternatives, if any, he proposed on the spot are a matter of some controversy[80] – no transcript of this famous meeting of South America's liberators exists. What we know is that after leaving Guayaquil, San Martín resigned his command of the mixed Argentine and Peruvian patriot army in Lima and retired to Europe, leaving Bolívar to complete his campaign against the last Spanish holdouts in South America.

Leading his troops across the former colonial administrative boundaries between Quito and Peru, and eventually climbing the high plateau known as Upper Peru (present-day Bolivia) raised novel philosophical and political issues for Bolívar. Lima had been the capital of a viceroyalty with jurisdiction over present-day Peru and Chile, and Upper Peru had been subject to the viceroyalty of the Río de la Plata, seated in Buenos Aires, since 1776. The assumption made by most of the period's legal scholars was that the borders of the Spanish viceroyalties would become the borders of sovereign American states, if and when independence was established.[81] A large Colombian military presence in Peru and Upper Peru, then, constituted a challenge to these assumptions, and raised objections from many Peruvians.

Bolívar himself was aware of this distinction, later lamenting that "The war in Peru presents difficulties that appear insuperable ... the difference is that this is not Colombia and I am not Peruvian."[82] However, he understood the push into Peru as a continuation of his general campaign, and when the Colombian Congress demanded an explanation for the absence of their army and elected president from the national territory, he justified it by reference to a familiar doctrine of anti-imperial imperialism:

I should be permitted to advance on territories occupied by the Spanish in Peru, because the enemy will come here if I do not contain him there, and because enemy territory should not be considered foreign territory, but conquerable territory,... just as New Granada was for Venezuela. Anyone who denies this is a fool, and a fool is no authority.[83]

In August 1823, Congress assented to this terse logic and granted Bolívar permission to proceed into Peru. He met a warm welcome in Lima, but had trouble advancing against well-fortified Spanish positions, and struggled constantly to maintain the loyalty of the soldiers under his command, most of whom were being asked to fight far from their homes in Argentina, Chile, and Colombia. In February 1824, a betrayal by one of his Peruvian generals allowed the Spanish to retake Lima, marking a low point. The Peruvian Congress in exile granted Bolívar dictatorial authority to conduct the war. This set off further alarm bells back in Bogotá, but Bolívar insisted on accepting the office "for the good of Colombia."[84] A lapsed colony on the country's southern border simply constituted too grave a threat to ignore; in order to make independence safe at home, he would have to establish independence abroad, by any means necessary.

Gradually, and with Sucre providing most of the military leadership, the Army of Liberation struggled back, winning an important battle in December, and receiving shortly thereafter the capitulation of the main royalist force in Peru. It took almost another year of fierce fighting to overcome holdouts in Lima and in Upper Peru, but in October 1825, Bolívar climbed to the summit of the famous "silver mountain" of Potosí to declare a final end to the wars of independence: "After fifteen years of colossal battles we have destroyed a tyrannical edifice formed over three centuries of usurpation and violence." The fantastic riches he stood over, the source of a huge portion of the mineral wealth Spain had extracted from the Americas, were "worth nothing, when compared to the glory of having brought the flag of liberty all the way from the steaming Orinoco to plant it here, in the peak of this mountain."[85] The tension between anti-imperial aims and imperial means is palpable here; in planting a "flag of liberty" in Potosí, Bolívar laid claim to a profound symbol and valuable asset of Spain's American empire for himself and his Creole Revolution.

With the edifice of the old regime in ruins, it still remained to establish a new one capable of calming the endemic instability Spanish America's internal social hierarchy produced, which external enemies would surely seek to exploit. Indeed, cracks had already begun to appear in Colombian unity, and the threat of caste warfare continued. "The south hates the north, the coast hates the highlands, Venezuela hates Cundinamarca; and

Cundinamarca suffers from the disorders in Venezuela," Bolívar lamented, "and in the midst of all this disturbance *pardocracia* flourishes."[86] At the same time, a small detachment of Brazilian troops entered the Bolivian territory and skirmished briefly with Colombian troops, causing Bolívar to become concerned that Pedro I, the heir to the Portuguese throne who had ruled Brazil as emperor since 1822, might be collaborating with Europe's Holy Alliance to reconquer the Americas.[87]

As a response, in two private letters, Bolívar proposed a permanent "union of the three republics" – Colombia, Peru, and Bolivia – that his armies had liberated and still occupied. Colombia would be redivided into Venezuela, Cundinamarca, and Quito, and Peru would be split into two smaller departments. Each of the six component states would adopt the Bolivian Constitution, which would also be applied, with some modifications, to the general government of the union. Bolívar himself would assume the title of "Liberator-President" and in this role ride on an annual circuit throughout all of the states, calming their disorders by his very presence.

Though allowing some autonomy to each state, the "intention of this pact would be the most perfect union possible under the federal form" of government; "there will be one flag, one army, and one single nation." Bolívar summarized by describing the proposed Andean union as an intellectual and institutional "synthesis [*transacción*] of Europe with America, of the army with the people, of democracy with aristocracy, and of empire with republicanism."[88] It would be hard to find a more complete and succinct statement of the internal contradictions of the ideology of Creole Revolution than this one, or a better institutional illustration of anti-imperial imperialism than Bolívar's Andean union.

4.6 CREOLE COSMOPOLITANISM

Bolívar's idea of a union encompassing all of Andean South America never advanced beyond the short sketches cited earlier, but not for the reasons he himself most feared. Instead of race war, partisan political conflicts amongst committed Creole revolutionaries began to undermine Bolívar's influence within Colombia over the course of the 1820s, making it impossible for him to continue imposing his institutional preferences at will.[89] Even as his star fell at home, though, it continued to rise abroad, so the most successful efforts of Bolívar's late career took place in the realm of international diplomacy. Especially important was the convocation of Panama Congress, a meeting of ambassadors from the independent

American states held in June and July 1826. Bolívar's primary role in the organization of this event, regarded ever since as a prototype of inter-American cooperation, has earned him a deserved place in the pantheon of cosmopolitan philosophers,[90] though as I will show here, Bolívar's was a peculiarly Creole cosmopolitanism, rife with the same tensions we've traced throughout his thought.

Bolívar began laying the groundwork for the Panama Congress in 1822, when, still on the cusp of completing Colombia's liberation, he sent emissaries to the equally embattled independent governments of Mexico, Peru, Chile, and the Río de la Plata (present-day Argentina and Uruguay). Each bore an invitation to join a "bilateral treaty of union, league, and perpetual confederation" with Colombia, pledging mutual military support for the completion of the war against Spain.[91] Even the very language of his invitation, though, betrays the more ambitious plans Bolívar already had in mind:

Of all of the epochs of American history, none is as glorious as the present moment, when the empires of the New World are escaping the chains placed on them by another hemisphere, and beginning their national existence. But America's greatest day has yet to arrive. We have expelled our oppressors, broken their tyrannical tablets of laws, and founded legitimate institutions, but it still remains to lay the foundations of our social pact, and to make of this world a nation of republics.[92]

As in his constitutional thought, the fundamental aim of Bolívar's diplomatic efforts was to smooth Spanish America's transition from an oppressive system of imperial rule to a stable and prosperous independent existence. In his mind, this would require not only well-designed domestic institutions, but also a pan-Spanish American "social pact" – an institutionalized system of interstate relations capable of coordinating its member states' interactions with the outside world, with each other, and with the heterogeneous populations that made up their citizenry. Unfortunately, Bolívar did not elaborate upon exactly what he meant by "a nation of republics," but this intriguing phrase suggests a very close pact indeed.

The Colombian ambassadors' official instructions directed them to "urge incessantly" upon their hosts "the necessity of founding an assembly of plenipotentiaries," a congress of representatives from each new nation, authorized to enter agreements with the others that could give collective "impulse to the common interests of the American states." In the immediate term, this meant negotiating for recognition of an independence that had been established on the ground, and, more provocatively, coordinating strategies for collaborative assaults on the remaining Spanish bastions of South America (Peru and Upper Peru), North America (San Juan de Ulúa, off the coast of Mexico), and, most provocatively of all, the Caribbean (Cuba and Puerto Rico).

Even at this early stage, Bolívar and his administration emphasized that the proposed Spanish American assembly "should not be formed simply on the principles of an ordinary offensive and defensive alliance." Instead, it should structure much closer connections, creating "a society of sister nations, separated by the course of human events in the exercise of their sovereignty, but powerfully united against external aggression."[93] Colombia offered to make the first contribution of men and munitions to a single, shared standing army, to be filled out and funded proportionally according to the population of each member state.[94] With an eye on present threats from Europe's Holy Alliance and the emperor of Brazil, and possible future ones from France and the United States, Bolívar later spoke of this force, and the assembly that would oversee it, as the "shield" of Spanish America's "new destiny ... a fundamental base that will eternalize, if possible, the duration of our governments."[95] Here, Bolívar seems to anticipate an important strand of twentieth-century anticolonial thinking, proposing collaboration amongst former colonies as a means of mutually assuring independence.[96]

Though the proposed assembly's attentions were mostly to be trained overseas, its architects described a role in Spanish America's interstate relations as well, mediating territorial disputes amongst member states and establishing uniform commercial regulations for the region. The Congress could "calm the discords that can arise between peoples who share the same customs and habits, which, in the absence of such a saintly institution, might ignite destructive wars like those that have desolated less fortunate regions."[97] The argument here is not unlike the one developed by Alexander Hamilton in the *Federalist*, described in the last chapter. Bolívar's invitation cited the same history of incessant European warfare as a warning against what Spanish America would encounter if it failed to enter into independence substantially united, offering the same solution: the "saintly institution" of union.[98]

Every bit as ambitious as Hamilton, Bolívar viewed the assembly as an opportunity for Spanish America to model interstate relations unlike any the world had ever seen. As he invited his fellow Americans to meet for the first time on the Isthmus of Panama, he spoke of a new "Amphictyonic League" even more impressive than the one that united Greeks and Macedonians in the fourth century BC. He imagined a future in which the entire world had adopted an institutionalized system of interstate relations modeled on Spanish America's.

> When, after a hundred centuries, posterity searches for the origins of their public law, and reviews the pacts that consolidated their destiny, they will respectfully recall the protocols of the Isthmus; there they will find the plan of our first alliance, which guided the progress of global relations. What then will the Isthmus of Corinth be, when compared with that of Panama?[99]

At his most zealous, Bolívar imagined a future in which the union forged in Panama itself expanded, adding new members from outside Spanish America, and then throughout the world, until it constituted a truly global government: "with the march of centuries, we will perhaps found a single, federal nation, encompassing the world [*una sola nación, cubriendo al universo, la federal*]."[100] Here, Bolívar seems to have grasped, even more profoundly than any of his fellow Creole revolutionaries, the novelty of union as a means of organizing interstate relations, and the great promise this alternative to the European balance of powers offered in a rapidly globalizing world.[101]

But even in the midst of such stirring cosmopolitan reflections, Bolívar failed to escape the characteristic contradictions of his political thought. In his most urgent pleas for support for the Congress of Panama, he invoked neither foreign aggression nor interstate conflict but a "domestic inferno devouring our blessed homelands": the constant rebellions of the colonies' non-white castes.[102] Later, he was more specific, listing amongst the advantages of confederation, "9th, America would no longer need to fear the terrifying monster that has consumed the island of Santo Domingo, nor the numerical preponderance of its primitive inhabitants."[103] The congress, he suggested, could coordinate not only its members' efforts to repulse external attackers, but also aggregate resources to suppress internal resistance to Creole rule.

As we've seen, concerns with slave revolt, *pardocracia*, and indigenous royalism were central to Bolívar's considerations of independence, constitutionalism, and territorial expansion. The appearance of similar strains in his diplomatic thought was not an aberration. The Panama Congress was essentially an effort to preserve, after independence, the external power, internal peace, and stable social hierarchy that imperial rule previously made possible in Spanish America. Thus, in the last analysis, even the Panama Congress, undoubtedly Bolívar's most inspiring idea, must be understood as a reflection of the Creole Revolutions' internal tensions, an instance of the anti-imperial imperialism that characterized all of Bolívar's political thought.

4.7 CONCLUSION

As the invitations for the Panama Congress were being finalized, Colombia's Vice President Francisco de Paula Santander wrote to Bolívar to suggest that the United States be included amongst the invitees. Such "intimate allies" he argued, "cannot but view with satisfaction an opportunity to take part in deliberations regarding common interests amongst sincere and enlightened friends."[104] But Santander's seemingly ingenuous expression of the "Western Hemisphere idea" – the belief that the common ideals that animated the American independence movements should facilitate their alliance[105] – met with derision from the Liberator. Like the great powers of Europe with whom they were competing for dominance of the hemisphere, "the North Americans are unreliable and entirely self-interested as allies [*aliados eventuales y muy egoístas*]."[106] If anybody beyond the formerly Spanish Americas was to be invited, it should be the British, who in Bolívar's view were, if no more reliable or less self-interested, at least better positioned to be helpful in the short term and less well positioned to threaten Spanish America's autonomy in the long term than the United States.

There may have been more behind Bolívar and Santander's disagreement than meets the eye. As I shall describe in more detail in Chapter 6, Santander was undergoing a political transformation in this period, positioning himself less and less as Bolívar's faithful lieutenant and more and more as the leader of an opposition committed to pursuing the "liberal" ideas and institutions that Bolívar seemed willing to set aside in his search for post-colonial stability. As a result, Santander was more open to the influence of the United States within Colombia, and less concerned with the prospect that, as Bolívar would famously put it, "the United States seems destined by Providence to plague the Americas with miseries in the name of liberty."[107] Whether for domestic or international reasons, though, Santander decided to override Bolívar's preferences, and, invoking his powers as acting president while Bolívar was away at war, dispatched an invitation to the United States to send delegates to the Panama Congress.

Arriving in late spring, 1825, Santander's invitation divided the cabinet of President John Quincy Adams. Noting the abolitionist currents swirling in each of the newly independent Spanish American states, and their interest in liberating the plantation colony of Cuba, Vice President John C. Calhoun argued forcefully against participation in the congress. He insisted that the United States should maintain the policy of neutrality toward Spain's remaining New World possessions announced only two years earlier in President James Monroe's famous State of the Union address, and leave Cuba alone until it could be added to the slaveholding states of the south.[108] On the other side, Secretary of State Henry Clay urged Adams to send representatives and take a leading role at Panama, viewing the congress as an opportunity to construct the "American System" he had long envisioned: "It is in our power to create a system of which we shall be the centre, and in which all South America will act with us."[109] At a deeper level, the invitation presented Adams with a dilemma, forcing him to decide whether the unionist solution to the problem of interstate relations his predecessors had applied to the former British colonies of North America in Philadelphia in 1787 should be extended to encompass the rest of the hemisphere.[110]

Ultimately, Adams elected to split the difference between his advisors, and leaven his forefathers' unionist ideal with a strong measure of American chauvinism. He sent representatives to Panama, defending his decision to do so against the energetic opposition of southern congressmen, but ultimately instructed them not only to decline any invitation to join a permanent union of American states, but also to work actively against the construction of a strictly Spanish American union. "All notion is rejected of an amphictyonic council," read the representatives' instructions, "invested with power finally to decide controversies between the American States or to regulate in any respect their conduct." The United States would not consent to any constraints on its ability to project power unilaterally when its interests dictated that it should.

Nor would it countenance the construction of any institution that might subject it to unequal terms of trade within its hemisphere. Lucas Alamán, Mexico's minister of external affairs, whom we shall meet in the next chapter, had proposed that the Spanish American nations should adopt a free-trade system amongst themselves, while excluding or taxing foreign competitors in industries that had not yet had a chance to mature. Adams rejected this idea out of hand. The starting point for commercial negotiations should consist in the principle that "No American nation shall grant any favors, in commerce or navigation, to any foreign power whatever, either upon this or any other continent, which shall not extend to every other American nation." Thus, he instructed his representatives to "resist in every form" an exclusively Spanish American free-trade pact if it should be proposed. The language the representatives were to use to respond to such proposals was stipulated in their instructions:

It may, perhaps, be objected that the marine of the other American nations is yet in its infancy; that ours has made great advances; and that they cannot be prepared for this reciprocal liberty of navigation until they have made some further progress in establishing theirs. The difference in the condition of the marine of the respective countries, assumed in the supposed argument, certainly exists. But how is it to be remedied? ... If the new States would build up for themselves powerful marines they must seek for their elements not in a narrow and contracted legislation, ... but in the abundance and excellence of their materials for ship building, in the skill of their artisans and the cheapness of the manufacture, in the number of their seamen, and in their hardy and enterprising character ... invigorated by a liberal, cheerful, and fearless competition with foreign powers.[111]

The instructions are remarkable, not only for how forthrightly they deny Spanish Americans the right to adopt protectionist measures that the United States had availed itself of in the not-too-distant past, but for how exactly they anticipate, in both tone and substance, what would only in the late twentieth century come to be known as the "Washington consensus" on international trade.[112]

Ultimately, Adams and his ministers probably need not have concerned themselves so much with the proceedings at Panama. The United States' representatives were delayed in their travel so drastically that they missed the meeting entirely, but even without their intervention, the congress adjourned without accomplishing anything more than an agreement to reconvene at an unspecified date in a more salubrious locale. The bilateral agreements that Columbia had initiated with each of the other former Spanish American states also languished, with the single exception of Mexico, to which we turn in the next chapter.

5

The Creole Conservatism of Lucas Alamán

In a happy coincidence of timing, research for this book brought me to Mexico City in the fall of 2010, just as Mexicans were preparing to celebrate the bicentennial of their country's independence. On the evening of September 15, I joined an immense crowd packed into the city's *zócalo*, or central plaza. At midnight, as electrically amplified peals rang from a ceremonial bell, then-President Felipe Calderón led revelers through a traditional series of cheers from the balcony of the national palace: "*¡Vivan los heroes que nos dieron patria! ...¡Viva la independencia nacional! ...¡Viva México!*"; "Long live the heroes that gave us our homeland! ... Long live national independence! ... Long live Mexico!" Fireworks burst from the tops of the surrounding buildings, beginning a long night of festivities, followed the next morning by a military parade and patriotic speeches.

Though emotionally exhilarating, my experience of Mexico's two-hundredth independence day was intellectually unsettling. The holiday commemorates an early morning in 1810 when a provincial priest rang his church's bells to call a small congregation to arms, telling them to round up and imprison the few Spanish inhabitants of their town. The two central heroes to whom the cheers make reference were Miguel Hidalgo, the bell-ringing insurgent priest who initiated the struggle and led its first military actions, and José María Morelos, a seminary student who took up his teacher's banner after Hidalgo was captured and executed. Both Hidalgo and Morelos considered themselves Creoles, but it would be very difficult to claim that their insurgency was a Creole Revolution. The forces they led were comprised of indigenous and *mestizo*, or mixed race, farmers and laborers from villages and small cities in the provinces, far from the capital where the colony's Creole population was concentrated.[1]

Though there were some Creole sympathizers and a few prominent Creole collaborators amongst the insurgent leadership, New Spanish Creoles mainly rejected the rebellion. Indeed, working in concert with European Spaniards, many actively sought to suppress the insurgents, perceiving in their plebeian character and egalitarian pronouncements a definite threat to a social order in which Creoles occupied an advantageous position.[2] Thus, the fact that Mexicans celebrate the year 1810 as the origin of their country's independence, giving Hidalgo and Morelos pride of place amongst the pantheon of the struggle's heroes, presents a definite problem for this book's central argument. In Mexico, independence does not appear to have resulted from a Creole Revolution, but an insurgency with a constituency and ideology radically different from those of the movements examined in previous chapters.

Nor do the difficulties end here. In standard accounts of Mexican history, the country's first decades of independence are characterized by near-constant conflict between implacable opponents: Liberals, the patriotic heirs of Hidalgo and Morelos, who sought to create an egalitarian republic, free from the oppressive legacies of Spanish domination; and the traitorous Conservatives, elitist opponents of independence bent on returning the country to shameful colonial submission.[3] The constitutional ideas I've presented as central to the ideology of Creole Revolution, which aimed to insulate politics against popular influence by centralizing authority in a union of former colonies and establishing a strong executive check upon the legislative branch, were supported in Mexico by the leaders of the Conservative, pro-Spanish faction. Thus, it is hard to argue that Mexican debates on constitutional design paralleled those in the United States and Colombia, where, as we've seen, Creole political theorists like Alexander Hamilton and Simón Bolívar argued that union and presidentialism would reinforce, rather than undermine, American independence.

Finally, far from adopting an aggressive, expansionist posture upon throwing off the Spanish yoke, in the usual telling, independent Mexico was immediately beset by foreign adventurers eager to snatch away its homeland, none more ravenous than those from the grasping colossus to the north, the United States of America. Even as they lament the loss of more than half the national territory in the Mexican–American War of 1846–1848, many Mexican intellectuals have taken a certain pride in defeat, viewing their country's repeated subjection to their overbearing neighbor's insults and abuses as the basis for a tradition of opposition to imperialism active even today. So in Mexico we seem to find an exception to the expansionist ambitions that I've claimed characterized the ideology of Creole Revolution as well.

However, recent studies have shown that Mexico's official history has its own history. The apotheosis (literal and figurative) of Hidalgo and Morelos, the Manichean presentation of ideological conflict during the nineteenth century, and the depiction of Mexico as a nation born under siege date to the late nineteenth and early twentieth centuries, when they met the ideological demands of regimes installed by the Wars of Reform (1857–1861) and the Revolution of 1910.[4] We now know that the participants and firsthand observers of the break with Spain viewed independence as a more ambiguous accomplishment, as the only partially successful last resort of Americans seeking equal representation and autonomy within a Spanish system that was itself undergoing dramatic changes, rather than the triumphant self-assertion of a Mexican nation suffering under Spanish oppression.[5] Scholars have also called the standard Liberal–Conservative binary into question, demonstrating that the supposed paragons of Mexican Conservatism actually drew much inspiration from European liberalism, seeking institutions that would hasten Mexico's political and economic modernization and rise into the first ranks of world nations.[6] Finally, new work on the independence of Texas and the Mexican–American War, by escaping the American diplomatic archives that long dominated both English- and Spanish-language studies, has traced the profound effects of domestic politics on the events that culminated in Mexico's 1848 cession of more than half its territory to the United States.[7]

These interventions have undermined the problematic commonplaces of the official history, clearing the way for this chapter's study of Mexico's struggle for independence as a Creole Revolution similar in many ways to the others examined in this book. From within this framework, some persistent historiographical problems become tractable. The skepticism and even hostility with which Creole revolutionaries regarded the indigenous insurgency of Hidalgo and Morelos can be understood as a reflection of the colonial social order. Mexican Creoles' contradictory class position inspired them to oppose a movement aimed at independence even as they sought to achieve the same goal on more favorable terms. The criticisms of a broad franchise, a powerful congress, a limited executive, and decentralized federalism voiced by influential constitutional thinkers become recognizable as efforts to consolidate Creoles' authority within the heterogeneous society independent Mexico inherited from its colonial predecessor, intended to stabilize the social order and make economic development and political progress possible. Finally, the military defeat Mexico suffered at the hands of the United States, a product of Mexican disorganization as much as *yanqui* avariciousness, illustrates the contingent outcome of a perhaps inevitable clash between competing Creole empires with mutually exclusive designs on hemispheric preeminence.

I focus my examination of the intellectual history of Mexico's Creole Revolution on the writings of Lucas Alamán, one of the most prominent statesmen and political thinkers of the period. Alamán is best known today for his multivolume works on Mexican history, and especially for his account of Mexico's independence movement, which remains an important reference.[8] But Alamán was no "mere" historian. An engineer by training and miner by inheritance, he traveled extensively in Europe as a young man, studying modern mining techniques and technologies that he hoped would revitalize the industry in his home country. Later, he represented New Spain at the reconvened Spanish *Cortes*, and so impressed his fellow American delegates that he became the group's unofficial scribe, drafting a proposal that would have transformed the Spanish Empire into a trans-Atlantic commonwealth. After independence, he served multiple terms as a representative in the national congress, and headed presidential cabinets as minister of internal and external relations on three separate occasions, participating in the drafting of Mexico's first two republican constitutions and overseeing the establishment of a national investment bank, the national archive, and a number of important cultural institutions. He also edited a newspaper and founded the country's first political party.

Reflecting on this record, an eminent historian has asserted that Alamán was "undoubtedly the major political and intellectual figure of independent Mexico until his death in 1853."[9] However, he has never been an iconic figure in the country he helped found, or attracted the international regard accorded his colleagues throughout the hemisphere. Alamán is almost certainly less familiar to most readers of this book than either Alexander Hamilton or Simón Bolívar. In large measure, this is due to Alamán's association, in the standard historiography I've described earlier, with political conservatism, a side of the ideological spectrum mostly neglected by historians and social scientists until very recently. Indeed, Alamán's thought is often presented as the quintessence of Mexican conservatism, and his best-known work, the *Historia de Méjico*, has long been read as the classic expression of conservative nostalgia for

Spanish domination and opposition to American independence. I show, however, that the *Historia* actually makes a case *for* Mexican independence and that it does so in terms that would have been familiar to other Creole revolutionaries, centered on the unequal station imposed on the descendants of European settlers born in the Americas by the economic policies and political structures of the Spanish Empire.

This is not to say that Alamán sympathized in all respects with the exemplars of Creole political thinking I've examined in previous chapters. His ideas definitely evince a different philosophical mien. Edmund Burke, rather than Hume or Montesquieu, is the most commonly cited figure in his writings.[10] For Alamán, independence represented an inevitable step in the gradual, progressive evolution of the New Spain's economy and society, the only possible resolution of a historical process that unavoidably placed Spanish and American interests at odds. He distinguished sharply between this justification for separation and the one announced by Hidalgo and Morelos and their insurgent supporters, who sought radical political and economic reforms that Alamán thought Mexican society was wholly unprepared to undergo.

Thus, I shall suggest that the *Historia*'s infamous critique of the Hidalgo insurgency, often read as an apology for Spanish rule and an argument against Mexican independence, is actually a particularly sharp instance of the anti-imperial imperialism that characterized patriotic Creoles' political thought throughout the hemisphere. As we will see, having witnessed a very different sort of independence movement made Alamán a more self-conscious Creole revolutionary than either Hamilton or Bolívar. Burke's *Reflections on the Revolution in France* provided the language and basic concepts that Alamán employed in his conservative variation on the ideology of Creole Revolution, but the background problems that Alamán addressed were distinctively American. In his writings, an indigenous peasantry replaced the Parisian *sans-culottes* and a form of Mexican patriotism that elevated pre-Hispanic society to an ideal replaced theories of natural right as the objects of skeptical rejection. Ultimately, like his counterparts on both continents, Alamán sought a path toward Mexican independence that would minimize disruptions of New Spain's internal social hierarchy.

Burke's influence was also apparent in Alamán's constitutional thinking, both in the *Historia*, which contains extensive analyses of the constitutions adopted after Mexico's independence, and in works written during and after Alamán's second, and longest, term as minister of relations. There, I shall show, Alamán was already arguing that a firm political union would better serve the needs of the new nation than a loose federation, because it was more congruent with New Spain's colonial experience, and thus better suited to the habits of its people. For the same reasons, but also because of his profound, and long-standing dislike of the "political metaphysics" that underlay the constitutionalism of revolutionary France, Alamán also sought to empower Mexico's executive and judicial branches, at the expense of the legislative, and to institute strict property qualifications for the franchise and other forms of political participation. Here again, the sympathies Alamán shared with Hamilton and Bolívar are as apparent as his distinctive philosophy. As we will see, like these other Creole constitutional theorists, Alamán adapted European intellectual traditions to confront a set of common problems inherent in the consolidation of American independence under Creole leadership.

Perhaps the most striking point of convergence I shall describe between Alamán and the figures considered in previous chapters, though, lies in his international outlook, an aspect of his thought that has been neglected even in the recent, revisionist literature. Like Hamilton and Bolívar in regard to their own countries, Alamán thought Mexico was capable of assuming a preeminent position in American, and indeed, global affairs. Also like Hamilton and Bolívar, he thought that empowering independent Mexico's central government and expanding its sphere of influence were indispensable means of achieving this end. He was one of the most enthusiastic supporters of Bolívar's efforts to stimulate cooperation amongst, or even form a union of the formerly Spanish Americas, but he hoped Mexico City, rather than Bogotá, would become the league's capital. Unlike Hamilton and Bolívar, however, Alamán lived to see the inter-American conflicts foreshadowed in Hamilton's dealings with Miranda and emerging in the United States' reaction to Bolívar's Panama Congress become dramatic reality. This chapter closes by considering the policies Alamán sought to institute in the territory known as *Tejas* while it still remained a part of Mexico, describing his attempts to establish a firmer Mexican presence in these contested territories as expressions of an imperial ambition analogous to those we've encountered elsewhere in the hemisphere.

On the whole, then, this chapter's analysis of Lucas Alamán's political thought should shed light on the complexities of Creole conservatism, which was both revolutionary and reactionary, both egalitarian and elitist, and both anti-imperialist and imperialist, reflecting the tensions present in the institutional position from which it arose.

5.1 MEXICO'S TWO REVOLUTIONS

Lucas Alamán was born in 1792 in Guanajuato, a prosperous city in the central highlands of New Spain, a viceroyalty of the Spanish Empire encompassing the present-day countries of Mexico, Guatemala, Honduras, El Salvador, Nicaragua, and Costa Rica, as well as much of what is now the western United States.[11] His family was wealthy and prominent within the city's high society, where Creoles from long-established American lineages mixed with more recent arrivals from Spain. Young Lucas showed early promise in his studies of Greek and Latin, but his father steered him toward mathematics, natural science, and engineering, preparing for the day when he would assume control of the family's extensive mining interests. He continued his humanistic explorations, though, under the personal tutelage of the Spanish intendant assigned to the city, Juan Antonio de Riaño, an unusually learned bureaucrat and a book collector.

A cloud settled over this peaceful existence with Napoleon's 1807 invasion of the Iberian Peninsula, which set off a conflict in the viceregal capital of Mexico City not unlike the one in Caracas I described in the last chapter. The Creole-dominated *ayuntamiento* and the European-dominated *audiencia* split over the proper response to the news from across the Atlantic, with Creoles proposing to form a provisional *junta* and Spaniards insisting upon recognition of the *Junta Central* convened in Sevilla. As in Venezuela, swift and decisive action by the peninsular faction, joined by Creole merchants financially attached to the empire's mercantilist policies, suppressed the autonomist faction and achieved a tense stalemate.[12]

Even in this climate of uncertainty, the comfortable denizens of Guanajuato were surprised when word came in September 1810 that a parish priest named Miguel Hidalgo had raised a rebellion in nearby Dolores, imprisoned European-born Spaniards and sacked their houses, and was now marching their way at the head of a large army. Alamán's European-born neighbors fortified themselves inside the city's granary along with their money and valuables, but to no avail. Farmers and laborers from the surrounding countryside joined Hidalgo's forces, overwhelming the granary, massacring the Spaniards inside, and looting their homes and businesses.[13] Alamán himself was led out of his family's home by a group of insurgents who took him for a European, only to be saved by the intervention of local residents who vouched for his American birth. This threat prompted Alamán's mother to appeal directly to Hidalgo for protection, calling upon the insurgent priest with an eighteen-year-old Lucas in tow. As he would later recount:

It was very risky for well-dressed persons to cross the streets, now full of a crowd drunk on fury and liquor. Nonetheless we arrived without incident at the Quarters of the Royal Guard, where Hidalgo was staying.... The priest was sitting at a small table.... He received us warmly, assured my mother of his continued friendship, and gave us an escort to defend the house.[14]

Alamán's personal experience of Hidalgo's insurgency was formative in his political thinking. When, almost forty years later, he wrote his history of the period, he focused on the insurgency's ideology and social basis, stressing fundamental differences between the insurgency and the forestalled push for autonomy authored by Mexico City's Creole elite, which after years of Spanish intransigence would eventually decide for independence and win that aim. That there were two revolutions in Mexico – one popular, radical, and ultimately unsuccessful, and another elite, moderate, and triumphant – is perhaps the central argument of Alamán's *Historia de Méjico*. Here, I show how this historiographical contention can be read as an instance of the ideology of Creole Revolution.

In Alamán's account, one basic point of disagreement between Mexico's two revolutions concerned the nature and origins of Mexico itself. For his part, he emphasized the profound and multiple senses in which Spanish rule had shaped the country.[15] Not only did Spain bring civilization, in the form of the Catholic faith, political institutions, modes of economic production and exchange, and the very cities and towns that defined the colony's human geography, but also, and even more importantly, Alamán insisted, Spanish colonization had created the Mexican people and structured its social classes:

The conquest introduced elements into the population of New Spain, and in general, over the entire American continent: ... the Spaniards and the blacks that they brought from Africa. In little time, the Spaniards born in Spain, and those born in America, were distinguished, the latter for this reason were given the name *criollos*, which with the passage of time came to be considered an insult, but which in its origin meant nothing more than born and raised in this land. From the mix of Spaniards and Indians came the *mestizos*, and with the blacks the *mulattos*, *zambos*, *pardos* and all the various nomenclature, which are generically referred to with the term *castas*. The European Spaniards ... were called *gachupines* ... and this name, just as with that of *criollo*, came to be considered offensive, as the rivalry between these two groups progressed.[16]

Mexico's population was irrevocably a product of imperial rule, its various "elements" and the relations between them defined by race and birthplace. Crucially, for Alamán, as for Simón Bolívar, three centuries of imperial rule had thoroughly erased Mexico's pre-Hispanic traditions. When the prospect of independence appeared in the first decade of the nineteenth century, there was no indigenous legacy left to recover that could form the basis of a new society.

In a departure from Bolívar, though, Alamán not only argued that the Spanish imperial system was all Mexico had, but also that it was also tried and true, and thus valuable. The system of government established in Spanish America, he wrote, "was not the work of one single conception, nor did it proceed from speculative theories of legislation, which pretend to subject the human species to imaginary principles." Rather, it reflected "the knowledge and experience of three centuries," gained by "long and repeated proofs." Only by virtue of their gradual evolution were the structures of Spanish rule capable of bringing order to the New World's heterogeneous society. Imperial institutions had proven their worth by making "all of the immense continent of America ... move with uniformity, without violence, one can even say without force, in a progressive direction with continuous improvement."[17]

Here, we can clearly see Edmund Burke's influence on Alamán's ideas. Not one to embrace black legends of Spanish depravity, Alamán describes the empire in terms taken directly from Burke's own description of the English constitution. For Burke, the wisdom of the Glorious Revolution's reformers lay in their forbearance, their decision not to "dissolve the whole fabric" of political life as they "regenerated the deficient part of the old constitution through the parts which were not impaired."[18] Similarly, Alamán admired the Bourbon reformers because, while making "great alterations and improvements" to problematic aspects of the inherited Spanish imperial system, they "always left the rest untouched."[19] In his retelling, Bourbon rule brought better administration to the Americas, curbed the abuses of local officials, improved public education, reduced public drunkenness and nudity, improved infrastructure, public health, and led to cultural advances, reflected in the visual, literary, and performing arts.[20] In all, then, Alamán viewed the Spanish Empire very differently than Bolívar, seeing the Bourbon kings, in particular, as enlightened monarchs, who had achieved great, if gradual social progress, and thus enabled whatever civilizational accomplishments New Spaniards could claim at the end of the eighteenth century.

Alongside this effusive praise, though, Alamán traced sources of emerging conflict in the Spanish Empire. Unlike their Hapsburg predecessors, who had viewed the empire as "multiple independent nations, whose crowns were united on the head of a single monarch," the Bourbon kings, building on their French experiences, "considered Spain a single nation, governed by an absolute and sovereign authority, and the overseas possessions as their colonies ... destined to provide funds and commercial advantages to her."[21] This new attitude, particularly when embodied in restrictions on agriculture, manufacturing, and commerce in the colonies, could not but cause resentments amongst New Spanish Creoles, who were accustomed to thinking of themselves as the equal subjects of a common king and entitled to the reciprocal rights and privileges that this position entailed.

Alamán recognized that the advantages and disadvantages reaped by Americans from Bourbon rule were two sides of the same coin, noting that the same steps toward royal absolutism and reforms to the imperial bureaucracy that "promoted to a great extent the well-being of the people" had also exacerbated the rivalry between New Spain's European and American Spaniards. In lines reminiscent of Bolívar and other Creoles' complaints, he noted that the 70,000 European Spaniards who resided in New Spain on the eve of the wars of independence "occupied all of the principal positions in the administration, the church, the magistracy, and the army." The Bourbon reforms had accelerated the exclusion of Creoles from the colonial administration, not only by making a greater number of posts direct appointments of the Crown, but by rationalizing the educational system used to create an efficient bureaucracy. While wealthy Creoles continued to receive the traditional, liberal education of Spanish aristocrats, the European Spaniards coming to the American colonies were increasingly products of specialized academies. These expert administrators viewed the liberally educated Creoles "depreciatively" while, conversely, Creoles from established families termed the new arrivals *advenedizos*, or upstarts.[22] By the turn of the century, all that was required to shift Creole–Peninsular rivalry from grumbled resentments over ministerial posts and taxes into open conflict was a spark.

Fittingly, the secretary of the world spirit himself would be the one to provide it. Alamán argues that disagreements between Creole and Peninsular Spaniards over the appropriate response to Napoleon's invasion reflected deeper divisions, that the two camps held "different concepts of America, each of which was valid in its time. The *Audiencia* and the Spaniards, according to principles adopted by the Bourbons, viewed New Spain as a colony, while the *Ayuntamiento* and the Americans," recalling an earlier Hapsburg notion, "supposed that Mexico was independent," a component kingdom of a composite monarchy, "and could function as a sovereign nation,"[23] if exigencies demanded that it do so.

As time went on, this gap widened. In Alamán's account, the gradually intensifying conflict between New Spain's Creole and Peninsular populations acquires an inevitable, even foreordained, quality. "The ancients would have called this chain of events, which followed one upon another in an irresistible manner, fate.... Ourselves, guided by the truths of the Christian faith, can recognize and adore in all human events the decrees of divine providence ... It appears that everything conspired toward the ruin of Spanish dominion in New Spain."[24] The conception of historical change evident in these remarks is a critical feature of Alamán's political thought, reflecting once again the influence of Edmund Burke and distinguishing his particular case for the justice of American independence from the others we have considered.[25] Like Burke, Alamán distinguished between events for which the time was ripe and those for which it was not. He felt that Mexican, and more broadly, American independence was justified, fundamentally, because its time had come. Steady progress in New Spain's economy, changes in Madrid's conception of its overseas provinces, Americans' developing sense of their potential prominence in the world, and Europe's shifting alliances had all conspired in conjunction to produce both Creole demands for equal status and Spanish reluctance to concede. By the second decade of the nineteenth century, the sheer mechanical difficulties involved in maintaining an empire across the Atlantic while fighting off foreign occupation at home made Mexican independence a foregone conclusion. Importantly, though, the terms on which this historical inevitability would be realized remained very much in play.

Father Miguel Hidalgo was in some ways an unlikely figure to initiate an uprising of Mexico's poor and outcaste masses. He had a comfortable, Creole upbringing on a *hacienda* near Guanajuato, and was a frequent guest at salons hosted by the city's elite. The story excerpted in the preceding text, of Alamán and his mother's personal appeal to the insurgent leader, seems to indicate that Hidalgo was a familiar figure, even a friend of the family. However, he was also known for having mastered several indigenous languages, and for his willingness to publicly criticize the racial prejudice inherent in New Spanish society.

During the conflicts between Creole and Peninsular Spaniards that followed the forced abdication of Fernando VII, Hidalgo became involved in a conspiracy against Spanish rule initiated by other influential and well-to-do Creoles. When the plot was discovered and arrest warrants were issued for its participants, he decided that mobilizing the Indigenous and mixed-race peasantry that patronized his rural church was the only means of preventing defeat. Over the objections of his co-conspirators, Hidalgo delivered the sermon described at this chapter's outset, inciting his Indigenous parishioners to overthrow what he described as a French-dominated, and consequently atheistic Spain in the name of the Catholic religion and the legitimate king. He led his growing army out of Dolores and across New Spain under a banner displaying the Virgin of Guadalupe, who according to myth had appeared to an indigenous peasant in 1531 and addressed him in his native Nahuatl, and who, by the late eighteenth century, had already come to symbolize a syncretic Mexican identity submerged by Spanish oppression.[26]

This began seven years of near-continuous insurgent warfare in Mexico. When Hidalgo was captured, defrocked, excommunicated, and executed in 1811, he was succeeded by José María Morelos, also a priest, but of more humble extraction and more certain egalitarian principles. While he preserved the pious Catholicism of his mentor, Morelos abandoned the pretense of fighting in the name of Fernando VII and incorporated new political and economic planks – land reform, the abolition of slavery and caste distinctions, and universal male suffrage – into the insurgency's platform.[27] Though at some moments his forces seemed poised to take Mexico City, in 1815, Morelos too was captured, and without his influence, the insurgency gradually dispersed. By 1817, it was decisively suppressed, though as Mexico's independence day attests, defeat on the battlefield did not forestall Hidalgo and Morelos's eventual veneration as the country's founding fathers.[28]

Alamán, arguing against those who even in his own day would have linked independence to the insurgency, insisted that the latter "not only did not win independence, but retarded and impeded it, while the principles that it propagated have been the cause of the fact that once [independence] was won, it did not produce any of the fruits that it should have."[29] The insurgency's failure was, in his analysis, an inevitable result of its plebian constituency. While a few individuals amongst the masses that followed Hidalgo and Morelos might have been inspired by the idea of independence, the majority, Alamán asserted, were "attracted to nothing more than the prospect of pillage,"[30] under which heading he grouped both the direct attacks on property that accompanied the insurgency's movements across the country, and the land reforms Morelos hoped to pursue.

Alamán denied that the insurgency could be described as a war between "Spaniards and Americans," or between "those who wanted independence and those who did not," or least of all, "the heroic effort of a people that fought for its liberty to throw off the yoke of an oppressive power." Rather, the movement Hidalgo and Morelos led was, at best, a "rising of the proletarian class against property," and at worst, an "eruption of barbarians who laid waste to everything."[31] The threat the insurgency posed

produced a reaction on the part of the respectable portion of society, in defense of their goods and their families, and gave their forces and resources to the government: this was what suffocated the general desire for independence, and led many men to fight under royalist banners, who sympathized with the idea [of independence], but did not want it brought about accompanied by crime and disorder.[32]

Thus, despite the fact that historical forces and divine providence had conspired to interest New Spain's Creoles in greater autonomy, the insurgency's radicalism alienated any possible support from this sector of society, causing renewed cooperation between European and American Spaniards and delaying the colony's gradual march toward independence.

In Alamán's analysis, the insurgency was not only ineffective, but ideologically unsound, built on problematic principles whose ill effects persisted even after the movement was decisively suppressed. He reserved some of his sharpest critiques for the philosophically sophisticated Creoles who sympathized with Hidalgo and Morelos' cause. Prominent amongst this group was Servando Teresa de Mier, a Dominican friar who had been excommunicated, imprisoned, and expelled from Mexico for heresy after a contentious sermon on the Virgen of Guadalupe's origins in 1794, only to return in the midst of an insurgency inspired by his interpretation. In a famous 1813 pamphlet, which influenced Simón Bolívar amongst others, Mier presented a familiar list of Creole grievances – deprecatory European attitudes, limitations on free trade, denial of high offices, and unequal political representation – as violations of an implicit constitution or "social compact," contained in the agreements Spanish monarchs had concluded with the Americas' conquistadors and their descendants.[33] These infractions, Mier argued, combined with the forced abdication of Fernando VII, decisively broke the link between Spain and America, leaving Americans free to decide for themselves whether to recognize the authority of the *Junta Central*, or to organize independent polities for themselves.

However, Mier added new arguments to this standard defense of Creole Revolution in order to accommodate the insurgency. He drew comparisons between the brutal tactics employed by royalist commanders fighting against the insurgents and the infamous acts of cruelty committed by the conquistadors against America's Indigenous inhabitants, describing both as expressions of the consistently depraved view Spain took of its American possessions, and denouncing the empire's history as three centuries of oppression. Finally, he depicted the insurgents' demand for Mexican independence as the re-emergence of *Anáhuac*, a unified nation long submerged by Spanish domination, using an indigenous term for the region surrounding Mexico City. Mier's arguments were spread and popularized by Carlos María Bustamante, a newspaper editor who also survived imprisonment on several occasions. By incorporating references to Aztec emperors and nobles into the peroration of a speech he wrote for José Morelos to deliver before an assembly of insurgent leaders, Bustamante made correcting the injustice of the conquest into the central mission of the movement.[34]

Alamán called Mier's work "instructive, but in a manner completely contrary to its purpose." He pointed out that the constitutionalist argument for independence, based as it was on royal concessions to the conquistadors, was impossible to reconcile with the insurgents' critique of the conquest itself. Under the first,

It was not the remains of the nations that ruled the land [before the conquest] that demanded independence, nor [was this demand] an attempt to recover rights usurped during the conquest; Independence was demanded by the descendants of the conquistadors, who had no other rights than those they gained in the same conquest, against which they had declaimed with an intensity difficult to explain, as if they were the heirs of the conquered peoples and were obligated to revenge their grievances.[35]

So, in attempting to lend constitutionalist legitimacy to the insurgency, Mier had committed a critical error, eliding an ineradicable difference between Mexico's two revolutions. According to Alamán, Mier and other Mexican Creoles could cogently seek autonomy or independence if they were denied the rights they enjoyed as specially entitled subjects of the Spanish Crown, but they could not simultaneously claim to have been harmed in an illegitimate conquest, since it was precisely in the conquest that their forefathers won their special titles. The empire's laws, far from eroding these distinctions, had established different sets of rights for its heterogeneous subjects:

That the Spaniards born in America and Asia had equal rights as those born in Europe, cannot be doubted, and had always been recognized, but this could not be maintained of the other natives of the country.... None of the precedents establish an equal right of Indians with Spaniards, ... [Laws treating the

indigenous population of New Spain] were made in their favor as protective legislation, based on the principle that they were weak of spirit and body; they were
perpetually bearers of the privileges of minors; they were not allowed a place in
the *ayuntamientos* of the Spanish cities, nor permitted to use horses or arms,...
[and] the African descended races, were excluded by the same measures.[36]

New Spain's various classes had always been considered differently under
imperial law. Though Alamán sympathized with Creole complaints of
unequal treatment, and even more importantly, believed that the time
was right for a Creole Revolution, he argued that it was deeply problematic to extend the same sympathy to the complaints of other New Spanish
populations. He draws precise distinctions between the rights accorded
to various groups under the Spanish imperial constitution, thereby con-
structing a historical basis for Creoles' complaints of violated pacts,
while undermining attempts to extend the same rights to New Spain's
Indigenous and African-descended peoples.

Alamán also doubted that a case for independence premised on the
injustice of the conquest could stand on its own. His criticism of this
aspect of Mier and Bustamante's argument takes us back to the nature
and origins of the Mexican people. The insurgent publicists' error, on his
account,

was to take for granted that the Mexican nation had existed before the conquest,
and was now "escaping from three-hundred years of oppression".... Though it
had an ancient name, [that is, *México*, also derived from an indigenous term] the
Mexican nation was an entirely different thing from that which had been conquered, and it was with the conquest that it began to incorporate the elements
that compose it.[37]

For Alamán, as we've seen, Mexico was created in the conquest. Its population, with its social divisions and customary practices, and its political
system, with its laws and institutions were established by the empire.
There was no ancient Mexico, submerged in Spanish oppression, waiting
to become independent.

In this forceful dismissal of Mier and Bustamante's attempts to make
indigenous symbols and customs central to a new Mexican identity, we see
Alamán adapting Edmund Burke's early satires of Rousseau and other's
idyllic depictions of pre-political human societies.[38] For Burke, famously,
"art is man's nature." There was no natural man to recover under the
layers of habituation to custom and society. For Alamán, Mexico was
a civilization created by three centuries of Spanish rule. There was no
pre-Hispanic nation ready and waiting to demand its independence. Like
Burke, Alamán understood the insurgents' use of indigenous words and

their elevation of indigenous ideals as a threat to the social and cultural advances that had been achieved under the empire, a call to abandon the policies and practices that had distanced modern Mexico from its barbaric past.

Thus, Alamán's conservative opposition to the insurgents' radicalism was, like Burke's conservative critique of the French Revolution, not premised on a romantic nostalgia for the past. Burke cautiously celebrated progress, praising the English constitution for "leav[ing] acquisition free, but secur[ing] what it acquires."[39] In the *Historia*, Alamán acknowledged that in order to conserve his colony's "entailed inheritance," the fruits of the gradual social, scientific, economic, and artistic progress acheived under Spanish rule, the imperial system would have to change, allowing Americans greater autonomy in order to defuse growing tensions.

5.2 ANOTHER COMMONWEALTH SOLUTION
TO THE AMERICAN QUESTION

Lucas Alamán spent most of the period during which the insurgency was actually active abroad. Shortly after the sack of Guanajuato, his family moved to Mexico City, where he continued his studies of natural science and engineering at the Colegio de Minería, an institution embodying the late Bourbon contribution to Mexican letters that Alamán praised so highly. In 1814, he departed alone for Europe, traveling through Spain, France, Britain, Italy, Switzerland, and Germany, observing modern mining techniques in action. In his absence, the insurgency passed its high point under the leadership of José María Morelos and then swiftly declined after his capture and execution. By the end of the decade, insurgents were operating in only a few, peripheral areas of the colony. Alamán returned home in early 1820 with plans for a new, more efficient process of separating silver ore, but he was promptly turned around and sent back across the Atlantic as the deputy from Guanajuato to the reconvened *Cortes* of Madrid.

As I noted in Chapter 1, the *Cortes* – an ancient Spanish representative institution – were first recalled in 1810 by the provisional organizing committee that led the resistance against Napoleon's armies. Its deputies met in Cádiz, on Spain's southwestern coast, while the rest of the country was under occupation. In 1812, the *Cortes* adopted a new and, for its time, remarkably liberal Constitution, giving itself a permanent position in the government alongside a limited monarchy, establishing universal male suffrage and protecting a slate of civil rights.[40] After his restoration to the throne in 1814, Fernando VII abolished the Constitution of 1812 and dissolved the *Cortes*, reclaiming absolute authority in Spain and its overseas kingdoms. But, in 1820, a revolt begun in Cádiz by Spanish soldiers bound for Venezuela swept across Spain, forcing Fernando VII to recognize the 1812 Constitution and reestablish the *Cortes*.

The return of constitutional monarchy to Spain had a very limited impact in South America, where by then a decade of bitter fighting had all but established independence outside of loyalist bastions in Peru. New Spaniards, however, having only recently suppressed Hidalgo and Morelos's insurgency, held elections and sent a delegation to the reconvened *Cortes*, with Alamán amongst them.[41]

Gathered in the metropole, the American deputies formed a bloc, concerning themselves almost exclusively with the unequal representation, poor administration, and trade restrictions imposed upon the Spanish provinces of the New World. Their attempts to raise what came to be known as the "American Question" – the appropriate place of the American colonies within the reformed constitutional monarchy that Spain had become – were largely frustrated by peninsular deputies opposed to any diminution of either their majority within the *Cortes* or the metropole's authority overseas. A special committee was established to study the issues, comprised of four peninsular and four American deputies, but the two sides were unable to reach any agreement on a way forward. Meeting separately, out of chambers, the American deputies resolved to present a unified exposition of their views and a plan for reform. They charged Alamán with drafting the "Exposition of the Overseas Deputies," which was read before the *Cortes* on June 25, 1821.[42]

In a manner reminiscent of the passages from Alexander Hamilton's pre-Revolutionary writings treated in Chapter 3, Alamán's Exposition made clear from the first that he and his fellow New Spanish deputies, far from decided upon following South America into independence, sought reforms of the empire's political institutions that would "reestablish tranquility and assure the conservation and wellbeing of this great and interesting part of the monarchy, while maintaining the integrity of the latter."[43] At the same time, and again not unlike Hamilton, Alamán did not hesitate to note that the American Question would not be susceptible to a military solution:

After so many and such costly efforts by the government to maintain these regions in dependency, after so much blood and desolation, nothing has worked. Buenos Aires, Chile, Santa Fé [de Bogota], and a great part of Venezuela are in fact emancipated, Peru is invaded, Quito alarmed, and a new revolution of a much more fearsome character has been recently established in Mexico. Thus, it is clear that the violent means that until now have been employed have not produced their desired effect, and that even if it were possible to continue using them, they would not produce this effect.[44]

Clearly, Alamán was confident that, with South America's independence already a *fait accompli*, the American deputies held an advantageous bargaining position. His Exposition offered Spain a final chance to address New Spaniards' complaints before another overseas colony was lost.

Alamán also went to great pains to demonstrate political moderation, emphasizing that Americans did not object to the form of government the Constitution of 1812 established – after all, "one cannot improve upon moderate monarchy"[45] – but to the manner in which it was applied to the Americas and the inequalities inevitably produced in the process. "The Americans are free men," he reminded the deputies, "they are Spaniards. They have the same rights as the *peninsulares*; and they know and have sufficient virtues and resources to sustain them. How, then, could they hope to do without them and remain in peace?"[46]

The causes of their disquiet were multiple, but not irreparable: imperial administrators, thousands of miles away from their superiors, often abused their power. Alamán argued that Americans should have greater autonomy in hiring and firing their own public employees, "because it is indisputable that men, having a strong tendency to put themselves above the law, need a continuous brake that keeps them within the sphere they are allotted." The great distance between Madrid and Mexico City also imposed immense expenses and great inconvenience upon the men chosen to represent America in the *Cortes*, depriving the latter of the "service of its most distinguished subjects." As a result, even if the unequal apportionment of deputies were rectified, Americans would remain underrepresented so long as they had to cross the Atlantic. Thus, greater legislative authority should be given to exclusively American assemblies to deal with exclusively American issues.[47]

Apart from increasing convenience, imperial decentralization would improve policy, since local legislators were more apt to understand the needs of their fellow citizens: "There would be nothing easier in the world than legislation, if one could give the same laws to all countries, but unfortunately it is not so, and we know that the institutions of Solon, Minos, Lycurgus, and Penn were amongst themselves as different as the customs and location of the peoples they gave them to." Flipping the typical revolutionary script, Alamán implied that the true radicalism lay in the peninsular deputies' refusal to consider modifying the Constitution to accommodate the American provinces, reflecting a doctrinaire attitude characteristic of the French Revolution. "Happily," he noted, "the time when nations were condemned to be victims of insulated and theoretic principles has passed," superseded by new era governed by the "truly wise, liberal, and philanthropic axiom, that laws are formed for the happiness of peoples, rather than the latter being formed to be sacrificed to institutions."[48]

Here, the Exposition's debts to Burke's 1775 "Resolutions for Conciliation with the Colonies" are apparent.[49] Burke, too, had asked his fellow members of Parliament whether they would "chuse to abide by a profitable experience," accommodating British North Americans' demands, or pursue the "mischievous theory" of parliamentary sovereignty even as it led them into war.[50] Alamán retrospectively shared the outlook Burke developed as the crisis in North America deepened, suggesting that the United States "would not have separated from the metropolis ... had they been presented with a government that had all of the advantages of league and liberty."[51] Today, scholars regard Burke's confederal solution to the developing colonial crisis as naïve, and perhaps it was, but as we know from Alexander Hamilton's debate with Samuel Seabury, there is reason to give it some credence.

Throughout the Americas, Creoles demanded reforms of imperial constitutions, not to rectify unjust conquests or to create equal societies unmarked by social divisions, but to assure that they themselves were "granted ... the same rights enjoyed by the *peninsulares*." Alamán and his fellow Creole deputies at the *Cortes* did not seek independence as members of incipient American nations, but rather recognition as descendants of the European conquerors of the New World, born overseas, but possessed nonetheless of the material and societal requisites to participate in the governance of their own communities.[52]

In fifteen points attached to the end of the Exposition, Alamán described exactly what would be required to satisfy this demand.[53] Three new *Cortes* should be established in the Americas, governing New Spain, including all of Central America, New Granada, including Venezuela and Ecuador, and the Río de la Plata, including Peru and Chile. This would solve the numerous financial and logistical difficulties involved in sending a slate of deputies across the Atlantic every two years and assure that the "laws given to peoples four or five thousand leagues distant from one another" would be made by legislators in full possession of the knowledge necessary to tailor them to the specific requirements of their subjects.[54] Executive "delegations" would be established in Mexico City,

Bogotá, and Lima, headed by persons named by and serving at the will of the king, and containing ministries of government, finance, justice, and war. The judicial power, too, would be reformed, its offices filled without respect for national provenance, rather than reserved for peninsular appointees.

In sum, Alamán argued, only a significant devolution of authority to the New World could check the "natural tendency toward mutual separation," which resulted from Creoles' knowledge that their "union with the peninsula, in its present terms, is not advantageous."[55] In its attempt to describe a reform of the Spanish imperial constitution that, without breaking all ties between the metropole and its colonies, would raise American colonists to equal status with their European counterparts within the empire, Alamán's Exposition bears a striking resemblance to the confederations and commonwealths proposed by British North American Creoles in the years leading up to their revolution. Like these proposals, it sparked outrage in the *Cortes* and was rejected by the peninsular majority without discussion. Thus, as in British North America, metropolitan intransigence forced Mexican Creoles to seek independence as the only means of escaping their marginal status.

By the time Alamán returned from Spain, independence had already been won. A Creole colonel of the Spanish Royal Army, Agustín Iturbide, who had participated with great effectiveness in the suppression of Hidalgo's insurgency since its outset, decided quite suddenly to abandon this cause and lead Mexico to freedom.[56] He published a document stating the principles of his revolution in February 1821, known as the Plan of Iguala, in which he outlined "Three Guarantees," which would serve as basic law: the establishment of the Roman Catholic Apostolic religion, without tolerance for any other; the absolute independence of Mexico; and the unity of European and American Mexicans, entailing the abolition of all distinctions drawn between them by the Spanish Empire. The plan also stated that Mexico would be governed by a constitutional monarchy and invited Fernando VII to come and occupy its throne, providing that in the case of his refusal, other members of the royal family would be invited. By August, Iturbide had forced the newly appointed captain-general and superior political chief of New Spain, Juan O'Donojú, to sign a treaty recognizing Mexico's independence under the terms of the plan. In September, he oversaw the "Mexican Empire's" official declaration of independence.[57]

While Alamán was not present to participate in the drafting of these documents or in the debates that would later ensue over their implementation, his *Historia* praised Iturbide's actions. The Plan of Iguala made its case for independence "without odious acrimony, without unfounded or exaggerated complaints" against the metropole, while "recognizing the great advantages that America had gained from Spanish conquest and domination." Iturbide had declared that since "now the branch is equal to the trunk," it was time for Mexicans to control their own destiny, placing independence within "the ordinary course of human events." This gradual, peaceful separation, akin to the process by which children become independent of their parents, was Alamán's ideal, clearly preferable to a radical break, with all its attendant violence and disruption.[58]

5.3 GOVERNING A POSTCOLONIAL SOCIETY

In its first thirty years of independence, Mexico was governed by twenty-six different administrations and at least four distinct constitutional arrangements.[59] The extraordinary instability of the period has long caused scholars to regard it with wariness.[60] Even Lucas Alamán, a firsthand observer and a prominent participant in the period's politics, described Mexico's first thirty years as the "era of Santa Anna's revolutions."[61] He referred, here, to General Antonio López de Santa Anna, who personally led six successful coups d'état and served as president or interim president seven times. Because Santa Anna was a man of flexible political convictions, who relied on a very diverse series of constituencies for support during his various regimes, it is tempting to regard the era as one of pure ideological chaos or, at the very least, one in which personal charisma, local connections, and brute strength – a combination captured in the term *caudillo*, which Santa Anna exemplified – mattered much more than ideas or institutions. However, as in the rest of the Americas, in Mexico the struggle for independence gave way to intense reflection and debate on the best manner of governing the country. When we look past Santa Anna's oscillating interventions, Mexico's first thirty years emerge as a period of fascinating constitutional thinking worthy of extensive study.

While recognizing that Mexico's early independence was more than meaningless tumult and upheaval, it is also essential to complicate the long-accepted account of the period as one in which the struggle over independence itself continued between Liberals seeking to eliminate the remaining vestiges of Spanish rule and Conservatives who sought to return the country to its colonial status. As I noted on the preceding text, a series of interventions by historians of Mexico has mostly dismantled this portrayal, in large part by showing that Conservatives were as dedicated as their Liberal counterparts to creating a system in which Mexicans could defend themselves against internal and external threats to their independence.[62] Here, building on this literature's findings, I show that Mexico's early constitutional debates closely resembled the debates we have reviewed in the United States and Andean South America, suggesting that nineteenth-century Mexican conservatism would be better understood as an instance of Creole constitutional thinking, rather than an effort to resurrect Spanish rule. No figure better exemplifies this position than Alamán, who consistently sought to consolidate the authority of Mexico City's *hombres de bien*, or Creole elite,[63] and increase their capacity to control the country as a whole, precisely because he thought that this was the surest means of establishing stable self-government in a postcolonial society.

While near-constant turmoil characterized the politics around him, Alamán joined the company of Creole revolutionary ideologists across the hemisphere, producing a constitutional theory whose central tenets included limitations on the authority of the legislative branch, vis-à-vis the executive and judicial branches, and on the authority of provincial governments, vis-à-vis the general government. His case for these institutional arrangements was not, as was Alexander Hamilton's, based upon a proto-political economy of individual interests, nor, as was Simón Bolívar's, on a re-nascent classical republican account of virtues and vices, but rather on a belief in the capacity of tradition to produce legitimacy, which he frequently elaborated by reference to Edmund Burke. Despite Burke's influence, Alamán's constitutional thought is clearly grounded in a distinctively postcolonial, American setting, in which the question of establishing a government capable of providing stability for Mexico's diverse population takes first place. Thus, Alamán's ideas provide an excellent illustration of how the shared characteristics of the Creole revolutionaries' social position produced ideological convergence despite differences in philosophical starting points.

As I've already noted, Alamán praised Agustín de Iturbide's efforts to secure Mexican independence above all for the respect that Iturbide accorded to Mexico's Hispanic heritage. For the same reason, he appreciated the constitution outlined in the Plan of Iguala, which in his evaluation,

[a]ttended to customs formed over three hundred years; to the opinions established, interests created, and respect invested in the name and authority of the monarch.... It is difficult enough to merely make a nation independent: if at the

same time one tries to change everything with respect to the established form of government,... the difficulty becomes insuperable. In the United States of America, they only undertook the former task, and the good order and stability with which things have continued, the grandeur that the country has achieved, has come from nothing else but the fact that they did not undertake the latter. Iturbide rightly believed that the faithful imitation of those states [the U.S.] consisted not in copying their political constitution, for which the ground in Mexico was less prepared than even in Russia or Turkey, but in following the prudent principle of making independence while leaving the form of government to which the nation was accustomed intact.[64]

As we saw with Simón Bolívar, the idea that a relative lack of experience in self-government made Spanish America unfit for what was presented as the radically republican and federal constitution of the United States was central to Creole constitutional thought. Here, Alamán presents a particularly sophisticated version of the case, recognizing that the framers of the US Constitution had also resisted calls for more totalizing revolutionary reform, and arguing that their country had benefited from their moderation.

Alamán acknowledged explicitly that "it is noteworthy that the two most prominent men that Spanish America has produced in this series of revolutions, Iturbide and Bolívar, have coincided on the same idea," while citing "a notable difference in favor of the great man of Mexico: this conviction, which in Bolívar was the result of sad experience, was in Iturbide a prudent prior belief."[65] Once again, then, Alamán emerges as an extraordinarily self-conscious theorist of Creole Revolution, grasping features of the Americas' shared experience that largely eluded his counterparts elsewhere, and stating very explicitly his conception of the particular problems raised throughout the hemisphere.

This impression is reinforced when we consider the other major advantage Alamán cited in support of Iturbide's plan: he argues that Mexico differed from its neighbor to the north not only in its relatively scant experience of self-government, but because it was not, like the United States, "composed of homogenous elements," but rather "divided by nature and by laws that have reigned for many years over diverse nations, one of which pretends to have exclusive right to the territory." Here he refers, of course, to the racial composition of Mexico's population, and to the indigenous majority's assertion of an original claim on lands lost in the conquest. Whereas in the United States, a Creole majority could adopt republican institutions without fear, in Mexico, it was "necessary to provide against institutions that in their nature would make one race predominant,... as the example of Haiti demonstrates." This protection, he thought, can only be accomplished by establishing a power superior to all others and independent of them, which although composed of persons of one or another of the diverse races which are subject to it, by the legal preeminence which it enjoys, can view them all as equals and attend, without difference to the wellbeing and prosperity of each one, as happened in America with the authority of the kings with respect to the Indians. Only a power of this nature can inspire equal respect for all and count on the support of all when it is demanded by the circumstances of the nation.[66]

In other words, only a strong, independent executive, bearing the traditional legitimacy of the Spanish Crown and operating within a mixed regime that represented the country's various castes and classes could govern Mexico. Alamán's Burkean attention to the importance of custom and habit and a thoroughly Creole attention to the difficulties presented in adopting a popular government for a people divided by race and class constituted the basic elements of his constitutional thought, the base upon which he would advocate, throughout his life, for a constitutional system comprised by political union and a presidentialist system of separated powers.

5.4 CONSTITUTIONALISM IN EXILE

Despite the advantages that Alamán claimed for it, Iturbide's tenure was short-lived. Though he was able to consolidate a de facto Mexican independence quickly and with relatively little bloodshed, Spain refused to recognize his accomplishment and declined to send a prince to Mexico. In the confusion that ensued, Iturbide took the newly erected throne himself, becoming Emperor Agustín I in July 1822. Initially popular, he was soon beset by a rebellion headed by an ambitious officer from Veracruz, Antonio López de Santa Anna, who the emperor had removed from command following numerous complaints of insubordination and embezzlement. Santa Anna's cause received support from Mexico City's elite of Creoles and European Spaniards who had supported independence but opposed Iturbide's accession,[67] and from prominent regional politicians, who viewed the rebellion as a path to acquiring greater autonomy in provincial matters for the local governments in which they were dominant.[68] In March 1823, overwhelmed by opposition, Agustín I abdicated the throne and departed for exile.

After the fall of the empire, a depleted national government in Mexico City was left in the hands of a provisional executive council, on which Alamán, only recently returned from Spain, served as minister of internal and external relations. The council's main work was to organize elections for a constituent congress that would draft a constitution for the Republic of Mexico. This prospect occasioned intense debate in the capital, organized for the first time around a division between centralists and federalists. Mexico City's Creole elite of property owners, professionals, intellectuals, and statesmen were quite unified in their centralist convictions, believing that a unified political system that consolidated their own authority and projected it over the entire country was the only means of setting independent Mexico on a path toward progress and prosperity. They were opposed by the representatives of local governments – the *ayuntamientos* of the Spanish Empire and the provincial deputations established by the *Cortes* – who also sought to consolidate their own power and were more likely to present federalism as the embodiment of a long-standing custom of provincial self-government than as a means of achieving egalitarian reforms.

Following the debacle of Iturbide's empire and the important role of the provincial deputations in bringing about its end, the federalists counted on a decided advantage in popular support.[69] The elections returned a federalist majority in the constituent congress, which, over centralist objections, ratified the Constitution of the United States of Mexico in October 1824. The Constitution of 1824 made the general government of the federation substantially dependent upon the state governments for the exercise of its powers, and imposed strict limitations on the executive powers it invested in a president and vice president.[70] Though prospects for the republic seemed bright at its outset, competition over posts quickly enveloped the country in partisan conflict.[71] Only one president, Guadalupe Victoria, served a full term in office under the new constitution, from 1824 to 1829. In his second coup, Santa Anna forcibly overturned the results of the election of 1828, installing his preferred candidate, Vicente Guerrero, in office. Guerrero was, in turn, removed and replaced by his vice president, Anastasio Bustamante, less than a year later.[72]

Bustamante named Alamán minister of relations, from which post he directed the administration, overseeing a series of reforms that, while outwardly conforming to the Constitution of 1824, had the effect of concentrating power in Mexico City's Creole elite. State politicians who refused to implement the central government's policies were removed and replaced by extraconstitutional means, and suffrage was limited in the capital to those possessing property or a trade. By all accounts, Alamán was actually successful in his central aim of reforming the economy and the treasury, with a substantial increase in public revenues permitting the first balanced budgets in the country's independent history.[73] But even the promise of fiscal stability was not enough to overcome the federalist opposition in the states, and in 1832, Santa Anna rode yet another wave of dissent back into the presidential palace, whereupon he promptly left matters in the hands of his vice president, Valentín Gómez Farías, who cleansed the state and federal governments of Alamán's allies and initiated a series of laws designed to undermine the Church and the army, which he presented as oppressive legacies of Spanish domination.[74] Alamán and his fellow ministers went into hiding to avoid prosecution.

It was during this period of internal exile that Alamán wrote the single most systematic statement of his constitutional thought, ostensibly as part of a case for his own rehabilitation. In 1835, he published a detailed defense of his actions as minister and an "Impartial Examination" of the administration he had served.[75] Both documents illuminate the political history of the period, but the Impartial Examination transcends its momentary purpose, containing both an analysis and critique of the Constitution of 1824 and a more general statement of principles, which in one scholar's opinion, slices through "the Gordian knots of the liberal constitutional model as it developed in the West, particularly in France, Spain, and Latin America."[76] While it is certainly true that at some points Alamán's writing rises into this global register, and that his arguments draw upon examples from each of these places, his ideas are best understood within a merely hemispheric context: the problems Alamán identified in the Constitution of 1824 and the solutions he proposed exemplify the constitutional dimensions of the ideology of Creole Revolution, converging in several important respects with the ideas I have already described in this book's studies of Alexander Hamilton and Simón Bolívar.

Alamán opens the Impartial Examination with an extended quotation from Burke's *Reflections on the Revolution in France*, and indeed, Burke's influence is clear throughout the essay.[77] Alamán's fundamental critique of the Constituent Congress was that in "blindly following the theoretical principles of speculative philosophy," it had failed to produce a constitution "congruent with [Mexico's] customs and uses." Their deepest error was to think that the federal constitution of the United States, "even exactly copied, would produce the same effects while working on different elements." Federalism, he argues, had deep roots in the United States that did not exist in Mexico. The former colonies that comprised the union to the north were "originally formed independent of one another," each with its "unique constitution, modeled in general upon the principles adopted in England." When, with independence, British North Americans "broke the tie" of English rule, "all that the legislators had to do was to substitute for the common tie of external domination a national union, and this is what they did with the Federal Constitution." In adopting this form of government, then, they "did not alter at all the particular existence of the states, nor vary their constitutions," and as a result, their new system profited from its compatibility with the "habitual customs, the ordinary mode of living for all individuals." In sum, "Independence did not change that Republic except incidentally, it left intact all with respect to the primordial constitution. From this resulted the fact that since its independence the United States has proceeded forward every day without incident on the road to their prosperity."[78]

The Spanish Empire, Alamán insisted, was organized very differently, with much greater centralization and uniformity in its structure. As a result, the attempt to introduce federalism had produced very different results: "while they found themselves constituted from the moment they were liberated, we, destroying everything that had previously existed, found ourselves independent and in anarchy."[79] Federalism simply represented too radical a break with Mexico's colonial experience; as such, ironically, it presented a grave threat to Mexico's continued independence.

Alamán devotes even more space in the Impartial Examination to criticizing the division of powers between the branches of the federal government than to the one between the state and federal governments. The Constitution of 1824 allowed such a "monstrous accumulation of powers in the bodies called legislative" that its result was "nothing more than a passage from the tyranny of one to the infinitely more unbearable tyranny of many."[80] Notably, he describes the problem as a result of important departures from, rather than adherence to, the example of the United States:

from this model [that is, the US Constitution] we took barely a tint, while what we actually practiced was the Spanish Constitution, itself nothing else than an imitation of that of the Constituent Assembly of France, and this the result of all the extravagant metaphysics of the philosophers of the past century. Thus it was that, without being clear, all of the spirit of the Spanish Constitution was transferred to our Federal Constitution under the form of the Constitution of the United States,... The constitution which the Constituent Assembly gave France, which was copied in a servile manner by the *Cortes* of Cádiz, not only did not distinguish properly between the powers, not only did not establish a well-balanced equilibrium amongst them, but excessively debilitating the Executive, transferred all authority to the Legislature, creating in the place of the absolute power of the monarchy a power as absolute and entirely arbitrary, not even having to contain it the brakes that can in some manner impede the arbitrariness of monarchs.[81]

In these passages, the convergence of Alamán's thought with Hamilton's arguments in defense of a "partial intermixture of powers" borne by the branches of the federal government is striking.[82] For both, the prospect of popular tyranny formed the main argument on behalf of a constitutional system in which the legislature was checked and balanced by its coordinate branches, and above all, by the executive.

And, indeed, when Alamán comes to specifics, the advantages he cites in favor of the division of powers established by the US Constitution are the same ones Hamilton defended in the *Federalist Papers*. In establishing the executive branch, the Mexican Constitution "assigns certain faculties and many obligations to the government,... without calculating whether the faculties were sufficient to fulfill [the obligations]." The Mexican president was much more limited, compared to his US counterpart, in his authority to discharge cabinet members and military leaders, to pardon or commute criminal charges, and to initiate legal causes or defend himself from legal causes initiated against him by others. "Is it so strange, then," he asks, "that a government so weakly organized is unable to carry out the objectives for which it was created, repressing the wicked, protecting the good and peaceful, assuring order, reinforcing military discipline, and allowing the nation to enjoy the benefits of society, the primordial objective of all human institutions?"[83]

Alamán also recognized the advantages the United States derived from the capacity of the judicial branch to limit the powers of Congress: "How different is the power of a congress that ... must submit its acts to the judgment of an immovable [because life-tenured] tribunal, one for this reason less susceptible to momentary impressions!" He argued that if laws passed by Congress were reviewable by the Supreme Court, Mexico would not have seen "the decrees of expatriation of persons and their families, without any appeal" or the series of "sequestrations and confiscations, one more embarrassing than the next," which had contributed so greatly to persistent instability.[84] But the Constituent Congress, subscribing to "extravagant and flattering ideas of sovereignty" had invested the legislative branch with an unlimited authority, with the ironic result that "in the same era in which the infallibility of the pope is most ridiculed, the principle of the infallibility of congresses is consecrated."[85] Here, Alamán's own, markedly traditionalist version of Creole constitutional thought is clear, deriving support for familiar institutions from unique first principles.

If Alamán is positively Hamiltonian in his discussion of the separation of powers, he strikes a more Bolivarian note when he turns to consideration of the related issue of emergency powers:[86] "[T]he habitual weakness of the government, although always damaging to the interests of the nation, would be less so if it only existed in ordinary and tranquil times, giving place in those of danger and revolution to a more energetic [government]." He supports this case with a comparison between England, where, "in times of public inquietudes the law protecting personal security, known as the *Law of Habeas Corpus*, is suspended" and France, which, "constituted according to the enlightenment of the age," was forced "to authorize the government with a terrible military law" to meet whatever emergencies it encountered.

Like Bolívar, Alamán thought that a strong executive was absolutely requisite to meet the particular challenges presented by independence in the Americas and that only a "general rule within the Constitution or later laws, [regarding] what should be done in not-infrequent cases of public turbulence," could establish stable self-government, in which "revolutions would not be so frequent or so dangerous." He decried the error, common to "modern systems" of thinking that "it is enough, to secure liberty, to restrict the faculties of those who until then have been the depositories of power," arguing that without constitutions that provided the executive with the authority to meet, legally, the unique difficulties encountered by the new nations of Spanish America, the latter would succumb to internal rebellion or external conquest.[87]

Finally, the Impartial Examination turns to the Congress itself, arguing that not only should the authority of the legislative branch be lessened, vis-à-vis its coordinate branches, but that the structure of the branch itself should be modified, so as to improve the "quality" of its membership: "When a power is extensive, the good or ill use of it depends solely on the personal qualities of the men in whom it is deposited." For Alamán, the fact that Congress was a "numerous body" presented the most serious problem. He cites Burke to the effect that popular assemblies are "less under responsibility to one of the greatest controlling powers on earth, the sense of fame and estimation.... A perfect democracy is therefore the most shameless thing in the world."[88]

The only check upon congressional shamelessness, for Alamán as well as for Burke, was to give "property, above all in land, which is the most stable and intimately related to the prosperity of the nation, a direct influence in legislation."[89] To this end, Alamán suggested that property requirements be established for the rights to vote and hold public office, and that the requirements for service in the upper house of the legislature should be higher, so as to make it the special province of propertied interests: "[T]he division of Congress into two chambers can never fulfill the function [of limiting abuses of power] as long as the two chambers only differ in the mode of their election or for some incidental feature such as the duration of their terms [in office], but do not represent essentially different interests whose combination produces a general convenience in the laws."[90] Here, Alamán employs an argument that would have been very familiar to the framers of the Constitution of the United States, in which "balanced government" is presented as a result of the representation of different social orders. Of course, it is for precisely its capacity to achieve this balance that Burke so effusively praised the English Constitution.[91]

Though they were often presented in Burkean terms or elaborated with quotes from Burke, it is important that we understand that Alamán's arguments for political centralization, a limited legislative authority, and institutional representation of property owners were not simple reiterations of Burke, nor even a straightforward application of Burke's analysis of the French Revolution to Mexico, though the latter comes closer to the truth. Rather, in the *Examen Imparcial*, a uniquely Creole concern with governing a heterogeneous population divided by imperial social and ethnic categories is as strongly apparent as the more properly Burkean concern with institutional continuity. Alamán's arguments for property requirements, in particular, are clearly grounded in the specific problems presented in an attempt to establish republican institutions in the newly independent Americas:

These and other restrictions are never, it seems to me, more necessary than when passing from a system in which there is not the least idea of popular elections to one in which all depends upon them, in which one proposes to give such an important faculty to a people that does not have any well-formed conception of its objective, consequences, or importance.[92]

This passage inevitably calls to mind Simón Bolívar's worry, discussed in the last chapter, that Spanish Americans' lack of experience in self-government had deprived them of the virtues he thought were necessary to sustain self-government; here we can see how Creole revolutionaries from very different parts of the New World, with very different educational experiences and philosophical influences, deployed similar descriptions of the Spanish American experience to defend the constitutional consolidation of their own class's authority within independent states.

5.5 PERFECTING THE UNION

Alamán saw most of his constitutional aims realized almost immediately. By early 1834, the near-continuous coups, a number of regional secessions, two radical administrations, persistent economic decline and financial instability, and a general atmosphere of lawlessness and violence had convinced Mexico City's *hombres de bien* to put aside their philosophical differences in order to construct a system that would better consolidate their control over the country. Santa Anna, sensing the change in political winds, returned to the city, removed Gómez Farías from office along with most of the ministry, nullified the reforms they had put in place, and dissolved Congress.

Alamán's Impartial Examination joined a number of newspaper editorials and pamphlets in calling for constitutional changes that would address Mexico's post-colonial problems.[93] Santa Anna decreed that elections for a new congress should be held and, following an effective campaign of intimidation and censorship, they returned two houses dominated by the city's Creole elite.[94] Debate began immediately on whether these representatives had the power to change the constitution. In the summer of 1835, it was decided that they did, and by October of that year, a draft of a new constitution was published. Over the course of 1836, parts of this draft were codified and ratified, eventually forming *Las Siete Leyes*, or the Seven Laws, which replaced the Constitution of 1824 as the basic law of the land.[95]

Under the *Siete Leyes*, the idea of Mexico as a federation of sovereign states was definitively abolished: The "states" in the Constitution of 1824 were replaced with "departments," whose "interior government" is assigned to a governor appointed by the general government. Whereas the Constitution of 1824 allowed the states substantial autonomy with respect to the regulation of elections, commerce, and criminal justice, the *Siete Leyes* explicitly establishes the "subjection" of the departments in these matters. The *ayuntamientos* were suspended and the state militias reduced in number.

The federal government's separation of powers was also modified to limit the authority of the legislative branch, particularly with respect to private property and criminal justice. The president's term in office was doubled, but with the specter of Santa Anna haunting their proceedings, the constituents declined to grant the executive greater emergency powers. A Supreme Court with eleven life-term members was granted final appellate authority in all criminal and civil matters, but no power of judicial review. This power went to a new, fourth branch of government established by the Second Law. The "Supreme Conservative Power" was charged with "guarding the Constitution of the Republic" and "maintaining the balance between the coordinate powers" of the federal government. This tribunal, clearly inspired by Simón Bolívar's Constitution of 1826, was authorized to nullify acts by any of the three branches to declare the president unfit for service, to dissolve the Supreme Court, to temporarily suspend Congress, and to reinstate any of the branches in the event that they be "revolutionarily dissolved."

The *Siete Leyes* also distinguished between "Mexicans" and "Mexican Citizens," establishing an annual income requirement for the latter (100 pesos), as well as for local and departmental offices (500–2,000 pesos), for federal deputies (1,500 pesos), senators (2,500 pesos), members of the Supreme Conservative Power (3,000 pesos), and for the presidency (4,000 pesos). In one scholar's estimate, based on a broad survey of studies, these limits would have disenfranchised 80 percent of Mexico City's population and an even larger proportion of Mexicans living outside the city, completely excluding small-holding indigenous farmers, peons, and domestic servants.[96]

On paper, then, the *Siete Leyes* represented a major consolidation of authority by Mexico's Creole elite vis-à-vis the Constitution of 1824, which when considered from a hemispheric perspective bears a close resemblance to the shift accomplished by the adoption of the Constitution of 1787 in the United States, or the one intended by Bolívar's Constitution of 1826. Their fate, however, much more closely resembled that of the latter, in that they never really became effective, and certainly never accomplished their aim of bringing order and progress to the country.

Even before the *Siete Leyes* had been ratified, several provinces launched rebellions in the name of federalism. This forced the government to commit already scarce funds to their suppression, in which project it had very partial success. The first and only president elected under the *Siete Leyes*, Anastasio Bustamante, managed to serve only half of his eight-year term before chaos had consumed the capital. While he managed, at the cost of many lives and much property, to hold out against one serious rebellion, he succumbed to the next one, led, of course, by Santa Anna. The *Siete Leyes* were scrapped in favor of a new constitution, known as the *Bases Orgánicas*,[97] which awarded Santa Anna virtually dictatorial powers, but did not bring the country peace. His regime was succeeded by two more dictatorships, the reestablishment of the Constitution of 1824, and, finally, the war with the United States, during which Mexico had five different presidents and lost more than half of its territory.

5.6 TEXAS AND THE CLASH OF CREOLE EMPIRES

As with all of the states that comprise the Americas, there is a tendency to view Mexico's current territorial dimensions as natural, as if the country's long history of provincial secessions and foreign conquests inevitably produced the familiar present-day nation, its boundaries, and population. But we miss a fascinating dimension of Mexico's nineteenth-century formation by imposing this teleological frame. Here I shall show that the country's frontiers are a contingent product of conflicts between rival Creole imperialists, each aspiring to hemispheric dominance.

Again, Lucas Alamán provides us with a crucial insight into these ideologies. From the first lines of his *Historia*, he imparts a distinctly imperial conception of Mexico, a vast aggregation of territories accumulated in a long series of conquests:

The Viceroyalty of New Spain comprehended, in the era in which this story begins, not just the territory to which Don Hernando Cortés gave this name when he discovered and conquered it, but also the ancient kingdoms of Michoacan and New Galicia, conquered by Nuño de Guzman, which formed the intendency of Guadalajara, as well as others, successively added: the interior provinces of the east and west, the Californias, and the Yucatan peninsula. In the north it was bounded by the United States of America, from the Gulf of Mexico to the Pacific Ocean, with uncertain borders until these were clearly fixed in the celebrated treaty between Spain and that country of 22 February 1819. It extended to the South until it touched the province of Chiapas and its annex of Soconusco, dependents of the captaincy-general of Guatemala. The coasts of the Yucatan, from the Gulf of Honduras, through the vast stretch of the breast [*seno*] of Mexico, delimited its eastern territories, and in the west, [it extended] from the Isthmus of Tehuantepec to the North, in Alta California.[98]

Nor did Mexico relinquish this imperial status upon becoming independent. Even before ascending to the throne, Agustín Iturbide had declared independence in the name of an "Empire of Mexico," and shortly brought the former kingdom of Guatemala – present-day Guatemala, Honduras, El Salvador, Nicaragua, and Costa Rica – under Mexican dominion. Alamán wrote that "with this addition, the Mexican Empire became an extensive territory, fertile and situated most advantageously for commerce with both oceans, a nation of the first importance."[99] However, even by the time Alamán wrote these lines, the Mexican Empire had been dismembered by secession and foreign conquest, its territories reduced by more than half, and its global preeminence severely eroded.

Thus, in the *Historia*, the explicitly imperial dimension of the Creole revolutionary ideology, the defenses to territorial expansion and internal colonization that we traced in the ideas of Alexander Hamilton and Simón Bolívar, is transformed into mourning for an empire lost and an effort to identify the causes of its downfall. The work's penultimate chapter compares, to rather tragic effect, the state of the country in 1808 and 1852, noting diminished "territorial extension" as the first and foremost manifestation of a steady decline from global prominence to insignificance. Some readers take Alamán's *Historia* as a whole, and this chapter in particular, to be a critique of independence itself or even a call for Mexico to return to European rule. I think this reading is mistaken. Alamán, like Hamilton and Bolívar, sought to create a novel American empire precisely as a means of consolidating independence. He lamented the loss of Mexico's claims in Central America and the North American west because he feared that a diminished Mexico would gradually fall under foreign influence or be reconquered outright.

As Alamán notes in the passage excerpted in the preceding text, the northern borders of the Empire of Mexico were fixed shortly before its independence, in a treaty signed on February 22, 1819 by the president of the United States, John Quincy Adams, and the Spanish foreign minister, Luis de Onís. The Adams–Onís Treaty, as it came to be known, ceded Spanish claims to the Floridas, parts of the Louisiana Territory, and the lands north and east of a line comprised by the Arkansas River and the 42nd parallel to the United States, in exchange for the latter's relinquishment of any claim to Texas.[100] The recently reconvened *Cortes* ratified the treaty in 1820, over the protests of New Spanish deputies, who thought it overly generous.[101]

Despite these concessions, upon gaining independence Mexico inherited a vast territory, over which it could claim only formal control. In fact, the northern reaches of the country were mostly inhabited by Indigenous peoples, few of whom spoke Spanish, belonged to the Catholic Church, or felt any particular loyalty to the newly declared Empire of Mexico. Agustín I's ministers recognized this problem early on, recommending that measures be taken to consolidate Mexican control over the north, but any action on these recommendations was delayed by the emperor's abdication.[102] Thus, in 1823, when Alamán assumed the post of minister of relations under the interim government that succeeded Iturbide, there was still no policy regulating settlement in the north. In his first official report to Congress, delivered in November of that year, Alamán stressed the potential that was going unrealized in the northern *baldíos*, or "unoccupied" lands:

The almost magical transformation that lands of this kind have undergone in the new states of the Union in the North of our continent [that is, the United States], where deserts continually exposed to the barbarian invasions have been in a few years changed into populous and flourishing provinces, cannot but invite our country to seek similar rewards.... The colonization of these provinces, by their situation, demands the preferential attention of Congress and the government. This matter is made all the more urgent, because while it has remained unresolved a number of foreigners have established themselves there without any order whatsoever, and without the nation taking all of the advantage that it should. The civilization of the barbaric Indians and the security of our borders ... will be additional benefits of these measures.[103]

With Iturbide's abdication, Mexico formally became a "republic," but as Alamán's remarks evidence, it maintained an intrinsically imperial orientation to its territories. In language reminiscent of imperialist political thinkers both before and since his time, Alamán urges Mexico to "civilize" its barbarian citizens, and to seize the profits that their lands and labor would furnish.[104] But, in the same passage, Alamán's invocation of the United States as both an example and a mounting threat betrays the other edge of his concerns. In Alamán's distinctively Creole anti-imperial imperialism, territorial expansion and internal colonization are presented as indispensible means of responding to the threat of conquest presented by the New World's other imperial aspirants.

Alamán finally succeeded in pushing a colonization law through Congress in August 1824, which gave the government some authority to regulate the rapidly expanding population of illegal Anglo-American settlers in Texas.[105] However, discussion of the proper policies to pursue with respect to the north was soon consumed by the broader constitutional debate between federalists and centralists. As we might suspect, Alamán sympathized with the latter camp and pressed this position in newspaper editorials published while the Constituent Congress debated the matter over the course of 1824. Specifically, he argued that Texas, along with New Mexico and Upper California, should be admitted to the union as territories, rather than states, placing them under the direct jurisdiction of the general government, which would more effectively oversee their settlement and defense. Alamán's efforts succeeded with respect to Upper California and New Mexico, but the federalist majority in the Constituent Congress made Texas part of the new state of Coahuila y Tejas, passing jurisdiction over settlement to the provincial government head-quartered in Saltillo.[106]

Alamán's next report, read to both houses of Congress in January 1825, was still optimistic. He detailed the general government's ongoing colonization and conversion efforts in California, as well as nationwide policies designed to improve the administration of justice, public health, public schooling, and record keeping, to support the press, scientific and artistic institutions, and the national army, and infrastructure programs that would stimulate agricultural production, industrialization, and commerce. He noted, ruefully, that "if rebuilding were as easy as destroying, we would have reason to be dismayed that ... we have not reclaimed the state of abundance and prosperity" enjoyed before independence, but he insisted that "when we consider that in this period commotions and political upheaval have been continuous, ... we have a motive for admiring the progress that we have made."[107] Once again, Alamán invoked the example of the United States, where federal oversight of settlement in western territories produced "great progress in civilization, industry, and commerce," suggesting that "with similar legislation, we can hope for the same."[108]

After 1825, however, Alamán's reports were increasingly dedicated to describing the barriers that federalism placed in the way of progress thoughout the nation, and effective settlement policy in Texas. The easternmost portions of the region, he noted with apprehension, were experiencing a rapid influx of Anglo-American settlers, who sometimes acquired land and documents by legal means, but often purchased land from unauthorized sellers or corrupt state officials, and entered the country illegally. Once there, they "observed the laws of the country that they came from" rather than the one they inhabited, working the land using the slaves they brought with them across the border, even though Mexico had abolished slavery in 1825.[109]

Alamán helped write a new Law of Colonization in 1830, which proscribed additional immigration from the United States, offered free land and direct support to Mexicans willing to move north, and asserted federal control over the licensing of new colonies, but once again, federalism undermined enforcement of the law. Provincial politicians in Coahuila y Tejas were making a tidy profit from land sales to illegal Anglo-American immigrants, and refused to comply with the new regulations, declaring the law an unconstitutional intrusion of the federal government upon state authority.

Mexico's difficulties in consolidating control over Texas were only exacerbated by the arrival of the United States' minister plenipotentiary, Joel Roberts Poinsett. Poinsett immediately made it clear that the United States had expansive designs on the Mexican north, unabashedly showing a Mexican contact a map he had drafted which incorporated Texas, New Mexico, and Upper California, as well as parts of Lower California, Sonora, Coahuila, and Nuevo León into the United States.[110] His official instructions were to press Mexico to sell all or part of Texas in the short term. He found Alamán receptive to talks about reformulating the boundaries established in 1819, but was dismayed when Alamán refused to consider any change until a binational commission had completed a thorough survey of the land, a process that might take as long as two years.

This was the beginning of poor relations between the two ministers, which only worsened as Poinsett sought to achieve his ends by involving himself in Mexico's contentious partisan politics. Poinsett personally secured a charter for the York Rite Masonic Lodge of Mexico City, which quickly filled with federalist members, and even held meetings in his home. Soon after, Alamán, not a mason himself but a sympathizer with the rival, centralist Scotch Rite Lodge, was forced out of his cabinet post.[111] He would continue his battle with Poinsett in the editorial pages of the centralist newspaper, *El Sol*, writing article after article describing US designs on Texas and other parts of northern Mexico.[112] To his dismay, though, Alamán would live to see these designs fulfilled in the aftermath of the Mexican–American War, which I shall describe in Chapter 6.

5.7 PAN-LATIN AMERICANISM AND THE ORIGINS OF *ANTIYANQUISMO*

In a point of striking ideological convergence with Simón Bolívar, as partisan politics and masonic intrigues undermined his influence over Mexico's domestic affairs, Alamán turned increasingly to international diplomacy as a means of pursuing his aims. Specifically, and again, like Bolívar, Alamán began to think that the only way that Mexico would be able to meet the threats that not only the United States, but also a number of European powers posed to its territorial integrity and economic autonomy, was by forming common cause with its fellow Spanish American states. Indeed, it was Bolívar himself who planted this seed. In his 1823 report to Congress, Alamán wrote that

If politics and commerce put us in contact with European nations, some of which are our neighbors as a result of their establishments on our continent and adjacent islands, even more powerful motives unite us with the newly formed states of our America [*nuestra América*]. Having the same origin, being bound by the same interests and threatened by the same dangers, we are unified in our fate and we should be [unified] in our forces. Convinced of these reasons, the Republic of Colombia proposed forming a general confederation of all the formerly Spanish American states.... This will be a true family pact [*pacto verdaderamente de familia*] that will unify all Americans in the defense of their liberty and independence, and stimulate commerce and our mutual interests.[113]

On October 3, 1823, Alamán and Miguel Santa María, minister plenipotentiary of Colombia in Mexico, signed a "Treaty of Union, League and Perpetual Confederation," obligating each nation to "sustain with their influence and maritime and terrestrial forces, as circumstances permit, their [mutual] independence from the Spanish nation or any other foreign domination."[114] The treaty also laid plans for a meeting of ministers plenipotentiary from all of the newly independent states – the Congress of Panama discussed in the last chapter. For all they shared, though, Alamán had differences with Bolívar in regard to the ideal capital of the Spanish Americas: His private instructions to ministers sent to Central and South America, specified that "all should contribute to giving Mexico decisive influence over the other new republics, making it the political center of everything.... Mexico will become in foreign relations the metropolis of all America."[115]

As the language of the treaty makes clear, in 1823, for Alamán as much as for Bolívar, the primary benefit to be derived from "confederation" was a superior bargaining position with Spain, which had not yet recognized the independence of any of its American colonies, and still occupied a number of strategically important areas, including an island fortress off the coast of Veracruz, Mexico. At this stage, it was possible for Bolívar to consider inviting Britain to send a representative to the Congress, and for Alamán to direct his minister in the United States to issue a similar invitation.[116] However, as time passed and the less-than-friendly intentions of the neighbor to the north became apparent, the idea of a Spanish American league became, for both Bolívar and Alamán, more exclusive and more directly defensive.[117] For Alamán, this exclusive "Spanish Americanism" came much more naturally than for Bolívar. Rather than the regional starting point for expansive federation that might one day take in the entire world, for Alamán Spanish American unity was a "family pact." In his later writings on the subject, the importance of the long-standing historical ties amongst the formerly Spanish states receive even greater emphasis:

> The nature, uniformity of interests, and the causes borne by all of the coun-tries of America that have shaken off the yoke of Spain, bind them together in such a manner that it could be said that although they are divided and recognize diverse centers of government, they form a whole composed of homogeneous parts. These circumstances make their relations much more intimate, so that they cannot be indifferent to one another's reverses and successes, and so that all are disposed to mutually aid the reaching of the object that all uniformly seek.[118]

It is remarkable that Alamán, whom I cited in the preceding text insist-ing that imperial rule had left Mexico a fundamentally *heterogeneous* society, could propose here that all of Spanish America in fact formed a "whole composed of *homogenous* parts." Of course, for Alamán, the Spanish Americas were homogenous precisely in their heterogeneity. The external threats and internal conflicts unleashed by the overthow of Spanish rule were *the* common problems confronting Creole statesmen across the hemisphere. Alamán hoped that the reunification of the former colonies would provide a solution to both. In this sense, we can say that Alamán's Spanish Americanism was, like Hamilton's American system and Bolívar's Panama Congress, an effort to establish a new empire, which would match and exceed the old one in its capacity to create inter-nal order and win external respectability.

5.8 CONCLUSION

In the next chapter, I will detail the partisan politics that undermined Alamán's plans and, ultimately, left Mexico unable to respond to the threat to its territorial integrity posed by the United States. For the moment, it suffices to note that the cumulative effect of so much instability was pro-found disillusionment with popular government amongst Mexico City's Creole elite. In 1840, a public letter to President Bustamante proposed that only a European monarch on a Mexican throne could bring order to the country, causing much uproar in the capital.[119] By 1846, an anon-ymous newspaper editorial, often attributed to Alamán, stated that "We want a Representative Monarchy; we want National Unity, order along with political and civil liberty, and the integrity of Mexican territory; we want, in sum, all of the promises and guarantees of the Plan of Iguala, to assure a stable foundation for our glorious independence."[120] Though Alamán never signed his name to any call for the creation of a monarchy, his political opinions did become explicitly "conservative" following the war. Indeed, he founded a Conservative Party and published its official newspaper, *El Universal*, where he argued that

Those who oppose the bloody propaganda of appalling republicanism are called *Conservatives*; and this name is fitting, because it is counterpoised to the name which best describes their opponents: *destructors*. Yes, destructors are those who fanatically aspire to regenerate society with barbarous means, attempting to arrive at this end by tearing down every monument to science, civilization and art, erasing history and tradition, and drowning in a lake of blood an entire innocent generation.... In the end, we call ourselves *conservatives*. Do you know why? Because we want most of all to *conserve* the weak life that is left in this poor society, which you have wounded almost to the point of death; and then to give it back the vigor and youth it can and should have, which you have beaten out of it and which we will bring back.[121]

There is some debate on the extent to which Alamán's views changed over time, whether he was at one time a convinced "liberal," a "moderate liberal," a "typical Cadiz Liberal," or a "liberal centralist," and when and in what stages his transition to conservatism took place.[122] What is clear is that in the last years of his life, Alamán was ready to experiment with drastic measures, supporting Santa Anna's return for a final dictatorship in 1853, and agreeing to serve once again as his minister of relations, only to die two months after he took office.

6

The End of Creole Revolution

The Creole Revolutions remade the New World, banishing the British and Spanish Empires to the margins of the hemisphere and transforming their former colonies into independent American states. It is tempting, after examining the ideas that animated these movements, to suggest that the Creole Revolutions made our New World, but history belies such a neat conclusion. Though many legacies of the Creole Revolutions remain with us today, in our political ideas and institutions, our internal patterns of social stratification, and our external relations with the world, after winning their independence, the Americas departed dramatically from the path envisioned by the political thinkers discussed in this book's previous chapters.

The ideology of Creole Revolution emerged from an important moment of hemispheric convergence, as similarly situated political thinkers sought to address similar political and philosophical problems by developing similar critiques of European rule, designing similar constitutions, and adopting similar approaches to foreign policy. But the most prominent pattern in the subsequent history of the Americas is divergence. In the years following its independence, the United States added new territories to its union until it stretched across a continent, built the world's largest economy, and became first a hemispheric and then a global superpower. In the same period, the unions forged by Spanish America's Creole revolutionaries succumbed to secessions and civil wars, disintegrating into smaller polities that experienced persistent political instability, uneven economic development, and frequent foreign interventions.

Because the United States' gains in territory, wealth, and global preeminence so often came at the expense of other Americans, the Creole Revolutions' heirs in different parts of the hemisphere have come to think of one another in sharply divergent ways as well. Once an exemplar and a partner in a common venture to remodel the world's politics and political institutions, the United States now often features in Latin American political thought as the "colossus of the north": a self-interested and aggressive threat to the freedom and an impediment to the prosperity of those who live beyond its borders but within its sphere of influence.

Retrospect tends to wrap this history of economic, political, and ideological divergence in an undeserved air of inevitability, allowing contemporary observers to assume that the seeds of the Americas' present-day differences were planted deep in the past, if not embedded in the very soil, rocks, and rivers of the northern and southern continents themselves. But the important ideological commonalities that this book has described in the American independence movements make the contrasting post-independence fortunes of the United States and the countries of Spanish America appear more puzzling. Why were the Creole Revolutions' common ideals and ambitions realized to dramatically different degrees in different parts of the hemisphere? Why did similar political institutions and constitutional designs perform better and persist longer in Britain's former colonies than in Spain's? In this chapter, I argue that the causes of the disparities that divide our Americas today are both more recent and more contingent than has commonly been assumed, locating the origins of the Americas' divergence in the political conflicts that emerged in the immediate aftermath of independence throughout the hemisphere, bringing an end to the Creole Revolutions.

6.1 IMPERIAL INSTITUTIONS AND POST-INDEPENDENCE DEVELOPMENT IN THE AMERICAS

In claiming that the Americas only decisively parted ways after independence, the account I offer here challenges existing explanations of the political and economic "gaps" between the contemporary United States and the countries of Latin America. For much of its history, the large and long-standing scholarly literature dedicated to explaining why the United States has achieved greater economic prosperity, more stable political institutions, and a broader global influence than Latin America was dominated by explanations rooted in the superior qualities of the Anglo-Saxon race, which doubled as a justification for the territorial depredations that the United States visited upon its neighbors throughout the nineteenth and early twentieth centuries.[1]

As the foundations of "scientific" racism were undermined by improved accounts of human genetic variation, and as the social scientific literature shed its more overt ideological intentions, scholars turned to environmental factors, especially climate and geography, to explain the different developmental trajectories traced by the two halves of the hemisphere.[2] This paradigm also succumbed to the weight of problematic facts, especially the observation that, over a very long time period, the Americas have undergone a striking "reversal of fortunes," as once-prosperous and densely populated regions of pre-Columbian Spanish America were gradually overtaken and then decisively outpaced by the former wilds and imperial backwaters of British North America.[3]

The inability of invariant climatic and geographic variables to account for this shift has inspired scholars, in recent years, to emphasize the effects of "institutions": informal rules and norms of social interaction as well as formal laws and forms of political organization that channel conflicts, structure investments, and thereby determine patterns of political and economic development.

But even as social scientists have abandoned explanations of differential economic and political development centered on fixed factors such as race, climate, or geography in favor of alternatives focused on more mutable institutions, they have continued to insist that the origins of the Americas' divergence lie very deep in their history, at the onset of European colonization. Specifically, they argue that the United States' relatively stable politics and relatively early industrialization are attributable to institutional advantages established when the country was a British colony, while Latin America's endemic disorders and developmental delays stem from problematic institutional legacies left behind by Spanish and Portuguese rule. Where imperial institutions enforced contracts, protected property rights, and limited social stratification – as in the British colonies that became the United States – capital investment, technological innovation, industrialization, and growth followed. Meanwhile, where institutions made property rights contingent upon membership in a small, well-connected elite and created a durable caste system – as in much of Latin America and the Caribbean – investment and trade were inhibited, and industrialization and development were delayed.[4]

Institutional explanations differ as to why European empires established different institutions in different parts of the Americas. Some scholars point to the institutional traditions that different imperial powers carried over the Atlantic and into their colonies, contrasting Spain's political absolutism and economic mercantilism with England's constitutionalism and economic liberalism.[5] Others emphasize the conditions that colonists encountered upon arriving in the Americas. Where they found a difficult disease environment, a large, sedentary indigenous population, or soil and climate conditions convenient to commercial agriculture, settlers of every European origin built hierarchical institutions designed to extract labor and maximize remittances, while those who settled in more salubrious, sparsely populated zones ended up living in more homogenous, equal societies under more liberal governments.[6] Proponents of both theories agree, though, that once these imperial institutions were established, they became "locked-in": subject to path-dependent processes of reproduction that propagated their advantageous or disadvantageous economic effects across the centuries, through the disjuncture of independence, and up to the present day.[7]

This is the contention that I shall question here. Though it is in many ways compelling, the institutional explanation of the Americas' post-independence divergence entails an important methodological and substantive difficulty. It takes for granted the territorial boundaries that define where the United States ends and Mexico begins, or that distinguish Venezuela from Colombia, and Argentina from Uruguay, using them to delimit empirical units of analysis. But it was not always inevitable that the United States would extend across a continent, as it does today, or that the former Spanish Americas would be comprised by nineteen separate states. The political borders of the Americas were not established along with other institutions under imperial rule.[8] Rather, they are a product of the often-violent partisan contention that arose everywhere in the Creole Revolutions' immediate aftermath.

While, as I detail in the following text, these post-colonial political conflicts were in many ways very similar throughout the Americas, they had very different outcomes. Regional resistance to political centralization and partisan opposition to incumbent administrations shattered the unions that Creole revolutionaries built throughout Spanish America, while the union forged at Philadelphia in 1787 survived the trials of its early years territorially intact. I have shown elsewhere that the success or failure of these parallel projects in political unification had significant effects on subsequent patterns of political and economic development in the Americas.[9] In the following text, I argue that fortune, rather than fate, decreed that the United States should persist and even expand after independence, despite experiencing conflicts not unlike the ones that tore apart the United Provinces of the Río de la Plata (comprising present-day Argentina, Uruguay, Paraguay, and Bolivia), Gran Colombia (comprising present-day Venezuela, Colombia,

Ecuador, and Panama), and the Empire of Mexico (comprising present-day Mexico, Guatemala, Honduras, El Salvador, Nicaragua, Costa Rica, and the western United States). The endurance of union in the north, and its breakdown in the south shaped the institutional, economic, and ideological legacies of the Creole Revolutions, initiating the long process of differentiation visible in our Americas today.

6.2 RISE OF A CREOLE OPPOSITION

In the last three chapters, we've seen that despite their different philosophical influences, Alexander Hamilton, Simón Bolívar, and Lucas Alamán all converged on a shared set of political ideas, an ideology that justified their analogous efforts to establish and maintain Creole rule in the Americas. Despite their monumental achievements, at the end of their lives, they also shared a deep sense of despair. In 1802, Hamilton remarked in a letter that his was "an odd destiny": "Perhaps no man in the United States has sacrificed or done more for the present Constitution than myself.... Yet I have the murmurs of its friends no less than the curses of its foes for my rewards. What can I do better than withdraw from the Scene? Every day proves to me more and more that this American world was not made for me."[10] Many of Hamilton's fellow Creole revolutionaries did, in fact, withdraw, embarking on voluntary or forced exiles in Europe or in other parts of the Americas. Simón Bolívar was on his way out of the country when he succumbed to tuberculosis on the Caribbean coast of Colombia. One of his last letters summarizes lessons learned in twenty years of revolutionary leadership in six sober bullet points:

(1) America is ungovernable, for us; (2) Those who serve revolution plough the sea; (3) the only thing one can do in America is emigrate; (4) This country will fall inevitably into the hands of the unrestrained multitudes and then into the hands of insignificant tyrants of all colors and races; (5) Once we've been eaten alive by every crime and extinguished by ferocity, the Europeans won't even bother to conquer us; (6) If it were possible for any part of the world to revert to primitive chaos, it would be America in her last hour.[11]

Lucas Alamán resisted the urge to abandon the Americas, but for his part, in 1850, he described Mexico as "a country that proceeded directly from infancy to decrepitude, without having enjoyed more than a glimmer of the freshness of youth nor given any other sign of life than violent convulsions," concluding that "there appears to be reason to believe with the great Bolívar that independence has been bought at the cost of all the goods that Spanish America enjoyed."[12]

The cause of each man's late depression was the same: the emergence of partisan and sectional opposition parties that contested incumbent revolutionaries' hold on power within newly independent American governments, challenging the main tenants of their political thinking, and threatening to undo their lives' work. These parties did not arise, as one might expect, in order to pursue the interests of the millions of African and Indigenous Americans whose situation had, in some cases, actually worsened after independence. Rather, the leadership and constituencies of the Americas' first opposition parties were predominately Creole. These opposition parties were formed, as I shall emphasize in the following text, not in order to contest the racial exclusions and hierarchies that the Creole Revolutions had been so concerned to preserve and defend, but rather, in large part, to contest the ways in which those exclusions and hierarchies were preserved and defended.

In speaking of the Americas' "first" opposition parties, and of the "emergence" of intra-Creole disagreements regarding constitutional design, I do not wish to overstate the point, or to suggest that a complete consensus ever existed amongst the Creole revolutionaries within any region. As the three previous chapters have shown, the ideology of Creole Revolution emerged in its local variations throughout the hemisphere from contexts marked by intense debate, disagreement, and, often, armed conflict. However, I do aim to highlight a notable breakdown in what consensus did exist amongst patriotic Creoles, and to describe a shift in the intensity of these debates after independence had been won.

Perhaps the clearest evidence of this breakdown is the fact that, in several instances, the principal intellectual leaders of opposition parties were once close allies or even members of the incumbent administrations they began to bitterly contest. When he took up his post as secretary of the treasury in the early 1790s, Hamilton found himself under attack by Thomas Jefferson and James Madison, figures with whom he had worked closely as late as the debates on the ratification of the Constitution of 1787. In the late 1820s, Bolívar had to contend with the less concerted, but equally devastating, defection of two of his main lieutenants, Francisco de Paula Santander, who served as vice president during each of Bolívar's terms in office, and José Antonio Páez, a longtime ally whom Bolívar had made military commander of Venezuela. Alamán, finally, grappled throughout the 1820s and 1830s with opponents led first by Lorenzo de Zavala, a fellow delegate to the Spanish *Cortes* in 1820, who had supported both the constitutional monarchy of Iturbide and the Constitution of 1824, and then José María Luis Mora, who, like

Alamán, was born in Guanajuato, suffered material harm at the hands of the insurgency, and sought more stringent franchise restrictions and greater political centralization in 1824, before he became the main ideologue of a radical reformist party in 1833.

From one perspective, this turn of events is unsurprising. Politics in the newly independent Americas followed a pattern that can be found in the aftermath of most successful revolutions, particularly anti-imperial struggles. "As a general rule," writes Bruce Ackerman, "the retreat of the imperial power permits the ascendant revolutionary elite to indulge in the luxury of disagreement." The sudden absence of a common enemy dissolves patriotic unity and exposes latent disagreements, whether based on separate regional loyalties, incompatible economic interests, or bare individual ambition. "During the period of national liberation, these disagreements are suppressed by the ever-present threat of defeat; but after the revolution, they take on a pressing urgency as the new nation defines its affirmative direction."[13]

There were certainly more than enough latent cleavages in American societies to stimulate conflict amongst triumphant Creole revolutionaries, but the American republics were perhaps uniquely unprepared for partisan conflict, their leaders and political thinkers being almost universally convinced that factionalism of any kind was unacceptable and dangerous. As Seymour Martin Lipset noted in his perceptive study of postcolonial politics,

> To accept criticism as proper requires the prior acceptance of the view that opposition and succession are normal, and that men may be loyal to the polity and yet disapprove of the particular set of incumbents. This view does not come easily to men who have themselves created a polity, and cannot, therefore, conceive of it functioning properly without them or in ways other than they think best.[14]

In the Americas, both incumbent administrations and their challengers reacted badly to the rise of partisan conflict amongst former patriots. Incumbents refused to concede any legitimacy to their opponents and sought to employ the governmental powers at their disposal to suppress dissent and exile dissenters. In response challengers deepened the stakes of these conflicts, making effective use of rapidly expanding independent press outlets to portray their enemies as would-be aristocrats or tyrants and betrayers of the revolutions they had so recently led. As a result, party politics brought all of the hemisphere's newly independent polities to the brink of dissolution, and it is at this brink that we find the origins of American divergence. While the United States negotiated a treacherous passage through its post-colonial conflicts, the new states of Spanish America broke apart on the reefs of partisan infighting.

6.3 POSTCOLONIAL CONFLICT
IN THE UNITED STATES

The partisan divisions that defined what historians now call the "first party system" of the United States first arose in response to policies Alexander Hamilton pursued as secretary of the treasury, especially his efforts to place the new nation's finances on a firmer footing through the federal assumption of state war debts and the chartering of a national bank.[15] Both issues were particularly apt to arouse antagonism: The federal assumption of outstanding debts divided debtor states that would benefit from more solvent states that would be forced to take on the debtors' burdens, while the national bank was seen as a boon to financial speculators and would-be industrialists concentrated in the northern states and a challenge to southern commercial agriculturalists' dominance of the economy.

The Commonwealth of Virginia, the most populous state in the union, with few outstanding debts of its own and a thriving commercial agricultural economy, was naturally positioned to lead the opposition on both matters. On December 16, 1790, the state's General Assembly sent a resolution to Congress, arguing that Hamilton's plans would "erect and concentrate and perpetuate a large moneyed interest," leading to "the prostration of agriculture at the feet of commerce, or a change in the present form of Federal Government fatal to the existence of American liberty."[16] Here we can already see how rapidly debate over the design of the new nation's financial institutions could shift to more fundamental terrain. For both Hamilton and for his opponents, nothing less than independence itself was at stake.

Hamilton's allies, who continued to call themselves "Federalists," as they had during the debate on ratification of the Constitution, believed that a well-managed public debt was an indispensable instrument for an ambitious new nation in a world of aggressive empires. Only the steady support of the federal government, they argued, could enable the United States' incipient industries to compete with longer-established manufacturers across the Atlantic and allow the country to achieve the economic autonomy necessary to sustain its political independence. The opposition, led by Thomas Jefferson and James Madison, took to calling themselves "Democratic-Republicans," arguing that Hamilton's true aim was to corrupt the United States' uniquely virtuous populace, empower and enrich a small class of financial speculators, and ultimately return the United States to monarchical submission.

Ideological conflict between the warring camps of the first party system reached its greatest intensity in the latter half of the 1790s, as new domestic and foreign policy questions arose to divide Creoles who had only recently fought together for independence. The concatenated pressure of frequent and scurrilous denunciations in the opposition press, turbulence and outright violence in the Napoleonic Wars' Caribbean theater, and the addition of a northern wing to the of the Republican Party attracting the affiliation of recent immigrants[17] forced the Federalist administration of John Adams into a desperate move: the notorious "Alien and Sedition Acts," passed in the summer of 1798. In effect, these measures turned the federal government, and particularly its executive branch, into a weapon for partisan combat, criminalizing speech critical of the government and permitting the president to arrest and deport non-citizens deemed dangerous to national security.

In response, Jefferson and Madison drafted resolutions to be sent to Congress, Jefferson's by the legislature of Kentucky and Madison's by Virginia. Madison's resolution denounced the Federalists in the strongest possible terms, describing their policies as an effort to "transform the present republican system of the United States, into an absolute, or at best a mixed monarchy."[18] Jefferson went still further, asserting a novel state prerogative to nullify, or declare "unauthoritative, void, and of no force," federal laws which were determined to have exceeded the federal government's delegated authority. He also drew a line in the sand, threatening that the federal government's continuation in its present path would "necessarily drive these States into revolution and blood."[19] Thus, on the eve of the new century, the US Constitution was under assault from both sides, with an incumbent party employing all means at its disposal to silence its opponents, and an opposition party ready to dissolve the union to escape federal tyranny.

Matters worsened when the presidential election of 1800 returned an ambiguous result. The indirect selection process prescribed by the Constitution for the office of the president was designed to produce national consensus around a luminary of truly superior virtue, in the mold of George Washington, but it performed poorly in the first presidential election contested by two distinct political factions. The two Republican candidates, Thomas Jefferson and Aaron Burr, tied in the lead with seventy-three electoral college votes apiece, activating a backup provision that empowered the House of Representatives to choose a president in an unusual vote by state delegations. Federalists in the House rallied for Burr, whom they perceived to be the more pliable contender, producing another deadlock, with Republicans coming up one vote short of the nine they required for an absolute majority in favor of Jefferson.

At this point, possibilities proliferated: The radical members of the Federalist majority in the lame duck Congress considered passing a statute that would push the Federalist John Marshall, then secretary of state, into office. More moderate members sought policy assurances from Jefferson in exchange for their votes. Jefferson refused to negotiate terms, declaring "unequivocally, that [he] would not receive the government on capitulation, that [he] would not go into it with [his] hands tied." He also appealed to his old friend John Adams in no uncertain terms, letting him know that his failure to veto any measure that handed the election to a Federalist party stalwart would "produce resistance by force, and incalculable consequences" for the young republic. The Republican governors of Virginia and Pennsylvania began to arm their militias, readying local forces to impose the outcome they viewed as just upon a federal government they did not trust or regard as legitimate.[20]

And then, when the crisis seemed ready to explode, it was over. On February 17, 1801, in the 36th round of voting, Federalist representatives from Delaware, Maryland, and Vermont cast blank ballots, giving the election to Jefferson. It is still unclear what changed their minds. Representative James Bayard of Delaware later indicated that he had received policy assurances from Jefferson through an intermediary, but Jefferson denied that any such exchange took place. Alexander Hamilton also played a role, organizing not so much for Jefferson as against Burr, whom he regarded as venal and opportunistic, and whom he described as such in letters that would help precipitate the duel that prematurely ended his life three years later.

If the causes of the compromise of 1801 remain murky, its results are quite clear: But for the fateful abstention of three representatives, the United States would have seen civil war, and in all likelihood, the collapse of the union only twenty-five years after it was declared independent. Nor was this the last time the United States approached the brink of dissolution. By 1809, the tables had turned, and trade embargoes imposed by the Madison administration on the eve of the War of 1812 inspired New England Federalists to embrace first nullification and then, eventually, to contemplate secession at a convention called for the purpose at Hartford in 1814.[21]

Southerners went back into the opposition during the presidency of John Quincy Adams, and again threatened nullification in response to protective tariffs imposed in 1828. South Carolina's legislature passed an actual "Ordinance of Nullification" in 1832, and readied its state militia to resist federal enforcement if necessary.[22] Traveling in America at the time, Alexis de Tocqueville observed that, "If conflict were to erupt today between the sovereignty of the Union and the sovereignty of the states, it is easy to foresee that the former would succumb."[23]

In the late 1830s, the annexation of Texas, a slave state, and the resulting shift in congressional representation led northerners to contemplate dissolution once again, and only last-minute compromises forestalled armed conflict over further territorial acquisitions in the Mexican–American War.[24] Given this prelude, David Hendrickson writes, the fact that regional struggles did finally cause civil war in the United States in 1861 "should not be considered as an accident or an anomaly but a reversion to the mean suggested by the historical experience of previous ages – a resumption of history, as it were, among a people (or peoples) who had entertained the enthralling but ultimately naïve hope that they had found history's end."[25]

It is impossible to observe the counterfactual trajectory the United States would have followed if any of these conflicts prior to 1861 had produced a civil war, or if the actual Civil War had not ended in a Union victory, but the experience of Spanish America suggests that the effects of early breakdown on political economic development would have been very large and very negative. Apart from the direct benefits of size – in the form of complementary regional comparative advantages unmitigated by customs duties or regulations, economies of scale in the provision of public goods and the collection of taxes, and insurance against shocks to particular industries – unity placed the new nation in a much better position to pursue its interests abroad.

A smaller, less stable set of polities would not have secured the loans from foreign, and especially English, investors at rates that enabled the United States to make large investments in industry, infrastructure, and territorial expansion through the Louisiana Purchase. A group of warring neighbors would not have created the navy that protected American ships from French and English depredations in the Caribbean and from pirates in the Mediterranean, or the army that conquered Mexico and the indigenous communities of the west, allowing Americans to realize their manifest destiny.[26]

There are many reasons to think, then, that the development gaps that separate the United States from Latin America today are as much contingent products of post-colonial political conflicts as the inescapable legacy of imperial institutions. If the Union had collapsed on any of the numerous occasions in which contemporaneous observers were concerned it might, the United States would have traced a post-independence path much more like the ones followed in Spanish America, to which I turn now.

6.4 THE PLATINE PROVINCES FAIL TO UNITE

Though I have not examined the Creole Revolution that began in Buenos Aires in 1810 and eventually liberated all of the Southern Cone in previous chapters, I briefly describe its history here as an instructive comparison with the cases we've already considered. *Porteños*, as the inhabitants of Buenos Aires are known, were amongst the noisiest Creoles in Spanish America on the eve of independence, issuing regular editorials, reports, and petitions proposing institutional and economic reforms of the Spanish system. Their precociousness in this respect was not random; Spain had made Buenos Aires the centerpiece of its efforts to revive the empire's profitability after years of steady decline. In 1776, it created the viceroyalty of the Río de la Plata, bringing a massive portion of South America – comprising present-day Argentina, Uruguay, Paraguay, and Bolivia – under the command of a bureaucracy headed in Buenos Aires, which also took over transport of Andean silver to the metropole. A relaxed trade policy permitted ranchers in the city's hinterlands to begin exporting hides and salted beef directly to other Spanish colonies, though trade with other European states and their colonies remained illicit.

These policies transformed Buenos Aires from a backwater into a major commercial hub, and for a time made its inhabitants rich. But Spain's entanglement in the Napoleonic Wars introduced serious strains, disrupting trade and transport even as the Royal Treasury became more desperate for colonial remittances. Though the city's best-connected merchants increased efforts to keep commerce within the empire's mercantilist channels, a new, reformist impulse emerged to argue for an entirely new, more modern conception of property and trade.[27]

The reformist spokesmen were Creole professionals with close ties to commerce, trained in traditional Spanish canon law but familiar with the new thinking of the French physiocrats and Italian and Scottish political economists. Writing on behalf of a group of Buenos Aires landowners,

Mariano Moreno sought to convince the viceroy that "with the Royal Treasury having run out of funds and resources,... and your Government without effective means of sustaining our security,... there is no other option than to grant English merchants permission to conduct business in this city."[28] The recommendation does not appear particularly radical in retrospect, especially given Spain's incapacity to engage in much commerce itself, but Moreno recognized that permitting English trade would represent an institutional sea change, from a colonial system designed to maximize transfers of wealth, mainly in precious metals, to the metropole, to one that permitted a broader, and freer trade primarily in agricultural products that would enrich both sovereign and subjects.

Moreno's argument on behalf of this reform closely resembles the critiques that other Americans lodged against European rule, highlighting the inequalities that empire imposed upon the colony's Creole elite. He gave "thanks to God that we do not live in those obscure centuries when, the interests of vassals being separate from those of their Lords, the stockpiling of treasures was esteemed even when it left the people in misery."[29] In defending a policy permitting Buenos Aires to trade with England, then, Moreno was recommending reform of precisely the mercantilist system that institutionalist accounts of the Americas' development gap have blamed for the relative underdevelopment of Spain's former colonies.

Though the viceroy did assent to Moreno's proposed revisions, the change in policy was as short-lived as the empire itself. On May 25, 1810, following news of serious setbacks to the Spanish resistance against Napoleon, a *Junta* of Buenos Aires notables assumed provisional authority over the viceroyalty of the Río de la Plata. Moreno, writing as their secretary, promised publicly to maintain "these possessions in the most constant fidelity and adherence to [their] much loved King, Sr. D. Fernando VII, and his legitimate successors,"[30] but he also circulated a private "Plan of Operations" for the government of what he called the "United Provinces of the Río de la Plata," specifying the measures that should be taken, "now that South America has proclaimed its independence, so that it can enjoy a just and complete liberty."[31]

Moreno's "Plan" is notorious for its frank Jacobinism, recommending that a network of spies be established to identify royalists and other dissenters, and calling upon revolutionaries to "cut off heads, spill blood, and sacrifice at any cost" for their cause.[32] But more notable for present purposes are the dimensions the "Plan" proposed for the territory of the United Provinces. Moreno detailed strategies for the liberation and annexation of the entirety of the former viceroyalty, including the regions then known as *Alto Peru* (present-day Bolivia) and the *Banda Oriental* (present-day Uruguay), both of which were then controlled by royalist forces. He also outlined a scheme to collaborate with England in the "dismemberment of [Portuguese] Brazil," proposing that the United Provinces and the United Kingdom should divide its territories between themselves.[33]

Like his colleagues throughout the hemisphere, Moreno defended this expansionist effort as a means of securing independence; the liberation and annexation of Brazil would deprive Portugal of a foothold that it might use to aid Spain in the reconquest of America after Napoleon's armies ended their occupation of the Iberian peninsula.[34] Though Moreno's plan was never carried out, it stands as a testament to the ubiquity of anti-imperial imperialism in the newly independent Americas, and provides us with new perspective on the alternative arrangements of political boundaries that were possible in this critical period of upheaval.

Other members of Moreno's circle emphasized the importance of maintaining the integrity of the former viceroyalty for the long-term economic prosperity of the United Provinces. In an article written in the midst of the May Revolution, on the "Causes of the destruction or the conservation and growth of nations," the lawyer, economist, and general Manuel Belgrano argued that "lack of religion, poor institutions and laws, abuses of governmental authority, and the corruption of traditions" were "no more than side-effects, or antecedents of … disunion," the true cause of national decline. Only a union of former colonies, Belgrano insisted, could remove them "from the state of oppression in which their enemies placed them, return them to their splendor, and keep them on the banks overlooking the void" of anarchy to which revolution exposed them.[35]

For the United Provinces' future economic prospects, it was particularly important to maintain control of *Alto Peru*, the primary source of silver in South America and the fount of Buenos Aires' late-colonial wealth. Belgrano personally led a liberating army into the Andes in 1812, but was unable to overcome local opponents of the revolution and their Spanish allies. Deprived of the income that *Alto Peru* had provided, the provisional government in Buenos Aires was forced to take on debt at ruinous rates of interest. Farmers, ranchers, traders, and textile manufacturers suffered from the loss of an important market for their goods, and worse was yet to come. The United Provinces lost control of Paraguay to a regional strongman, and became entangled in a prolonged, three-sided contest with local insurgents and Portuguese Brazil over the *Banda*

Oriental, eventually agreeing to a compromise that created the autonomous state of Uruguay. Finally, Buenos Aires faced a revolt of the interior
provinces of what would become Argentina, leading to a complete collapse of unified government in 1819.

The idea of a greater union emerged once more during a short period of
relative peace in the 1820s, under the influence of Bernardino Rivadavia.
Rivadavia had spent the first decade of the revolution overseas, as a representative of the United Provinces to the courts of England and France.
There he absorbed most of Europe's contemporary intellectual currents
and became a devotee of Jeremy Bentham. He returned to Buenos Aires
in 1821 to serve as minister of government and foreign affairs under
the province's governor, ready to apply utilitarian principles to a complete renovation of the country's political and economic institutions. In a
famous 1822 letter to Bentham, he described his efforts to eliminate

ancient abuses of all kinds found in our administration, and to prevent the establishing of others ... to favour the establishment of a national bank upon a solid
basis; to retrench (after having allowed them a just indemnity) those civilians and
military who incumber uselessly the state; to protect individual property; to cause
to be executed all public works of acknowledged utility; to protect commerce, the
sciences and the arts; [and] to promulgate a law ... that reduces very materially
the custom-house duties.[36]

Rivadavia and his supporters, known as *unitarios* for their commitment to strong, centralized government within the old viceregal territory, eventually managed to push through a new constitution, reuniting
the provinces and giving the president broad powers to oversee the
nation's economy. Rivadavia was the first man elected to the post, and
he announced an ambitious program of reforms. However, he was soon
overcome by a new wave of provincial opposition, and once again the
country descended into civil war.

Though almost entirely ineffective, Rivadavia's ideas still deserve
our attention, because they help us contemplate an important counterfactual developmental trajectory, providing a glimpse of the institutional reforms and economic growth the United Provinces might have
achieved, had they not been torn asunder by regional separatists and
reactionaries. In the Americas, the persistence of imperial institutions
after independence depended critically on the shape of the states that
eventually emerged from foreign struggles and civil wars. The United
States narrowly escaped the fate that the United Provinces suffered,
so the question must arise: Would we still be trying to explain the

Americas' development "gaps" if leaders like Moreno, Belgrano, and Rivadavia been able to pursue the reforms they recommended within the union they strove to create?

6.5 THE COLLAPSE OF GRAN COLOMBIA

As I showed at length in Chapter 4, Creole revolutionaries' efforts to forge a union of former colonies advanced much further in northern South America than in the south, under the tireless leadership of Simón Bolívar. From 1821, a single constitution governed greater Colombia (comprising present-day Colombia, Venezuela, Ecuador, and Panama), and Bolívar's efforts to add additional territories, including present-day Peru and Bolivia, to the union were well underway by the middle of the 1820s. As in the United States and in the United Provinces, though, regional resistance to the revolutionary regime arose almost as soon as independence had been won.

In Caracas, local elites grumbled about directives handed down from Bogotá, playing on Venezuelans' low opinion of their neighbors and resentments about the differential costs born during the struggle for independence. The large population of New Granada gave the province an overbearing influence in national policy making, providing ammunition for *federalistas*, who argued that the Union forged by the 1821 Constitution was overly centralized, demanding a looser arrangement that would allow *Caraqueños* more autonomy in the management of their affairs.

In Quito, elites also "had reason to 'feel [themselves] reduced from [their] ancient dignity' by the mere fact of joining ... Gran Colombia." The city lost control of its economic policy, and was thus unable to protect its profitable, but pre-industrial, textile trade from imported competition. The neighboring cities of Cuenca and Guayaquil, formerly subordinated to Quito, were made into separate and equal departmental capitals.

Even within the newly empowered national capital at Bogotá, politicians became disenchanted with Bolívar's endless military campaigning and his habitual invocations of extraconstitutional powers to invalidate lawfully enacted statutes. They were extremely wary of the Bolivian Constitution, which as we noted in Chapter 4, Bolívar hoped to apply throughout an enlarged Colombia or "Federation of the Andes." The institution of the life presidency aroused particularly sharp and perhaps inevitable resistance from ambitious elites who cherished their own designs on the new nation's highest office.[37]

In 1826, despite growing divisions, Colombia's Congress convened according to its constitutionally mandated schedule, and reelected Simón Bolívar as president and Francisco de Paula Santander as vice president. Perhaps as a result of their growing, but ultimately ill-founded, confidence in the union's stability, the Congress also initiated impeachment hearings against the country's most prominent provincial *caudillo*, José Antonio Páez, *Comandante General* of the Department of Venezuela. Páez had long since begun to use his post to acquire productive land on favorable terms and to extend his influence throughout the province through a policy of forced conscriptions into local militias, activities that provided the primary basis for his prosecution.

Páez at first appeared ready to submit to Congress's judgment, but then abruptly changed course and, allying himself with Caracas's radical federalists, denounced the impeachment proceedings as a *Granadiño* plot to reduce Venezuelans to submission. He appealed to Bolívar directly, asking for greater provincial autonomy as a means of protecting himself and his fellow "poor militiamen" from the "lawyers and merchants" who dominated the capital at Bogotá.[38] Instead, Bolívar marched a sizable force all the way back from Peru to confront the rebellion, which dissolved as soon as his troops crossed the border into Venezuela. Believing that he needed Páez to preserve stability in Venezuela, though, Bolívar granted the rebel leader and his followers a full amnesty, assurances that they would not be deprived of their offices or properties, and even promised to call a convention to consider reforms to the constitution, in direct contravention of the document's explicit provision against any reforms before 1831.

Of course, Bolívar had his own reasons for calling a constitutional convention, which he hoped would apply his Bolivian Constitution to all of Colombia. Bolívar's unconstitutional promise precipitated a final break with the more liberal factions in the capital, including Vice President Santander, who now openly announced his opposition to the Bolivian Constitution. Nonetheless, Bolívar's supporters in Congress pushed through a bill summoning a convention to meet in the city of Ocaña in 1828, setting the stage for a definitive contest between Colombia's nascent parties.

Throughout 1827 and 1828, problems multiplied: a Granadan military unit stationed in Lima mutinied in the name of the Constitution and imprisoned their Venezuelan officers; a group of elites in Guayaquil, Colombia's southernmost city, declared an intention to secede and join Peru; and in Cartagena, on the Carribbean coast, José Prudencio Padilla raised an uprising of the area's mixed-race population, reigniting Creoles' fear of *pardocracia*. In this context, elections for the Constitutional Convention returned a spare majority for Santander's federalist faction, which proposed to retain the 1821 Constitution in whole, save for Article 128, which gave the president extraordinary powers in the event of a crisis. To prevent a quorum, Bolívar's supporters left the convention, returned to Bogotá, and circulated a petition calling for Bolívar to take supreme authority, gaining five hundred signatures. This was followed by a plebiscite of thirty-one towns, all agreeing that Bolívar should be granted absolute power. He accepted dictatorial powers, with the title of Liberator President, on August 27, 1828.

Bolívar had finally become the tyrant his detractors had always accused him of being, but even plenary powers were not enough to hold the union together. Despite strict controls instituted on everything from the press to university curricula, conflicts with federalists continued. In Caracas, Páez went once again into revolt, this time declaring for total independence. On May 6, 1830, a Constituent Congress founded the sovereign republic of Venezuela. Quito followed soon after, creating the independent state of Ecuador on May 13. Unable and unwilling to mount a defense of Colombian unity on two fronts at once, the national Congress recognized both states, retaining the name Colombia now for only the former province of New Granada (present-day Colombia and Panama).[39]

As I noted in the preceding text, familiarity tends to grant the political boundaries of Andean South America a natural quality, but as the brief account indicates, the borders we know today were not inevitable. Rather, they are the results of the collapse of Gran Colombia, the contingent outcome of postcolonial conflicts that might have been resolved in ways that maintained the union, or even made Bolívar's larger visions of Spanish American unity a reality. Ultimately, though neither came to fruition, Bolívar's writings make it clear that institutional alternatives were available to Andean South Americans in the aftermath of their independence that might have positioned the region to assume a more prominent place in international affairs and global commerce.

6.6 THE DECLINE AND FALL OF THE FIRST MEXICAN REPUBLIC

In Mexico, as I've already noted in Chapter 5, party politics emerged from fierce competition for offices between two rival masonic lodges, the

centralist, establishmentarian Scottish Rite, or *Escoceses*, and the federalist, radical York Rite, or *Yorkinos*.[40] The Scottish Rite Lodge had been
formed by Spanish military officers around the turn of the century, and
still counted many Europeans amongst their membership. Though the
remaining population of Spaniards in independent Mexico was small –
estimates put the figure at around 10,000[41] – it was influential, occupying
the highest rungs of the former colony's merchant, military, and ecclesiastical hierarchies. Thus, the York Rite, newer and with closer ties to
the United States (through its ambassador Joel Poinsett, a Yorkino himself) than to the former metropole, made "Hispanophobia" into a wedge
issue, pushing, first in the press and then in Congress, for the expulsion
of Spaniards from government posts and then from the country itself.
Escoceses, who opposed the expulsion acts, were denounced for sympathies toward a fifth column ready to support a Spanish reconquest.[42]

   Mexico's first president, Guadalupe Victoria, began his term with broad
support from across the political spectrum, but by the end of his time in
office, his cabinet had been purged of *Escoceses* and their allies, including Lucas Alamán, who was forced out of his post as minister of interior
and foreign relations. In response to the purging of the cabinet, and generally fierce Masonic infighting, the vice president of the republic and
the Grand Master of the Scottish Rite Lodge, Nicolás Bravo, embarked
on an armed revolt, demanding the expulsion of the US ambassador, the
reinstatement of dismissed ministers, and the abolition of secret societies.
General Vicente Guerrero, an old insurgent, put down the rebellion with
very little bloodshed. Bravo was exiled and the Scottish Rite lodge was
thoroughly and permanently discredited, but tense partisanship persisted
into the presidential election of 1828.

   During the presidential campaigns, the radical wing of the Yorkino
faction supported Guerrero's candidacy, and for a time, it seemed he
would win the presidency in a landslide. But a more moderate group of
Yorkinos broke off, and, joining with former *Escoceses*, began to organize for the minister of war, Manuel Gómez Pedraza, a deputy to the
Cortes and formerly a strong supporter of Iturbide's imperial administration. As in the United States, Mexico's indirect election procedure for
the presidency produced confusion, with several legislators choosing to
depart from their constituents' preference, and give their votes to elect
Gómez Pedraza, who won, eleven states to nine. Before the results even
became widely known, Antonio López de Santa Anna, then governor
of Veracruz, declared a revolt and began marching toward the capital.
Within the city, Lorenzo de Zavala, governor of the state of Mexico,

organized a barracks rebellion and occupied the armory. Gómez Pedraza fled, and rioting took hold, with a mob destroying the Parián, a shopping district where many Spaniards still owned properties. The election results were annulled, and Guerrero became the second president of Mexico.[43]

The experience of 1828 initiated a troubling pattern in Mexican politics. Coups succeeded in dislodging the president in 1829, 1832, 1834, 1841, 1845, twice in 1846, 1853, and 1855.[44] This political instability, scholars have argued, was a direct cause of the country's slow economic growth during its early independence.[45] Deprived of revenues from previously profitable mining and agriculture, the federal government was unable to mount an effective response when both internal and external threats arose to tear apart the union.

The trouble was most acute in the *baldíos*, or vacant lands, which made up Mexico's northern territories. As I noted in Chapter 5, most of the north's Indigenous inhabitants felt as little loyalty for the new government in Mexico City as they had for its predecessor in Madrid, and the Anglo-American settlers that were illegally crossing the border with their slaves in tow hoped that the region would soon be sold to the United States. In the meantime, they gladly used the influence their money bought in the provincial government of Coahuila y Tejas to evade federal restrictions on immigration, land sales, and slavery. When Mexico adopted a more centralized constitution in 1836, and sent federal troops northward to secure the border, Anglo-American settlers rioted, forming an "Army of the People" and declaring the independence of the "Lone Star Republic" or Texas. None other than Lorenzo de Zavala, an instigator of Guerrero's fateful 1828 coup d'état, was elected Texas's first vice president.

Crippled by infighting, and suffering from increasingly straightened finances, Mexico failed to dislodge the separatists by force, but also refused to recognize Texan independence for almost a decade. In 1845, the stalemate was broken when the United States, over strenuous objections from its neighbor's ambassadors, annexed the territory. War between Mexico and the United States ensued, culminating in the US Army's occupation of Mexico City in 1847. The United States and Mexico signed the Treaty of Guadalupe Hidalgo on February 2, 1848. Under its terms, Mexico yielded the present-day states of Texas, California, Utah, New Mexico, and Arizona, as well as parts of Colorado and Wyoming – 55 percent of Mexican territory in all – in exchange for $15 million and debt relief.[46]

There is perhaps no crisper illustration of the effects of union's success in the north and its failure in the south than the outcome of the

Mexican–American War. On the eve of the Creole Revolutions, no one would have predicted that prosperous and populous New Spain, the "jewel in the crown" of the Spanish Empire, would one day be conquered by the collection of small colonies on North America's Atlantic seaboard. In the first decade of the nineteenth century, Spain collected an average of $20 million annually in tax receipts from New Spain, while in 1770 England collected only $150,000 from the thirteen colonies that would become the United States. In both countries, Creole revolutionaries built unions of former colonies after winning independence as a means of organizing their new nations' defense against external foes and internal instability, hoping to quickly surpass their imperial predecessors' capacity for revenue collection. In the United States, the federal government's tax receipts increased dramatically, but regional defiance impoverished the federal government of Mexico, so that by the middle of the nineteenth century a military contest between the two countries over land each sought to control was a foregone conclusion.[47]

6.7 CREOLE REVOLUTION AS TRAGEDY AND FARCE

With the rise of intra-Creole partisanship and political conflict, the framework I've developed throughout this book becomes less relevant to the explanation of ideological variation and change in the Americas. Once the revolutions were won and American independence consolidated, economic sectors, regional rivalries, and personal ambitions replaced the institutions of European imperialism as fundamental contextual determinants of political ideas. At a certain point in the history of each of the countries I've considered here, it becomes impossible to speak of a unified Creole interest or a distinctively Creole mode of political thought. Nonetheless, the foregoing studies can still help explain two interesting features of the Americas' early party politics.

First, because the Americas' first opposition parties were reacting to incumbents defending a common set of positions, their own ideologies converged on certain points, especially in regard to constitutional design. As I've shown, shared background problems inspired Alexander Hamilton, Simón Bolívar, and Lucas Alamán to defend political unions and presidentialist systems that they believed would insulate Creole rule in the Americas against both European reconquest and internal unrest. In a sense, they were too successful in the latter project, designing institutions that not only disenfranchised and excluded Indigenous and African Americans, but diminished the capacity of provincial

Creoles to influence policy making and thus exciting opposition parties that viewed the destruction of unions, decentralized federalism, and legislative supremacy as means of regaining influence within independent states.

For some prominent opposition leaders, adopting these positions meant abandoning earlier views. In the United States, James Madison reversed himself completely, from arguing for a federal veto on state laws during the Constitutional Convention of 1787 to insisting, by 1798, that the state governments had the right to "interpose" their own authority against that of the federal government, unilaterally halting the execution of federal laws that by their lights appeared to exceed the Constitution's delegations of authority.[48] In Colombia, Vice President Francisco de Paula Santander followed a similar trajectory, dispensing with his long-held preference for centralism, which at times had led him into fierce conflicts with prominent federalists, to recommend "federalism as the only recourse left to us to save the national liberties" in 1827.[49] In Mexico, provincial politicians sought autonomy for state governments where their influence was more concentrated, and nationally prominent ideologues switched positions on the issue depending on which faction controlled the capital.[50]

In the United States, this constitutional debate overlapped with a foreign policy division, as Thomas Jefferson's Republican Party increasingly came to define itself by its support for the French cause in Europe, and to cast the Federalists' policy of neutrality as sympathetic, not only to the English side of the conflict with France, but to the English model of political organization.[51] In private correspondence, Jefferson described waiting "with great anxiety for the firm establishment of the new government in France, being perfectly convinced that if it takes place there, it [would] spread sooner or later" not only "all over Europe" but to the United States as well, which he worried was "falling back to that kind of Half-way house, the English constitution."[52] Across the hemisphere, opposition parties attacked powerful executives as "monarchical" and bicameral legislatures as "aristocratic," demanding constitutional reforms that they claimed would more fully realize the revolutions' calls for popular sovereignty.[53]

However forceful and frequent their invocations of the "rights of man," though, these opposition parties' objections to hierarchy and exclusivity were sharply circumscribed by their attitudes toward African and Indigenous Americans. This is a second sense in which the studies in the preceding text can help explain early partisan politics in the Americas. As Creole

Revolutionary unity dissolved, and intra-Creole ideological divisions emerged, Creoles' institutional position continued to influence their political thought by structuring the boundaries of possible disagreement between contending factions. While rising opposition parties rejected the models of anti-imperial imperialism that Hamilton, Bolívar, and Alamán developed, they did not seek, generally, to undermine Creole rule in the Americas, or, in particular, to abolish African slavery or protect Indigenous communities from expropriation and genocide. Indeed, as Gordon Wood notes, in the United States,

the new Republican party seemed to be exclusively a Southern party, with most of its leaders, including Jefferson and Madison, being members of the slaveholding aristocracy.... Yet paradoxically these slaveholding aristocratic leaders of the Republican party were the most fervent supporters of liberty, equality, and popular republican government in the nation.[54]

Again, it is not difficult to find analogies throughout the hemisphere. The federalist radicals of Caracas also "abandoned liberal orthodoxy" in their "indifference and even hostility toward the abolition of slavery,"[55] while in Mexico, self-declared liberals "recoiled from egalitarianism ... when confronted with the 'social question'" presented by the desperate conditions in which most of the country's non-Creole inhabitants lived.[56]

The frontier territories of the western United States, northern Mexico, and eastern Venezuela were all hotbeds of early opposition politics, as Creole settlers resisted incumbent administrations' attempts to regulate the terms on which they interacted with indigenous peoples and acquired indigenous lands.[57] Argentina provides perhaps the clearest illustration of this phenomenon of frontier opposition. Both of the region's primary federalist leaders, José Gervasio Artigas, who led Uruguay out of the United Provinces, and Juan Manuel de Rosas, whose rebellion precipitated the union's final collapse, learned their military trade as Indian fighters.[58] The freedom that these and other Creole frontiersmen demanded from their national governments was, in part, the freedom to oppress and expropriate indigenous Americans with impunity. Thus, early opposition political thought presents contradictions similar to those of the Creole Revolutions: Here once again, fervent invocations of revolutionary patriotism, popular sovereignty, and individual rights are paired with even more desperate defenses of imperial social hierarchies.

In the opening lines of a famous essay, Karl Marx amended a Hegelian adage to read, "all great world-historic facts and personages appear, so to speak, twice ... the first time as tragedy, the second time as farce."[59] The post-colonial conflicts that brought an end to the Americas' Creole Revolutions conformed to this pattern. Hamilton, Bolívar, and Alamán were classic tragic heroes, reaching extraordinary heights before excessive ambitions brought them crashing down to earth. The very institutions they proposed as means of consolidating independence and pushing the Americas into the vanguard of global history alienated fellow Creole patriots, aroused organized dissent, and ultimately undid their schemes, with particularly tragic consequences for Spanish America, where the collapse of unions constructed by Creole Revolutionaries initiated patterns of political instability and economic underdevelopment that persist even to the present day.

Meanwhile, the Creole opposition parties that were the agents of this undoing cast their eventual triumphs as new revolutions,[60] fresh declarations of independence not from European metropoles but from American imperial aspirants. Their principled stand for popular sovereignty was farcically hollow, however, emptied of any critical force by racial exceptions and exclusions even more radical than the ones embraced by the original ideologues of Creole Revolution.

7

Conclusion: From the Creole Revolutions to Our Americas

Though neither the success of the union of former colonies forged in Philadelphia, nor the failure of counterparts constructed in Mexico City, Bogota, and Buenos Aires was inevitable, this point of divergence in the Americas' political development was extremely consequential. Over the course of the nineteenth century, the United States reaped the advantages of its union, which not only helped insulate the new nation from foreign aggression and domestic unrest, but also facilitated rapid economic development and allowed the United States to project its influence over an ever-larger portion of the hemisphere. First the continent of North America, then the Caribbean and Central America, and finally many parts of South America fell under the formal control or informal hegemony of a rising industrial and military superpower. The absence of political unity in these regions – an absence attributable to the postcolonial conflicts recounted in the last chapter – impeded their own economic development and prevented their inhabitants from mounting an effective resistance to the United States' repeated incursions.

The different paths the Americas followed after independence changed the background problems that American political thinkers addressed as the century progressed. The United States' earliest interventions in Spanish American affairs were justified in terms familiar from the ideology of Creole Revolution, evincing the same contradictory mix of anti-imperial and imperial commitments.[1] In his 1823 message to Congress, in response to rumors that the allied Catholic monarchies of Europe were discussing plans to reconquer Spanish America, President James Monroe warned that his administration would "consider any attempt on [the Holy Allies'] part to extend their system to any portion of this hemisphere as dangerous to our peace and safety."² Though he stopped short of committing the United States to liberating the Americas from European rule, Monroe offered a strong statement of solidarity with the newly independent republics of the south, while also asserting a sphere of influence for the United States coextensive with the Americas.

As the United States' wealth and military might increased, Monroe's successors invoked his "doctrine" to defend expansions of territory and influence increasingly disconnected from any credible anti-imperial agenda. In 1845, President James K. Polk used his own annual message to describe the proposed annexation of Texas as "a peaceful and effective rebuke" to French and British efforts to assure that the breakaway Mexican province retained its independence. "From this example," he crowed, "European Governments may learn how vain diplomatic arts and intrigues must ever prove upon this continent against that system of self-government which seems natural to our soil, and which will ever resist foreign interference."³ Polk expressed no sympathy for Mexico's claim to its northern territory, massing forces along the border in preparation for an inter-American conflict that would permit the United States to realize its manifest destiny at its neighbor's expense. As Reginald Horsman has shown, by mid-century, both the United States' aggressive territorial expansion and its determination not to incorporate all of Mexico into the union were underwritten by a belief in the racial superiority of the north's Anglo-Saxon inhabitants, vis-à-vis the "mongrel race" that made up Mexico's population.⁴

The United States finally fulfilled Alexander Hamilton's call to "aim at an ascendance in American affairs" by defeating Spain in war and turning its strategically located former colonies on the islands of Cuba, Puerto Rico, Guam, and the Philippines into protectorates and unincorporated territories. Reflecting on these actions in his 1904 annual message, President Theodore Roosevelt conceded that "there are points of resemblance in our work to the work which is being done by the British in India and Egypt, by the French in Algiers, by the Dutch in Java, by the Russians in Turkestan, [and] by the Japanese in Formosa." But Roosevelt insisted that US foreign policy still pursued the distinctive ideals of its independence movement. He returned to and elaborated upon the Monroe Doctrine, arguing that the chronic political instability and frequent financial crises that plagued Spain's former American colonies presented open invitations to European intervention. Maintaining the independence of the New World would require the United States to exercise "an international police power" throughout its hemisphere. In countries like Cuba and the Philippines, whose inhabitants were, in Roosevelt's analysis, "utterly incapable of existing in independence at all or of building up a civilization of their own," the United States might need to shoulder the burden of a prolonged civilizing mission, "endeavoring to develop the natives themselves so that they shall take an ever-increasing share in their own government."[5] Here, alongside a still-more radical sense of Anglo-Saxon supremacy, the anti-imperial imperialism characteristic of the Creole Revolutions still echoes, informing Roosevelt's efforts to define and defend the new kind of empire the United States had become by the turn of the twentieth century.

Spanish America's distinctive political and economic development after independence fostered a distinctive evolution of anti-imperial imperialism. In 1891, the Cuban poet, patriot, and political thinker José Martí published a famous essay in a Spanish-language New York newspaper. From a young age, Martí was intensely devoted to the liberation of his native island, one of the last redoubts of Spanish rule in the Americas. His essay was addressed to his fellow Americans, entreating their support for a struggle that had, for decades, seemed always on the cusp of victory, only to fall short again and again. Martí's account of the obstacles encountered in the effort to achieve and sustain independence struck a familiar chord, denouncing would-be statesmen wedded to foreign models of government:

The good governor in America is not he who knows how to govern the Germans or the French, but he who knows what elements make up his own country, and how to bring them together ... using methods and institutions originating within the country itself.... Government is nothing more than the balance of the country's natural elements.[6]

Like his predecessors, who elaborated the ideology of Creole Revolution described in this book, Martí sought solutions to the unique philosophical and political problems presented by the Americas' histories of imperial rule and racially stratified societies. For Martí, as for his mentors, the institutional ideal to be pursued was "balance," a system capable of inducing post-colonial populations with opposed interests to pursue common goods and collective liberty.

However, the half-century that separated Martí from the first generation of Creole revolutionaries had introduced new hazards, as well. Alongside imperial powers across the Atlantic and restless masses within its borders, "Our America is running another risk that does not come from itself," he wrote, "but from the difference in origins, methods, and interests between the two parts of the continent." He warned that "the time is near when an enterprising and vigorous people, who are ignorant and disdainful of Our America, will approach and demand a close relationship."[7] Here, the wariness we noted in Simón Bolívar and Lucas Alamán's attitudes toward the United States has blossomed into outright opposition.

Born just after the Mexican–American War, witness to the first Yankee filibusters in Central America, and well aware of North Americans' longstanding designs on Cuba, Martí was under no illusions regarding his island's colossal neighbor. He understood that achieving independence would entail not only extricating Cuba from the Spanish Empire, and not only pacifying its diverse castes and classes, but also resisting formal or informal conquest by the United States. His essay's title – *Nuestra América*, or "Our America" – underlined the disparities of wealth and power that defined the New World's new reality, describing rivalries internal to a hemisphere that, as this book has argued, once faced common dilemmas.

The threat posed by the United States forced Creole political thinkers like Martí to confront the contradictions that characterized their predecessors' ideas, and, in some cases, to forge a common cause with their countries' Indigenous and African-descended inhabitants. As North American ideologues drew on pseudoscientific doctrines of Anglo-Saxon supremacy to defend the United States' expanding hegemony, Martí insisted that in his America, "There are no racial animosities, because there are no races.... The soul, equal and eternal, emanates from bodies of various shapes and colors. He who foments and spreads opposition and hatred between the races sins against humanity." Martí made this rejection of scientific racism central to his case for Cuban independence, casting his island's simultaneous struggle against Spain and the United States as an effort to abolish the colonial hierarchies that had survived the Creole Revolutions.[8]

But while Martí encountered a profoundly changed hemisphere, and introduced important changes into Latin American political thought, he remained attached to his predecessors' efforts to unite Spain's former American colonies, presenting this old idea as an indispensable means of overcoming new threats to independence.

We should not hide the patent truth, that the problem can be resolved, for the peace of centuries to come, by appropriate study, and by tacit and immediate union of the continental spirit. With a single voice the hymn is already being sung; the present generation is carrying industrious America along a road laid down by their sublime fathers; from the Río Grande to the Straits of Magellan, the Great Semí, astride his condor, is sowing the seed of a new America throughout the Latin nations of the continent and the sorrowful islands of the sea![9]

Though Martí's own generation would come up as short in its efforts to unite Spanish America as the previous one, their ideal would not die. "Our America" stands at the origins of a tradition that persisted in Latin American political thought throughout the twentieth century and up to the present day. Here, the anti-imperial imperialism of the Creole Revolutions, and in particular, the Creole revolutionaries' attachment to union as a means of consolidating independence, is combined with a defensive opposition to the foreign policy of the United States, and a newfound pride in Latin America's racially mixed population. Drawing inspiration from Martí and the original Creole revolutionaries, these latter-day Latin American intellectuals present their own nations as the true heirs to a revolutionary American project that, in its pursuit of power and wealth, and its attachment to racial hierarchy, the United States had failed to fulfill.[10]

The account I've provided here should give pause to those who would canonize the ideologists of Creole Revolution, revealing the particularity of their political thinking, the specificity of the conjuncture in which it arose, and the partiality of the interests it served. When we recognize that preserving and justifying hierarchy was the aim of our Creole founders, we will be less enchanted by their ideas and thus less apt to be permanently enchained by their institutions. We will be better prepared to propose and undertake reforms that can contribute to dismantling the persistent inequalities of our American societies.

But we can also find grounds for hope in the Creole Revolutions, regaining a vision of once-possible histories of the hemisphere that can help us imagine real alternatives to its current dispositions of authority and divisions of wealth. The ideology of Creole Revolution, for all its internal contradictions, emancipated the New World once; perhaps it can still inspire those who would seek to emancipate it once again.

Notes

1 John Stuart Mill, "On Liberty," in Stefan Collini, ed., *On Liberty and Other Writings* (Cambridge: Cambridge University Press, 1989), 4.

1. INTRODUCTION: THE IDEAS OF AMERICAN
INDEPENDENCE IN COMPARATIVE PERSPECTIVE

1 John Adams to James Lloyd, Quincy, March 27 and 30, 1815, in Charles Francis Adams, ed., *The Works of John Adams, Second President of the United States*, 10 Vols. (Boston: Little, Brown, and Co., 1856), X, 144–145.

2 Ibid., 149. The instance for Adams' reflections on Spanish America was apparently his correspondent's interest in the efforts of the Venezuelan patriot Francisco Miranda to obtain the US support for an assault on then Spanish South America, efforts which Adams rebuffed but which were much more warmly received by Alexander Hamilton. I return to these interesting events in Chapter 3.

3 Edmund Burke, *Reflections on the Revolution in France* [1790], Conor Cruise O'Brien, ed. (London: Penguin Books, 2004); and Alexis de Tocqueville, *Democracy in America* [1835]. Trans. Arthur Goldhammer (New York: The Library of America, 2004).

4 R. R. Palmer, *The Age of Democratic Revolutions: A Political History of Europe and America, 1760–1800*, 2 Vols. (Princeton: Princeton University Press, 1959 and 1964); Eric Hobsbawm, *The Age of Revolution, 1789–1848* (London: Wiedenfeld & Nicolson, 1962); Barrington Moore, Jr., *The Social Origins of Dictatorship and Democracy: Lord and Peasant in the Making of the Modern World* (Boston: Beacon Press, 1966); and Perry Anderson, "The Notion of a Bourgeois Revolution" [1976] in *English Questions* (London: Verso, 1992), 105–118.

5 Caroline Robbins, *The Eighteenth-Century Commonwealthman: Studies in the Transmission, Development, and Circumstance of English Liberal*

Thought from the Restoration of Charles II Until the War with the Thirteen Colonies [1959] (Indianapolis: Liberty Fund, 2004); Bernard Bailyn, *The Ideological Origins of the American Revolution,* enlarged edition (Cambridge, MA: Harvard University Press, 1992); Hannah Arendt, *On Revolution* [1963] (New York: Penguin Books, 2006); Gordon S. Wood, *The Creation of the American Republic, 1776–1787* (New York: W. W. Norton, 1972) and *The Radicalism of the American Revolution* (New York: Vintage Books, 1993); J. G. A Pocock, *The Machiavellian Moment: Florentine Political Thought and the Atlantic Republican Tradition* (Princeton: Princeton University Press, 1975); John M. Murrin, "The Great Inversion, or Court versus Country: A Comparison of the Revolution Settlements in England (1688–1721) and America (1776–1816)," in J. G. A. Pocock, ed., *Three British Revolutions: 1641, 1688, 1776* (Princeton: Princeton University Press, 1980), 368–453; and Paul Anthony Rahe, *Republics Ancient and Modern: Classical Republicanism and the American Revolution* (Chapel Hill: University of North Carolina Press, 1992).

6 Louis Hartz, *The Liberal Tradition in America: An Interpretation of American Political Thought since the Revolution* (New York: Harcourt, Brace, 1955). For the wide range of theories offered as explanations for the United States' uniqueness, vis-à-vis Europe, see also: Seymour Martin Lipset, *American Exceptionalism: A Double-Edged Sword* (New York: W. W. Norton, 1996); and Deborah Madsen, *American Exceptionalism* (Edinburgh: Edinburgh University Press, 1998).

7 In recent decades, two important exceptions to this rule have appeared. First, a revisionist current in Latin American, and particularly Mexican, intellectual history has scholars tracing the connections between the French Revolution, Spanish liberalism, and the Spanish Americas' independence movements; see François-Xavier Guerra, "Revolución Francesa y Revoluciones Hispánicas: Una Relación Compleja," in *Modernidad e Independencias: Ensayos Sobre Las Revoluciones Hispánicas,* revised and expanded edition (Madrid: Ediciones Encuentro, 2009), 35–77; Jaime E. Rodríguez O., "Two Revolutions: France 1789 and Mexico 1810," *The Americas,* Vol. 47, No. 2 (Oct. 1990), 161–176; and *The Independence of Spanish America* (Cambridge: Cambridge University Press, 1998); and Roberto Breña, *El Primer Liberalismo Español y los Procesos de Emancipación de América, 1808–1824: Una Revisión Historiográfica del Liberalismo Hispánico* (Mexico City: El Colegio de México, 2006). Second, "Atlantic" and "Global" historians have included Latin America in their description of the "seismic waves [that] traveled through the Atlantic world after 1775, linking uprisings on either side." See Wim Klooster, *Revolutions in the Atlantic World: A Comparative History* (New York: New York University Press, 2009), 158 for the quoted portion; Lester D. Langley, *The Americas in the Age of Revolution* (New Haven: Yale University Press, 1996); John H. Elliott, *Empires of the Atlantic World: Britain and Spain in America, 1492–1830* (New Haven: Yale University Press, 2006); and the essays collected in David Armitage and Sanjay Subrahmanyam, eds., *The Age of Revolutions in Global Context, c. 1760–1840* (Houndsmills: Palgrave MacMillan, 2010).

8 Spanish America's nationalism is early, here, in relation to emergence of nationalism as an organizing force of politics throughout the rest of the world, particularly in the twentieth-century decolonization movements of Asia and Africa. See the citations in notes 9 and 10. For the term "incipient nationalism" and the best-known English-language exposition of this thesis, see John Lynch, *The Spanish American Revolutions, 1808–1826*, 2nd edition (New York: W. W. Norton and Co., 1973), 24–37. See also: D. A. Brading, *The First America: The Spanish Monarchy, Creole Patriots, and the Liberal State, 1492–1867* (Cambridge: Cambridge University Press, 1991); and the essays assembled in Nicholas Canny and Anthony Pagden, eds., *Colonial Identity in the Atlantic World, 1500–1800* (Princeton: Princeton University Press, 1987).

9 For a defense of the practice of adopting Latin America's present-day nations as units of analysis, which has the virtue of recognizing the problem involved, see James Mahoney, *Colonialism and Postcolonial Development: Spanish America in Comparative Perspective* (Cambridge: Cambridge University Press, 2010), 38–42.

10 Benedict Anderson, *Imagined Communities: Reflections on the Origin and Spread of Nationalism*, revised edition (London: Verso, 1991), 46.

11 Arturo Escobar, *Encountering Development: The Making and Unmaking of the Third World* (Princeton: Princeton University Press, 1995); Walter D. Mignolo, *The Darker Side of Western Modernity: Global Futures, Decolonial Options* (Durham: Duke University Press, 2011); Mabel Moraña, Enrique Dussel, and Carlos A. Jáuregui, eds., *Coloniality at Large: Latin America and the Postcolonial Debate* (Durham: Duke University Press, 2008). Though a few notable works analyze the independence movement of the United States using something like the incipient nationalism thesis, they have done so in order to emphasize the qualities that made it fundamentally exceptional – and ultimately exceptionally successful – amongst the larger group of nations that emerged from imperial rule. See: Louis Hartz, ed., *The Founding of New Societies: Studies in the History of the United States, Latin America, South Africa, Canada, and Australia* (New York: Harcourt, Brace, 1964); Thomas C. Barrow, "The American Revolution as a Colonial War for Independence," *The William and Mary Quarterly*, Third Series, Vol. 25, No. 3 (July 1968), 452–464; Seymour Martin Lipset, *The First New Nation: The United States in Historical and Comparative Perspective* (New York: W. W. Norton, 1979).

12 For example, in his magisterial intellectual history of the United States' early republican period, Gordon Wood notes at several points that the British North American Revolution "was no simple colonial rebellion against English imperialism," each time emphasizing the relatively greater importance of republican ideals in the founders' motivations. Wood, *Creation of the American Republic*, 91, 128, and 395. Scholars of Spanish American independence who have adopted the age of revolutions thesis display the same tendency. Jaime Rodríguez, for example, goes even further than Wood, insisting that "Spanish America was not a colony of Spain," nor Spain itself an "Empire," and that consequently the Spanish American revolutions are better understood as a "civil war," a conflict over the future of the

Spanish monarchy, than an anticolonial or anti-imperial conflict. Rodríguez, *Independence of Spanish America*, xii, 107–168.

13 As Rogers Smith has argued, these accounts "falter because they center on relationships among a minority of Americans – white men, largely of northern European ancestry – analyzed in terms of categories derived from the hierarchy of political and economic status such men held in Europe.... But the relative egalitarianism that prevailed among white men [in the early United States] ... was surrounded by an array of fixed, ascriptive hierarchies, all largely unchallenged by the leading American revolutionaries." *Civic Ideals: Conflicting Visions of Citizenship in U.S. History* (New Haven: Yale University Press, 1997), 17.

14 It has proven difficult to find evidence of nationalist identities in the documentary residues of the independence movements, and as a result, in recent years, historians of Spanish America have rejected both the incipient nationalism thesis, and related attempts to draw comparisons between American independence and later struggles for national liberation. See Rodríguez, *Independence of Spanish America* and Tomás Pérez Vejo, *Elegía Criolla: Una Reinterpretación de las Guerras de Independencia Hispano Americanas* (Mexico City: Tusquets, 2010). Claudio Lomnitz "Nationalism as a Practical System: Benedict Anderson's Theory of Nationalism from the Vantage Point of Spanish America," in *Deep Mexico, Silent Mexico* (Minneapolis: University of Minnesota Press, 2001), 3–34; Eric Van Young, "The Limits of Atlantic-World Nationalism in a Revolutionary Age: Imagined Communities and Lived Communities in Mexico, 1810–1821," in Joseph Esherick, Hasan Kayalı, and Eric Van Young, eds., *Empire to Nation: Historical Perspectives on the Making of the Modern World* (Oxford: Rowman and Littlefield, 2006); and the essays collected in Sara Castro-Klarén and John Charles Chasteen, eds., *Beyond Imagined Communities: Reading and Writing the Nation in Nineteenth-Century Latin America* (Baltimore: Johns Hopkins University Press, 2003).

15 Diego von Vacano, *The Color of Citizenship: Race, Modernity, and Latin American/Hispanic Political Thought* (New York: Oxford University Press, 2012).

16 For useful overviews of the interdisciplinary literature on "settler colonialism," see: Caroline Elkins and Susan Pedersen, "Settler Colonialism: A Concept and Its Uses," in Elkins and Pedersen, eds., *Settler Colonialism in the Twentieth Century* (New York: Routledge, 2005); Lorenzo Veracini, *Settler Colonialism: A Theoretical Overview* (London: Palgrave Macillan, 2010), 17–18; Veracini, "'Settler Colonialism': Career of a Concept," *The Journal of Imperial and Commonwealth History*, Vol. 41, No. 2 (2013), 313–333. A few notable works have used the concept of settler colonialism to interpret the independence movement of the United States, and even to frame interesting comparisons between the American Revolution and other "settler revolts" in Australia, New Zealand, South Africa, French Algeria, and Israel/Palestine. See, especially, Aziz Rana, *The Two Faces of American Freedom* (Cambridge, MA: Harvard University Press, 2010). Unfortunately, the literature on settler colonialism has focused largely on the former British empire, to the exclusion of Latin America, sometimes even suggesting that

settler colonialism was a uniquely British form of imperialism. See, for example, James Belich, *Replenishing the Earth: The Settler Revolution and the Rise of the Anglo World, 1783–1939* (Oxford: Oxford University Press, 2009). Notably, some of the early literature on the subject broke with this tendency: Louis Hartz, ed., *The Founding of New Societies: Studies in the History of the United States, Latin America, South Africa, Canada, and Australia* (New York: Harcourt Brace, 1964); Donald Denoon, *Settler Capitalism: The Dynamics of Dependent Development in the Southern Hemisphere* (Oxford: Clarendon Press, 1983); and Immanuel Wallerstein, *The Modern World System, Volume III: The Second Era of Great Expansion of the Capitalist World-Economy, 1730s–1840s*, revised and expanded edition (Berkeley: University of California Press, 2011), 191–256.

17 See, for this use of the term in political theory: Jane Anna Gordon and Neil Roberts, eds., *Creolizing Rousseau* (London: Rowman and Littlefield, 2015).

18 "Creole, n. and adj." OED Online. December 2015. Oxford University Press. www.oed.com/view/Entry/44229?redirectedFrom=creole& (accessed March 3, 2016).

19 See especially the work of the Venezuelan historian Germán Carrera Damas, who places the fact that the protagonists of the independence movements were Creoles at the center of his important studies: *Venezuela: Proyecto Nacional y Poder Social* (Barcelona: Editorial Crítica, 1986); and *De la Dificultad de Ser Criollo* (Caracas: Grijalbo, 1993).

20 Anderson, *Imagined Communities*, 47–65.

21 See citations at note 16.

22 Anderson, *Imagined Communities*, 57.

23 Interested readers can consult C. L. R. James's classic *The Black Jacobins: Toussaint L'Ouverture and the San Domingo Revolution* (London: Secker and Warburg, 1938); and the essays assembled in David P. Geggus, ed., *The Impact of the Haitian Revolution in the Atlantic World* (Columbia: University of South Carolina Press, 2001).

24 Illustrative examples include Roxanne L. Euben, *Enemy in the Mirror: Islamic Fundamentalism and the Limits of Modern Rationalism* (Princeton: Princeton University Press, 1999); Andrew F. March, *Islam and Liberal Citizenship: The Search for an Overlapping Consensus* (Oxford: Oxford University Press, 2009); Leigh Jenco, *Making the Political: Founding and Action in the Political Theory of Zhang Shizhao* (Cambridge: Cambridge University Press, 2010); Karuna Mantena, "Another Realism: The Politics of Gandhian Nonviolence," *American Political Science Review*, Vol. 106, No. 2 (May 2012), 455–470; and Farah Godrej, *Cosmopolitan Political Thought: Method, Practice, Discipline* (Oxford: Oxford University Press, 2014). For a recent review, see Diego von Vacano, "The Scope of Comparative Political Theory," *Annual Review of Political Science*, Vol. 18 (2015), 465–480.

25 For "scholarly" and "engaged" comparative political theory, see Andrew F. March, "What Is Comparative Political Theory?" *The Review of Politics*, Vol. 71 (2009), 531–65. For alternative accounts of the field's normative importance, see Anthony J. Parel, "The Comparative Study of Political Philosophy," in Parel and Ronald C. Keith, eds., *Comparative Political Philosophy: Studies*

under the Upas Tree, 2nd edition (Lanham: Lexington Books, 2003); Fred Dallmayr, "Beyond Monologue: For a Comparative Political Theory," *Perspectives on Politics*, Vol. 2, No. 2 (June 2004), 249–257; Leigh Kathryn Jenco, "'What Does Heaven Ever Say?': A Methods-Centered Approach to Cross-Cultural Engagement," *The American Political Science Review*, Vol. 101, No. 4 (Nov. 2007), 741–755; Farah Godrej, "Towards a Cosmopolitan Political Thought: The Hermeneutics of Interpreting the Other," *Polity*, Vol. 41, No. 2 (Apr. 2009), 135–165; Michael Freeden and Andrew Vincent, "Introduction: The Study of Comparative Political Thought," in Freeden and Vincent, eds., *Comparative Political Thought: Theorizing Practices* (Oxford: Routledge, 2013); and Melissa S. Williams and Mark E. Warren, "A Democratic Case for Comparative Political Theory," *Political Theory*, Vol. 42, No. 1 (Jan. 2014), 26–47.

26 For important exceptions see: Courtney Jung, *The Moral Force of Indigenous Politics: Critical Liberalism and the Zapatistas* (Cambridge: Cambridge University Press, 2008); Paulina Ochoa Espejo, "Paradoxes of Popular Sovereignty: A View from Spanish America," *The Journal of Politics*, Vol. 74, No. 4 (2012), 1053–1065; von Vacano, *Color of Citizenship*; Angélica M. Bernal, "The Meaning and Perils of Presidential Refounding in Latin America" *Constellations* vol. 21, no. 4 (Dec. 2014), 440–456; Katherine Gordy, *Living Ideology in Cuba: Socialism in Principle and Practice* (Ann Arbor: University of Michigan Press, 2015); Juliet Hooker, *Theorizing Race in the Americas: Douglass, Sarmiento, Du Bois, and Vasconcelos* (Oxford: Oxford University Press, 2017).

27 Though the language of causality here is new, the connection suggested between political ideas and background "problems" is not. See: R. G. Collingwood. *An Autobiography* (Oxford: Clarendon Press, 1939), 29–43; Quentin Skinner, "The Rise of, Challenge to and Prospects for a Collingwoodian Approach to the History of Political Thought," in Dario Castiglione and Iain Hampsher-Monk, eds., *The History of Political Thought in National Context* (Cambridge: Cambridge University Press, 2001), 175–188; David Scott, *Conscripts of Modernity: The Tragedy of Colonial Enlightenment* (Durham: Duke University Press, 2004), 3–8; Michael Rosen, "The History of Ideas as Philosophy and History," *History of Political Thought*, Vol. 22, No. 4 (Winter 2011), 691–720; and Mark Bevir, *The Logic of the History of Ideas* (Cambridge: Cambridge University Press, 1999), 221–264.

28 Jack Knight, *Institutions and Social Conflict* (Cambridge: Cambridge University Press, 1992).

29 James Mahoney, *Colonialism and Postcolonial Development: Spanish America in Comparative Perspective* (Cambridge: Cambridge University Press, 2010), 17.

30 The effects of "context," in this sense, on political ideas has traditionally been emphasized in studies influenced by Karl Marx's account of "ideology." I shall elaborate upon the account of ideology underlying this study in the next chapter. For other attempts to adapt Marx's concept to the study of political thought, see Richard Ashcraft, "On the Problem of Method and the Nature of Political Theory," *Political Theory*, Vol. 3, No. 1 (Feb. 1975),

5–25; "Political Theory and the Problem of Ideology," *The Journal of Politics*, Vol. 42, No. 3 (Aug. 1980), 687–705; "Marx and Political Theory," *Comparative Studies in Society and History*, Vol. 26, No. 4 (Oct. 1984), 637–671; Neal Wood, "The Social History of Political Theory," *Political Theory*, Vol. 6, No. 3 (Aug. 1978), 345–367; Ellen Meiksins Wood and Neal Wood, "Socrates and Democracy: A Reply to Gregory Vlastos," *Political Theory*, Vol. 14, No. 1 (Feb. 1986), 55–82; and Ellen Meiksins Wood, *Citizens to Lords: A Social History of Western Political Thought from Antiquity to the Middle Ages* (London: Verso, 2008), 1–16.

31 See Mark M. Blyth, "Any More Bright Ideas? The Ideational Turn of Comparative Political Economy," *Comparative Politics*, Vol. 29, No. 2 (Jan. 1997), 229–250; Robert C. Lieberman, "Ideas, Institutions, and Political Order: Explaining Political Change," *American Political Science Review*, Vol. 96, No. 4 (Dec. 2002), 697–712; Daniel Béland and Robert Henry Cox, eds., *Ideas and Politics in Social Science Research* (New York: Oxford University Press, 2011).

32 Quentin Skinner, *Liberty before Liberalism* (Cambridge: Cambridge University Press, 1998), 101. See also Skinner, *Visions of Politics, Volume 1: Regarding Method* (Cambridge: Cambridge University Press, 2002), especially 103–127; and J. G. A. Pocock, *Virtue, Commerce, and History: Essays on Political Thought and History, Chiefly in the Eighteenth Century* (Cambridge: Cambridge University Press, 1985), 1–34.

33 Bevir, *Logic of the History of Ideas*, 174–220.

34 Michael Freeden, *Ideologies and Political Theory: A Conceptual Approach* (Oxford: Oxford University Press, 1996). Notably, Freeden has also proposed an approach to "comparative political thought" focused on the analysis of "combinations of conceptual arrangements." See "The Comparative Study of Political Thinking," *Journal of Political Ideologies*, Vol. 12, No. 1 (Feb. 2007), 1–9; and Freeden and Vincent, eds., *Comparative Political Thought*, 1–22.

35 John Stuart Mill, "A System of Logic, Raciocinative and Inductive," in J. M. Robson, ed., *The Collected Works of John Stuart Mill* (Toronto: University of Toronto Press, 1974), VII, especially 388–390. The literature on the relevance of Mill's methods to social science is, predictably, huge. For influential discussions, see Charles C. Ragin, *The Comparative Method: Moving beyond Qualitative and Quantitative Strategies* (Berkeley: University of California Press, 1987); and Gary King, Robert O. Keohane, and Sidney Verba, *Designing Social Inquiry: Scientific Inference in Qualitative Research* (Princeton: Princeton University Press, 1994).

36 The method of agreement suffers from certain difficulties, but serves its purpose well in this application. For the danger of biased inference associated with "selecting on the dependent variable," see Barbara Geddes, "How the Cases You Choose Affect the Answers You Get: Selection Bias in Comparative Politics," *Political Analysis*, Vol. 2, No. 1 (1990), 131–150; and, for a more general critique, see Stanley Lieberson, "Small N's and Big Conclusions: An Examination of the Reasoning in Comparative Studies Based on a Small Number of Cases," *Social Forces*, Vol. 70, No. 2 (Dec. 1991), 307–320.

Though I cannot claim to have completely avoided the problems identified in these important articles, I seek to mitigate their effects by providing as much evidence as possible for the general interpretation of Creole political thinking that I propose within each individual case study, a method akin to "process tracing." See Andrew Bennett, "Process Tracing and Causal Inference," in Henry E. Brady and David Collier, eds., *Rethinking Social Inquiry: Diverse Tools, Shared Standards*, 2nd edition (Lanham: Rowman and Littlefield, 2010), 207–220; and James Mahoney, "The Logic of Process Tracing Tests in the Social Sciences," *Sociological Methods Research*, Vol. 41, No. 4 (Nov. 2012), 570–597.

37　For a portrait of the United States on the eve of independence, see Gordon Wood, *The Radicalism of the American Revolution* (New York: Vintage Books, 1993), 11–94. For Venezuela, see P. Michael McKinley, *Pre-Revolutionary Caracas: Politics, Economy, and Society, 1777–1811* (Cambridge: Cambridge University Press, 1985). For Mexico, see D. A. Brading, *Miners and Merchants in Bourbon Mexico, 1763–1810* (Cambridge: Cambridge University Press, 1971). For a comparative discussion of variation in the forms of imperial rule established by the British and Spanish in the Americas, see J. H. Elliott, *Empires of the Atlantic World: Britain and Spain in America, 1492–1830* (New Haven: Yale University Press, 2006); and James Mahoney, *Colonialism and Postcolonial Development: Spanish America in Comparative Perspective* (Cambridge: Cambridge University Press, 2010).

38　For Hamilton's biography, see Ron Chernow, *Alexander Hamilton* (New York: Penguin, 2004). For Bolívar, see John Lynch, *Simón Bolívar: A Life* (New Haven: Yale University Press, 2006). Unfortunately, we still lack a biography of Alamán in English, though Stanley C. Green, *The Mexican Republic: The First Decade, 1823–1832* (Pittsburgh: University of Pittsburgh Press, 1987) provides most of the relevant facts. Spanish readers can consult José C. Valadés, *Alamán: Estadista e Historiador* (Mexico City: José Porrua e Hijos, 1938).

2. THE IDEOLOGY OF CREOLE REVOLUTION

1　Simón Bolívar, "Contestación de un Americano Meridional ...," Kingston, September 6, 1815, in Vicente Lecuna and Esther Barret de Nazaris, eds., *Obras Completas*, 2nd edition, 3 Vols. (Havana: Editorial Lex, 1950), Vol. I, 166.

2　For a systematic presentation of these variations, see John Gerring, "Ideology: A Definitional Analysis," *Political Research Quarterly*, Vol. 50, No. 4 (Dec. 1997), 957–994.

3　See Kathleen Knight, "Transformations of the Concept of Ideology in the Twentieth Century," *American Political Science Review*, Vol. 100, No. 4, (Nov. 2006), 619–626; Keith T. Poole and Howard Rosenthal, *Ideology and Congress* (New Brunswick: Transaction Publishers, 2007); Philip E. Converse, "The Nature of Belief Systems in Mass Publics," in David E. Apter, ed., *Ideology and Discontent* (London: Free Press of Glencoe, 1964), 206–261.

4 See Steven B. Smith, *Reading Leo Strauss: Politics, Philosophy, Judaism* (Chicago: Chicago University Press, 2006), 13. In his influential work, Michael Freeden disavows any pejorative intention in his use of the term "ideology," but does acknowledge that ideologies "will be more hasty [than political philosophies] in ending discussion if rational persuasion proves inconclusive. They will be less thorough in pursuing the detailed implications of their arguments. After all, ideologies have to deliver conceptual social maps and political decisions, and they have to do so in language accessible to the masses as well as the intellectuals, to amateur as well as professional thinkers." *Ideologies and Political Theory: A Conceptual Approach* (Oxford: Oxford University Press, 1996), 30.

5 For historical overviews of the concept of ideology that foreground Marx's contributions, see Jorge Larraín, *The Concept of Ideology* (Athens: University of Georgia Press, 1979); and Terry Eagleton, *Ideology: An Introduction*, updated edition (London: Verso, 2007). For analytical treatments that have informed the account I develop here, see G. A. Cohen, *Karl Marx's Theory of History: A Defence*, expanded edition (Oxford: Oxford University Press, 2000), 216–248; and Jon Elster, *Making Sense of Marx* (Cambridge: Cambridge University Press, 1985), 459–510.

6 Karl Marx and Friedrich Engels, "The German Ideology: Part I" [1845–6], in Robert C. Tucker, ed., *The Marx-Engels Reader*, 2nd edition (New York: W. W. Norton, 1978), 154–155.

7 Karl Marx, *A Contribution to the Critique of Political Economy* [1859], in Tucker, ed., *Marx-Engels Reader*, 4. On the stabilizing functions of institutional and ideological superstructures, see also: Louis Althusser, "Ideology and Ideological State Apparatuses (Notes Toward an Investigation)," in *Lenin and Philosophy and Other Essays*. Trans. Ben Brewster (New York: Monthly Review Press, 1971), 127–186.

8 Marx, "The German Ideology," in Tucker, ed., *Marx-Engels Reader*, 174. It bears noting that there is some debate amongst Marx's many interpreters as to whether, for Marx, the term "ideology" should be reserved as a description exclusively for the efforts of a dominant class to obscure the conditions of its rule, or rather, as I've suggested here, that the arguments dominated classes make in the course of challenging the rule of dominant classes can also be usefully regarded as ideologies. See Larraín, *Concept of Ideology*, 74–77.

9 Marx, "The German Ideology," in Tucker, ed., *Marx-Engels Reader*, 160–161.

10 Richard Ashcraft "Political Theory and the Problem of Ideology," *The Journal of Politics*, Vol. 42, No. 3 (Aug. 1980), 692.

11 Calls for the replacement of Marx's original, economic theories of class-conflict with more flexible, institutional ones has been common amongst comparative political scientists and historical sociologists. See Frank Parkin, *Marxism and Class Theory: A Bourgeois Critique* (New York: Columbia University Press, 1979) and Theda Skocpol, "Bringing the State Back In: Strategies of Analysis in Current Research," in Peter Evans, Dietrich Rueschemeyer, and Theda Skocpol, eds., *Bringing the State Back In* (Cambridge: Cambridge University Press, 1985), 3–38. The approach

I adopt here has been inspired, particularly, by the "distributional approach" to historical institutionalism described by James Mahoney. See: *Colonialism and Postcolonial Development: Spanish America in Comparative Perspective* (Cambridge: Cambridge University Press, 2010), 14–17.

12 Jack P. Greene, *Peripheries and Center: Constitutional Development in the Extended Polities of the British Empire and the United State, 1607–1788* (Athens: University of Georgia Press, 1986), 67–68.

13 Karl Marx and Friedrich Engels, "Manifesto of the Communist Party" [1848], in Tucker, ed., *Marx-Engels Reader*, 473–474.

14 Anderson, *Imagined Communities*, 58.

15 For a very useful comparative survey, interested readers may consult J. H. Elliott, *Empires of the Atlantic World: Britain and Spain in America, 1492–1830* (New Haven: Yale University Press, 2006), 153–183.

16 Tulio Halperín-Donghi, *Politics, Economics, and Society in Argentina in the Revolutionary Period*. Trans. Richard Southern (Cambridge: Cambridge University Press, 1975), 42. For an interesting account of the gradual replacement, within Britain's North American colonies, of a system in which "Anglo settlers – simply by virtue of being settlers – were not clearly demarcated as a qualitatively separate group" with one that "marked a fundamental divide between free Anglo subjects and mere imperial subjects." See: Aziz Rana, *The Two Faces of American Freedom* (Cambridge, MA: Harvard University Press, 2010), 37–62.

17 Edmund S. Morgan, *American Slavery, American Freedom: The Ordeal of Colonial Virginia* (New York: W. W. Norton, 1975), 295–362.

18 Rogers M. Smith, *Civic Ideals: Conflicting Visions of Citizenship in U.S. History* (New Haven: Yale University Press, 1997), 64.

19 Magnus Mörner, "Economic Factors and Stratification in Colonial Spanish America with Special Regard to Elites," *The Hispanic American Historical Review*, Vol. 63, No. 2 (May 1983), 335–369; Jorge Cañizares-Esguerra, "Racial, Religious, and Civic Creole Identity in Colonial Spanish America," *American Literary History*, Vol. 17, No. 3 (Fall 2005), 420–437; Ana Luz Ramírez Zavala, "Indio/Indígena, 1750–1850," *Historia Mexicana*, Vol. 60, No. 3 (Jan.–Mar. 2011), 1643–1681.

20 See, for the conflicts attendant upon the "New Laws" of 1542, Lewis Hanke, *The Spanish Struggle for Justice in the Conquest of America* (Philadelphia: University of Pennsylvania Press, 1949); and, for the *cédula de gracias a sacar* offered in 1795: Marixa Lasso, *Myths of Harmony: Race and Republicanism during the Age of Revolution, Columbia 1795–1831* (Pittsburgh: University of Pittsburgh Press, 2007), 19–33.

21 John H. Elliott, "A Europe of Composite Monarchies," *Past and Present*, Vol. 137 (Nov. 1992), 48–71.

22 The British American Revolution has been extensively analyzed in these terms. See Greene, *Peripheries and Center*; Greene, *Negotiated Authorities: Essays in Colonial Political and Constitutional History* (Charlottesville: University of Virginia Press, 1994); Mary Sarah Bilder, *The Transatlantic Constitution: Colonial Legal Culture and the Empire* (Cambridge, MA: Harvard University Press, 2004); Daniel J. Hulsebosch,

Constituting Empire: New York and the Transformation of Constitutionalism in the Atlantic World, 1664–1830 (Chapel Hill: University of North Carolina Press, 2005); Allison L. LaCroix, *The Ideological Origins of American Federalism* (Cambridge, MA: Harvard University Press, 2011). The literature on Spanish America is somewhat more spare, though much has been inspired of late by the pioneering analysis of François-Xavier Guerra, *Modernidad e Independencias: Ensayos sobre las Revoluciones Hispánicas* (Madrid: Ediciones Encuentro, 2009), 78–112.

23 David C. Hendrickson, *Peace Pact: The Lost World of the American Founding* (Lawrence: University Press of Kansas, 2003), 70–74; Mark A. Burkholder and D. S. Chandler, *From Impotence to Authority: The Spanish Crown and the American Audiencias, 1687–1808* (Columbia: University of Missouri Press, 1977).

24 Erik Olin Wright, *Classes* (London: Verso, 1985), 43–44. See also Wright, ed., *The Debate on Classes* (London: Verso, 1989).

25 See Colin M. MacLachlan, *Spain's Empire in the New World: The Role of Ideas in Institutional and Social Change* (Berkeley: University of California Press, 1988); John Lynch, *Bourbon Spain, 1700–1808* (Oxford: Basil Blackwell Press, 1989); and Guillermo Pérez Sarrión, ed., *Más Estado y Más Mercado: Absolutismo y Economía en la España del Siglo XVIII* (Madrid: Sílex Ediciones, 2011).

26 Rodríguez, *Independence of Spanish America*, 19; emphasis in the original.

27 See citations in note 26, and, for Lucas Alamán's nuanced contemporary impression of the Bourbon reforms, see Chapter 5.

28 See, for a fascinating empirical study of Creole representation in the *Audiencias*, Burkholder and Chandler, *From Impotence to Authority*, and more generally Guerra, *Modernidad e Independencias*, 78–112.

29 Jack P. Greene, "The Seven Years' War and the American Revolution: The Causal Relationship Reconsidered," in Peter Marshall and Glyn Williams, eds., *The British Atlantic Empire before the American Revolution* (London: Frank Cass & Co., 1980), 101.

30 Ibid., 92.

31 Edmund S. Morgan and Helen M. Morgan, *The Stamp Act Crisis: Prologue to Revolution* (Chapel Hill: University of North Carolina Press, 1953).

32 For Buffon, De Pauw, and Raynal, see Antonello Gerbi, *The Dispute of the New World: The History of a Polemic, 1750–1900* [1955]. Trans. Jeremy Moyle (Pittsburgh: University of Pittsburgh Press, 1973) and Jorge Canizares-Esguerra, *How to Write the History of the New World: Histories, Epistomologies, and Identities in the Eighteenth Century Atlantic World* (Palo Alto: Stanford University Press, 2001). For Diderot, see Sankar Muthu, *Enlightenment against Empire* (Princeton: Princeton University Press, 2003), 72–121.

33 Gerbi, *Dispute of the New World*, 74–79; Anthony Pagden, *Spanish Imperialism and the Political Imagination* (New Haven: Yale University Press, 1990), 13–36 and *Lords of All the World: Ideologies of Empire in Spain, Britain, and France, c. 1500–c.1800* (New Haven: Yale University Press, 1995), 63–102; Thomas McCarthy, *Race, Empire, and the Idea of*

Human Development (Cambridge: Cambridge University Press, 2009); Brett Bowden, *Empire of Civilization: Evolution of an Imperial Idea* (Chicago: University of Chicago Press, 2009).

34 Gerbi, *Dispute of the New World*, 194–233, 240–268, 289–324; Pagden, *Spanish Imperialism*, 91–116.

35 For the contributions of the debate on New World degeneration to the development of "Creole patriotism," see David Brading's magisterial *The First America: The Spanish Monarchy, Creole Patriots, and the Liberal State, 1492–1867* (Cambridge: Cambridge University Press, 1991), 422–464. For an interesting collection of comparative essays, see Nicholas Canny and Anthony Pagden, eds., *Colonial Identity in the Atlantic World, 1500–1800* (Princeton: Princeton University Press, 1989).

36 See Lewis Hanke, *The Spanish Struggle for Justice in the Conquest of America* (Philadelphia: University of Pennsylvania Press, 1949).

37 Stuart Banner, *How the Indians Lost their Land: Law and Power on the Frontier* (Cambridge, MA: Harvard University Press, 2005), 85–111. See also Jack M. Sosin, *Whitehall and the Wilderness: The Middle West in British Colonial Policy, 1760–1775* (Lincoln: University of Nebraska Press, 1961).

38 The seventh such abuse cited reads, "He has endeavoured to prevent the population of these States; for that purpose obstructing the Laws for Naturalization of Foreigners; refusing to pass others to encourage their migrations hither, and raising the conditions of new Appropriations of Lands." For the connection between the Proclamation of 1763 and the independence movement, see also Rana, *Two Faces of American Freedom*, 64–69.

39 John W. Compton and Karen Orren "Political Theory in Institutional Context: The Case of Patriot Royalism," *American Political Thought*, Vol. 3, No. 1 (Spring 2014), 10. See Morgan and Morgan's classic account in *The Stamp Act Crisis*, and, for a recent argument that the "constitutional positions taken by patriot writers … were primarily the products of debate," as opposed to the "institutional peculiarities of political life on the periphery of an Atlantic empire," see Eric Nelson, "Patriot Royalism: The Stuart Monarchy in American Political Thought, 1769–75," *The William and Mary Quarterly*, Vol. 68, No. 4 (Oct. 2011), 533–572; and Nelson, *The Royalist Revolution: Monarchy and the American Founding* (Cambridge, MA: Harvard University Press, 2014).

40 Xavier-Guerra, *Modernidad e Independencias*, 148–188; Rodríguez, *Independence of Spanish America*, 49–74; Roberto Breña, "Relevancia y Contexto del Bienio 1808–1810: El Ciclo Revolucionario Hispánico: Puntos de Referencia e Historiografía Contemporánea," in Roberto Breña, ed., *En el Umbral de las Revoluciones Hispánicas: El Bienio 1808–1810* (Mexico City: El Colegio de México, 2010).

41 Michael W. Doyle, *Empires* (Ithaca: Cornell University Press, 1986), 19.

42 Pagden, *Lords of All the World*, 12–23.

43 Hannah Arendt, "On Violence," in *Crises of the Republic* (New York: Harcourt Brace, 1972), 153; and *The Origins of Totalitarianism* (New York: Harcourt Brace, 1968), 123–302. See also Karuna Mantena, "Genealogies of Catastrophe: Arendt on the Logic and Legacy of Imperialism," in Seyla

Benhabib, ed., *Politics in Dark Times: Encounters with Hannah Arendt* (Cambridge: Cambridge University Press, 2010), 83–112.

44 Jane Burbank and Frederick Cooper, *Empires in World History: Power and the Politics of Difference* (Princeton: Princeton University Press, 2010), 8.

45 See also Lauren Benton and Richard J. Ross, "Empires and Legal Pluralism: Jurisdiction, Sovereignty, and Political Imagination in the Early Modern World," in Benton and Ross, eds., *Legal Pluralism and Empires, 1500–1850* (New York: New York University Press, 2013), 1–17.

46 See Bernard Bailyn, *The Ideological Origins of the American Revolution*, enlarged edition (Cambridge, MA: Harvard University Press, 1992), 160–229; Luis Villoro, *El Proceso Ideológico de la Revolución de Independencia* (Mexico City: Fondo de Cultura Económica, 2010), 132–172.

47 Smith, *Civic Ideals*, 70–86.

48 Thomas Jefferson, "A Summary View of the Rights of British America," 1774, in Merrill D. Peterson, ed., *Writings* (New York: The Library of America, 1984), 105–106.

49 As Barbara Arneil has shown, Jefferson's account of how the conquest and settlement of the New World invested the conquerors and settlers, and their Creole descendants, with new rights was inspired in part by John Locke's famous chapter *"On Property"* in the second *Treatise on Government*; see *John Locke and America: The Defence of English Colonialism* (Oxford: Oxford University Press, 1996), 190.

50 Jefferson, "A Summary View," in Peterson, ed., *Writings* 108, 112, 121–122.

51 Camilo Torres, "Memorial de Agravios," 1809 in José Luis Romero and Luis Alberto Romero, eds., *Pensamiento Político de la Emancipación*, 2 Vols. (Caracas: Biblioteca Ayacucho, 1977), I, 27.

52 Ibid., I, 29.

53 Simon Collier, *Ideas and Politics of Chilean Independence, 1808–1833* (Cambridge: Cambridge University Press, 1967), 6–7.

54 Simón Bolívar, "Al Congreso Constituyente de Bolivia," 1826, in *El Pensamiento Constitucional Hispanoamericano hasta 1830* (Caracas: Academia Nacional de la Historia, 1961), I, 172.

55 I owe this observation to Roberto Gargarella, *Los Fundamentos Legales de la Desigualdad: El Constitucionalismo en América, 1776–1860* (Madrid: Siglo XXI, 2005), 167–169.

56 My use of the term is inspired by David C. Hendrickson, *Peace Pact: The Lost World of the American Founding* (Lawrence: University Press of Kansas, 2003), 14–23.

57 For this definition of presidentialism, see Juan J. Linz, "The Perils of Presidentialism," *Journal of Democracy*, Vol. 1, No. 1 (Winter 1990), 51–69.

58 David Bushnell, "Los Usos del Modelo: La Generación de la Independencia y la Imagen de Norteamérica," *Revista de Historia de América*, No. 82 (July–Dec. 1976), 7–27; Robert J. Kolesar, "North American Constitutionalism and Spanish America," in George Athan Billias, ed., *American Constitutionalism Abroad* (New York: Greenwood Press, 1990). Jonathan M. Miller, "The Authority of a Foreign Talisman: A Study of U.S. Constitutional Practice as Authority in Nineteenth Century Argentina and the Argentine Elite's Leap

of Faith," *American University Law Review*, Vol. 46, No. 5 (June 1997), 1483–1572.

59 David Pantoja Morán, *El Supremo Poder Conservador: El Diseño Institucional en las Primeras Constituciones Mexicanas* (Mexico City: El Colegio de México, 2005), 13–50.

60 In his celebrated 1852 *Bases y puntos de partida para la organización política de la República Arjentina*, the Argentinian constitutional thinker Juan Bautista Alberdi insisted that "The Federation of the United States of North America is not a simple federation but a mixed federation [*federación compuesta*], a unitary and centralized federation, as we would say here; and it is precisely for this reason that it has survived up to the present day.... As is known, it was preceded by a Confederation, or a pure and simple federation, which in eight years brought those states to the edge of ruin. For their part, the Argentine federalists in 1826 poorly understood the system that they hoped to apply to their country.... They confused the Confederation of the United States of 9 July 1778 with the Constitution of the United States of America, promulgated by Washington on 17 September 1787. Between these two systems, nonetheless, there is this difference: the first ruined the United States in eight years, and the other restored it to life and guided it to the opulence that it now enjoys." *Obras Completas de J.B. Alberdi*, 8 Vols. (Buenos Aires: Imprenta de La Tribuna Nacional, 1886), III, 468–469.

61 Alexander Hamilton, "Federalist No. 11," November 24, 1787, in Terence Ball, ed., *The Federalist, with Letters of "Brutus"* (Cambridge: Cambridge University Press, 2003), 52.

62 James Madison, "Federalist No. 10," November 22, 1787, in Ball, ed., *The Federalist*, 40–46.

63 Simón Bolívar, "Convocatoria del Congreso de Panamá," Lima, December 7, 1824, in Bolívar, *Doctrina*, 211.

64 Bolívar, "Un Pensamiento sobre el Congreso de Panamá," undated, in Bolívar, *Doctrina*, 260–261.

65 See Guerra, *Modernidad e Independencias*, 19–54; Klooster, *Revolutions of the Atlantic World*; Carrera Damas, *Venezuela*, 80; David Geggus, ed., *The Impact of the Haitian Revolution in the Atlantic World* (Columbia: University of South Carolina Press, 2001); Ada Ferrer, *Freedom's Mirror: Cuba and Haiti in the Age of Revolution* (Cambridge: Cambridge University Press, 2014).

66 Lucas Alamán, "Examen Imparcial de La Administración del General Vicepresidente Don Anastasio Bustamante, Con Observaciones Generales sobre el Estado Presente de la Republica y Consecuencias que éste debe Producir," 1834, in José Antonio Aguilar Rivera, ed., *Examen Imparcial de la Administración de Bustamante* (Mexico City: Consejo Nacional para la Cultura y las Artes, 2008), 201.

67 John Adams, *A Defense of the Constitutions of Government of the United States of America*, 1787, in Adams, ed., *The Works of John Adams*, IV, 271-VI, 223.

68 Alexander Hamilton, "Federalist No. 70," March 15, 1788, in Ball, ed., *Federalist Papers*, 341–342.

69 Alexander Hamilton, "Speech in the Constitutional Convention on a Plan of Government" (version recorded by James Madison), June 18, 1787, in Joanne B. Freeman, ed., *Writings* (New York: Library of America, 2001), 157.

70 J. M. Gutiérrez Estrada, "Carta Dirigida al Excelentísimo Señor Presidente de la República," Tacubaya, August 25, 1840, in Elías José Palti, *La Política del Disenso: La Polémica en torno al Monarquismo (México, 1848–1850) … y las Aporías del Liberalismo* (Mexico City: Fondo de Cultura Económica, 1998), 61–71.

71 See Hendrickson, *Peace Pact*, 274.

72 For the period's imperial entanglements, see especially William W. Kaufmann, *British Policy and the Independence of Latin America, 1804–1828* (New Haven: Yale University Press, 1951); Thomas Bender, *A Nation amongst Nations* (New York: Hill and Wang, 2006), 61–115; Jeremy Adelman, *Sovereignty and Revolution in the Iberian Atlantic* (Princeton: Princeton University Press, 2006); Carlos Marichal, *Bankruptcy of Empire: Mexican Silver and the Wars between Spain, Britain, and France, 1760–1810* (Cambridge: Cambridge University Press, 2007); Eliga Gould, *Among the Powers of the Earth: The American Revolution and the Making of a New World Empire* (Cambridge, MA: Harvard University Press, 2012); Susanna Hecht, *The Scramble for the Amazon and the Lost Paradise of Euclides da Cunha* (Chicago: University of Chicago Press, 2013); and Matthew Brown and Gabrielle Paquette, "Between the Age of Atlantic Revolutions and the Age of Empire," in Brown and Pacquette, eds., *Connections after Colonialism: Europe and Latin America in the 1820s* (Tuscaloosa: University of Alabama Press, 2013), 1–28.

73 George Washington, "Farewell Address," 1796. Available at http://avalon .law.yale.edu/ 18th_century /washing.asp (accessed October 20, 2014).

74 "Acta de Independencia de las Provincias Unidas en Sud-América," July 9, 1816 in Romero and Romero, eds., *Pensamiento Político de la Emancipación*, II, 205.

75 Halperín-Donghi, *Argentina in the Revolutionary Period*, 239–307.

76 Mark R. Anderson, *The Battle for the Fourteenth Colony: America's War of Liberation in Canada, 1774–1776* (Lebanon: University Press of New England, 2013).

77 Timothy E. Anna, *The Mexican Empire of Iturbide* (Lincoln: University of Nebraska Press, 1990).

78 David Bushnell, *The Santander Regime in Gran Colombia* (Newark: University of Delaware Press, 1954).

79 Thomas Jefferson to James Monroe, Washington, November 24, 1801, in Petersen, ed., *Writings*, 1097.

80 Mariano Moreno, "Plan de Operaciones," undated, in Gustavo Varela, ed., *Plan de Operaciones y Otros Escritos* (La Plata: Terramar 2007), 38, 81.

81 Bolívar to Francisco de Paula Santander, Lima, March 12–14, 1823. *Archivo del Libertador*, Document No. 7256.

82 Bolívar to Antonio José de Sucre, Magdalena, May 12, 1826, and Bolívar to Antonio Gutiérrez de la Fuente, Magdalena, May 12, 1826, *Archivo* Documents Nos. 1087 and 1089. See Chapter 4, Section 4.5, for a detailed analysis of these plans.

83 William Appleman Williams, *The Tragedy of American Diplomacy* (New York: W. W. Norton, 1972), 19–57. See also Jay Sexton, *The Monroe Doctrine: Empire and Nation in Nineteenth-Century America* (New York: Hill and Wang, 2011), 5–8.

84 Gerbi, *Dispute of the New World*, 194–288; David A. Brading, *The First America: The Spanish Monarchy, Creole Patriots, and the Liberal State, 1492–1867* (Cambridge: Cambridge University Press, 1991).

85 Thomas Paine, "Common Sense," 1776, in Bruce Kucklick, ed., *Political Writings* (Cambridge: Cambridge University Press, 2000), 44.

86 Cited in Collier, *Chilean Independence*, 240.

87 For a comprehensive overview, see Jennifer Pitts, "Political Theory of Empire and Imperialism," *Annual Review of Political Science*, No. 13 (2010), 211–235.

88 Uday Singh Mehta, *Liberalism and Empire: A Study in Nineteenth-Century British Liberal Thought* (Chicago: University of Chicago Press, 1999), 46.

89 Pitts, "Political Theory of Empire and Imperialism," 216. Here, I should note, Pitts very neatly describes a position that she does not herself endorse, but actually refutes, in her own important contribution to the literature on liberal imperialism; see *A Turn to Empire: The Rise of Imperial Liberalism in Britain and France* (Princeton: Princeton University Press, 2005), 4.

3. ALEXANDER HAMILTON IN HEMISPHERIC PERSPECTIVE

1 The chapter's title, and this terminology, were inspired by Jack P. Greene, "Hemispheric History and Atlantic History," in Jack P. Greene and Philip D. Morgan, eds., *Atlantic History: A Critical Appraisal* (Oxford: Oxford University Press, 2009), 299–315.

2 The two poles of this argument are well represented by John Burgess's 1891 *Political Science and Comparative Constitutional Law* (Boston: Ginn & Company) and Woodrow Wilson's 1885 *Congressional Government* (Boston: Houghton, Mifflin, and Co.). For a discussion, see Karen Orren and Stephen Skowronek, *The Search for American Political Development* (Cambridge: Cambridge University Press, 2004), 37–45.

3 Charles A. Beard, *An Economic Interpretation of the Constitution of the United States* [1913] (New York: The Free Press, 1986), 325, 27–50.

4 For the emergence of the category "bourgeois revolution" amongst Beard's contemporaries, see Perry Anderson, "The Notion of a Bourgeois Revolution" [1976], in *English Questions* (London: Verso, 1992), 105–118.

5 See Clyde W. Barrow, *More Than Just a Historian: The Political and Economic Thought of Charles A. Beard* (New Brunswick: Transaction Publishers, 2000); and Max M. Edling, "Introduction to the Centennial Symposium on Charles Beard's *Economic Interpretation*," *American Political Thought*, Vol. 2, No. 2 (Fall 2013), 259–263.

6 Robert E. Brown, *Charles Beard and the Constitution: A Critical Analysis of "An Economic Interpretation of the Constitution"* (Princeton: Princeton University Press, 1956); Forrest McDonald, *We the People: The Economic*

Origins of the Constitution (Chicago: University of Chicago Press, 1958). See also Robert A. McGuire and Robert L. Ohsfeldt, "Economic Interests and the American Constitution: A Qualitative Rehabilitation of Charles A. Beard," *Journal of Economic History*, Vol. 44, No. 2 (1984), 487–519; and Woody Holton, "The Readers Reports Are In," *American Political Thought*, Vol. 2, No. 2 (Fall 2013), 264–273.

7 Louis Hartz, *The Liberal Tradition in America: An Interpretation of American Political Thought since the Revolution* (New York: Harcourt, 1991), 4, 10, 67–86.

8 See Mark Hulliung, "Louis Hartz, His Day and Ours," in Hulliung, ed., *The American Liberal Tradition Reconsidered: The Contested Legacy of Louis Hartz* (Lawrence: University Press of Kansas, 2010), 11–52.

9 See, especially, Bernard Bailyn, *The Ideological Origins of the American Revolution* [1967], enlarged edition (Cambridge, MA: Harvard University Press, 1992); Gordon Wood, *The Creation of the American Republic, 1776–1787* [1969], reprint (Chapel Hill: University of North Carolina Press, 1998); and J. G. A. Pocock, *The Machiavellian Moment: Florentine Political Thought and the Atlantic Republican Tradition* (Princeton: Princeton University Press, 1975). Two essays by Robert Shalhope are particularly helpful in understanding the historiographic stakes of this intervention: Robert Shalhope, "Toward a Republican Synthesis: The Emergence of an Understanding of Republicanism in American Historiography," *William and Mary Quarterly*, No. 29 (1972), 49–80; and Shalhope, "Republicanism and Early American Historiography," *William and Mary Quarterly*, No. 39 (1982), 334–356. For a critique, see Isaac Kramnick, "Republican Revisionism Revisited," *The American Historical Review*, Vol. 87, No. 3 (June 1982), 629–664. Pocock elaborated on his disagreement with Hartz and latter-day Hartzians in a response to critics of the *Machiavellian Moment*; see "Between Gog and Magog: The Republican Thesis and the Ideologia Americana," *Journal of the History of Ideas*, Vol. 48, No. 2 (Apr.–June 1987), 325–346.

10 Gordon S. Wood, "Rhetoric and Reality in the American Revolution," *The William and Mary Quarterly*, Vol. 23, No. 1 (Jan. 1966), 3–32; and Wood, "Interests and Disinterestedness in the Making of the Constitution," in Richard Beeman, Stephen Botein, and Edward C. Carter II, eds., *Beyond Confederation: Origins of the Constitution and American National Identity* (Chapel Hill: University of North Carolina Press, 1987), 69–109. See also Alan Gibson, "Louis Hartz and Study of the American Founding: The Search for New Fundamental Categories," in Hulliung, ed., *American Liberal Tradition Reconsidered*, 159–160.

11 Gordon Wood, *Empire of Liberty: A History of the Early Republic, 1789–1815* (Oxford: Oxford University Press, 2009), 29.

12 Wood, "Interests and Disinterestedness," 72.

13 Wood, *Empire of Liberty*, 102–103.

14 David C. Hendrickson, *Peace Pact: The Lost World of the American Founding* (Lawrence: University Press of Kansas, 2003), 281–297; Max M. Edling, "Charles Beard and the Internationalist Interpretation of the American Founding," *American Political Thought*, Vol. 2, No. 2 (Fall 2013), 292–301.

15 Peter S. Onuf and Nicholas G. Onuf, *Federal Union, Modern World: The Law of Nations in an Age of Revolutions, 1776–1814* (Madison: Madison House, 1993); Linda Colley, "The Difficulties of Empire: Present, Past and Future," *Historical Research*, Vol. 79, No. 1 (Winter 1998), 367–382; David Armitage, *The Declaration of Independence: A Global History* (Cambridge, MA: Harvard University Press, 2007); Eliga Gould, *Among the Powers of the Earth: The American Revolution and the Making of a New World Empire* (Cambridge, MA: Harvard University Press, 2012).

16 Hendrickson, *Peace Pact*; Daniel H. Deudney, "The Philadelphian System: Sovereignty, Arms Control, and Balance of Power in the American States-Union, circa 1787–1861," *International Organization*, Vol. 49, No. 2 (Mar. 1995), 191–228; Max M. Edling, *A Revolution in Favor of Government: Origins of the U.S. Constitution and the Making of the American State* (Oxford: Oxford University Press, 2003; Daniel J. Hulsebosch, *Constituting Empire: New York and the Transformation of Constitutionalism in the Atlantic World, 1664–1830* (Chapel Hill: University of North Carolina Press, 2005); David M. Golove and Daniel J. Hulsebosch, "A Civilized Nation: The Early American Constitution, the Law of Nations, and the Pursuit of International Recognition," *New York University Law Review*, Vol. 85 (Oct. 2010), 932–1066.

17 Max M. Edling, *A Hercules in the Cradle: War, Money, and the American State, 1783–1867* (Chicago: University of Chicago Press, 2014), 6–7.

18 Rogers M. Smith, *Civic Ideals: Conflicting Visions of Citizenship in U.S. History* (New Haven: Yale University Press, 1997), 15. See also Smith, "Beyond Tocqueville, Myrdal, and Hartz: The Multiple Traditions in America," *The American Political Science Review*, Vol. 87, No. 3. (Sept. 1993), 549–566; and, for a useful review of related literature, Marc Stears, "The Liberal Tradition and the Politics of Exclusion," *Annual Review of Political Science*, No. 10 (2007), 85–101.

19 Aziz Rana, *The Two Faces of American Freedom* (Cambridge, MA: Harvard University Press, 2010), 21–22.

20 See Rogers Smith, "Understanding the Symbiosis of American Rights and American Racism," in Hulliung, ed., *The American Liberal Tradition Reconsidered*, 55–89.

21 A recent volume of essays nicely described Hamilton's popular and scholarly reputation as both "enigmatic and suspect." See Douglas Ambrose, "Introduction," in Ambrose and Robert W. T. Martin, eds., *The Many Faces of Alexander Hamilton: The Life and Legacy of America's Most Elusive Founding Father* (New York: New York University Press, 2006), 19.

22 Beard, *Economic Interpretation*, 100–114.

23 Hartz, *Liberal Tradition*, 103.

24 Wood, *Empire of Liberty*, 110.

25 Ron Chernow, *Alexander Hamilton* (New York: Penguin Press, 2004), 6.

26 Karl-Friedrich Walling, *Republican Empire: Alexander Hamilton on War and Free Government* (Lawrence: University Press of Kansas, 1999), 115.

27 Gerald Stourzh insightfully observed that one of Hamilton's "most revealing utterances was his reference, in 1790, to the Spanish possessions on 'our

right' and the British possessions (Canada) on 'our left,'" inferring from this that Hamilton instinctively oriented himself toward the east, and envisioned an American empire engaged, commercially and otherwise, with the great European powers of his day, unlike Thomas Jefferson's "westward-looking 'Empire of Liberty,' agrarian, pacificist, isolationist." Stourzh, *Alexander Hamilton and the Idea of Republican Government* (Stanford: Stanford University Press, 1970), 195. As I shall show, Hamilton was also more likely to look south, toward Spanish America, than Jefferson, or indeed, any of his colleagues.

28 Chernow, *Hamilton*, 16–17.

29 Svend Erik Green-Pedersen, "The History of the Danish Negro Slave Trade, 1733–1807: An Interim Survey Relating in Particular to its Volume, Structure, Profitability, and Abolition," *Revue Française d'Histoire d'Outre-Mer*, Vol. 62 (1975), 196–220.

30 Hamilton to Edward Stevens, St. Croix, November 11, 1769. From Alexander Hamilton, in Joanne B. Freeman, ed., *Writings* (New York: The Library of America, 2001), 3.

31 "Account of a Hurricane," *The Royal Danish American Gazette*, September 6, 1772. Ibid., 6–9.

32 Cited in Forrest McDonald, *Alexander Hamilton: A Biography* (New York: W. W. Norton, 1979), 12.

33 See Daniel Huslebosch's excellent account in *Constituting Empire: New York and the Transformation of Constitutionalism in the Atlantic World, 1664–1830* (Chapel Hill: University of North Carolina Press, 2005), 15–105.

34 My version of Hume's political thought has been informed especially by Sheldon S. Wolin, "Hume and Conservatism," *The American Political Science Review*, Vol. 48, No. 4 (Dec. 1954), 999–1016; Russell Hardin, *David Hume: Moral and Political Theorist* (Oxford: Oxford University Press, 2007); and Andrew Sabl, *Hume's Politics: Coordination and Crisis in the History of England* (Princeton: Princeton University Press, 2012). For Hume's influence on Hamilton, see Douglass Adair, "'That Politics May Be Reduced to a Science': David Hume, James Madison, and the Tenth Federalist," *The Huntington Library Quarterly*, Vol. 20, No. 4 (Aug. 1957), 343–360; Stourzh, *Alexander Hamilton*; John M. Werner, "David Hume and America," *Journal of the History of Ideas*, Vol. 33, No. 3, (July–Sep. 1972), 439–456; McDonald, *Alexander Hamilton*, 35–38; Morton White, *Philosophy, The Federalist, and the Constitution* (New York: Oxford University Press, 1987); and Clement Fatovic, "Reason and Experience in Alexander Hamilton's Science of Politics," *American Political Thought* Vol. 2, No. 1 (Spring 2013), 1–30.

35 See Barbara Arneil, *John Locke and America: The Defence of English Colonialism* (Oxford: Oxford University Press, 1996), 88–117.

36 Jack P. Greene, "The Origins of the New Colonial Policy, 1748–1763," in Jack P. Greene and J. R. Poole, eds., *A Companion to the American Revolution* (Malden: Blackwell, 2000), 101–111.

37 For the reforms undertaken by the Grenville ministry, see John L. Bullion, *A Great and Necessary Measure: George Grenville and the Genesis of the*

Stamp Act (Columbia: University of Missouri Press, 1982). For the Royal Proclamation of 1763, see Stuart Banner, *How the Indians Lost Their Land: Law and Power on the Frontier* (Cambridge, MA: Harvard University Press, 2005), 91–111.

38 For a complete account of these disagreements, see John Phillip Reid, *Constitutional History of the American Revolution*, abridged edition (Madison: Wisconsin University Press, 1995).

39 Rana, *Two Faces of American Freedom*, 37.

40 Hulsebosch, *Constituting Empire*, 57–58.

41 Rana, *Two Faces of American Freedom*, 66–69.

42 Edmund S. Morgan and Helen M. Morgan, *The Stamp Act Crisis: Prologue to Revolution* (Chapel Hill: University of North Carolina Press, 1953).

43 Bernard Bailyn, "The Transforming Radicalism of the American Revolution," in Bernard Bailyn ed., *Pamphlets of the American Revolution, Volume 1: 1750–1765* (Cambridge, MA: Harvard University Press, 1965).

44 Robert Middlekauff, *The Glorious Cause: The American Revolution, 1763–1789* (New York: Oxford University Press, 1982), 219–249.

45 Eric Nelson, *The Royalist Revolution: Monarchy and the American Founding* (Cambridge, MA: Harvard University Press, 2014). See also the important critiques of Nelson's account by Gordon Wood, Pauline Maier, and Daniel Hulsebosch in the "Forum on Patriot Royalism," *William and Mary Quarterly*, Vol. 68, No. 4 (Oct. 2011), 533–596; and in John W. Compton and Karen Orren, "Political Theory in Institutional Context: The Case of Patriot Royalism," *American Political Thought*, Vol. 3, No. 1 (Spring 2014), 1–31.

46 Nelson, *Royalist Revolution*, 39; and more broadly, Mark G. Spencer, *David Hume and Eighteenth-Century America* (Rochester: University of Rochester Press, 2005).

47 David Hume "Of the Independency of Parliament" [1742], in Knud Haakonssen, ed., *Hume: Political Essays* (Cambridge: Cambridge University Press, 1994), 24. See also: Albert O. Hirschman, *The Passions and the Interests: Political Arguments for Capitalism before Its Triumph* (Princeton: Princeton University Press, 1977), 70–75.

48 Alexander Hamilton, "The Farmer Refuted ...," New York, February 23, 1775, in Harold C. Syrett, ed., *The Papers of Alexander Hamilton*, 27 Vols. (New York: Columbia University Press, 1961–1987) [hereafter *PAH*] I, 94–95.

49 Ibid., *PAH* I, 92.

50 Hamilton, "A Full Vindication of the Measures of Congress," December 15, 1774. *PAH* I, 53–54.

51 Hamilton, "The Farmer Refuted ...," *PAH* I, 164.

52 Ibid. *PAH* I, 98–99. See also Nelson, *The Royalist Revolution*, 53–55; and Gordon Wood, "The Problem of Sovereignty," *The William and Mary Quarterly*, Vol. 68, No. 4 (Oct. 2011), 573–577.

53 Hamilton, "The Farmer Refuted," *PAH* I, 98–99, emphasis added.

54 Here again, Hamilton cites Hume as his authority: "Mr. Hume, in enumerating those political maxims, which will be eternally true, speaks thus: 'It may easily be observed, that though free governments have been commonly the most happy, for those who partake of their freedom, yet are they the most ruinous and oppressive to *their provinces*'" (Hamilton, "The Farmer Refuted", *PAH* I, 100–101).

55 Hamilton, "A Full Vindication," *PAH* I, 54.

56 Seabury, "A View of the Controversy."

57 A Westchester Farmer [Rev. Samuel Seabury], "A View of the Controversy between Great-Britain and her Colonies ...," New York, January 5, 1775 (White Plains: Westchester County Historical Society, 1930). Available at http://anglicanhistory.org/usa/seabury/farmer/03.html (accessed August 10, 2010).

58 Hamilton, "The Farmer Refuted," *PAH* I, 107; emphasis added.

59 For a judicious weighing of the evidence, see Michelle DuRoss, "Somewhere in Between: Alexander Hamilton and Slavery," *The Early America Review*, Vol 9, No. 4 (Winter/Spring 2011), 1–8.

60 For the reaction to *Somerset* in the colonies, see George William Van Cleve, *A Slaveholders Union: Slavery, Politics, and the Constitution in the Early American Republic* (Chicago: University of Chicago Press, 2010), 31–40.

61 Philip Lawson, *The Imperial Challenge: Quebec and Britain in the Age of the American Revolution* (Montreal: McGill-Queen's University Press, 1989); David Milobar, "Quebec Reform, the British Constitution, and the Atlantic Empire, 1774–1775," *Parliamentary History*, Vol. 14, No. 1 (Feb. 1995), 65–88.

62 Rana, *Two Faces of American Freedom*, 73–79.

63 Hulsebosch, *Constituting Empire*, 134–135.

64 Hamilton, "Remarks on the Quebec Bill," June 1775, in Richard B. Vernier, ed., *The Revolutionary Writings of Alexander Hamilton* (Indianapolis: Liberty Fund, 2008), 145, 148, 150–152.

65 See Edling, *Hercules in the Cradle*, 20–28, for an account of the military and financial difficulties the Articles engendered during the war.

66 Hamilton to George Clinton, Valley Forge, February 13, 1778, *PAH* I, 425.

67 Hamilton to James Duane. Liberty Pole, New Jersey, September 3, 1780. *PAH* II, 401–402.

68 Ibid., *PAH* II, 403; emphasis added.

69 For Hamilton's use of the term "empire," see Stourzh, *Alexander Hamilton*, 189–201; J. G. A Pocock, *The Machiavellian Moment: Florentine Political Thought and the Atlantic Republican Tradition* (Princeton: Princeton University Press, 1975), 528–533; Walling, *Republican Empire*. For the Union as a midpoint between empire and international system, see Hendrickson, *Peace Pact*, 274; Max M. Edling, "'A Mongrel Kind of Government': The U.S. Constitution, the Federal Union, and the Origins of the American State," in Peter Thompson and Peter S. Onuf, eds., *State and Citizen: British America and the Early United States* (Charlottesville: University of Virginia Press, 2013), 150–177.

70 "The Continentalist, No. I." *New-York Packet, and the American Advertiser,* July 12, 1781. *PAH* II, 649–651.

71 "The Continentalist, No. VI." *New-York Packet, and the American Advertiser,* July 4, 1782. *PAH* III, 103.

72 "The Continentalist, No. II." *New-York Packet, and the American Advertiser,* July 19, 1781. *PAH* II, 655–656.

73 "The Continentalist, No. IV." *New-York Packet, and the American Advertiser,* August 30, 1781. *PAH* II, 670; emphasis removed.

74 "The Continentalist, No. III." *New-York Packet, and the American Advertiser,* August 9, 1781. *PAH* II, 665; emphasis in the original.

75 Chernow, *Hamilton,* 221.

76 Proceedings of Commissioners to Remedy Defects of the Federal Government, Annapolis Maryland, September 11, 1786. Available at: http://avalon.law .yale.edu/18th_century/ annapoli.asp (accessed January 21, 2016).

77 There is no complete transcript of this speech. As records of its contents, we have only Hamilton's very scanty notes, and the notes taken on the speech by four members of its audience: James Madison, Robert Yates, John Lansing, and Rufus King. All five can be found in *PAH* IV, 178–207.

78 Ibid., 180–194.

79 Hamilton, "Speech on a Plan of Government," Philadelphia, June 18, 1787, *PAH* IV, 191.

80 Ibid.

81 Ibid., 185. Here again, Eric Nelson's account of the continuities between the "patriot royalism" of Hamilton's pre-independence pamphlets and his constitutional designs is very useful. See *The Royalist Revolution,* 191–193.

82 Ibid., 191.

83 Stourzh, *Alexander Hamilton,* 51.

84 Chernow, *Hamilton,* 232.

85 Hamilton to Thomas Pickering, September 16, 1803. *PAH* XXVI, 148. Hamilton's deduction was based on the Convention's voting rules, which gave one vote to each state delegation without recording the individual votes of the delegates. Since two of Virginia's six delegates – George Mason and Edmund Randolph – had loudly opposed Hamilton's proposal, Madison must have numbered amongst the four that delivered his delegation's concurrence.

86 Nelson, *Royalist Revolution,* 194.

87 Hamilton, "Conjectures about the New Constitution," c. late September 1787, in *Writings,* 169.

88 Max M. Edling, *A Revolution in Favor of Government: Origins of the U.S. Constitution and the Making of the American State* (Oxford: Oxford University Press, 2003). For the "fiscal-military state," see also John Brewer, *The Sinews of Power: War, Money and the English State* (London: Unwin Hyman, 1989).

89 Edling, *A Revolution in Favor of Government,* 8. For the "national state," see also Charles Tilly, *Coercion, Capital, and European States, AD 990–1992* (Malden: Blackwell Publishing, 1992).

90 For the European antecedents to the "unionist paradigm" pioneered by Hamilton and others in the United States, see Hendrickson, *Peace Pact.*

91 Alexander Hamilton, "Federalist No. 1," in Terence Ball, ed., *The Federalist, with Letters of "Brutus"* (Cambridge: Cambridge University Press, 2003) [hereafter *Federalist*], 40–46, 1–2.

92 Hamilton, *Federalist No. 6*, 19.

93 Hamilton, *Federalist No. 8*, 30–35.

94 Hamilton, *Federalist No. 6*, 21.

95 The "doux commerce" thesis, which claims that international trade should have a general "softening" effect on international relations, receives its most famous formulation in Montesquieu, and also appears in Turgot, Mirabeau, William Robertson, Hume, Adam Smith, and later, Kant. See Hirschman, *Passions and the Interests*, 56–63; Anthony Padgen, *Lords of All the World: Ideologies of Empire in Spain, Britain and France, c. 1500–c. 1800* (New Haven: Yale University Press, 1995), 178–195; and Turkuler Isiksel, "The Dream of Commercial Peace," in Luuk van Middelaar and Philippe van Parijs, eds., *After the Storm: How to Save Democracy in Europe* (Tielt: Lannoo, 2015), 27–40. Thomas Jefferson, with his vision of an "Empire of Liberty," would later become the most famous American proponent of this view; see Wood, *Empire of Liberty*, 189–192.

96 Hamilton, *Federalist No. 6*, 22. See also Stourzh, *Alexander Hamilton*, 140–153. For the historical precedents of Hamilton's skepticism toward the "*doux commerce*" thesis, see Istvan Hont, *Jealousy of Trade: International Competition and the Nation-State in Historical Perspective* (Cambridge, MA: Harvard University Press, 2005), 51–57, 185–187.

97 Hamilton, *Federalist No. 7*, 25.

98 See Chernow, *Alexander Hamilton*, 344–345 for Hamilton as the "clear-eyed apostle of America's economic future," but compare Stourzh, *Alexander Hamilton*, 7, or Wood, *Empire of Liberty*, 102–103.

99 Hamilton, *Federalist No. 11*, 51.

100 James Winthrop, "Agrippa XIV," January 29, 1788. Available at: http:// teachingamericanhistory.org/library/ index.asp?document=1648 (accessed March 2, 2012).

101 Stourzh, *Alexander Hamilton*, 187.

102 See also Wood, *Creation of the American Republic*, 505–506.

103 Hamilton, *Federalist No. 9*, 35–39.

104 Hamilton, *Federalist No. 27*, 125–126.

105 Hamilton, *Federalist No. 35*, 159–161.

106 As Eric Nelson observes, then, even as Britain, "with its kings and queens, would consolidate the whig constitution against which patriots had rebelled, eventually placing supreme, unchecked political power in a single legislative chamber elected by the people.... The new American republic ... would evolve and perfect a recognizably Royalist constitution, investing its chief magistrate with the very same prerogative powers that Charles I had defended against the great whig heroes of the seventeenth century. On one side of the Atlantic, there would be kings without monarchy; on the other, monarchy without kings." *The Royalist Revolution*, 232. Note, though that while Nelson views this rather remarkable case of divergent constitutional development as a result of purely intellectual causes, here I've tried to show how

the context of the American founding, and in particular, the contradictory institutional position occupied by its Creole protagonists, provided the background problems to which Presidentialism provided a solution.

107 See Brutus, Letters XI–XV, in Ball, ed., *The Federalist*, 501–529; Herbert J. Storing, *What the Anti-Federalists Were For: The Political Thought of the Opponents of the Constitution* (Chicago: University of Chicago Press, 1981), 53–63.

108 David Hume, "Of the Independency of Parliament" [1742], in Haakonssen, ed., *Hume: Political Essays*, 26.

109 Hamilton, *Federalist No. 66*, 322.

110 Hamilton, *Federalist No. 71*, 350.

111 Hamilton, *Federalist No. 68*, 331–333.

112 Hamilton, *Federalist No. 70*, 341.

113 Hamilton, *Federalist No. 71*, 349.

114 Hamilton, *Federalist No. 78*, 377.

115 Hamilton, *Federalist No. 78*, 381.

116 Hamilton, *Federalist No. 11*, 51–52. We can trace Hamilton's quadripartite geographical system to the influence of Murray Postlethwayt's *Universal Dictionary of Trade and Commerce*, which was organized under these categories. Hamilton made extensive notes from the work in the back of his 1777 pay book, employing the same headings. Under "AMERICA," for example, he wrote: "Its boundaries yet unascertained. The part known little less in extent than all the other three parts together contains the greatest part of their productions and a variety of others peculiar to itself." *PAH* I, 373 n. 2.

117 Hamilton, *Federalist No. 11*, 52. Hamilton attributes the notion "that even dogs cease to bark after having breathed a while in our atmosphere" to the *Recherches philosophiques sur les Américains* by Cornelius de Pauw, the Dutch naturalist discussed in Chapter 2, who, following Georges-Louis Leclerc, Comte de Buffon, argued that American animal species were generally smaller and less vital than those of Europe and Asia, and even asserted that mere residence in the New World was sufficient to produce this effect in Old World species.

118 Ibid., 52.

119 Stourzh, *Alexander Hamilton*, 196. Here, it should be clear, the evidence seems to me to favor Stourzh's reading of Hamilton's plans for the hemisphere as "*imperialistic*," and to rather seriously attenuate Karl-Friedrich Walling's more recent attempt to deny this tendency in Hamilton especially and the American founding more generally. See Walling, *Republican Empire*, 97, 115.

120 Hamilton, *Federalist No. 11*, 51–52.

121 Jay Sexton observes, in his useful history, that "[t]he key to understanding the nineteenth-century Monroe Doctrine is the simultaneity and interdependence of anticolonialism and imperialism," *The Monroe Doctrine: Empire and Nation in Nineteenth-Century America* (New York: Hill and Wang, 2011), 5.

122 Hamilton to George Washington, November 18, 1788, *PAH* V, 234.

123 Hamilton complained, in private correspondence, of "that defect in the constitution, which renders it possible for the man intended for vice president may, in fact, turn up president." Hamilton to James Wilson, January 25, 1789, *PAH* V, 248. I discuss the constitutional crisis that arose in the presidential election of 1800 in Chapter 6.

124 Chernow, *Alexander Hamilton*, 286–287.

125 There are three such reports which are held to be particularly consequential: the "Report on Public Credit" delivered January 9, 1790, the "Report on a National Bank" delivered December 13, 1790, and the "Report on Manufactures" delivered December 5, 1791. Here I focus mainly on the last one, widely considered Hamilton's greatest work.

126 Alexander Hamilton, "Report on Manufactures," in Freeman, ed., *Writings*, 691–692.

127 Ibid., 651.

128 Ibid., 661.

129 Ibid., 648.

130 Ibid., 670–671.

131 Jennifer Pitts, *A Turn to Empire: The Rise of Imperial Liberalism in Britain and France* (Princeton: Princeton University Press, 2005), 20–21.

132 Hamilton, "The French Revolution" (unpublished manuscript) Philadelphia, 1794. *PAH* XVII, 586.

133 Hamilton, "The Cause of France" (unpublished manuscript) Philadelphia, 1794. *PAH* XVII, 586.

134 "Pacificus No. II," *Gazette of the United States*, Philadelphia, July 3, 1793. *PAH* XV, 56–58.

135 Ibid., 59–60. All emphases in the original.

136 See Stanley Elkins and Eric McKitrick *The Age of Federalism: The Early American Republic, 1788–1800* (Oxford: Oxford University Press, 1993), 303–373, 498–513, 537–690, 711–719 and Alexander DeConde, *The Quasi-War: The Politics and Diplomacy of the Undeclared War with France, 1797–1801* (New York: Charles Scribner and Sons, 1966).

137 "The Warning No. I," *Gazette of the United States*, New York, January 27, 1797. *PAH* XX, 494.

138 "The Warning No. II," *Gazette of the United States*, New York, February 7, 1797. *PAH* XX, 512.

139 "The Stand, No. II," *The New York Commercial Advertiser*, New York, April 4, 1798. *PAH* XXI, 396.

140 Stourzh, *Alexander Hamilton*, 122.

141 For Miranda, see Karen Racine, *Francisco de Miranda: A Transatlantic Life in the Age of Revolution* (Wilmington: Scholarly Resource Books, 2003).

142 Hamilton to Francisco de Miranda, New York, January–July, 1784. *PAH* III, 504, 585–587.

143 Miranda to Hamilton, Paris, November 4, 1792, ["the 1t. year of the Republic"]. *PAH* XIII, 16.

144 Miranda to Hamilton, London, April 6, 1798. *PAH* XXI, 399.

145 Hamilton to King, New York, August 22, 1798. *PAH* XXII, 154–155. Emphasis in original.

146 On the duel, and the early republic's "culture of honor," see Joanne Freeman, *Affairs of Honor: National Politics in the New Republic* (New Haven: Yale University Press, 2001).

147 Hamilton to Theodore Sedgwick, New York, July 10, 1804, in Freeman, ed., *Writings*, 1022.

4. SIMÓN BOLÍVAR AND THE CONTRADICTIONS
OF CREOLE REVOLUTION

1 For an account of the enduring importance of Bolívar's image in Venezuelan politics, see Germán Carrera Damas, *El Culto a Bolívar: Esbozo para un Estudio de la Historia de las Ideas en Venezuela* (Caracas: Universidad Central de Venezuela, 1970). For an interesting selection of Chávez's writings on Bolívar in English, see the "Introduction" to Matthew Brown, ed., *Hugo Chávez Presents: The Bolivarian Revolution* (London: Verso, 2009).

2 Martí's 1893 speech on Bolívar to the Latin American Literary Society of New York was later published in his journal, *Patria*, on November 4, 1893; see: *José Martí: Obras Completas*, 26 Vols. (Havana: Centro de Estudios Martianos, 2001), VIII, 241–248. Neruda's "Un Canto para Bolívar" was first published in the collection *Tercera Residencia*, in 1947. García Márquez's fictionalized, but well-researched account of Bolívar's final trip up the Magdalena River, *El General en su Laberinto*, was published in 1989.

3 See the fascinating account of Bolívar's popular reception in the United States in Caitlin Fitz, *Our Sister Republics: The United States in an Age of American Revolution* (New York: Liveright Publishing Co., 2016), 116–155. See also David Sowell, "The Mirror of Public Opinion: Bolívar, Republicanism, and the United States Press, 1821–1831," *Revista de Historia de América*, No. 134 (Jan.–Jun. 2004), 165–183.

4 Selections from their correspondence can be found in Pedro Schwartz and Carlos Rodríguez Braun, "Las Relaciones entre Jeremías Bentham y S. Bolívar," *Telos: Revista Iberoamericana de Estudios Utilitaristas*, Vol. 1, No. 3 (1992), 45–68.

5 In early 1829, Constant contributed two pieces to a debate with the Abbé de Pradt in the pages of the *Le Courrier Français*, arguing that the "dictatorial" features of Bolívar's 1826 Constitution for Bolivia, were not necessary, even in light of the region's difficult political experiences. See Benjamin Constant, *Actes du Congrès de Lausanne* (Geneva: Librarie Droz, 1968), 69–74.

6 Marx was commissioned to write an entry on Bolívar for the *New American Cyclopaedia* in 1857, but his submission was rejected for its "partisan style." He sent the manuscript to Friedrich Engels for help with the citations, noting in a prefatory letter that "To see the dastardly, most miserable and meanest of blackguards described as Napoleon I was altogether too much." Both the entry and excerpts from Marx's letter can be found at www.marxists .org/archive/marx/works/1858/01/bolivar.htm. See also Hal Draper's indispensable analysis of Marx's opinions, "Karl Marx and Simón Bolívar," *New Politics*, Vol. 7, No. 1 (Winter 1968), 64–77.

7 In a still-influential mid-twentieth-century exchange, the Spaniard Salvador de Madariaga argued that Bolívar's true institutional ideal should be described as "monocracy" rather than democracy or republic. See: *Bolívar* (Mexico City: Editorial Hermes, 1951). He was exhaustively and emphatically refuted by the Vicente Lecuna, President of Venezuela's *Sociedad Bolivariana*, a government-run historical and archival organization; *Catálogo de Errores y Calumnias en la Historia de Bolívar*, 3 Vols. (New York: Colonial Press, 1956–1958). For a more recent statements on the same controversy, see Frank Safford, "Bolívar as Triumphal State Maker and Despairing 'Democrat,'" in David Bushnell and Lester D. Langley, eds., *Simón Bolívar: Essays on the Life and Legacy of the Liberator* (Lanham: Rowman and Littlefield, 2008), 99–120.

8 In his excellent recent biography, John Lynch presents Bolívar as a pragmatic politician, who "preferred a successful deal to the constraints of dogma"; *Simón Bolívar: A Life* (New Haven: Yale University Press, 2006), 281. But equally excellent scholars have sought to show that Bolívar was so deeply committed to outmoded republican principles that he failed to confront the realities of his time and place. See Anthony Pagden, *Spanish Imperialism and the Political Imagination* (New Haven: Yale University Press, 1990), 133–154; and Luis Castro Leiva, *Gran Colombia: Una Illusión Ilustrada* (Caracas: Monte Avila Editores, 1985).

9 Compare Diego A. von Vacano, *The Color of Citizenship: Race, Modernity and Latin American/Hispanic Political Thought* (Oxford: Oxford University Press, 2012), 56–82 with Aline Helg, "Simón Bolívar and the Spectre of Pardocracia: José Padilla in Post-Independence Cartagena," *Journal of Latin American Studies*, Vol. 35, No. 3 (Aug. 2003), 447–471. In an analysis which, as will become apparent, exerted significant influence on my own, the Venezuelan historian Germán Carrera Damas shows that Bolívar was simultaneously an innovative theorist of colonial emancipation *and* an opponent of serious social reform. See *Venezuela: Proyecto Nacional y Poder Social* (Barcelona: Editorial Crítica, 1986).

10 Some scholars have sought to avoid this problem by organizing their intellectual histories around a turn in Bolívar's thinking, whether from an early democratic idealism to a later dictatorial decadence, or from an early collectivist republicanism to a late individualist liberalism. See, for the former, Víctor Andrés Belaúnde *Bolívar and the Political Thought of the Spanish American Revolution* (Baltimore: Johns Hopkins University Press, 1938), 231–258; and, for the latter, Luis Barrón, "La tradición republican y el nacimiento del liberalism en Hispanoamérica después de la Independencia: Bolívar, Lucas Alamán y el 'Poder Conservador,'" in José Antonio Aguilar and Rafael Rojas, eds., *El Republicanismo en Hispanoamérica: Ensayos de Historia Intellectual y Política* (Mexico City: CIDE, 2002), 275. Though I find the former account more persuasive than the latter, the very difference between these two interpretations suggests, I think, that it is more plausible to read Bolívar's thought as consistently contradictory, as I do here.

11 Lynch, *Simón Bolívar*, 24.

12 Bolívar's debts to the classical republican tradition have been explored in David Brading, *The First America: The Spanish Monarchy, Creole*

Patriots, and the Liberal State (Cambridge: Cambridge University Press, 1991), 603–620; Pagden, *Spanish Imperialism*, 133–154; Barrón "La tradición republicana," 244–288; Rafael Rojas, *Las Repúblicas de Aire: Utopía y Desencanto en la Revolución de Hispanoamérica* (Mexico City: Taurus, 2009); and von Vacano, *Color of Citizenship*, 56–82. The literature on the classical republican tradition itself is enormous. The following works have particularly informed my analysis: J. G. A. Pocock, *The Machiavellian Moment: Florentine Political Thought and the Atlantic Republican Tradition* (Princeton: Princeton University Press, 1975); Quentin Skinner, "Machiavelli on the Maintenance of Liberty," *Australian Journal of Political Science*, Vol. 18, No. 2. (Nov. 1983), 3–15; "Machiavelli's Discorsi and the Pre-Humanist Origins of Republican Ideas," in Gisela Bock, Quentin Skinner, and Maurizio Viroli, eds., *Machiavelli and Republicanism* (Cambridge: Cambridge University Press, 1990), 121–142; *Liberty before Liberalism* (Cambridge: Cambridge University Press, 1998) and Paul Rahe, *Republics Ancient and Modern: Classical Republicanism and the American Revolution* (Chapel Hill: University of North Carolina Press, 1992).

13 In his recent book, Diego Von Vacano argues that despite his many direct references to Montesquieu and Rousseau, Bolívar's thought actually displays a "greater affinity" with that of Machiavelli than either Montesquieu or Rousseau. There is much in this insight, particularly in the admiration of "martial" qualities common to both Bolívar and Machiavelli's republicanisms, though as I shall show, both Montesquieu and Rousseau's influence upon Bolívar are quite clear in his conception of the "balanced constitution" of England, his insistence upon matching regimes to the people they are meant to govern, and in his account of the role of the president within the Bolivian constitution of 1826. We have interesting indirect testimony regarding Bolívar's rather ambivalent relationship to Machiavelli from his longtime Irish aide-de-camp, Daniel O'Leary, who recounted the following exchange in his memoirs: "a few months before his death, Bolívar visited me in Cartagena, and seeing on my table a volume of a new edition of the works of Machiavelli, observed that I should have better things to do with my time. We discussed the merits of the work, and noticing that Bolívar seemed to know its contents very well, I asked him whether he had read it recently; he responded that he had not read a line of Machiavelli since he left Europe 25 years ago." *Memorias del General Daniel Florencio O'Leary: Narración* (Caracas: Imprenta Nacional, 1952), 66–67.

14 Mikael Hörnqvist has shown that the attempt to balance internal liberty and external conquest and dominion – and, indeed, the belief that these two aims might be complimentary rather than contradictory, as they were for Bolívar – are traceable all the way to Rennaissance Italian republicanism. See *Machiavelli and Empire* (Cambridge: Cambridge University Press, 2004). See Judith N. Shklar, "Montesquieu and the New Republicanism," in Bock, Skinner, and Viroli, eds., *Machiavelli and Republicanism*, 265–279; and David Armitage, "Empire and Liberty: A Republican Dilemma," in Martin Van Gelderen and Quentin Skinner, eds. *Republicanism: A Shared European Heritage*, 2 Vols. (Cambridge: Cambridge University Press, 2004), II,

29–46, for useful discussions of how these concerns evolved in later republican writings.

15 The degree to which the institutional changes associated with the Bourbon Reforms contributed to the growth of tensions between Caracas's Creole elite and the Spanish metropole, and thus to the eventual movement for independence, has been the subject of some historiographical debate. See, for contrasting views, John Lynch, *The Spanish American Revolutions, 1808–1826*, 2nd edition (New York: W. W. Norton, 1986), 4–24, 190–195; and P. Michael McKinley, *Pre-Revolutionary Caracas: Politics, Economy, and Society, 1711–1811* (Cambridge: Cambridge University Press, 1985), 90–145. For the neighboring, and important case of New Granada, see Anthony McFarlane, *Columbia before Independence: Economy, Society, and Politics under Bourbon Rule* (Cambridge: Cambridge University Press, 1993).

16 Cited in Marixa Lasso, *Myths of Harmony: Race and Republicanism during the Age of Revolutions, Colombia, 1795–1831* (Pittsburgh: University of Pittsburgh Press, 2007), 24–25.

17 Carrera Damas, *Venezuela*, 42–55.

18 For an exhaustive account of Miranda's efforts to attract funding in support of this mission, first in the United States, and then throughout the British Caribbean, as well as an analysis of Miranda's reception in Venezuela, see William Spence Robertson, *Francisco de Miranda and the Revolutionizing of Spanish America* (Washington, D.C.: Government Printing Office, 1909), 361–398.

19 Simón Bolívar, "Discurso pronunciado en la Sociedad Patriótica de Caracas," July 3–4, 1811, from Manuel Pérez Vila, ed., *Doctrina del Libertador*, 3rd edition (Caracas: Biblioteca Ayacucho, 2009), 9. Whenever possible, I shall cite from this useful collection of Bolívar's writings (hereafter *Doctrina*), which is available for free download from the Biblioteca Ayacucho Online: www.bibliotecayacucho.gob.ve. For rarer texts not included therein, I will cite from the *Obras Completas*, Vicente Lecuna and Esther Barret de Nazaris, eds., *Simón Bolívar: Obras Completas*, 2nd edition, 3 Vols. (Havana: Editorial Lex, 1950); or the nearly complete digital collection of the *Archivo del Libertador* (hereafter *Archivo*), available at www.archivo dellibertador.gob.ve. Readers interested in English translations of Bolívar's most important writings should consult the excellent new collection edited by David Bushnell, *El Libertador: Writings of Simón Bolívar* (Oxford: Oxford University Press, 2003).

20 For an English translation, see David Armitage, *The Declaration of Independence: A Global History* (Cambridge, MA: Harvard University Press, 2007), 199–207. Notably, the preamble offers to "generously forget the long series of ills, injuries, and privations, which the sad right of conquest has indistinctly caused, to all the descendants of the Discoverers, Conquerors, and Settlers of these Countries," thereby neatly connecting independence to injuries suffered specifically by Creoles.

21 Bolívar, "Carta de Jamaica," Kingston, September 6, 1815, from *Doctrina*, 74–75. Bolívar takes a good measure of rhetorical license in his characterization of the regime; the exceptions to the rule of American exclusion

226 *Notes to Pages 96–103*

he describes were numerous in each of the posts he names, though there is evidence that peninsular appointees were systematically preferred to Americans at the end of the eighteenth century. See: Mark A. Burkholder and D. S. Chandler, *From Impotence to Authority: The Spanish Crown and the American Audiencias, 1687–1808* (Columbia: University of Missouri Press, 1977).

22 Bolívar, "Carta de Jamaica," Kingston, September 6, 1815, from *Doctrina*, 74–75, emphasis added.

23 David Young, "Montesquieu's View of Despotism and His Use of Travel Literature," *The Review of Politics*, Vol. 40, No. 3 (July 1978), 392–405.

24 Bolívar, "Carta de Jamaica," Kingston, September 6, 1815, from *Doctrina*, 75–76.

25 Ibid., 73. Bolívar's complete rejection of any "usable" pre-Hispanic broke sharply from an intellectual tradition some scholars have referred to as "Creole Patriotism," which sought to recover and revalue Aztec and Incan institutions or practices as the basis for independent American nation-states. See Pagden, *Spanish Imperialism*, 133–139 and Brading, *The First America*, 253–464.

26 J. G. A. Pocock describes the "Machiavellian moment" at the center of classical republican political thought in *Machiavellian Moment*, vii.

27 Lynch, *Spanish American Revolutions*, 197–199.

28 Peter Blanchard, *Under the Flags of Freedom: Slave Soldiers and the Wars of Independence in Spanish South America* (Pittsburgh: University of Pittsburgh Press, 2008), 17–36.

29 For the racial politics of revolution in Cartagena, see Aline Helg, *Liberty and Equality in Caribbean Colombia* (Chapel Hill: University of North Carolina Press, 2004); and Lasso, *Myths of Harmony*.

30 The Venezuelan historian Germán Carrera Damas has done the most to reconstruct the social and racial basis of conflict under the Second Republic and the aims of Boves and his forces. See *Boves: Aspectos Socioeconómicos de la Guerra de Independencia* (Caracas: 1972); and "Algunos Problemas Relativos a la Organización del Estado durante la Segunda República Venezolana," in *Tres Temas de Historia* (Caracas: Universidad Central de Venezuela, 1961).

31 Sibylle Fischer, "Bolívar in Haiti: Republicanism in the Revolutionary Atlantic," in Carla Calargé, Raphael Dalleo, Luis Duno-Gottberg, and Clevis Headley, eds., *Haiti and the Americas* (Jackson: University Press of Mississippi, 2013), 25–53.

32 Bolívar, "Discurso pronuciado ... ante el Congreso de Angostura," February 15, 1819, *Doctrina* 130.

33 Ibid., 124.

34 Ibid., 128–129. For an interesting account of Bolívar's "aristocratic" attraction to education and social reform, see also Karen Racine, "Simon Bolivar, Englishman: Elite Responsibility and Social Reform in Spanish American Independence," in Bushnell and Langley, eds., *Simón Bolívar*, 55–72.

35 Bolívar, "Discurso pronuciado ... ante el Congreso de Angostura," February 15, 1819, *Doctrina* 141.

36 See O. Carlos Stroetzer, "Bolívar y el Poder Moral," *Revista de Historia de América*, No. 95 (Jan.–June 1983), 139–158; Barrón, "La Tradición Republicana," 244–88; and, for Bolívar's influence in Mexico, David Pantoja Morán, *El Supremo Poder Conservador: El Diseño Institucional en las Primeras Constituciones Mexicanas* (Mexico City: El Colegio de México, 2005).

37 Belaúnde, *Bolívar*, 194.

38 For the similar considerations on this subject in Machiavelli's political thought, see: Skinner, "Machiavelli on the Maintenance of Liberty," 3–15.

39 For a perceptive account of how republican notions of unity and the common good became central to Creole efforts to suppress *pardo* political and social mobility, see Lasso, *Myths of Harmony*.

40 Bolívar, "Discurso pronunciado … ante el Congreso de Angostura," February 15, 1819, *Doctrina*, 129–130.

41 Bolívar to Francisco de Paula Santander, Lima, April 7, 1825, *Archivo*, Document 10215.

42 Bolívar, "Discurso pronunciado … ante el Congreso de Angostura," February 15, 1819, *Doctrina*, 130.

43 Bolívar, "Memoria dirigida a los ciudadanos de la Nueva Granada," Cartagena de Indias, December 15, 1812, *Doctrina*, 13–14.

44 David Bushnell, "Los Usos del Modelo: La Generación de la Independencia y la Imagen de Norteamérica," *Revista de Historia de América*, No. 82 (June–Dec. 1976), 7–27.

45 Bolívar, "Discurso pronunciado … ante el Congreso de Angostura," February 15, 1819, *Doctrina*, 126–127.

46 I have been unable to find any evidence in Bolívar's writings that he was familiar with the debates preceding ratification of the US Constitution of 1787 in general, or with the *Federalist Papers* in particular. As I suggest here, though, one has the sense that he might have found Publius's arguments congenial.

47 Bolívar, "Discurso pronunciado … ante el Congreso de Angostura," February 15, 1819, *Doctrina*, 127.

48 Lynch, *Simón Bolívar*, 104–107.

49 For Bolívar's later handling of another *pardo* critic, see Aline Helg, "Simón Bolívar and the Spectre of *Pardocracia*: José Padilla in Post-Independence Cartagena," *Journal of Latin American Studies*, Vol. 35, No. 3 (Aug. 2003), 447–471.

50 Matthew Brown, *Adventuring through Spanish Colonies: Simón Bolívar, Foreign Mercenaries, and the Birth of New Nations* (Liverpool: University of Liverpool Press, 2006).

51 David Bushnell, *The Santander Regime in Gran Colombia* (Newark: University of Delaware Press, 1954), 13–14.

52 Bolívar to Francisco de Paula Santander, San Carlos, July 13, 1821. *Doctrina*, 184–186.

53 Ibid., 184–186.

54 Constitución de la República de Colombia, Cúcuta, August 30, 1821, in Nelson Chávez Herrera, ed., *Primeras Constituciones de Latinoamérica*

y el Caribe (Caracas: Fundación Biblioteca Ayacucho y Banco Central de Venezuela, 2011), 284–312.

55 On the use of colonial boundaries in Spanish America after independence, see Suzanne Lalonde, *Determining Boundaries in a Conflicted World: The Role of Uti Possidetis* (Montreal: McGill-Queens University Press, 2002).

56 Article 128, Constitución de la República de Colombia, in Herrera, ed., *Primeras Constituciones,* 302.

57 Cited in Lynch, *Bolívar,* 145.

58 Bolívar, "Discurso pronuciado ... ante el Congreso de Angostura" February 15, 1819, *Doctrina,* 132.

59 Bolívar to General Pedro Antonio Olañeta, May 21, 1824. In *Obras Completas,* II, 9.

60 Bolívar, "Discurso pronuciado ... ante el Congreso de Angostura," February 15, 1819, *Doctrina,* 133–134.

61 Ibid., 134. Bolívar's use of the term "neutral body [*cuerpo neutro*]" as a description for the Hereditary Senate's position between the government and the people is likely derived from Benjamin Constant, who argued that in pre-revolutionary France, the king had served as a "neutral power" between the people and the nobility, and who sought to introduce a replacement *pouvoir préservatuer,* or "conservative power" into post-revolutionary constitution-alism. See Barrón, "La Tradición Republicana."

62 Bolívar, "Discurso pronuciado ... ante el Congreso de Angostura," February 15, 1819, *Doctrina,* 134–135.

63 See, especially, Pocock, *Machiavellian Moment,* passim, and, for the problems inherent in applying this conception to the supposedly classless Americas, see Gordon Wood, *The Creation of the American Republic, 1776–1787,* revised edition (Chapel Hill: University of North Carolina Press, 1998) 3–45, 197–255.

64 Ibid., 135–139.

65 The powers of the Executive Branch were defined in Title VI of the Bolivian Constitution of 1826. I quote from, Art. 82, § 24, in Herrera, ed., *Primeras Constituciones,* 352.

66 Bolívar, "Mensaje al Congreso de Bolivia," Lima, May 25, 1826, *Doctrina,* 80.

67 Jean-Jacques Rousseau, "The Social Contract, Book II, Chapter VII," in Victor Gourevitch, ed., *The Social Contract and Other Later Political Writings* (Cambridge: Cambridge University Press, 1997), 71.

68 See, especially, Madariaga, *Bolívar,* passim.

69 Bolívar, "Mensaje al Congreso de Bolivia," Lima, May 25, 1826, *Doctrina,* 280.

70 Ibid., 282.

71 For an important revisionist account of the interests and ideology of Popayán's indigenous and enslaved royalists, see Marcela Echeverri, "Popular Royalists, Empire, and Politics in Southwestern New Granada, 1808–1819," *Hispanic American Historical Review,* Vol. 91, No. 2 (May 2011), 237–269; and "Popular Royalists and Revolution in Colombia: Nationalism and Empire, 1780–1820" (PhD dissertation, New York University, 2008).

72 Bolívar, "Proclama en Pasto," June 8, 1822, *Archivo del Libertador*, Document 5765.

73 Von Vacano, *Color of Citizenship*, 70. It is worth noting that on at least one important occasion Bolívar retreated to a more conventional, less interventionist republicanism. From his Jamaican exile in 1815, he remarked, with palpable disappointment, that though he, "more than anyone, wished to see [Spanish] America formed into the greatest nation on earth ... I cannot persuade myself that the New World can, in this moment, be ruled as one large republic.... M. de Pradt [the French clergyman and intellectual who wrote extensively on the Americas] has wisely subdivided [Spanish] America into 15 or 17 independent states, each governed by its own monarch. I agree with the first part, as America is fit for the creation of seventeen nations, but as to the second, though it would be easier to achieve, I am not a supporter of American monarchies. Here are my reasons: the interest of a republic, properly understood, is circumscribed by the sphere of self-preservation, prosperity, and glory. Not evincing an imperial will, because it is precisely its opposite, the republic has no reason to extend its boundaries, and diminish its own resources, merely in order to force its neighbors to participate in a liberal constitution." From the "Carta de Jamaica," Kingston, September 6, 1815. *Doctrina*, 80–81.

74 Bolívar, "Memoria dirigida a los ciudadanos de la Nueva Granada," Cartagena de Indias, December 15, 1812, *Doctrina*, 10–11, emphasis added.

75 Ibid., 17.

76 Ibid., 82.

77 See Claudia L. Bushman, *America Discovers Columbus: How an Italian Explorer Became an American Hero* (Lebanon: University Press of New England, 1992).

78 Bolívar, "Discurso de Angostura," February 15, 1819, *Doctrina*, 146.

79 Bolívar to José Joaquín de Olmedo, Cali, January 2, 1822, *Doctrina*, 192.

80 Gerhard Masur's classic account of the meeting, and the historiographic debate surrounding even in the mid-twentieth century is still valuable. See "The Conference of Guayaquil," *The Hispanic American Historical Review*, Vol. 31, No. 2 (May 1951), 189–229.

81 The Roman legal doctrine of *uti possidetis* is often cited in this connection, though as recent work has shown, it did not often appear in contemporary documents; see Lalonde, *Determining Boundaries*, 24–60. A more plausible basis for the assumption has been found in Spanish customary law, which prescribed that in the absence of a legitimate monarch, such as the one caused by Napoleon's conquest of the Iberian peninsula, sovereignty returned to the constitutive kingdoms of the realm, the viceroyalties, in the case of the Americas. See John H. Elliott, "A Europe of Composite Monarchies," *Past and Present*, No. 137 (1992), 48–71; Guerra, *Modernidad y Independencias*.

82 Bolívar to Francisco de Paula Santander, Lima, September 11, 1823. *Archivo*, Document No. 7767.

83 Bolívar to Francisco de Paula Santander, Lima, March 12–14, 1823. *Archivo*, Document No. 7256.

84 Cited in Lynch, *Bolívar*, 189.

85 Bolívar, "Palabras en Potosí" *OC* III, 756.

86 Cited in Lynch, *Bolívar*, 218.

87 For a full treatment of the dynamics of this extremely interesting relationship, see: Thomas Millington, *Colombia's Military and Brazil's Monarchy: Undermining the Republican Foundations of South American Independence* (Wesport: Greenwood Press, 1996).

88 Bolívar to Antonio José de Sucre, Magdalena, May 12, 1826, and Bolívar to Antonio Gutiérrez de la Fuente, Magdalena, May 12, 1826, *Archivo* Documents Nos. 1087 and 1089.

89 Chapter 6 provides a comparative account of the political ideologies that divided Creole revolutionaries in the aftermath of independence and describes the consequences partisan conflict had on political and institutional development in Colombia.

90 For a fuller account of Bolívar's influences than I am able to give here, see German A. de la Reza, *La Invención de la Paz: De la República Cristiana del Duque de Sully a la Sociedad de Naciones de Simón Bolívar* (Mexico City: Ediciones Siglo XXI, 2009).

91 For Bolívar's more informal efforts to instigate cooperation amongst the various Spanish American independence movements, see Harold A. Bierck, "Bolívar and Spanish American Cooperation," *Pacific Historical Review*, Vol. 14, No. 2 (June 1945), 196–203.

92 Bolívar, "Invitación del Libertador ..." Cali, January 8–9, 1822, in German A. de la Reza, ed., *Documentos Sobre el Congreso Anfictiónico de Panamá* (Caracas: Fundación Biblioteca Ayacucho, 2010), 3–4.

93 Pedro Gual (Colombian Minister of Foreign Relations) "Instruccciones ...," Cúcuta, October 10–11, 1821, in De la Reza, ed., *Documentos*, 8–9.

94 Ibid., 6.

95 Bolívar, "Invitación ...," Lima, December 7, 1824, in De la Reza, ed., *Documentos*, 40.

96 See, for example, Kwame Nkrumah's 1963 classic *Africa Must Unite*. For studies of postcolonial unification efforts in Africa, see Frederick Cooper, *Citizenship between Empire and Nation: Remaking France and French Africa, 1945–1960* (Princeton: Princeton University Press, 2014); Gary Wilder, *Freedom Time: Negritude, Decolonization, and the Future of the World* (Durham: Duke University Press, 2015); and Adom Getachew, "The Rise and Fall of Self-Determination: Towards a History of Anti-Colonial World-Making" (PhD dissertation, Yale University, 2015).

97 Pedro Gual, "Instrucciones ...," Cúcuta, October 10–11, 1821. From De la Reza, ed., *Documentos*, 9.

98 See preceding, Chapter 2, notes 88–90.

99 Bolívar, "Invitación ...," Lima, December 7, 1824, in De la Reza, ed., *Documentos*, 42.

100 Bolívar, "Un Pensamiento sobre el Congreso de Panamá," Lima, February 1826, from De la Reza, *Documentos*, 52.

101 For an analogous, but rhetorically less ambitious line of thinking in the early republican United States, see: Peter S. Onuf and Nicholas G. Onuf, *Federal Union, Modern World: The Law of Nations in an Age of Revolutions, 1776–1814* (Madison: Madison House, 1993).

102 Bolívar to Francisco de Paula Santander, Lima, January 6, 1825. From *Doctrina*, 216.

103 Bolívar, "Un Pensamiento sobre el Congreso de Panamá," Lima, February 1826, from De la Reza, *Documentos*, 52.

104 Francisco de Paula Santander to Bolívar, Bogotá, February 6, 1825, from De la Reza, *Documentos*, 44–45.

105 Arthur P. Whitaker, *The Western Hemisphere Idea: Its Rise and Decline* (Ithaca: Cornell University Press, 1954).

106 Bolívar to Santander, Lima, March 8, 1825, Vicente Lecuna, ed., *Cartas del Libertador*, 2nd edition (Caracas: Banco de Venezuela, 1967), 272–275.

107 Bolívar to Colonel Patrick Campbell, British Chargé d'Affaires in Columbia, Guayaquil, August 5, 1829, in *Doctrina*, 355.

108 See, for a study of southern expansionism in the mid-nineteenth century, Robert E. May, *The Southern Dream of a Caribbean Empire, 1854–1861* (Baton Rouge: Louisiana State University Press, 1973).

109 Cited in Jay Sexton, *The Monroe Doctrine: Empire and Nation in Nineteenth-Century America* (New York: Hill and Wang, 2011), 75. For Clay's consistent advocacy of closer ties with Spanish America, see also Whitaker, *Western Hemisphere Idea*.

110 For this fascinating framing of the issue, see James E Lewis, Jr., *The American Union and the Problem of Neighborhood: The United States and the Collapse of the Spanish Empire, 1783–1829* (Chapel Hill: University of North Carolina Press, 1998).

111 Henry Clay, "General Instructions to Richard C. Anderson and John Sergeant, esqs., appointed Envoys Extraordinary and Ministers Plenipotentiary of the United States to the Congress at Panama," Washington, May 8, 1826, *The American Annual Register for the Years 1827–9*, 2nd edition (New York: William Hackson and E. & G. W. Blunt, 1835), 29–55.

112 See David Harvey, *A Brief History of Neoliberalism* (Oxford: Oxford University Press, 2005), 13.

5. THE CREOLE CONSERVATISM OF LUCAS ALAMÁN

1 See Eric Van Young, *The Other Rebellion: Popular Violence, Ideology, and the Mexican Struggle for Independence, 1810–1821* (Stanford: Stanford University Press, 2001), 39–65.

2 For the most important group of insurgent-sympathizers in Mexico City, see Virginia Guedea, *En Busca de un Gobierno Alterno: Los Guadalupes de México* (Mexico City: UNAM, 1992). For Mexico City's reaction to the insurgency, see Timothy E. Anna, *The Fall of Royal Government in Mexico City* (Lincoln: University of Nebraska Press, 1978), 64–97, 162–178.

3 For Mexico's "official history" of liberal-conservative conflict, see Jesús Reyes Heroles, *El Liberalismo Mexicano*, 3 Vols. (Mexico City: UNAM Press, 1957); for a more recent consideration, see Enrique Krauze, *Siglo de Caudillos: Biografía Política de México, 1810–1910* (Barcelona: Tusquets Editores, 1994).

4 Antonio Annino and Rafael Rojas, *La Independencia: Los Libros de la Patria* (Mexico City: CIDE and FCE, 2008), especially pp. 84–106.

5 See François-Xavier Guerra, *Modernidad e Independencias: Ensayos sobre las Revoluciones Hispánicas*, new edition (Madrid: Ediciones Encuentro, 2009); Jaime E. Rodríguez O., *The Independence of Spanish America* (Cambridge: Cambridge University Press, 1998); and Roberto Breña, *El Primer Liberalismo Español y los Procesos de Emancipación de América, 1808–1824: Una Revisión Historiográfica del Liberalismo Hispánico* (Mexico City: El Colegio de México, 2006). See also Annino and Rojas, *La Independencia*, 132–137, for a broader discussion of the "New Political History" and a fuller bibliography.

6 See Charles A. Hale, *Mexican Liberalism in the Age of Mora, 1821–1853* (New Haven: Yale University Press, 1968); Will Fowler, *Mexico in the Age of Proposals, 1821–1853* (Westport: Greenwood Press, 1998); Josefina Zoraida Vázquez, "Centralistas, Conservadores, y Monarquistas, 1830–1853," in William Fowler and Humberto Morales Moreno, eds., *El Conservadurismo Mexicano en el Siglo XIX* (Puebla: Benemérita Universidad Autónoma de Puebla, 1999); José Antonio Aguilar Rivera, *En Pos de la Quimera: Reflexiones sobre el Experimento Constituticional Atlántico* (Mexico City: FCE, 2000); Catherine Andrews, "Sobre Conservadurismo e Ideas Conservadoras en la Primera República Federal, 1824–1835," in Erika Pani, ed., *Conservadurismo y Derechas en la Historia de México*, Vol. 1 (Mexico City: FCE, 2009). For a full literature review, see Erika Pani, "'Las Fuerzas Oscuras': El Problema del Conservadurismo en la Historia de México," in Pani, ed., *Conservadurismo y Derechos*.

7 See Nettie Lee Benson, "Territorial Integrity in Mexican Politics, 1821–1833," in Jaime E. Rodríguez O., ed., *The Independence of Mexico and the Creation of the New Nation* (Los Angeles: UCLA Latin American Center, 1989); Pedro Santoni, *Mexicans at Arms: Puro Federalists and the Politics of War, 1845–1848* (Fort Worth: TCU Press, 1996); and Timothy J. Henderson, *A Glorious Defeat: Mexico and Its War with the United States* (New York: Hill and Wang, 2007).

8 Annino and Rojas describe Alamán's *Historia de Méjico desde los primeros movimientos que prepararon su Independencia en el año 1808 hasta la época presente*, published serially between 1849 and 1852, as the "best work of the era, and perhaps the entire nineteenth century." *La Independencia*, 57–58. I shall refer throughout to the five-volume fifth edition of the work: Lucas Alamán, *Historia de Méjico*, 5th edition, 5 Vols. (Mexico City: Editorial Jus, 1968) (hereafter *HM*).

9 Hale, *Mexican Liberalism*, 16.

10 Some recent scholarship, in an effort to rescue Alamán from the Liberal–Conservative binaries that long governed Mexican intellectual history, has deemphasized Burke's influence on Alamán, or presented it as a feature only of Alamán's late work. See José Antonio Aguilar's introductory essay in Lucas Alamán, *Examen Imparcial de la Administración de Bustamante*, José Antonio Aguilar Rivera, ed. (Mexico City: Consejo Nacional para la Cultura y las Artes, 2008); and Andrews, "Sobre Conservadurismo e

Ideas Conservadoras." Without denying that Alamán's thinking underwent changes over the course of his long career, here I shall try to show that Burke's influence was profound and consistent, appearing as early as the proposal Alamán drafted on behalf of the American delegation in the Spanish *Cortes* in 1820.

11 Unfortunately, we still lack a biography of Alamán in English, though Stanley C. Green, *The Mexican Republic: The First Decade, 1823–1832* (Pittsburgh: University of Pittsburgh Press, 1987) provides most of the relevant facts. The eminent historian Eric Van Young is at work rectifying this gap, and was generous enough to share some of his notes, which I draw on throughout. The standard biography in Spanish remains José C. Valadés, *Alamán: Estadista e Historiador* (Mexico City: José Porrua e Hijos, 1938).

12 See Anna, *Fall of Royal Government*, for a more detailed narration of events.

13 The fall of Guanajuato's *Alhóndiga de Granaditas* is still treated as the paradigmatic event of Hidalgo's revolt, in no small part because of Alamán's first-hand account; HM I, 261–292. An excerpt in English translation can be found in Gilbert M. Joseph and Timothy J. Henderson, eds., *The Mexico Reader: History, Culture, Politics* (Durham: Duke University Press, 2002), 171–188.

14 HM I, 282–283.

15 As Moisés Gonzáles Navarro puts it, for Alamán, "the origin of the Mexican nation was in the Conquest." *El Pensamiento Político de Lucas Alamán* (Mexico City: Fondo de Cultura Económica, 1952), 87.

16 HM I, 14.

17 HM I, 60–61.

18 Edmund Burke, "Reflections on the Revolution in France," 1790 in Iain Hampsher-Monk, ed., *Edmund Burke: Revolutionary Writings* (Cambridge: Cambridge University Press, 2014), 23.

19 HM I, 61.

20 HM I, 54–56, 80–84. Alamán's enthusiasm also no doubt reflected the immense expansion of mining and mineral exports presided over by the Bourbons, particularly notable during the latter half of the eighteenth century, from which his family would have profited directly. See D. A. Brading, *Miners and Merchants in Bourbon Mexico, 1763–1810* (Cambridge: Cambridge University Press, 1971).

21 HM I, 63–64.

22 HM I, 16–17.

23 HM I, 121–127.

24 HM I, 221–222.

25 Elías Palti, "Lucas Alamán y la involución política del pueblo mexicano. ¿Las ideas conservadoras 'fuera de lugar'?" in Pani, ed. *Conservadurismo y Derechas*, I, 305–306.

26 For a concise history of the Virgen de Guadalupe, and a nice account of her political and social evolution at the turn of the nineteenth century, see Margarita Zires, "Los Mitos de la Virgen de Guadalupe: Su Proceso de Construcción y Reinterpretación en el México Pasado y Contemporáneo," *Mexican Studies/Estudios Mexicanos*, Vol. 10, No. 2 (Summer 1994), 296–301.

27 Morelos declared for total independence in 1813 with a document titled "*Sentimientos de la Nación*" and shortly thereafter produced a constitution for independent Mexico. See Felipe Tena Ramirez, ed., *Leyes Fundamentales de México, 1808–1957* (Mexico City: Editorial Porrua, undated), 28–58. An English translation of the "Sentiments of the Nation" can be found in Joseph and Henderson, *The Mexico Reader*, 189–192.

28 For the general history of the insurgency, see Hugh M. Hamill, *The Hidalgo Revolt: Prelude to Mexican Independence* (Gainesville: University of Florida Press, 1966); and Timothy J. Henderson *The Mexican Wars for Independence* (New York: Hill and Wang, 2009). For more focused treatments of its social and ideological dimensions, see Villoro *Proceso Ideológico*, 69–102 and Van Young, *The Other Rebellion*.

29 *HM* II, 146.

30 *HM* I, 258.

31 *HM* I, 258, 310–311; *HM* II, 138–140; *HM* IV, 461.

32 *HM* IV, 461.

33 Mier published his *Historia de la revolución de Nueva España, antigua-menta Anáhuac* under the penname José Guerra. Simón Bolívar cited him by this name in support of his own constitutionalist defense of Creole Revolution, described in the last chapter. In reconstructing the arguments contained therein, I've relied here on D. A. Brading, *The First America: The Spanish Monarchy, Creole Patriots, and the Liberal State, 1492–1867* (Cambridge: Cambridge University Press, 1991), 590–595. For more on Mier, see also Annino and Rojas, *La Independencia*, 22–26; and Roberto Breña, "Pensamiento Político e Ideología en la Emancipación Americana: Fray Servando Teresa de Mier y la Independencia Absoluta de la Nueva España," in Francisco Colom, ed., *Relatos de Nación: La Construcción de las Identidades Nacionales en el Mundo Hispánico*, 2 Vols. (Madrid: Editorial Iberoamericana Vervuert, 2005). For the insurgency's adoption of Mier and Bustamante's indigenist arguments, see Luis Villoro, *El Proceso Ideológico de la Revolución de Independencia* [1953] (Mexico City: FCE, 2010), 132–172.

34 The original text of Morelos's "Discurso inaugural del Congreso de Chilpancingo" delivered in 1813, is available online in the digital collection of the Archivo General de la Nación: www.agn.gob.mx (accessed September 30, 2013).

35 *HM* I, 125–126.

36 *HM* III, 18.

37 *HM* V, 244.

38 See John C. Weston, Jr., "The Ironic Purpose of Burke's Vindication Vindicated," *Journal of the History of Ideas*, Vol. 19, No. 3 (June 1958), 435–441 and Iain Hampsher-Monk, "*Reflections on the Revolution in France*," in David Dwan and Christopher J. Insole, eds., *The Cambridge Companion to Edmund Burke* (Cambridge: Cambridge University Press, 2012), 200–202.

39 Burke, *Reflections*, in Hampsher-Monk, ed., *Revolutionary Writings*, 34.

40 Text can be found in Tena Ramírez, *Leyes Fundamentales*, 59–106.

41 See: Charles R. Berry, "The Election of the Mexican Deputies to the Spanish Cortes, 1810–1822," in Nettie Lee Benson, ed., *Mexico and the Spanish Cortes, 1810–1822* (Austin: University of Texas Press, 1966), 10–42.

42 "Exposición presentada a las Cortes por los diputados de ultramar en la sesion de 25 de Junio de 1821, sobre el estado actual de las provincias de que eran representantes, y medios convenientes para su definitiva pacificación; redactada por encargo de los mismos diputados por D. Lucas Alamán y D. José Mariano de Michelena." Document Number 19 in the Appendix to *HM* V. See also Valadés, *Alamán*, 105–116.

43 "*Exposición*," *HM* V, 642.

44 Ibid., 642.

45 Ibid., 649.

46 Ibid., 642–643.

47 Ibid., 643–644.

48 Ibid., 645–650.

49 Though Alamán did not cite Burke explicitly, we know that the American deputies at the *Cortes* had read Burke's speech and grasped its relevance to their own struggle, because Father Fernando Antonio Dávila, the deputy from Chiapas, read whole passages aloud later that day. See Mario Rodríguez, "The 'American Question' at the Cortes of Madrid," *The Americas*, Vol. 38, No. 3 (Jan. 1982), 310–311.

50 Edmund Burke, "Speech on Moving His Resolutions for Conciliation with the Colonies," delivered March 22, 1775, in David Bromwich, ed., *Edmund Burke on Empire, Liberty, and Reform: Speeches and Letters* (New Haven: Yale University Press, 2000), 115–116.

51 Alamán, "*Exposción*," 649.

52 Ibid., 642–643.

53 Ibid., 652–654.

54 Ibid., 644–645.

55 Ibid., 648–649.

56 Scholars debate the reasons Iturbide took this decision when he did. Alamán asserts that "Although Iturbide savagely prosecuted the war against the insurgents, he was not for this any less inclined toward independence than any other Americans," noting that like other Creoles, he felt that the insurgents presented such a grave threat to Mexico's social order that "it was necessary to finish them before proposing any new plan" for independence (*HM* V, 47). Later historians have derided Iturbide's rebellion as a counter-revolutionary response to events in Spain, spurred by perceived threats to the privileges of the clerical establishment and the military under reestablished constitutional government. See: Neill Macaulay, "The Army of New Spain and the Mexican Delegation to the Spanish Cortes," in Benson, ed., *Mexico and the Spanish Cortes*, 134–152. A more sympathetic view, resting on much more extensive research than any other available work, holds that Iturbide an his supporters "were conservative reformers, but not counterrevolutionaries." See Timothy E. Anna, *The Mexican Empire of Iturbide* (Lincoln: University of Nebraska Press, 1990), 39 for the quoted portion and pp. 1–26 for the interpretive controversy.

57 See Anna, *Iturbide*, 3–13 for the history and Tena Ramirez, *Leyes Fundamentales*, 107–119 for the text of both the Plan of Iguala and the Treaty of Córdoba. For an English translation of the Plan, see Joseph and Henderson, *The Mexico Reader*, 192–195. For the origins of the ideas contained in the plan, particularly that of establishing new princes in the Americas, see Nettie Lee Benson, "Iturbide y los Planes de Independencia," *Historia Mexicana*, Vol. 2, No. 3 (Jan.–Mar. 1953), 439–446.

58 *HM* V, 73.

59 My tally is based on the very useful chronology in Fowler, *Mexico in the Age of Proposals*, 271–276. The four "constitutional systems" I have in mind are (1) Iturbide's empire under the Plan of Iguala and the Treaty of Córdoba, (2) the First Republic under the Constitution of 1824, (3) the First Centralist Republic under the *Siete Leyes* of 1836, and (4) Santa Anna's dictatorship under the *Bases Orgánicas* of 1843. I say "at least" four because one might easily argue that within each of the periods when these documents were technically the basic law of the land, there were periods when Mexico was actually governed by distinctive de facto arrangements.

60 See Fowler, *Mexico in the Age of Proposals*, 1–2; Josefina Zoraida Vázquez, "Los años olvidados," *Mexican Studies/Estudios Mexicanos*, Vol. 5, No. 2 (Summer 1989), 313–326 and Michael P. Costeloe, *The Central Republic in Mexico, 1835–1846: Hombres de Bien in the Age of Santa Anna* (Cambridge: Cambridge University Press, 1993), 1–2.

61 *HM* V, 434.

62 See cites in note 6.

63 For the term "*hombres de bien*," see Costeloe, *The Central Reepublic*, 16–27.

64 *HM* V, 82.

65 *HM* V, 82–83.

66 *HM* V, 80–81.

67 Alamán, too, derided Iturbide's presumption, arguing that with the "false step" of taking the throne, he had "precipitated his own downfall." He wrote that a better path would have been to have Iturbide established as "First Regent," allowing him to exercise the same powers without giving Santa Anna and other opportunists to base their revolutionary appeal on republican principles in which they themselves did not believe (*HM* V, 404).

68 On Santa Anna's rebellion, and the importance of provincialism to Iturbide's demise, see Anna, *Iturbide*, 178–188; and Nettie Lee Benson, "The Plan of Casa Mata," *Hispanic American Historical Review*, Vol. 25, No. 1 (Feb. 1945), 45–56.

69 Jaime E. Rodríguez O., "The Struggle for the Nation: The First Centralist-Federalist Conflict in Mexico," *The Americas*, Vol. 49, No. 1 (July 1992), 1–22; Jaime E. Rodríguez O. and Virginia Guedea, "La Constitución de 1824 y la formación del Estado Mexicano," *Historia Mexicana*, Vol. 40, No. 3 (Jan.–Mar. 1991), 507–535. For the provincial origins of Mexican federalism, see Nettie Lee Benson, *La Diputación Provincial y el Federalismo Mexicano* (Mexico City: Colegio de México, 1955).

70 Tena Ramírez, *Leyes Fundamentales de México*, 153–198. An English translation can be found at http://tarlton.law.utexas.edu/constitutions/text /1824index.html (accessed April 4, 2011).

71 See Green, *The Mexican Republic*, passim and especially pp. 87–111.

72 In Chapter 6, I provide a more detailed narrative of Mexico's second presidential election and the parties whose conflict led first to a contested result and then civil war.

73 Ibid., 189–229. I discuss some of Alamán's policies as minister in more detail in the following text.

74 See Fowler, *Mexico in the Age of Proposals*, 189–196.

75 The "Defensa del Ex Ministro de Relaciones Don Lucas Alamán" and the "Examen Imparcial de la Administración del General Vicepresidente Don Anastasio Bustamante" have recently been republished, along with a very useful introductory essay, in José Antonio Aguilar Rivera, ed., *Examen Imparcial de la Administración de Bustamante* (Mexico City: Consejo Nacional para la Cultura y las Artes, 2008) (hereafter *EI*).

76 Aguilar, "Alamán en el Periodo de Bustamante," in *EI*, 20.

77 I say this while acknowledging the contributions of José Antonio Aguilar and Catherine Andrews, who have argued that Burke's influence on Alamán, in particular, and Mexican conservatism, in general, has been over-emphasized. See Aguilar "Alamán en el Periodo de Bustamante," in *EI*, passim and particularly 37–45; Andrews, "Conservadurismo e Ideas Conservadoras," 120–126; and Fowler, *Mexico in the Age of Proposals*, 60–69 for a very different view. Aguilar, in particular, is quite right to point out that Alamán's arguments in the *Examen Imparcial* resemble those of Hamilton and Madison as often as they do Burke's, though he does not cite them, and it is not clear that he had read the *Federalist Papers*. I do not, however, think that this means that Burke's influence was minimal, or merely rhetorical; I read Alamán's *Examen Imparcial* as a Burkean defense of constitutional ideas that were shared by Creole revolutionaries throughout the hemisphere. That Alamán converged on the same ideas as Hamilton and Madison while beginning from Burkean premises presents powerful evidence that the shared characteristics of Creoles' social position had a strong effect on their political thought.

78 *EI*, 199–200.

79 *EI*, 200.

80 *EI*, 204, 201.

81 *EI*, 201.

82 Hamilton, *The Federalist No. 66*.

83 *EI*, 203–207.

84 *EI*, 209–210.

85 *EI*, 210–211.

86 I owe this insight to José Antonio Aguilar, who has treated the theme of emergency powers in Latin American political thought in a number of works. See "Alamán en el Periodo de Bustamante," *EI*, 29–32; *En Pos de la Quimera*, passim and especially 167–201; and *El Manto Liberal: Los Poderes de Emergencia en México, 1821–1876* (Mexico City: UNAM Press, 2001).

87 *EI*, 207–209.

88 *EI*, 212, citing Burke, *Reflections on the Revolution in France*, 97.

89 *EI*, 214. For Burke on property, see *Reflections*, passim and particularly 140–141.

90 *EI*, 212–221; 215 for the quoted portion.

91 Catherine Andrews has argued quite convincingly that Alamán's ideal constitution was, in fact, much closer to the English model than that of the United States, and suggested that his enthusiasm for the latter was a result of misunderstanding the extent to which it too established a formal balance of powers between social classes. She notes, interestingly, that this misunderstanding may have come from reading John Adams's *Defence of the Constitutions of the United States*. See "In the Pursuit of Balance. Lucas Alamán's Proposals for Constitutional Reform (1830–1835)," *Historia Constitucional* (electronic edition), No. 8, 2007.

92 *EI*, 216.

93 See Costeloe, *The Central Republic*, 31–92 for the politics of the period and, particularly, 57–61 for the "political manifesto" laid out in mainly anonymous newspaper editorials and pamphlets over the course of 1834–1835. For a more focused study of the debate, which traces its roots back to the Bustamante administration of 1830–1832, see Catherine Andrews, "El Debate Político de la Década de 1830 y los Orígenes de las Siete Leyes," in Cecilia Noriega and Alicia Salmerón, eds., *México: Un Siglo de Historia Constitucional, 1808–1917* (Mexico City: Instituto Mora, 2010), 111–133; and Andrews, "Conservadurismo e Ideas Conservadoras," 117–126.

94 Costeloe, *The Central Republic*, 40–45.

95 Tena Ramírez, *Leyes Fundamentales de México*, 199–248.

96 Costeloe, *The Central Republic*, 107–109. For more on the *Siete Leyes*, see Alfonso Noriega, *El Pensamiento Conservador y el Conservadurismo Mexicano*, 2 vols. (Mexico City: UNAM, 1972) and David Pantoja Morán, *El Supremo Poder Conservador: El Diseño Institucional en las Primeras Constituciones Mexicanas* (Mexico City: El Colegio de México, 2005).

97 Tena Ramírez, *Leyes Fundamentales*, 403–438.

98 *HM* I, 11.

99 *HM* V, 306.

100 Henderson, *A Glorious Defeat*, 33–34.

101 Nettie Lee Benson, "Territorial Integrity in Mexican Politics, 1821–1833," in Jaime E. Rodríguez O., ed., *The Independence of Mexico and the Creation of the New Nation* (Los Angeles: UCLA Latin American Center, 1989), 275.

102 Ibid., 276–281.

103 Lucas Alamán, "Memoria del Secretario de Estado y del Despacho de Relaciones Esteriories é Interiories," November 8, 1823, in *Memorias de los Ministros del Interior y del Exterior* (Mexico City: Secretaria de Gobernación, 1987) (hereafter *MM*), 76–77.

104 For a history of the concept of civilization in imperial political thought, see Brett Bowden, *Empire of Civilization: Evolution of an Imperial Idea* (Chicago: University of Chicago Press, 2009).

105 Timothy Henderson estimates that in 1823 there were around 3,000 illegal Anglo-American settlers already in Texas and roughly the same number of Mexican citizens, some of whom were legal Anglo-American settlers. *A Glorious Defeat*, 49–50.

106 Benson, "Territorial Integrity," 285–286; Henderson, *A Glorious Defeat*, 29–30.

107 Alamán, "Memoria del Secretario de Estado y del Despacho de Relaciones Esteriories é Interiores," January 11, 1825, *MM*, 89–90.

108 Ibid., 137.

109 Lucas Alamán, "Memoria," Mexico City, January 8, 1831. From Magdalena Rivera, ed., *Memorias de los Ministros del interior y del exterior* (Mexico City: Instituto Nacional de Estudios Históricos de la Revolución Mexicana, 1987), 386.

110 Benson, "Territorial Integrity," 288.

111 Henderson, *A Glorious Defeat*, 40–47; Valadés, *Alamán*, 203–209.

112 Benson, "Territorial Integrity," 297.

113 "Memoria ...," November 8, 1823, in *MM*, 34–35.

114 Cited in Salvador Méndez Reyes, *El Hispanoamericanismo de Lucas Alamán, 1823–1853* (Toluca: Universidad Autonomo del Estado de Mexico, 1996), 129.

115 Cited in Méndez Reyes, *Hispanoamericanismo*, 239.

116 Ibid., 176–195.

117 The celebrated Mexican statesman José Vasconcelos, in his 1934 *Bolivarismo y Monroísmo: Temas Iberoamericanos* (Santiago: Biblioteca América), described Alamán's "Spanish Americanism" thus: "it is little known that the first attempt to deal a blow to the Monroe Doctrine was by the Mexican, Lucas Alamán ... Alamán believed in the race [*la raza*], believed in the language, believed in the religious community. In sum, Alamán gave Bolivarianism the content that it lacked.... With Alamán a Spanish Americanism in clear and defined opposition to [Monroeism] is born." For Vasconcelos's views of Alamán, see also Valadés, *Alamán*, passim; and Méndez Reyes, *Hispanoamericanismo*, 105–110.

118 Alamán, "Memoria ...," January 11, 1825 in *MM*, 95–96.

119 For an excellent introduction to and anthology of "the debate on monarchism," see Elías José Palti, *La Política del Disenso: La "Polémica en Torno al Monarquismo," México, 1848–1850, ... y las Aporías del Liberalismo* (Mexico City: Fondo de Cultura Económica, 1998). The letter to which I refer, J. M. Gutiérrez Estrada's "Carta Dirigida al Excelentísimo Señor Presidente de la República" (Aug. 25, 1840) can be found therein, at 61–71.

120 "Neustra Profesión de Fe al 'Memorial Histórico,'" *El Tiempo*, No. 12 (Feb. 12, 1846), ibid., 76.

121 "Los Conservadores y la Nación," *El Universal* (Jan. 9, 1850), ibid., 459–461.

122 See Valadés, *Alamán*, passim; Noriega, *El Pensamiento Conservador*, 76; Aguilar, "Lucas Alamán y La Constitución," 83–122; Zoraida Vázquez, "Centralistas, Conservadores y Monarchistas," 121–125; Fowler, *Mexico in the Age of Proposals*, 75–85.

6. THE END OF CREOLE REVOLUTION

1 See Reginald Horsman, *Race and Manifest Destiny: The Origins of American Racial Anglo-Saxonism* (Cambridge, MA: Harvard University Press, 1981), especially 208–248; and Louis A. Pérez, Jr., *Cuba in the American*

Imagination: Metaphor and the Imperial Ethos (Chapel Hill: University of Carolina Press, 2008), especially 95–174.

2 For recent attempts to revive geographic and climatic explanation of differential economic development, see Jared Diamond, *Guns, Germs, and Steel: The Fates of Human Societies* (New York: W. W. Norton, 1997); and Jeffrey D. Sachs, *Tropical Underdevelopment*, NBER Working Paper 8119 (Cambridge, MA: National Bureau of Economic Research, 2001).

3 Daron Acemoglu, Simon Johnson, and James A. Robinson, "Reversal of Fortune: Geography and Institutions in the Making of the Modern World Income Distribution," *The Quarterly Journal of Economics*, Nov. 2002.

4 See, for especially influential versions of this thesis: Douglass C. North, "Institutions and Economic Growth: An Historical Introduction," *World Development*, Vol. 17, No. 9 (1989), 1326–1330; John H. Coatsworth, "Notes on the Comparative Economic History of Latin America and the United States," in Walther L. Bernecker and Hans Werner Tobler, eds., *Development and Underdevelopment in America: Contrasts of Economic Growth in North and Latin America in Historical Perspective* (Berlin: Walter de Gruyter, 1993). Stanley L. Engerman and Kenneth L. Sokoloff, "Factor Endowments, Institutions, and Differential Paths of Growth among New World Economies," in Stephen H. Haber, ed., *How Latin America Fell Behind* (Palo Alto: Stanford University Press, 1997), 260–306; Douglass C. North, William Summerhill, and Barry R. Weingast, "Order, Disorder and Economic Change: Latin America vs. North America," in Bruce Bueno de Mesquita and Hilton Root, eds., *Governing for Prosperity* (New Haven: Yale University Press, 2000), 17–58; Daron Acemoglu, Simon Johnson, and James A. Robinson, "The Colonial Origins of Comparative Development: An Empirical Investigation," *The American Economic Review*, Vol. 91, No. 5 (Dec. 2001), 1369–1401; James Mahoney, *Colonialism and Postcolonial Development: Spanish America in Comparative Perspective* (Cambridge: Cambridge University Press, 2010), 229–242, 254–257; Adam Przeworski and Carolina Curvale, "Does Politics Explain the Economic Gap between the United States and Latin America?," in Francis Fukuyama, ed., *Falling Behind: Explaining the Development Gap between Latin America and the United States* (Oxford: Oxford University Press, 2008), 99–133.

5 North, *Institutions*; Matthew Lange, James Mahoney, and Matthias vom Hau, "Colonialism and Development: A Comparative Analysis of Spanish and British Colonies," *American Journal of Sociology*, Vol. 111, No. 5 (Mar. 2006), 1412–1462; Rafael La Porta, Florencio Lopez-de-Silanes, and Andrei Shleifer, "The Economic Consequences of Legal Origins," *Journal of Economic Literature*, Vol. 46, No. 2 (June 2008), 285–332.

6 Coatsworth, "Comparative Economic History"; Engerman and Sokoloff, "Factor Endowments"; Acemoglu, Johnson, and Robinson, "Colonial Origins"; "Reversal of Fortune"; Daron Acemoglu and James Robinson, *Why Nations Fail: The Origins of Power, Prosperity, and Poverty* (New York: Crown Publishers, 2012). Mahoney combines elements of each view,

arguing that the size and complexity of pre-colonial populations determined the intensity with which imperial powers with different economic orientations (mercantilist or liberal) established institutions in different parts of the Americas (Mahoney, *Colonialism and Postcolonial Development*).

7 As Adam Przeworski notes, that institutions are "endogenous," or sustained over time by self-reinforcing processes, is one of the new institutional literature's two definitive propositions. See: "The Last Instance: Are Institutions the Primary Cause of Development?," *European Journal of Sociology*, Vol. 45, Issue 2 (Aug. 2004), 165). See also Paul Pierson, "Increasing Returns, Path Dependence, and the Study of Politics," *American Political Science Review*, No. 94 (June 2000).

8 Here, it is worth clarifying my difference with Benedict Anderson's influential observation, following Gerhard Masur, that "each of the new Spanish American republics had been an administrative unit from the sixteenth to the eighteenth century"; see *Imagined Communities: Reflections on the Origins and Spread of Nationalism*, revised edition (London: Verso, 1991), 52. The problem, as the previous chapters have shown, is that the Spanish Empire contained many nested, overlapping administrative units, some of which became independent states and some of which did not. The doctrine of *uti possidetis*, usually cited as the relevant legal precedent, did not provide clear direction as to which sort of administrative unit – the *audiencia*, viceroyalty, captaincy-general, or kingdom – should determine the shape of the states that would eventually emerge. See Suzanne Lalonde, *Determining Boundaries in a Conflicted World: The Role of Uti Possidetis* (Montreal: McGill-Queen's University Press, 2002), 24–60.

9 Joshua Simon, "The Americas' More Perfect Unions: New Institutional Insights from Comparative Political Theory," *Perspectives on Politics*, Vol. 12, No. 4 (Dec. 2014), 808–828.

10 Alexander Hamilton to Gouverneur Morris, New York, February 29 1802, in Joanne B. Freeman, ed., *Writings of Alexander Hamilton* (New York: Library of America, 2001), 986.

11 Simón Bolívar to Juan José Flores. Barranquilla, November 9, 1830. OC III p. 501.

12 Lucas Alamán, *Historia de Méjico*, 5th edition, 5 Vols. (Mexico City: Editorial Jus, 1968), V, 567.

13 Bruce Ackerman, *The Failure of the Founding Fathers: Jefferson, Marshall, and the Rise of Presidential Democracy* (Cambridge, MA: Harvard University Press, 2005), 26.

14 Seymour Martin Lipset, *The First New Nation: The United States in Historical and Comparative Perspective* (New York: W. W. Norton, 1979), 43–44.

15 For a detailed account of the purposes of these programs, see Max Edling, *A Hercules in the Cradle: War, Money and the American State, 1783–1867* (Chicago: University of Chicago Press, 2014), 81–107. For a general account of the period's politics, see also Gordon Wood, *Empire of Liberty: A History of the Early Republic, 1789–1815* (Oxford: Oxford University Press, 2009), 140–314.

16 "Virginia's Remonstrance Against the Assumption of State Debts," December 16, 1790, in Lance Banning, ed., *Liberty and Order: The First American Party Struggle* (Indianapolis: Liberty Fund, 2004).

17 For an in-depth study of the northern Republicans, see Joyce Appleby, *Capitalism and a New Social Order: The Republican Vision of the 1790s* (New York: New York University Press, 1984).

18 James Madison, "Virginia Resolutions against the Alien and Sedition Acts," December 21, 1798, in Jack Rakove, ed., *James Madison: Writings* (New York: Library of America, 1999), 589.

19 Thomas Jefferson, "Draft of the Kentucky Resolutions," October 1798, in Merrill D. Peterson, ed., *Thomas Jefferson: Writings* (New York: The Library of America, 1984), 449–456.

20 Ackerman, *Failure of the Founding Fathers*, 16–108. The two Jefferson quotations are cited at 87 and 91.

21 Wood, *Empire of Liberty*, 692–696.

22 Daniel Walker Howe, *What Hath God Wrought: The Transformation of America, 1815–1848* (Oxford: Oxford University Press, 2007), 367–410.

23 Alexis de Tocqueville, *Democracy in America* [1835]. Translated by Arthur Goldhammer (New York: The Library of America, 2004), 425.

24 James McPherson, *Battle Cry of Freedom: The Civil War Era* (Oxford: Oxford University Press, 1988), 47–77.

25 David C. Hendrickson, *Union, Nation, or Empire: The American Debate over International Relations, 1789–1941* (Lawrence: University Press of Kansas, 2009), 202.

26 Edling, *Hercules in the Cradle*, passim.

27 Tulio Halperín-Donghi, *Politics, Economics, and Society in Argentina in the Revolutionary Period* (Cambridge: Cambridge University Press, 1975); Jeremy Adelman, *Republic of Capital: Buenos Aires and the Legal Transformation of the Atlantic World* (Stanford: Stanford University Press, 1999).

28 Mariano Moreno, "Representación de los Hacendados," Buenos Aires, September 30, 1809. From Mariano Moreno, in Gustavo Varela, ed., *Plan de Operaciones y Otros Escritos* (La Plata: Terramar 2007), 96.

29 Ibid., 108.

30 "Proclama de la Junta Provisional Gubernativa de Buenos Aires," May 26, 1810. From José Luis Romero and Luis Alberto Romero, eds., *Pensamiento Político de la Emancipación*, 2 Vols. (Caracas: Biblioteca Ayacucho, 1977), I, 255.

31 Mariano Moreno, "Plan de Operaciones," Buenos Aires, August 30, 1810. From Moreno, *Plan de Operaciones*, 38.

32 Ibid., 42.

33 Ibid., 81.

34 Ibid., 75–83.

35 Manuel Belgrano, "Causas de la destrucción o de la conservación y engrandecimiento de las naciones," Buenos Aires, May 19, 1810. From Manuel Belgrano, in Gregorio Weinberg, ed., *Escritos Económicos* (Buenos Aires: Editorial Raigal, 1954).

36 Bernardino Rivadavia to Jeremy Bentham, Buenos Aires, August 26, 1822. I quote here from the English translation of this letter, originally written in French, from Jeremy Bentham, in John Bowring, ed., *The Works of Jeremy Bentham*, 11 Vols. (Edinburgh: William Tait, 1838–1843), IV, 592–593.

37 David Bushnell, *The Santander Regime in Gran Colombia* (Newark: University of Delaware Press, 1954), passim, and 314 for the quoted portion.

38 Cited in John Lynch, *Simón Bolívar: A Life* (New Haven: Yale University Press, 2006), 223.

39 The narrative of this and the preceding paragraphs are drawn from Bushnell, *Santander Regime*, 318–359; and Lynch, *Bolívar*, 227–279.

40 See Michael P. Costeloe, *La Primera República Federal de México: Un Estudio de los Partidos Políticos en el México Independiente* (Mexico City: Fondo de Cultura Económica, 1983); Stanley C. Green, *The Mexican Republic: The First Decade, 1823–1832* (Pittsburgh: University of Pittsburgh Press, 1987); and Will Fowler, *Mexico in the Age of Proposals, 1821–1853* (Westport: Greenwood Press, 1998).

41 Green, *Mexican Republic*, 141.

42 See: Erika Pani, "Saving the Nation through Exclusion: Alien Laws in the Early Republic in the United States and Mexico," *The Americas*, Vol. 65, No. 2 (Oct. 2008), 217–246.

43 See Green, *Mexican Republic*, 140–161.

44 Fowler, *Mexico in the Age of Proposals*, 20–32.

45 Donald Fithian Stevens, *Origins of Instability in Early Republican Mexico* (Durham: Duke University Press, 1991).

46 Timothy J. Henderson, *A Glorious Defeat: Mexico and Its War with the United States* (New York: Hill and Wang, 2007).

47 For a fascinating comparison of the United States and Mexico's ability to raise revenues and defend their territory in the period surrounding the Mexican–American War, see Edling, *Hercules in the Cradle*, 145–177. Figures cited in the preceding text are at 167–168.

48 For Madison's "imposition" doctrine, a close cousin of Thomas Jefferson's better-known "nullification" doctrine, see Madison, "Virginia Resolutions," in Rakove, ed., *Writings*, 589. See also Forrest McDonald, *States Rights and the Union: Imperium in Imperio, 1776–1876* (Lawrence: University Press of Kansas, 2000), 17–18, 42.

49 Francisco de Paula Santander to Alejandro Vélez, May 17, 1827. Cited in Bushnell, *Santander Regime*, 357.

50 As Charles Hale suggests, over the course of the nineteenth century, "federalism as a juridical form was not a distinguishing feature of Mexican political liberalism," *Mexican Liberalism in the Age of Mora, 1821–1853* (New Haven: Yale University Press, 1968), 84–85. The same can be said of the United States, where even Hamilton's High Federalist allies eventually took up the states' rights banner to resist the policies of Thomas Jefferson's administration, which adopted a more expansive vision of the federal government's authority once it took office. See McDonald, *States Rights and the Union*, 59–61.

51 See Lance Banning, *The Jeffersonian Persuasion: Evolution of a Party Ideology* (Ithaca: Cornell University Press, 1978), 208–245; and Appleby, *Capitalism and a New Social Order*, 57–63.

52 Thomas Jefferson to George Mason, Philadelphia, February 4, 1791, in Peterson, ed., *Writings*, 971–972. See also Lawrence S. Kaplan, *Jefferson and France: An Essay on Politics and Political Ideas* (New Haven: Yale University Press, 1967), 37–59.

53 See Bushnell, *Santander Regime*, 291, for an account of the populist rhetoric employed by the "Caracas Club," a group of opposition pamphleteers and newspaper editorialists; and Fowler, *Mexico in the Age of Proposals*, 171–189, for analysis of the political thought of Lorenzo de Zavala, Mexico's most articulate populist politician of the early republican period.

54 Wood, *Empire of Liberty*, 167–168. One of the clearest illustrations of the Democratic-Republicans' racially limited commitment to democracy and republicanism is the contrary positions the party adopted in relation to the French and Haitian Revolutions, offering hearty support for the former while working to undermine the latter. See Gordon S. Brown, *Toussaint's Clause: The Founding Fathers and the Haitian Revolution* (Jackson: University Press of Mississippi, 2005). For Jefferson's evolving defense of indigenous expropriation, see Adam Dahl, "Commercial Conquest: Empire and Property in the Early U.S. Republic," *American Political Thought*, Vol. 5, No. 3 (Summer 2016), 421–445.

55 Bushnell, *Santander Regime*, 291.

56 Hale, *Mexican Liberalism*, 38.

57 See Aziz Rana, *The Two Faces of American Freedom* (Cambridge, MA: Harvard University Press, 2010), 131–148; and Stevens, *Origins of Instability*, 75–87.

58 The conquest of Buenos Aires "civilized" Creole revolutionaries by the "barbarian" gauchos from the provinces forms the main theme of Domingo Faustino Sarmiento's 1845 classic, *Facundo: Civilización y Barbarie*. See also John Street, *Artigas and the Emancipation of Uruguay* (Cambridge: Cambridge University Press, 1959); David Bushnell, *Reform and Reaction in the Platine Provinces, 1810–1852* (Gainesville: University of Florida Press, 1983); John Lynch, *Argentine Dictator: Juan Manuel de Rosas, 1829–1852* (Oxford: Oxford University Press, 1981); and Jorge Myers, *Orden y Virtud: El Discurso Republicano en el Régimen Rosista* (Buenos Aires: Universidad Nacional de Quilmes, 1995).

59 Karl Marx, "The Eighteenth Brumaire of Louis Bonaparte" [1852], in Robert C. Tucker, ed., *The Marx-Engels Reader*, 2nd edition (New York: W. W. Norton, 1978), 594.

60 Thomas Jefferson referred to his own election to the presidency as the "revolution of 1800," declaring it "as real a revolution in the principles of our government as that of 1776 was in its form." Jefferson to Judge Spencer Rome, Poplar Forest, September 6, 1819 in Peterson, ed. *Writings*, 1425.

7. CONCLUSION: FROM THE CREOLE REVOLUTIONS
TO OUR AMERICAS

1 For "imperial anticolonialism" in the nineteenth-century US foreign policy, see: William Appleman Williams, *The Tragedy of American Diplomacy* (New York: W. W. Norton, 1972); and Jay Sexton, *The Monroe Doctrine: Empire and Nation in Nineteenth-Century America* (New York: Hill and Wang, 2011).

2 James Monroe, "Seventh Annual Message," December 2, 1823. Online by Gerhard Peters and John T. Woolley, *The American Presidency Project.* www.presidency.ucsb.edu/ws/?pid=29465 (accessed February 1, 2016).

3 James K. Polk, "First Annual Message," December 2, 1845. Online by Gerhard Peters and John T. Woolley, *The American Presidency Project.* www.presidency.ucsb.edu/ws/?pid=29486 (accessed February 1, 2016).

4 Reginald Horsman, *Race and Manifest Destiny: The Origins of American Racial Anglo-Saxonism* (Cambridge, MA: Harvard University Press, 1981), 241. See also: Paul Frymer, "'A Rush and a Push and the Land Is Ours': Territorial Expansion, Land Policy, and U.S. State Formation," *Perspectives on Politics*, Vol. 12, No. 2 (2014), 119–144.

5 Theodore Roosevelt, "Fourth Annual Message," December 6, 1904. Online by Gerhard Peters and John T. Woolley, *The American Presidency Project.* www.presidency.ucsb.edu/ws/?pid=29545 (accessed February 1, 2016).

6 José Martí's essay "Nuestra América" was originally published in *La Revista Ilustrada de Nueva York*, on January 1, 1891. Here I translate from the version published in the Mexican newspaper *El Partido Liberal* on January 30, 1891, which is reprinted in Martí's *Obras Completas*, 26 Vols. (Havana: Editorial de Ciencias Sociales, 1991), VI, 17.

7 Ibid., 21.

8 Ibid., 22. See also Ada Ferrer, *Insurgent Cuba: Race, Nation, and Revolution, 1868–1898* (Chapel Hill: University of North Carolina Press, 1999).

9 Martí, "Nuestra América," from *Obras Completas*, VI, 22–23.

10 See Michel Gobat, "The Invention of Latin America: A Transnational History of Anti-Imperialism, Democracy, and Race," *The American Historical Review*, Vol. 118, No. 5 (Dec. 2013), 1345–1375; and Greg Grandin, "Your Americanism and Mine: Americanism and Anti-Americanism in the Americas," *The American Historical Review*, Vol. 111, No. 4 (Oct. 2006), 1042–1066.

Bibliography

COLLECTIONS OF PRIMARY SOURCES

Adams, Charles Francis, ed., *The Works of John Adams, Second President of the United States*, 10 Vols. (Boston: Little, Brown and Co., 1856), X, 149.

Aguilar Rivera, José Antonio, ed., *Examen Imparcial de la Administración de Bustamante* (Mexico City: Consejo Nacional para la Cultura y las Artes, 2008) [*EI*].

Archivo General de la Nación (Mexico), www.agn.gob.mx.

Ball, Terence, ed., *The Federalist, with Letters of "Brutus"* (Cambridge: Cambridge University Press, 2003) [*Federalist*].

Banning, Lance, ed., *Liberty and Order: The First American Party Struggle* (Indianapolis: Liberty Fund, 2004).

Bowring, John, ed., *The Works of Jeremy Bentham*, 11 Vols. (Edinburgh: William Tait, 1838–1843).

Bromwich, David, ed., *Edmund Burke on Empire, Liberty, and Reform: Speeches and Letters* (New Haven: Yale University Press, 2000).

Brown, Matthew, ed., *Hugo Chávez Presents: The Bolívarian Revolution* (London: Verso, 2009).

Bushnell, David, ed., *El Libertador: Writings of Simón Bolívar*. Trans. Frederick H. Fornoff (Oxford: Oxford University Press, 2003).

Catálogo Digital del Archivo del Libertador Simón Bolívar, www.archivo dellibertador.gob.ve/ [*Archivo*].

Chávez Herrera, Nelson, ed., *Primeras Constituciones de Latinoamérica y el Caribe* (Caracas: Fundación Biblioteca Ayacucho y Banco Central de Venezuela, 2011).

de la Reza, Germán A., ed., *Documentos Sobre el Congreso Anfictiónico de Panamá* (Caracas: Fundación Biblioteca Ayacucho, 2010).

Freeman, Joanne B., ed., *Alexander Hamilton: Writings* (New York: Library of America, 2001).

Gibson, William M., ed., *The Constitutions of Colombia* (Durham: Duke University Press, 1948).

Gourevitch, Victor, ed., *Jean-Jacques Rousseau: The Social Contract and Other Later Political Writings* (Cambridge: Cambridge University Press, 1997).

Haakonssen, Knud, ed., *David Hume: Political Essays* (Cambridge: Cambridge University Press, 1994).

Hampsher-Monk, Iain, ed., *Edmund Burke: Revolutionary Writings* (Cambridge: Cambridge University Press, 2014).

Joseph, Gilbert M. and Timothy J. Henderson, eds., *The Mexico Reader: History, Culture, Politics* (Durham: Duke University Press, 2002).

Kucklick, Bruce, ed., *Thomas Paine: Political Writings* (Cambridge: Cambridge University Press, 2000).

Lecuna, Vicente and Esther Barret de Nazaris, eds., *Simón Bolívar: Obras Completas*, 2nd edition, 3 Vols. (Havana: Editorial Lex, 1950).

Library of Economics and Liberty, www.econlib.org.

Lillian Goldman Law Library, Yale Law School, http://avalon.law.yale.edu.

Marxists Internet Archive, www.marxists.org.

Myers, Jorge, ed., *Orden y Virtud: El Discurso Republicano en el Régimen Rosista* (Buenos Aires: Universidad Nacional de Quilmes, 1995).

Palti, Elías José, ed., *La Política del Disenso: La "Polémica en Torno al Monarquismo," México, 1848–1850, ... y las Aporías del Liberalismo* (Mexico City: Fondo de Cultura Económica, 1998).

Pérez Vila, Manuel, ed., *Simón Bolívar: Doctrina del Libertador*, 3rd edition (Caracas: Fundación Biblioteca Ayacucho, 2009) [*Doctrina*].

Peters, Gerhard and John T. Woolley, *The American Presidency Project*, www.presidency.ucsb.edu.

Peterson, Merrill D., ed., *Thomas Jefferson: Writings* (New York: The Library of America, 1984).

Project Canterbury, http://anglicanhistory.org/.

Robson, John M., ed., *The Collected Works of John Stuart Mill*, 33 Vols. (Toronto: University of Toronto Press, 1963).

Romero, José Luis and Luis Alberto Romero, eds., *Pensamiento Político de la Emancipación*, 2 Vols. (Caracas: Biblioteca Ayacucho, 1977).

Rakove, Jack, ed., *James Madison: Writings* (New York: Library of America, 1999).

Syrett, Harold C., ed., *The Papers of Alexander Hamilton*, 27 Vols. (New York: Columbia University Press, 1961–1987) [*PAH*].

Teaching American History Library, http://teachingamericanhistory.org/library.

Tena Ramírez, Felipe, ed., *Leyes Fundamentales de México, 1808–1957* (Mexico City: Editorial Porrua, undated).

Tucker, Robert C., ed., *The Marx-Engels Reader*, 2nd edition (New York: W. W. Norton, 1978).

Varela, Gustavo, ed., *Mariano Moreno: Plan de Operaciones y Otros Escritos* (La Plata: Terramar 2007).

Vernier, Richard B., ed., *The Revolutionary Writings of Alexander Hamilton* (Indianapolis: Liberty Fund, 2008).

Weinberg, Gregorio, ed., *Manuel Belgrano: Escritos Económicos* (Buenos Aires: Editorial Raigal, 1954).

Unnamed editor, *The American Annual Register for the Years 1827–9*, 2nd edition (New York: William Hackson and E. & G. W. Blunt, 1835).

Unnamed editor, *Obras Completas de J.B. Alberdi*, 8 Vols. (Buenos Aires: Imprenta de La Tribuna Nacional, 1886).

Unnamed editor, *El pensamiento constitucional hispanoamericano hasta 1830: Compilación de Constituciones Sancionadas y Proyectos Constitucionales*, 5 Vols. (Caracas: Academia Nacional de Historia, 1961).

Unnamed editor, *Memorias de los Ministros del Interior y del Exterior* (Mexico City: Secretaría de Gobernación, 1987). [MM]

Unnamed editor, *José Martí: Obras Completas*, 26 Vols. (Havana: Centro de Estudios Martianos, 2001).

OTHER WORKS

Acemoglu, Daron and James Robinson, *Why Nations Fail: The Origins of Power, Prosperity, and Poverty* (New York: Crown Publishers, 2012).

Acemoglu, Daron, Simon Johnson, and James A. Robinson, "The Colonial Origins of Comparative Development: An Empirical Investigation." *The American Economic Review*, Vol. 91, No. 5 (Dec. 2001), 1369–1401.

"Reversal of Fortune: Geography and Institutions in the Making of the Modern World Income Distribution." *The Quarterly Journal of Economics*, Vol. 117, No. 4 (Nov. 2002), 1231–1294.

Ackerman, Bruce, *We the People: Foundations* (Cambridge, MA: Harvard University Press, 1991).

The Failure of the Founding Fathers: Jefferson, Marshall, and the Rise of Presidential Democracy (Cambridge, MA: Harvard University Press, 2005).

Adair, Douglass, "'That Politics May Be Reduced to a Science': David Hume, James Madison, and the Tenth Federalist." *The Huntington Library Quarterly*, Vol. 20, No. 4 (Aug. 1957), 343–360.

Adelman, Jeremy, *Republic of Capital: Buenos Aires and the Legal Transformation of the Atlantic World* (Stanford: Stanford University Press, 1999).

Sovereignty and Revolution in the Iberian Atlantic (Princeton: Princeton University Press, 2006).

Aguilar Rivera, José Antonio, *En Pos de la Quimera: Reflexiones sobre el Experimento Constitucional Atlántico* (Mexico City: Fondo de Cultura Económica, 2000).

El Manto Liberal: Los Poderes de Emergencia en México, 1821–1876 (Mexico City: UNAM Press, 2001).

"Alamán en el Periodo de Bustamante," in Aguilar Rivera, ed., *Examen Imparcial de la Administración de Bustamante* (Mexico City: Consejo Nacional para la Cultura y las Artes, 2008).

"Lucas Alamán y La Constitución." *Isonomía*, No. 33 (Oct. 2010), 83–122.

Aguilar Rivera, José Antonio and Rafael Rojas, eds., *El Republicanismo en Hispanoamérica: Ensayos de historia intellectual y política* (Mexico City: CIDE, 2002).

Alamán, Lucas, *Historia de Méjico*, 5th edition, 5 Vols. (Mexico City: Editorial Jus, 1968) [*HM*].

Althusser, Louis, "Ideology and Ideological State Apparatuses (Notes Toward an Investigation)," in *Lenin and Philosophy and Other Essays*. Trans. Ben Brewster (New York: Monthly Review Press, 1971), 127–186.

Ambrose, Douglas and Robert W. T. Martin, eds., *The Many Faces of Alexander Hamilton: The Life and Legacy of America's Most Elusive Founding Father* (New York: New York University Press, 2006).

Anderson, Benedict, *Imagined Communities: Reflections on the Origin and Spread of Nationalism*, revised edition (London: Verso, 1991).

Anderson, Mark R., *The Battle for the Fourteenth Colony: America's War of Liberation in Canada, 1774–1776* (Lebanon: University Press of New England, 2013).

Anderson, Perry, "The Notion of a Bourgeois Revolution" [1976] in *English Questions* (London: Verso, 1992), 105–118.

Andrews, Catherine, "In the Pursuit of Balance. Lucas Alamán's Proposals for Constitutional Reform (1830–1835)." *Historia Constitucional* (electronic edition), no. 8, 2007.

"Sobre Conservadurismo e Ideas Conservadoras en la Primera República Federal, 1824–1835," in Erika Pani, ed., *Conservadurismo y Derechas en la Historia de México*, Vol. 1 (Mexico City: FCE, 2009).

"El Debate Político de la Década de 1830 y los Orígenes de las Siete Leyes," in Cecilia Noriega and Alicia Salmerón, eds., *México: Un Siglo de Historia Constitucional, 1808–1917* (Mexico City: Instituto Mora, 2010), 111–133.

Anna, Timothy E., *The Fall of Royal Government in Mexico City* (Lincoln: University of Nebraska Press, 1978).

The Mexican Empire of Iturbide (Lincoln: University of Nebraska Press, 1990).

Annino, Antonio and Rafael Rojas, *La Independencia: Los Libros de la Patria* (Mexico City: CIDE and FCE, 2008).

Appleby, Joyce, *Capitalism and a New Social Order: The Republican Vision of the 1790s* (New York: New York University Press, 1984).

Arendt, Hannah, *On Revolution* [1963] (New York: Penguin Books, 2006).

The Origins of Totalitarianism (New York: Harcourt Brace, 1968).

"On Violence," in *Crises of the Republic* (New York: Harcourt Brace, 1972), 103–198.

Armitage, David, "Empire and Liberty: A Republican Dilemma," from Martin Van Gelderen and Quentin Skinner, eds., *Republicanism: A Shared European Heritage*, 2 Vols. (Cambridge: Cambridge University Press, 2004), II, 29–46.

The Declaration of Independence: A Global History (Cambridge, MA: Harvard University Press, 2007).

Armitage, David and Sanjay Subrahmanyam, eds., *The Age of Revolutions in Global Context, c. 1760–1840* (Houndsmills: Palgrave MacMillan, 2010).

Arneil, Barbara, *John Locke and America: The Defence of English Colonialism* (Oxford: Oxford University Press, 1996).

Ashcraft, Richard, "On the Problem of Method and the Nature of Political Theory." *Political Theory*, Vol. 3, No. 1 (Feb. 1975), 5–25.

"Political Theory and the Problem of Ideology." *The Journal of Politics*, Vol. 42, No. 3 (Aug. 1980).

"Marx and Political Theory." *Comparative Studies in Society and History*, Vol. 26, No. 4 (Oct. 1984), 637–671.

Bailyn, Bernard, "The Transforming Radicalism of the American Revolution," in Bernard Bailyn, ed., *Pamphlets of the American Revolution, Volume 1: 1750–1765* (Cambridge, MA: Harvard University Press, 1965).

The Ideological Origins of the American Revolution, enlarged edition (Cambridge, MA: Harvard University Press, 1992).

Banner, Stuart, *How the Indians Lost Their Land: Law and Power on the Frontier* (Cambridge, MA: Harvard University Press, 2005).

Banning, Lance, *The Jeffersonian Persuasion: Evolution of a Party Ideology* (Ithaca: Cornell University Press, 1978).

Barrón, Luis, "*La Tradición Republicana y el Nacimiento del Liberalismo en Hispanoamérica después de la Independencia: Bolívar, Lucas Alamán y el 'Poder Conservador,'*" in Aguilar Rivera, José Antonio and Rafael Rojas, eds., *El Republicanismo en Hispanoamérica: Ensayos de historia intellectual y política* (Mexico City: CIDE, 2002), 244–288.

Barrow, Clyde W., *More Than Just a Historian: The Political and Economic Thought of Charles A. Beard* (New Brunswick: Transaction Publishers, 2000).

Barrow, Thomas C., "The American Revolution as a Colonial War for Independence." *The William and Mary Quarterly*, Third Series, Vol. 25, No. 3 (July 1968), 452–464.

Beard, Charles A., *An Economic Interpretation of the Constitution of the United States* [1913] (New York: The Free Press, 1986).

Béland, Daniel and Robert Henry Cox, eds., *Ideas and Politics in Social Science Research* (New York: Oxford University Press, 2011).

Belaúnde, Víctor Andrés, *Bolívar and the Political Thought of the Spanish American Revolution* (Baltimore: Johns Hopkins University Press, 1938).

Belich, James, *Replenishing the Earth: The Settler Revolution and the Rise of the Anglo World, 1783–1939* (Oxford: Oxford University Press, 2009).

Bender, Thomas, *A Nation Amongst Nations* (New York: Hill and Wang, 2006).

Bennett, Andrew, "Process Tracing and Causal Inference," in Henry E. Brady and David Collier, eds., *Rethinking Social Inquiry: Diverse Tools, Shared Standards*, 2nd edition (Lanham: Rowman and Littlefield, 2010), 207–220.

Benson, Nettie Lee, "The Plan of Casa Mata." *Hispanic American Historical Review*, Vol. 25, No. 1 (Feb. 1945), 45–56.

"Iturbide y los Planes de Independencia." *Historia Mexicana*, Vol. 2, No. 3 (Jan.–Mar. 1953), 439–446.

La Diputación Provincial y el Federalismo Mexicano (Mexico City: Colegio de México, 1955).

ed., *Mexico and the Spanish Cortes, 1810–1822: Eight Essays* (Austin: University of Texas Press, 1966).

"Territorial Integrity in Mexican Politics, 1821–1833," in Jaime E. Rodríguez O., ed., *The Independence of Mexico and the Creation of the New Nation*, (Los Angeles: UCLA Latin American Center, 1989).

Benton, Lauren and Richard J. Ross, "Empires and Legal Pluralism: Jurisdiction, Sovereignty, and Political Imagination in the Early Modern World," in Benton and Ross, eds., *Legal Pluralism and Empires, 1500–1850* (New York: New York University Press, 2013), 1–17.

Berlin, Ira, "The Revolution in Black Life," in A. F. Young, ed., *The American Revolution: Explanations in the History of American Radicalism* (DeKalb: Northern Illinois University Press).

Bernal, Angélica M., "The Meaning and Perils of Presidential Refounding in Latin America." *Constellations* Vol. 21, No. 4 (Dec. 2014), 440–456.

Bevir, Mark, *The Logic of the History of Ideas* (Cambridge: Cambridge University Press, 1999).

Bierck, Harold A. "Bolívar and Spanish American Cooperation." *Pacific Historical Review*, Vol. 14, No. 2 (June 1945), 196–203.

Bilder, Mary Sarah, *The Transatlantic Constitution: Colonial Legal Culture and the Empire* (Cambridge, MA: Harvard University Press, 2004).

Blanchard, Peter, *Under the Flags of Freedom: Slave Soldiers and the Wars of Independence in Spanish South America* (Pittsburgh: University of Pittsburgh Press, 2008).

Blyth, Mark M., "Any More Bright Ideas? The Ideational Turn of Comparative Political Economy." *Comparative Politics*, Vol. 29, No. 2 (Jan. 1997), 229–250.

Bowden, Brett, *Empire of Civilization: Evolution of an Imperial Idea* (Chicago: University of Chicago Press, 2009).

Brading, D. A., *Miners and Merchants in Bourbon Mexico, 1763–1810* (Cambridge: Cambridge University Press, 1971.

The First America: The Spanish Monarchy, Creole Patriots, and the Liberal State, 1492–1867 (Cambridge: Cambridge University Press, 1991).

Breña, Roberto, "Pensamiento Político e Ideología en la Emancipación Americana: Fray Servando Teresa de Mier y la Independencia Absoluta de la Nueva España," in Francisco Colom, ed., *Relatos de Nación: La Construcción de las Identidades Nacionales en el Mundo Hispánico*, 2 Vols. (Madrid: Editorial Iberoamericana Vervuert, 2005).

El Primer Liberalismo Español y los Procesos de Emancipación de América, 1808–1824: Una Revisión Historiográfica del Liberalismo Hispánico (Mexico City: El Colegio de México, 2006).

"Relevancia y Contexto del Bienio 1808–1810: El Ciclo Revolucionario Hispánico: Puntos de Referencia e Historiografía Contemporánea," in Roberto Breña, ed., *En el Umbral de las Revoluciones Hispánicas: El Bienio 1808–1810* (Mexico City: El Colegio de México, 2010).

Brewer, John, *The Sinews of Power: War, Money and the English State* (London: Unwin Hyman, 1989).

Brown, Gordon S., *Toussaint's Clause: The Founding Fathers and the Haitian Revolution* (Jackson: University Press of Mississippi, 2005).

Brown, Matthew, *Adventuring through Spanish Colonies: Simón Bolívar, Foreign Mercenaries, and the Birth of New Nations* (Liverpool: University of Liverpool Press, 2006).

"Enlightened Reform after Independence: Simón Bolívar's Bolivian Constitution," in Gabriel Paquette, ed. *Enlightened Reform in Europe and Its Atlantic Colonies, c. 1750–1830* (Surrey: Ashgate, 2009), 339–360.

Brown, Matthew and Gabrielle Paquette, "Between the Age of Atlantic Revolutions and the Age of Empire," in Brown and Pacquette, eds., *Connections after Colonialism: Europe and Latin America in the 1820s* (Tuscaloosa: University of Alabama Press, 2013), 1–28.

Brown, Robert E., *Charles Beard and the Constitution: A Critical Analysis of "An Economic Interpretation of the Constitution"* (Princeton: Princeton University Press, 1956).

Bullion, John L., *A Great and Necessary Measure: George Grenville and the Genesis of the Stamp Act* (Columbia: University of Missouri Press, 1982).

Burbank, Jane and Frederick Cooper, *Empires in World History: Power and the Politics of Difference* (Princeton: Princeton University Press, 2010).

Burgess, John William, *Political Science and Comparative Constitutional Law*, 2 Vols. (Boston: Ginn & Company, 1890–1891).

Burkholder, Mark A. and D. S. Chandler, *From Impotence to Authority: The Spanish Crown and the American Audiencias, 1687–1808* (Columbia: University of Missouri Press, 1977).

Bushman, Claudia L., *America Discovers Columbus: How an Italian Explorer Became an American Hero* (Lebanon: University Press of New England, 1992).

Bushnell, David, *The Santander Regime in Gran Colombia*, 2nd edition (Westport: Greenwood Press, 1970).

"Los Usos del Modelo: La Generacion de la Independencia y la Imagen de Norteamerica." *Revista de Historia de América*, No. 82 (July–Dec. 1976).

Reform and Reaction in the Platine Provinces, 1810–1852 (Gainesville: University of Florida Press, 1983).

Cañizares-Esguerra, Jorge, *How to Write the History of the New World: Histories, Epistomologies, and Identities in the Eighteenth Century Atlantic World* (Palo Alto: Stanford University Press, 2001).

"Racial, Religious, and Civic Creole Identity in Colonial Spanish America," *American Literary History*, Vol. 17, No. 3 (Fall 2005), 420–437.

Canny, Nicholas and Anthony Pagden, eds., *Colonial Identity in the Atlantic World, 1500–1800* (Princeton: Princeton University Press, 1987).

Carrera Damas, Germán, *Tres Temas de Historia* (Caracas: Universidad Central de Venezuela, 1961).

El Culto a Bolívar: Esbozo para un Estudio de la Historia de las Ideas en Venezuela (Caracas: Universidad Central de Venezuela, 1970).

Boves: Aspectos Socioeconómicos de la Guerra de Independencia (Caracas: Ediciones de la Biblioteca Universidad Central de Venezuela, 1972).

Venezuela: Proyecto Nacional y Poder Social (Barcelona: Editorial Crítica, 1986).

De la Dificultad de Ser Criollo (Caracas: Grijalbo, 1993).

Castro-Klarén, Sara and John Charles Chasteen, eds., *Beyond Imagined Communities: Reading and Writing the Nation in Nineteenth-Century Latin America* (Baltimore: Johns Hopkins University Press, 2003).

Castro Leiva, Luis, *Gran Colombia: Una Illusion Ilustrada* (Caracas: Monte Avila Editores, 1985).

Chernow, Ron, *Alexander Hamilton* (New York: Penguin Press, 2004).

Chust Calero, Manuel, *La Cuestión Nacional Americana en las Cortes de Cádiz* (Valencia: Centro FCE Tomás y Valiente, 1999).

Coatsworth, John H., "Notes on the Comparative Economic History of Latin America and the United States," in Walther L. Bernecker and Hans Werner Tobler, eds., *Development and Underdevelopment in America: Contrasts of Economic Growth in North and Latin America in Historical Perspective* (Berlin: Walter de Gruyter, 1993).

Cohen, G. A., *Karl Marx's Theory of History: A Defence*, expanded edition (Oxford: Oxford University Press, 2000).

Colley, Linda, "The Difficulties of Empire: Present, Past and Future." *Historical Research*, Vol. 79, No. 1 (Winter 1998), 367–382.

Collier, Simon, *Ideas and Politics of Chilean Independence, 1808–1833* (Cambridge: Cambridge University Press, 1967).

"Nationality, Nationalism, and Supranationalism in the Writings of Simón Bolívar." *The Hispanic American Historical Review*, Vol. 63, No. 1 (1983), pp. 37–64.

Collingwood, R. G., *An Autobiography* (Oxford: Clarendon Press, 1939).

Compton, John W. and Karen Orren, "Political Theory in Institutional Context: The Case of Patriot Royalism." *American Political Thought*, Vol. 3, No. 1 (Spring 2014), 1–31.

Converse, Philip E., "The Nature of Belief Systems in Mass Publics," in David E. Apter, ed., *Ideology and Discontent* (London: Free Press of Glencoe, 1964), 206–261.

Constant, Benjamin, *Actes du Congrès de Lausanne* (Geneva: Librarie Droz, 1968).

Cooper, Frederick, *Citizenship between Empire and Nation: Remaking France and French Africa, 1945–1960* (Princeton: Princeton University Press, 2014).

Costeloe, Michael P., *La Primera República Federal de México: Un Estudio de los Partidos Políticos en el México Independiente* (Mexico City: Fondo de Cultura Económica, 1983).

The Central Republic in Mexico, 1835–1846: Hombres de Bien in the Age of Santa Anna (Cambridge: Cambridge University Press, 1993).

Dahl, Adam, "Commercial Conquest: Empire and Property in the Early U.S. Republic." *American Political Thought*, Vol. 5, No. 3 (Summer 2016), 421–445.

Dallmayr, Fred, "Beyond Monologue: For a Comparative Political Theory." *Perspectives on Politics*, Vol. 2, No. 2 (June 2004), 249–257.

de la Reza, Germán A., *La Invención de la Paz: De la República Cristiana del Duque de Sully a la Sociedad de Naciones de Simón Bolívar* (Mexico City: Ediciones Siglo XXI, 2009).

DeConde, Alexander, *The Quasi-War: The Politics and Diplomacy of the Undeclared War with France, 1797–1801* (New York: Charles Scribner and Sons, 1966).

Denoon, Donald, *Settler Capitalism: The Dynamics of Dependent Development in the Southern Hemisphere* (Oxford: Clarendon Press, 1983).

Deudney, Daniel H., "The Philadelphian System: Sovereignty, Arms Control, and Balance of Power in the American States-Union, circa 1787–1861." *International Organization*, Vol. 49, No. 2 (Mar. 1995), 191–228.

Diamond, Jared, *Guns, Germs, and Steel: The Fates of Human Societies* (New York: W. W. Norton, 1997).

Doyle, Michael W., *Empires* (Ithaca: Cornell University Press, 1986).

Draper, Hal, "Karl Marx and Simón Bolívar." *New Politics*, Vol. 7, No. 1 (Winter 1968), 64–77.

DuRoss, Michelle, "Somewhere in Between: Alexander Hamilton and Slavery." *The Early America Review*, Vol. 9, No. 4 (Winter/Spring 2011), 1–8.

Eagleton, Terry, *Ideology: An Introduction*, updated edition (London: Verso, 2007).

Echeverri, Marcela "Popular Royalists and Revolution in Colombia: Nationalism and Empire, 1780–1820" (PhD dissertation, New York University, 2008).

"Popular Royalists, Empire, and Politics in Southwestern New Granada, 1808–1819." *Hispanic American Historical Review*, Vol. 91, No. 2 (May 2011), 237–269.

Edling, Max M., *A Revolution in Favor of Government: Origins of the U.S. Constitution and the Making of the American State* (Oxford: Oxford University Press, 2003).

"Introduction to the Centennial Symposium on Charles Beard's *Economic Interpretation*." *American Political Thought*, Vol. 2, No. 2 (Fall 2013), 259–263.

"Charles Beard and the Internationalist Interpretation of the American Founding." *American Political Thought*, Vol. 2, No. 2 (Fall 2013), 292–301.

"'A Mongrel Kind of Government': The U.S. Constitution, the Federal Union, and the Origins of the American State," in Peter Thompson and Peter S. Onuf, eds., *State and Citizen: British America and the Early United States* (Charlottesville: University of Virginia Press, 2013), 150–177.

A Hercules in the Cradle: War, Money, and the American State, 1783–1867 (Chicago: University of Chicago Press, 2014).

Elkins, Caroline and Susan Pedersen, "Settler Colonialism: A Concept and Its Uses," in Elkins and Pedersen, eds., *Settler Colonialism in the Twentieth Century* (New York: Routledge, 2005).

Elkins, Stanley and Eric McKitrick, *The Age of Federalism: The Early American Republic, 1788–1800* (Oxford: Oxford University Press, 1993).

Elliott, John H., "A Europe of Composite Monarchies," *Past and Present*, No. 137 (Nov. 1992).

Empires of the Atlantic World: Britain and Spain in America, 1492–1830 (New Haven: Yale University Press, 2006).

Elster, Jon, *Making Sense of Marx* (Cambridge: Cambridge University Press, 1985).

Engerman, Stanley L. and Kenneth L. Sokoloff, "Factor Endowments, Institutions, and Differential Paths of Growth among New World Economies," in Stephen H. Haber, ed., *How Latin America Fell Behind* (Palo Alto: Stanford University Press, 1997), 260–306.

Escobar, Arturo, *Encountering Development: The Making and Unmaking of the Third World* (Princeton: Princeton University Press, 1995).

Euben, Roxanne L., *Enemy in the Mirror: Islamic Fundamentalism and the Limits of Modern Rationalism* (Princeton: Princeton University Press, 1999).

Fatovic, Clement, "Reason and Experience in Alexander Hamilton's Science of Politics." *American Political Thought*, Vol. 2, No. 1 (Spring 2013), 1–30.

Ferrer, Ada, *Insurgent Cuba: Race, Nation, and Revolution, 1868–1898* (Chapel Hill: University of North Carolina Press, 1999).

Freedom's Mirror: Cuba and Haiti in the Age of Revolution (Cambridge: Cambridge University Press, 2014).

Fieldhouse, D. K., *The Colonial Empires: A Comparative Survey from the Eighteenth Century* [1965], 2nd English edition (London: The MacMillan Press, 1982).

Fischer, Sibylle, "Bolívar in Haiti: Republicanism in the Revolutionary Atlantic," in Carla Calargé, Raphael Dalleo, Luis Duno-Gottberg, and Clevis Headley, eds., *Haiti and the Americas* (University Press of Mississippi, 2013), 25–53.

Fitz, Caitlin, *Our Sister Republics: The United States in an Age of American Revolution* (New York: W. W. Norton, 2016).

Flores Caballero, Romeo, *Counterrevolution: The Role of the Spaniards in the Independence of Mexico, 1804–38*. Trans. Jaime E. Rodríguez O. (Lincoln: University of Nebraska Press, 1974).

Fowler, Will, *Mexico in the Age of Proposals, 1821–1853* (Westport: Greenwood Press, 1998).

Freeden, Michael, *Ideologies and Political Theory: A Conceptual Approach* (Oxford: University of Oxford Press, 1996).

"Editorial: The Comparative Study of Political Thinking." *Journal of Political Ideologies*, Vol. 12, No. 1 (Feb. 2007), 1–9.

Freeden, Michael and Andrew Vincent, "Introduction: The Study of Comparative Political Thought," in Freeden and Vincent, eds., *Comparative Political Thought: Theorizing Practices* (Oxford: Routledge, 2013).

Freeman, Joanne, *Affairs of Honor: National Politics in the New Republic* (New Haven: Yale University Press, 2001).

Frymer, Paul. "'A Rush and a Push and the Land Is Ours': Territorial Expansion, Land Policy, and U.S. State Formation." *Perspectives on Politics*, Vol. 12, No. 2 (2014), 119–144.

Fukuyama, Francis, ed., *Falling Behind: Explaining the Development Gap between Latin America and the United States* (Oxford: Oxford University Press, 2008).

García Márquez, Gabriel, *El General en su Laberinto* (Spain: Editorial la Oveja Negra, 1989).

Gargarella, Roberto, *Los Fundamentos Legales de la Desigualdad: El Constitucionalismo en América, 1776–1860* (Madrid: Siglo XXI, 2005).

Gibson, Alan, "Louis Hartz and Study of the American Founding: The Search for New Fundamental Categories," in Mark Hulliung, ed., *The American Liberal Tradition Reconsidered: The Contested Legacy of Louis Hartz* (Lawrence: University Press of Kansas, 2010), 149–183.

Geddes, Barbara, "How the Cases You Choose Affect the Answers You Get: Selection Bias in Comparative Politics." *Political Analysis*, Vol. 2, No. 1 (1990), 131–150.

Geggus, David P., ed., *The Impact of the Haitian Revolution in the Atlantic World* (Columbia: University of South Carolina Press, 2001).

Gerbi, Antonello, *The Dispute of the New World: The History of a Polemic, 1750–1900* [1955]. Trans. Jeremy Moyle (Pittsburgh: University of Pittsburgh Press, 1973).

Gerring, John, "Ideology: A Definitional Analysis." *Political Research Quarterly*, Vol. 50, No. 4 (Dec. 1997), 957–994.

Getachew, Adom, "The Rise and Fall of Self-Determination: Towards a History of Anti-Colonial World-Making" (PhD dissertation, Yale University, 2015).

Gobat, Michel, "The Invention of Latin America: A Transnational History of Anti-Imperialism, Democracy, and Race." *The American Historical Review*, Vol. 118, No. 5 (Dec. 2013), 1345–1375.

Godrej, Farah, "Towards a Cosmopolitan Political Thought: The Hermeneutics of Interpreting the Other." *Polity*, Vol. 41, No. 2 (Apr. 2009), 135–165.

Cosmopolitan Political Thought: Method, Practice, Discipline (Oxford: Oxford University Press, 2014).

Golove, David M. and Daniel J. Hulsebosch, "A Civilized Nation: The Early American Constitution, the Law of Nations, and the Pursuit of International Recognition." *New York University Law Review*, Vol. 85 (Oct. 2010), 932–1066.

Gonzáles Navarro, Moisés, *El Pensamiento Político de Lucas Alamán* (Mexico City: Fondo de Cultura Económica, 1952).

Gordon, Jane Anna and Neil Roberts, eds., *Creolizing Rousseau* (London: Rowman and Littlefield, 2015).

Gordy, Katherine, *Living Ideology in Cuba: Socialism in Principle and Practice* (Ann Arbor: University of Michigan Press, 2015).

Gould, Eliga, *Among the Powers of the Earth: The American Revolution and the Making of a New World Empire* (Cambridge, MA: Harvard University Press, 2012).

Grandin, Greg, "Your Americanism and Mine: Americanism and Anti-Americanism in the Americas." *The American Historical Review*, Vol. 111, No. 4 (Oct. 2006), 1042–1066.

Green, Stanley C., *The Mexican Republic: The First Decade, 1823–1832* (Pittsburgh: University of Pittsburgh Press, 1987).

Green-Pedersen, Svend Erik, "The History of the Danish Negro Slave Trade, 1733–1807: An Interim Survey Relating in Particular to Its Volume, Structure, Profitability, and Abolition." *Revue Française d'Histoire d'Outre-Mer*, Vol. 62 (1975), 196–220.

Greene, Jack P., "The Seven Years' War and the American Revolution: The Causal Relationship Reconsidered," in Peter Marshall and Glyn Williams, eds., *The British Atlantic Empire before the American Revolution* (London: Frank Cass & Co., 1980), 87–108.

Peripheries and Center: Constitutional Development in the Extended Polities of the British Empire and the United States, 1607–1788 (Athens: University of Georgia Press, 1986).

Negotiated Authorities: Essays in Colonial Political and Constitutional History (Charlottesville: University of Virginia Press, 1994).

"The Origins of the New Colonial Policy, 1748–1763," in Jack P. Greene and J. R. Poole, eds., *A Companion to the American Revolution* (Malden: Blackwell, 2000).

"Hemispheric History and Atlantic History," in Jack P. Greene and Philip D. Morgan, eds., *Atlantic History: A Critical Appraisal* (Oxford: Oxford University Press, 2009), 299–315.

Guedea, Virginia, *En Busca de un Gobierno Alterno: Los Guadalupes de México* (Mexico City: UNAM, 1992).

Guerra, François-Xavier, *Modernidad e Independencias: Ensayos sobre las Revoluciones Hispánicas*, revised and expanded edition (Madrid: Ediciones Encuentro, 2009).

Hale, Charles A., *Mexican Liberalism in the Age of Mora, 1821–1853* (New Haven: Yale University Press, 1968).

Halperín-Donghi, Tulio, *Politics, Economics, and Society in Argentina in the Revolutionary Period.* Trans. Richard Southern (Cambridge: Cambridge University Press, 1975).

Hamill, Hugh M., *The Hidalgo Revolt: Prelude to Mexican Independence* (Gainesville: University of Florida Press, 1966).

Hampsher-Monk, Iain, "Reflections on the Revolution in France," in David Dwan and Christopher J. Insole, eds., *The Cambridge Companion to Edmund Burke* (Cambridge: Cambridge University Press, 2012), 195–208.

Hanke, Lewis, *The Spanish Struggle for Justice in the Conquest of America* (Philadelphia: University of Pennsylvania Press, 1949).

Hardin, Russell, *David Hume: Moral and Political Theorist* (Oxford: Oxford University Press, 2007).

Hartz, Louis, *The Liberal Tradition in America: An Interpretation of American Political Thought Since the Revolution* (New York: Harcourt, Brace, and World, 1955).

The Founding of New Societies: Studies in the History of the United States, Latin America, South Africa, Canada, and Australia (New York: Harcourt, Brace, 1964).

Harvey, David, *A Brief History of Neoliberalism* (Oxford: Oxford University Press, 2005).

Hecht, Susanna, *The Scramble for the Amazon and the Lost Paradise of Euclides da Cunha* (Chicago: University of Chicago Press, 2013).

Helg, Aline, "Simón Bolívar and the Spectre of Pardocracia: José Padilla in Post-Independence Cartagena." *Journal of Latin American Studies*, Vol. 35, No. 3 (Aug. 2003), 447–471.

Liberty and Equality in Caribbean Colombia, 1770–1835 (Chapel Hill: University of North Carolina Press, 2004).

Henderson, Timothy J., *A Glorious Defeat: Mexico and Its War with the United States* (New York: Hill and Wang, 2007).

The Mexican Wars for Independence (New York: Hill and Wang, 2009).

Hendrickson, David C., *Peace Pact: The Lost World of the American Founding* (Lawrence: University Press of Kansas, 2003).

Union, Nation, or Empire: The American Debate over International Relations, 1789–1941 (Lawrence: The University Press of Kansas, 2009).

Hirschman, Albert O., *The Passions and the Interests: Political Arguments for Capitalism before Its Triumph* (Princeton: Princeton University Press, 1977).

Hobsbawm, Eric, *The Age of Revolution, 1789–1848* (London: Wiedenfeld & Nicolson, 1962).

Holton, Woody, "The Readers Reports Are In." *American Political Thought*, Vol. 2, No. 2 (Fall 2013), 264–273.

Hont, Istvan, *Jealousy of Trade: International Competition and the Nation-State in Historical Perspective* (Cambridge, MA: Harvard University Press, 2005).

Hooker, Juliet, *Theorizing Race in the Americas: Douglass, Sarmiento, Du Bois, and Vasconcelos* (Oxford: Oxford University Press, 2017).

Hörnqvist, Mikael, *Machiavelli and Empire* (Cambridge: Cambridge University Press, 2004).

Horsman, Reginald, *Race and Manifest Destiny: The Origins of American Racial Anglo-Saxonism* (Cambridge, MA: Harvard University Press, 1981).

Howe, Daniel Walker, *What Hath God Wrought: The Transformation of America, 1815–1848* (Oxford: Oxford University Press, 2007).

Hulliung, Mark, "Louis Hartz, His Day and Ours," in Hulliung, ed., *The American Liberal Tradition Reconsidered: The Contested Legacy of Louis Hartz* (Lawrence: University Press of Kansas, 2010), 11–52.

Hulsebosch, Daniel J., *Constituting Empire: New York and the Transformation of Constitutionalism in the Atlantic World, 1664–1830* (Chapel Hill: University of North Carolina Press, 2005).

Isiksel, Turkuler, "The Dream of Commercial Peace," in Luuk van Middelaar and Philippe van Parijs, eds., *After the Storm: How to Save Democracy in Europe* (Tielt: Lannoo, 2015), 27–40.

James, C. L. R., *The Black Jacobins: Toussaint L'Ouverture and the San Domingo Revolution* (London: Secker and Warburg, 1938).

Jenco, Leigh Kathryn, "'What Does Heaven Ever Say?' A Methods-Centered Approach to Cross-Cultural Engagement." *The American Political Science Review*, Vol. 101, No. 4 (Nov. 2007), 741–755.

Making the Political: Founding and Action in the Political Theory of Zhang Shizhao (Cambridge: Cambridge University Press, 2010).

Jung, Courtney, *The Moral Force of Indigenous Politics: Critical Liberalism and the Zapatistas* (Cambridge: Cambridge University Press, 2008).

Kaplan, Lawrence S., *Jefferson and France: An Essay on Politics and Political Ideas* (New Haven: Yale University Press, 1967).

Kaufmann, William W., *British Policy and the Independence of Latin America, 1804–1828* (New Haven: Yale University Press, 1951).

King, Gary, Robert O. Keohane, and Sidney Verba, *Designing Social Inquiry: Scientific Inference in Qualitative Research* (Princeton: Princeton University Press, 1994).

Klooster, Wim, *Revolutions in the Atlantic World: A Comparative History* (New York: New York University Press, 2009).

Knight, Jack, *Institutions and Social Conflict* (Cambridge: Cambridge University Press, 1992).

Knight, Kathleen, "Transformations of the Concept of Ideology in the Twentieth Century." *American Political Science Review*, Vol. 100, No. 4 (Nov. 2006), 619–626.

Kolesar, Robert J., "North American Constitutionalism and Spanish America," in George Athan Billias, ed., *American Constitutionalism Abroad* (New York: Greenwood Press, 1990).

Kramnick, Isaac, "Republican Revisionism Revisited." *The American Historical Review*, Vol. 87, No. 3 (June 1982), 629–664.

Krauze, Enrique, *Siglo de Caudillos: Biografía Política de México, 1810–1910* (Barcelona: Tusquets Editores, 1994).

LaCroix, Alison L., *The Ideological Origins of American Federalism* (Cambridge, MA: Harvard University Press, 2010).

Lalonde, Suzanne, *Determining Boundaries in a Conflicted World: The Role of Uti Possidetis* (Montreal: McGill-Queens University Press, 2002).

Lange, Matthew, James Mahoney, and Matthias vom Hau, "Colonialism and Development: A Comparative Analysis of Spanish and British Colonies." *American Journal of Sociology*, Vol. 111, No. 5 (Mar. 2006), 1412–1462.

Langley, Lester D., *The Americas in the Age of Revolution* (New Haven: Yale University Press, 1996).

La Porta, Rafael, Florencio Lopez-de-Silanes, and Andrei Shleifer, "The Economic Consequences of Legal Origins." *Journal of Economic Literature*, Vol. 46, No. 2 (June 2008), 285–332.

Larrain, Jorge, *The Concept of Ideology* (Athens: University of Georgia Press, 1979).

Lasso, Marixa, *Myths of Harmony: Race and Republicanism during the Age of Revolution, Colombia 1795–1831* (Pittsburgh: University of Pittsburgh Press, 2007).

Lawson, Philip, *The Imperial Challenge: Quebec and Britain in the Age of the American Revolution* (Montreal: McGill-Queen's University Press, 1989).

Lecuna, Vicente, *Catálogo de Errores y Calumnias en la Historia de Bolívar*, 3 Vols. (New York: Colonial Press), 1956–1968.

Lewis, Jr., James E., *The American Union and the Problem of Neighborhood: The United States and the Collapse of the Spanish Empire, 1783–1829* (Chapel Hill: University of North Carolina Press, 1998).

Lieberman, Robert C., "Ideas, Institutions, and Political Order: Explaining Political Change." *American Political Science Review*, Vol. 96, No. 4 (Dec. 2002), 697–712.

Lieberson, Stanley, "Small N's and Big Conclusions: An Examination of the Reasoning in Comparative Studies Based on a Small Number of Cases." *Social Forces*, Vol. 70, No. 2 (Dec. 1991), 307–320.

Linz, Juan J. "The Perils of Presidentialism," *Journal of Democracy*, Vol. 1, No. 1 (Winter 1990), 52.

Lipset, Seymour Martin, *The First New Nation: The United States in Historical and Comparative Perspective* (New York: W. W. Norton, 1979).

American Exceptionalism: A Double-Edged Sword (New York: W. W. Norton, 1996).

Lomnitz, Claudio, "Nationalism as a Practical System: Benedict Anderson's Theory of Nationalism from the Vantage Point of Spanish America," in *Deep Mexico, Silent Mexico* (Minneapolis: University of Minnesota Press, 2001), 3–34.

Lynch, John, *The Spanish American Revolutions, 1808–1826*, 2nd edition (New York: W. W. Norton and Co., 1973).

Argentine Dictator: Juan Manuel de Rosas, 1829–1852 (Oxford: Oxford University Press, 1981).

Bourbon Spain, 1700–1808 (Oxford: Basil Blackwell Press, 1989).

Simón Bolívar: A Life (New Haven: Yale University Press, 2006).

Macaulay, Neill, "The Army of New Spain and the Mexican Delegation to the Spanish Cortes," in Benson, ed., *Mexico and the Spanish Cortes*.

MacLachlan, Colin M., *Spain's Empire in the New World: The Role of Ideas in Institutional and Social Change* (Berkeley: University of California Press, 1988).

Madariaga, Salvador de, *Bolívar* (Mexico City: Editorial Hermes, 1951).

Madsen, Deborah, *American Exceptionalism* (Edinburgh: Edinburgh University Press, 1998).

Mahoney, James, *Colonialism and Postcolonial Development: Spanish America in Comparative Perspective* (Cambridge: Cambridge University Press, 2010).

"The Logic of Process Tracing Tests in the Social Sciences." *Sociological Methods Research*, Vol. 41, No. 4 (Nov. 2012), 570–597.

Mantena, Karuna, "Genealogies of Catastrophe: Arendt on the Logic and Legacy of Imperialism," in Seyla Benhabib, ed., *Politics in Dark Times: Encounters with Hannah Arendt* (Cambridge: Cambridge University Press, 2010), 83–112.

"Another Realism: The Politics of Gandhian Nonviolence." *American Political Science Review*, Vol. 106, No. 2 (May 2012), 455–470.

March, Andrew F., *Islam and Liberal Citizenship: The Search for an Overlapping Consensus* (Oxford: Oxford University Press, 2009).

"What Is Comparative Political Theory." *The Review of Politics*, Vol. 71, No. 4 (Fall 2009), 531–565.

Marichal, Carlos, *Bankruptcy of Empire: Mexican Silver and the Wars between Spain, Britain, and France, 1760–1810* (Cambridge: Cambridge University Press, 2007).

Masur, Gerhard, "The Conference of Guayaquil." *The Hispanic American Historical Review*, Vol. 31, No. 2 (May 1951), 189–229.

Simón Bolívar, 2nd edition (Albuquerque: New Mexico University Press, 1969).

May, Robert E., *The Southern Dream of a Caribbean Empire, 1854–1861* (Baton Rouge: Louisiana State University Press, 1973).

McCarthy, Thomas, *Race, Empire, and the Idea of Human Development* (Cambridge: Cambridge University Press, 2009).

McDonald, Forrest, *We the People: The Economic Origins of the Constitution* (Chicago: University of Chicago Press, 1958).

Alexander Hamilton: A Biography (New York: W. W. Norton, 1979).

States Rights and the Union: Imperium in Imperio, 1776–1876 (Lawrence: University Press of Kansas, 2000).

McFarlane, Anthony, *Colombia before Independence: Economy, Society, and Politics under Bourbon Rule* (Cambridge: Cambridge University Press, 1993).

McGuire, Robert A. and Robert L. Ohsfeldt, "Economic Interests and the American Constitution: A Qualitative Rehabilitation of Charles A. Beard." *Journal of Economic History*, Vol. 44, No. 2 (1984), 487–519.

McKinley, P. Michael, *Pre-Revolutionary Caracas: Politics, Economy, and Society, 1777–1811* (Cambridge: Cambridge University Press, 1985).

McPherson, James, *Battle Cry of Freedom: The Civil War Era* (Oxford: Oxford University Press, 1988).

Mehta, Uday Singh, *Liberalism and Empire: A Study in Nineteenth-Century British Liberal Thought* (Chicago: University of Chicago Press, 1999).

Méndez Reyes, Salvador, *El Hispanoamericanismo de Lucas Alamán, 1823–1853* (Toluca: Universidad Autónomo del Estado de México, 1996).

Middlekauff, Robert, *The Glorious Cause: The American Revolution, 1763–1789* (New York: Oxford University Press, 1982).

Mignolo, Walter D., *The Darker Side of Western Modernity: Global Futures, Decolonial Options* (Durham: Duke University Press, 2011).

Miller, Jonathan M., "The Authority of a Foreign Talisman: A Study of U.S. Constitutional Practice as Authority in Nineteenth Century Argentina and the Argentine Elite's Leap of Faith." *American University Law Review*, Vol. 46, No. 5 (June 1997), 1483–1572.

Millington, Thomas, *Colombia's Military and Brazil's Monarchy: Undermining the Republican Foundations of South American Independence* (Westport: Greenwood Press, 1996).

Milobar, David, "Quebec Reform, the British Constitution, and the Atlantic Empire, 1774–1775." *Parliamentary History*, Vol. 14, No. 1 (Feb. 1995), 65–88.

Moore, Jr., Barrington, *The Social Origins of Dictatorship and Democracy: Lord and Peasant in the Making of the Modern World* (Boston: Beacon Press, 1966).

Moraña, Mabel, Enrique Dussel, and Carlos A. Jáuregui, eds., *Coloniality at Large: Latin America and the Postcolonial Debate* (Durham: Duke University Press, 2008).

Morgan, Edmund S., *American Slavery, American Freedom: The Ordeal of Colonial Virginia* (New York: W. W. Norton, 1975).

Morgan, Edmund S. and Helen M. Morgan, *The Stamp Act Crisis: Prologue to Revolution* (Chapel Hill: University of North Carolina Press, 1953).

Mörner, Magnus, "Economic Factors and Stratification in Colonial Spanish America with Special Regard to Elites." *The Hispanic American Historical Review*, Vol. 63, No. 2 (May 1983), 335–369.

Murrin, John M., "The Great Inversion, or Court versus Country: A Comparison of the Revolution Settlements in England (1688–1721) and America (1776–1816)," in J. G. A. Pocock, ed., *Three British Revolutions: 1641, 1688, 1776* (Princeton: Princeton University Press, 1980), 368–453.

Muthu, Sankar, *Enlightenment Against Empire* (Princeton: Princeton University Press, 2003).

Nelson, Eric, "Patriot Royalism: The Stuart Monarchy in American Political Thought, 1769–75." *The William and Mary Quarterly*, Vol. 68, No. 4 (Oct. 2011), 533–572.

The Royalist Revolution: Monarchy and the American Founding (Cambridge, MA: Harvard University Press, 2014).

Neruda, Pablo, *Tercera Residencia, 1935–1945* (Buenos Aires: Losada, 1947).

Nkrumah, Kwame, *Africa Must Unite* (New York: International Publishers, 1970).

Noriega, Alfonso, *El Pensamiento Conservador y el Conservadurismo Mexicano*, 2 Vols. (Mexico City: UNAM, 1972).

North, Douglass C., "Institutions and Economic Growth: An Historical Introduction." *World Development*, Vol. 17, No. 9 (1989), 1326–1330.

Institutions, Institutional Change, and Economic Performance (Cambridge: Cambridge University Press, 1990).

North, Douglass C., William Summerhill, and Barry R. Weingast, "Order, Disorder and Economic Change: Latin America vs. North America." in Bruce Bueno de Mesquita and Hilton Root, eds., *Governing for Prosperity* (New Haven: Yale University Press, 2000), 17–58.

Ochoa Espejo, Paulina, "Paradoxes of Popular Sovereignty: A View from Spanish America." *The Journal of Politics*, Vol. 74, No. 4 (2012), 1053–1065.

O'Leary, Daniel Florencio, *Memorias*, 3 Vols. (Caracas: Imprenta de 'El Monitor,' 1883).

Onuf, Peter S. and Nicholas G. Onuf, *Federal Union, Modern World: The Law of Nations in an Age of Revolutions, 1776–1814* (Madison: Madison House, 1993).

Orren, Karen and Stephen Skowronek, *The Search for American Political Development* (Cambridge: Cambridge University Press, 2004).

Pagden, Anthony, *Spanish Imperialism and the Political Imagination* (New Haven: Yale University Press, 1990).

Lords of All the World: Ideologies of Empire in Spain, Britain, and France, c. 1500–c.1800 (New Haven: Yale University Press, 1995).

Palmer, R. R., *The Age of Democratic Revolutions: A Political History of Europe and America, 1760–1800*, 2 Vols. (Princeton: Princeton University Press, 1959 and 1964).

Palti, Elías, "Lucas Alamán y la Involución Política del Pueblo Mexicano: ¿Las Ideas Conservadoras 'Fuera de Lugar'?," in Erika Pani, ed., *Conservadurismo y Derechas en la Historia de México*, Vol. 1 (Mexico City: FCE, 2009).

Pani, Erika, "Saving the Nation through Exclusion: Alien Laws in the Early Republic in the United States and Mexico." *The Americas*, Vol. 65, No. 2 (Oct. 2008), 217–246.

ed., *Conservadurismo y Derechas en la Historia de México*, 2 Vols. (Mexico City: FCE, 2009).

Pantoja Morán, David, *El Supremo Poder Conservador: El Diseño Institucional en las Primeras Constituciones Mexicanas* (Mexico City: El Colegio de México, 2005).

Parel, Anthony J., "The Comparative Study of Political Philosophy," in Parel and Ronald C. Keith, eds., *Comparative Political Philosophy: Studies under the Upas Tree*, 2nd edition (Lanham: Lexington Books, 2003).

Parkin, Frank, *Marxism and Class Theory: A Bourgeois Critique* (New York: Columbia University Press, 1979).

Pérez, Louis A., Jr., *Cuba in the American Imagination: Metaphor and the Imperial Ethos* (Chapel Hill: University of Carolina Press, 2008).

Pérez Sarrión, Guillermo, ed., *Más Estado y Más Mercado: Absolutismo y Economia en la España del Siglo XVIII* (Madrid: Sílex Ediciones, 2011).

Pérez Vejo, Tomás, *Elegía Criolla: Una Reinterpretación de las Guerras de Independencia Hispano Americanas* (Mexico City: Tusquets, 2010).

Phelan, John L., *The People and the King: The Comunero Revolution in Colombia, 1781* (Madison: University of Wisconsin Press, 1978).

Pierson, Paul, "Increasing Returns, Path Dependence, and the Study of Politics." *American Political Science Review*, Vol. 94, No. 2 (June 2000), 251–267.

Pitts, Jennifer, *A Turn to Empire: The Rise of Imperial Liberalism in Britain and France* (Princeton: Princeton University Press, 2005).

"Political Theory of Empire and Imperialism." *Annual Review of Political Science*, No. 13 (2010), 211–235.

Pocock, J. G. A., *The Machiavellian Moment: Florentine Political Thought and the Atlantic Republican Tradition* (Princeton: Princeton University Press, 1975).

Virtue, Commerce, and History: Essays on Political Thought and History, Chiefly in the Eighteenth Century (Cambridge: Cambridge University Press, 1985).

"Between Gog and Magog: The Republican Thesis and the *Ideologia Americana*." *Journal of the History of Ideas*, Vol. 48, No. 2 (Apr.–June 1987), 325–346.

Poole, Keith T. and Howard Rosenthal, *Ideology and Congress* (New Brunswick: Transaction Publishers, 2007).

Przeworski, Adam, "The Last Instance: Are Institutions the Primary Cause of Development?" *European Journal of Sociology*, Vol. 45, No. 2 (Aug. 2004), 165–188.

Przeworski, Adam and Carolina Curvale, "Does Politics Explain the Economic Gap between the United States and Latin America?," in Francis Fukuyama, ed., *Falling Behind: Explaining the Development Gap between Latin America and the United States* (Oxford: Oxford University Press, 2008), 99–133.

Racine, Karen, *Francisco de Miranda: A Transatlantic Life in the Age of Revolution* (Wilmington: Scholarly Resource Books, 2003).

"Simon Bolivar, Englishman: Elite Responsibility and Social Reform in Spanish American Independence," in David Bushnell and Lester Langley, eds., *Simon Bolivar: Essays on the Life and Legacy of the Liberator* (Lanham: Rowman and Littlefield, 2008).

Ragin, Charles C., *The Comparative Method: Moving Beyond Qualitative and Quantitative Strategies* (Berkeley: University of California Press, 1987).

Rahe, Paul Anthony, *Republics Ancient and Modern: Classical Republicanism and the American Revolution* (Chapel Hill: University of North Carolina Press, 1992).

Ramírez Zavala, Ana Luz, "Indio/Indígena, 1750–1850." *Historia Mexicana*, Vol. 60, No. 3 (Jan.–Mar. 2011), 1643–1681.

Rana, Aziz, *The Two Faces of American Freedom* (Cambridge, MA: Harvard University Press, 2010).

Reid, John Phillip, *Constitutional History of the American Revolution*, abridged edition (Madison: Wisconsin University Press, 1995).

Reyes Heroles, Jesús, *El Liberalismo Mexicano*, 3 Vols. (Mexico City: UNAM Press, 1957).

Rieu-Millan, Marie Laure, *Los Diputados Americanos en las Cortes de Cádiz* (Madrid: Consejo Superior de Investigaciones Científicas, 1990).

Robbins, Caroline, *The Eighteenth-Century Commonwealthman: Studies in the Transmission, Development, and Circumstance of English Liberal Thought from the Restoration of Charles II Until the War with the Thirteen Colonies* [1959] (Indianapolis: Liberty Fund, 2004).

Robertson, William Spence, *Francisco de Miranda and the Revolutionizing of Spanish America* (Washington, D.C.: Government Printing Office, 1909).

Rodríguez, Mario, "The 'American Question' at the Cortes of Madrid." *The Americas*, Vol. 38, No. 3 (Jan. 1982), 293–314.

Rodríguez O., Jaime E., "Two Revolutions: France 1789 and Mexico 1810." *The Americas*, Vol. 47, No. 2 (Oct. 1990), 161–176.

"The Struggle for the Nation: The First Centralist-Federalist Conflict in Mexico." *The Americas*, Vol. 49, No. 1 (July 1992), 1–22.

The Independence of Spanish America (Cambridge: Cambridge University Press, 1998).

Rodríguez O., Jaime E. and Virginia Guedea, "La Constitución de 1824 y la formación del Estado Mexicano." *Historia Mexicana*, Vol. 40, No. 3 (Jan.–Mar. 1991), 507–535.

Rojas, Rafael, *Las Repúblicas de Aire: Utopía y Desencanto en la Revolución de Hispanoamérica* (Mexico City: Taurus, 2009).

Rosen, Michael, "The History of Ideas as Philosophy and History." *History of Political Thought*, Vol. 22, No. 4 (Winter 2011), 691–720.

Sabl, Andrew, *Hume's Politics: Coordination and Crisis in the History of England* (Princeton: Princeton University Press, 2012).

Sachs, Jeffrey D., *Tropical Underdevelopment*, NBER Working Paper 8119 (Cambridge, MA: National Bureau of Economic Research, 2001).

Safford, Frank, "Bolívar as Triumphal State Maker and Despairing 'Democrat,'" in David Bushnell and Lester D. Langley, eds., *Simón Bolívar: Essays on the Life and Legacy of the Liberator* (Lanham: Rowman and Littlefield, 2008), 99–120.

Safford, Frank and Marco Palacios, *Colombia: Fragmented Land, Divided Society* (Oxford: Oxford University Press, 2002).

Santoni, Pedro, *Mexicans at Arms: Puro Federalists and the Politics of War, 1845–1848* (Fort Worth: TCU Press, 1996).

Sarmiento, Domingo Faustino, *Civilización I Barbarie: Vida de Juan Facundo Quiroga* (Santiago: Imprenta del Progresa, 1845).

Scott, David, *Conscripts of Modernity: The Tragedy of Colonial Enlightenment* (Durham: Duke University Press, 2004).

Schwartz, Pedro and Carlos Rodríguez Braun, "Las Relaciones entre Jeremías Bentham y S. Bolívar." *Telos: Revista Iberoamericana de Estudios Utilitaristas*, Vol. 1, No. 3 (1992), 45–68.

Sexton, Jay, *The Monroe Doctrine: Empire and Nation in Nineteenth-Century America* (New York: Hill and Wang, 2011).

Shalhope, Robert, "Toward a Republican Synthesis: The Emergence of an Understanding of Republicanism in American Historiography." *William and Mary Quarterly*, No. 29 (1972), 49–80.

"Republicanism and Early American Historiography." *William and Mary Quarterly*, No. 39 (1982), 334–356.

Shklar, Judith N., "Montesquieu and the New Republicanism," in Gisela Bock, Quentin Skinner and Maurizio Viroli, eds., *Machiavelli and Republicanism* (Cambridge: Cambridge University Press, 1990), 265–279.

Simon, Joshua, "The United States as Settler Empire." *Settler Colonial Studies,* Vol. 1, No. 2 (2012), 150–163.

"Simón Bolívar's Republican Imperialism: Another Ideology of American Independence." *History of Political Thought,* Vol. 33, No. 2 (2012), 280–304.

"The Americas' More Perfect Unions: New Institutional Insights from Comparative Political Theory." *Perspectives on Politics,* Vol. 12, No. 4 (Dec. 2014), 808–828.

Skinner, Quentin, "Machiavelli on the Maintenance of Liberty." *Australian Journal of Political Science,* Vol. 18, No. 2 (1983), 3–15.

"Machiavelli's *Discorsi* and the Pre-Humanist Origins of Republican Ideas," in Gisela Bock, Quentin Skinner, and Maurizio Viroli, eds., *Machiavelli and Republicanism* (Cambridge: Cambridge University Press, 1990), 121–142.

Liberty before Liberalism (Cambridge: Cambridge University Press, 1998).

"The Rise of, Challenge to and Prospects for a Collingwoodian Approach to the History of Political Thought," in Dario Castiglione and Iain Hampsher-Monk, eds., *The History of Political Thought in National Context* (Cambridge: Cambridge University Press, 2001), 175–188.

Visions of Politics, Volume 1: Regarding Method (Cambridge: Cambridge University Press, 2002).

Skocpol, Theda, "Bringing the State Back In: Strategies of Analysis in Current Research," in Peter Evans, Dietrich Rueschemeyer, and Theda Skocpol, eds., *Bringing the State Back In* (Cambridge: Cambridge University Press, 1985), 3–38.

Skocpol, Theda and Margaret Somers, "The Uses of Comparative History in Macrosocial Inquiry." *Comparative Studies in Society and History,* Vol. 22, No. 2 (Apr. 1980), 174–197.

Smith, Rogers, "Beyond Tocqueville, Myrdal, and Hartz: The Multiple Traditions in America." *The American Political Science Review,* Vol. 87, No. 3 (Sept. 1993), 549–566.

Civic Ideals: Conflicting Visions of Citizenship in U.S. History (New Haven: Yale University Press, 1997).

"Understanding the Symbiosis of American Rights and American Racism," in Mark Hulliung, ed., *The American Liberal Tradition Reconsidered: The Contested Legacy of Louis Hartz* (Lawrence: University Press of Kansas, 2010), 55–89.

Smith, Steven B., *Reading Leo Strauss: Politics, Philosophy, Judaism* (Chicago: Chicago University Press, 2006).

Sosin, Jack M., *Whitehall and the Wilderness: The Middle West in British Colonial Policy, 1760–1775* (Lincoln: University of Nebraska Press, 1961).

Sowell, David, "The Mirror of Public Opinion: Bolívar, Republicanism, and the United States Press, 1821–1831." *Revista de Historia de América,* No. 134 (Jan.–June 2004), 165–183.

Spencer, Mark G., *David Hume and Eighteenth-Century America* (Rochester: University of Rochester Press, 2005).

Stears, Marc, "The Liberal Tradition and the Politics of Exclusion." *Annual Review of Political Science,* No. 10 (2007), 85–101.

Stevens, Donald Fithian, *Origins of Instability in Early Republican Mexico* (Durham: Duke University Press, 1991).

Storing, Herbert J., *What the Anti-Federalists Were For: The Political Thought of the Opponents of the Constitution* (Chicago: University of Chicago Press, 1981).

Stourzh, Gerald, *Alexander Hamilton and the Idea of Republican Government* (Stanford: Stanford University Press, 1970).

Street, John, *Artigas and the Emancipation of Uruguay* (Cambridge: Cambridge University Press, 1959).

Stroetzer, O. Carlos, "Bolívar y el Poder Moral." *Revista de Historia de América* No. 95 (Jan.–June 1983), 139–158.

Tilly, Charles, *Coercion, Capital, and European States, AD 990–1992* (Malden: Blackwell Publishing, 1992).

Tocqueville, Alexis de, *Democracy in America* [1835]. Trans. Arthur Goldhammer (New York: The Library of America, 2004).

von Vacano, Diego, *The Color of Citizenship: Race, Modernity, and Latin American/Hispanic Political Thought* (New York: Oxford University Press, 2012).

"The Scope of Comparative Political Theory." *Annual Review of Political Science*, Vol. 18 (2015), 465–480.

Valadés, José C., *Alamán: Estadista e Historiador* (Mexico City: José Porrua e Hijos, 1938).

Van Cleve, George William, *A Slaveholders Union: Slavery, Politics, and the Constitution in the Early American Republic* (Chicago: University of Chicago Press, 2010).

Van Young, Eric, *The Other Rebellion: Popular Violence, Ideology, and the Mexican Struggle for Independence, 1810–1821* (Stanford: Stanford University Press, 2001).

"The Limits of Atlantic-World Nationalism in a Revolutionary Age: Imagined Communities and Lived Communities in Mexico, 1810–1821," in Joseph Esherick, Hasan Kayalı, and Eric Van Young, *Empire to Nation: Historical Perspectives on the Making of the Modern World* (Oxford: Rowman and Littlefield, 2006).

Vasconcelos, José, *Bolivarismo y Monroísmo: Temas Iberoamericanos* (Santiago: Biblioteca América, 1934).

Veracini, Lorenzo, *Settler Colonialism: A Theoretical Overview* (Houndmills: Palgrave Macmillan, 2010).

"'Settler Colonialism': Career of a Concept." *The Journal of Imperial and Commonwealth History*, Vol. 41, No. 2 (2013), 313–333.

Villoro, Luis, *El Proceso Ideológico de la Revolución de Independencia* [1953] (Mexico City: FCE, 2010).

Wallerstein, Immanuel, *The Modern World System, Volume III: The Second Era of Great Expansion of the Capitalist World-Economy, 1730s–1840s*, revised and expanded edition (Berkeley: University of California Press, 2011).

Walling, Karl-Friedrich, *Republican Empire: Alexander Hamilton on War and Free Government* (Lawrence: University Press of Kansas, 1999).

Werner, John M., "David Hume and America." *Journal of the History of Ideas*, Vol. 33, No. 3 (July–Sep. 1972), 439–456.

Weston, Jr., John C., "The Ironic Purpose of Burke's Vindication Vindicated." *Journal of the History of Ideas*, Vol. 19, No. 3 (June 1958), 435–441.

Whitaker, Arthur P., *The Western Hemisphere Idea: Its Rise and Decline* (Ithaca: Cornell University Press, 1954).

White, Morton, *Philosophy, The Federalist, and the Constitution* (New York: Oxford University Press, 1987).

Wilder, Gary, *Freedom Time: Negritude, Decolonization, and the Future of the World* (Durham: Duke University Press, 2015).

Williams, Melissa S. and Mark E. Warren, "A Democratic Case for Comparative Political Theory." *Political Theory*, Vol. 42, No. 1 (Jan. 2014), 26–47.

Williams, William Appleman, *The Tragedy of American Diplomacy* (New York: W. W. Norton, 1972).

Wilson, Woodrow, *Congressional Government* (Boston: Houghton, Mifflin and Co., 1885).

Wolin, Sheldon S., "Hume and Conservatism." *The American Political Science Review*, Vol. 48, No. 4 (Dec. 1954), 999–1016.

Wood, Ellen Meiksins, *Citizens to Lords: A Social History of Western Political Thought from Antiquity to the Middle Ages* (London: Verso, 2008).

Wood, Ellen Meiksins and Neal Wood, "Socrates and Democracy: A Reply to Gregory Vlastos." *Political Theory*, Vol. 14, No. 1 (Feb. 1986), 55–82.

Wood, Gordon S., "Rhetoric and Reality in the American Revolution." *The William and Mary Quarterly*, Vol. 23, No. 1 (Jan. 1966), 3–32.

The Creation of the American Republic, 1776–1787 (New York: W. W. Norton, 1972).

"Interests and Disinterestedness in the Making of the Constitution," in Richard Beeman, Stephen Botein, and Edward C. Carter II, eds., *Beyond Confederation: Origins of the Constitution and American National Identity* (Chapel Hill: University of North Carolina Press, 1987).

The Radicalism of the American Revolution (New York: Vintage Books, 1993).

Empire of Liberty: A History of the Early Republic, 1789–1815 (Oxford: Oxford University Press, 2009).

"The Problem of Sovereignty." *The William and Mary Quarterly*, Vol. 68, No. 4 (Oct. 2011), 573–577.

Wood, Neal, "The Social History of Political Theory." *Political Theory*, Vol. 6, No. 3 (Aug. 1978), 345–367.

Wright, Erik Olin, *Class, Crisis and the State* (London: Verso, 1978).

Classes (London: Verso, 1985).

ed., *The Debate on Classes* (London: Verso, 1989).

"The Shadow of Exploitation in Weber's Class Analysis." *American Sociological Review*, Vol. 67, No. 6 (Dec. 2002), 832–853.

Young, David, "Montesquieu's View of Despotism and His Use of Travel Literature." *The Review of Politics*, Vol. 40, No. 3 (July 1978), 392–405.

Zires, Margarita, "Los Mitos de la Virgen de Guadalupe: Su Proceso de Construcción y Reinterpretación en el México Pasado y Contemporáneo."

Mexican Studies/Estudios Mexicanos, Vol. 10, No. 2 (Summer 1994), 296–301.

Zoraida Vázquez, Josefina, "Los años olvidados." *Mexican Studies/Estudios Mexicanos*, Vol. 5, No. 2 (Summer 1989).

"Centralistas, Conservadores, y Monarquistas, 1830–1853," in William Fowler and Humberto Morales Moreno, eds., *El Conservadurismo Mexicano en el Siglo XIX* (Puebla: Benemérita Universidad Autónoma de Puebla, 1999).

Index

Ackerman, Bruce, 174
Adams, John, 4, 40, 88, 161
  Hamilton's attack on, 88
Adams, John Quincy
  Panama Congress and, 125–127
Agustín I. See Iturbide, Agustín
Alamán, Lucas, 12–14, 15, 46
  accomplishments of as major figure of
    his time, 131
  anti-imperial imperialism of, 162
  biographical overview, 134
  Burke's influence on, 132, 136, 138, 142,
    146, 149, 151
  constitutional design and theory of,
    148–151
  critique of insurgency of Hidalgo and
    Morelos by, 138–140
  critique of Mier and Bustamante
    (insurgency sympathizers), 140–142
  on disagreements between Creole and
    Peninsular Spaniards, 136–138
  education of, 143
  Examen Imparcial of, 153–158
  Exposición on American Question of,
    144–147
  on free trade, 126
  on French Constitution, 39–40
  Historia de Méjico of, 131–132, 143,
    160–161
  on historical inevitability of Mexican
    independence, 138
  international outlook of vs. Bolívar and
    Hamilton, 133

Joel Roberts Poinsett and, 164
Law of Colonization (1830) and, 163
  as Minister of Interior and Exterior
    Relations, 151
  Pan-Spanish Americanism of, 164–166
  personal experience of Hidalgo's
    insurgency, 134–135
  on Plan of Iguala, 147–148, 149–150
  political conservatism of, 131, 133,
    166–167
  on post-independence Mexico, 172
  on territorial expansion and internal
    colonization, 160–164
  time abroad during insurgency, 143
  on value of Spanish rule, 135–137
American independence movements
  age of revolutions thesis and, 3–6
  anti-imperial imperialism as justification
    for, 36
  as Creole Revolutions, 30
  Creole rights and, 33–37
  ideological and institutional similarities
    between, 1–3
  incipient nationalism thesis of, 5–7
  taxation by British Parliament and, 29
Anderson, Benedict, 8, 22
anti-imperial imperialism, 30–33,
    45–46
  of Alamán, 162
  of Bolívar, 46–47, 99, 117–121
  of Hamilton, 46–47, 87
  as justification of independence
    movements, 36